W9-DDD-489

METER *as* RHYTHM

METER *as* RHYTHM

Christopher F. Hasty

New York   Oxford   •   Oxford University Press   1997

Oxford University Press

Oxford   New York

Athens   Auckland   Bangkok   Bogota   Bombay   Buenos Aires
Calcutta   Cape Town   Dar es Salaam   Delhi   Florence   Hong Kong
Istanbul   Karachi   Kuala Lumpur   Madras   Madrid   Melbourne
Mexico City   Nairobi   Paris   Singapore   Taipei   Tokyo   Toronto

and associated companies in
Berlin   Ibadan

Published by Oxford University Press, Inc.
198 Madison Avenue, New York, New York 10016

Oxford is a registered trademark of Oxford University Press

Library of Congress Cataloging-in-Publication Data
Hasty, Christopher Francis.
Meter as rhythm / Christopher F. Hasty.
p.   cm.
Includes bibliographical references and index.
ISBN 0-19-510066-2
1. Musical meter and rhythm.   I. Title.
ML3850.H37   1997
781.2'2—dc20   96-24694

1 3 5 7 9 8 6 4 2

Printed in the United States of America
on acid-free paper

For
Olga and Kate

Preface

In thinking about music it is difficult to avoid representing any concrete instance as if it were a stable and essentially pre-formed entity composed of fully determinate and ultimately static objects or relations. Certainly, in the actual performance of music there is no escaping the contingency and indeterminacy that inhere in every temporal act. When we attempt to analyze the musical event, however, it is most convenient to imagine that the intricate web of relationships that comes into play on such an occasion has already been woven in a prior compositional act or in a determinate and determining order of values and beliefs. We can, for example, point to the score as a fixed set of instructions for the recreation of an essentially self-same work or as a repository wherein the traces of a composer's thought lie encoded awaiting faithful decoding by a receptive performer/listener. Or, with even greater abstraction, we can point to the presence of an underlying tonal system, the governing rules of a style or "common practice," the reflection of a set of existing social relations, or the role of hardened ideologies in music's production and reception.

It must be said that there is some truth in the variety of determinacies that intellectual analysis would ascribe to music (if little truth in the claims of any one perspective to speak for the whole). But it must also be said that, to the extent the abstractions of analysis deny or suppress the creativity, spontaneity, and novelty of actual musical experience, analysis will have misrepresented music's inescapably temporal nature. The challenge of taking this temporal nature into account lies in finding ways of speaking of music's very evanescence and thus of developing concepts that would capture both the determinacy and the indeterminacy of events in passage. Stated in this way, such an enterprise appears to be loaded with paradox. However, much of the paradox disappears if we can shift our attention from objects or products to process and from static being to dynamic becoming. Indeed, such a shift might provide a perspective from which the great variety of determinacies we ascribe to music could be seen as inseparable components of musical communication.

In the following pages I will focus on a single aspect of musical process —the metrical. Meter is an especially appropriate topic with which to begin an inquiry into the temporal character of musical experience. Of all music's features, meter (together with its customary companion, rhythm) seems to speak most directly of time and passage. This measuring of duration is one of the most viscerally immediate of music's powers and the most fleeting. In measured music we are riveted by each passing "beat," which in its passing seems to vanish without a trace. Nevertheless, this clear connection to immediate experience and real temporal passage has often been denied to meter in traditional theory's categorical opposition of meter and rhythm. Thus, it is customary to view rhythm as a rich and fully sensuous embodiment of music's temporal progress and meter as rhythm's shadowy, schematic counterpart—abstract, mechanical, and devoid of any intrinsic expression. Although this opposition has its own particular history and characteristics, it may be taken as emblematic of difficulties we face when we attempt to speak of musical passage.

In our attempts to speak of passage, to name its parts and describe the togetherness that allows us to conceive of parts, we are tempted to overlook the abstractions through which temporality is set aside for practical purposes of analysis and representation. Because meter as measure is so easily assimilated to number, it is especially susceptible to such abstraction. As the repetition of durational quantity, meter becomes eminently analyzable if the regularity of repetition is conceived deterministically and if duration is reduced to the spatial category of time span. However, what is lost in this simplification is the specifically temporal character of repetition and therefore the claim of meter to be regarded as fully sensible and intrinsically expressive. To the extent meter and rhythm are thus conceived as incommensurate, rhythm can be protected from the abstraction and schematicization of meter but will by the same token become inaccessible to close analysis. If vivid feelings of durational quantity are withdrawn from our concept of rhythm, we are left only with vague notions of "tension and relaxation" or "ebb and flow" for describing what is arguably the most complex and luxuriantly differentiated aspect of musical experience.

The problematical opposition of meter and rhythm will be the subject of the first part of this study. Chapter 1 undertakes a very general analysis of this complicated relationship, probing a variety of musical and nonmusical contexts in which the atemporal "law" of periodicity can be contrasted with the spontaneity of rhythm. The remainder of part I is devoted to critical readings of various theorists who have speculated on the relations of meter and rhythm. Although none of the positions reviewed here—not even the most sympathetic—will be taken as a model for our later theorizing, all are valuable as serious (if indirect) attempts to address fundamental human questions of compulsion and freedom, reason and feeling, time and the consolations of representation. The brief survey of opinion undertaken in part I will serve to identify crucial theoretical issues that are addressed anew in part II.

The second part of this book develops a theory of musical meter that would, as Alfred North Whitehead says, "take time seriously." This "taking seriously" means acknowledging a real past, present, and future—or, perhaps more to the point, acknowledging real potentiality, indeterminacy, and novelty, the conditions *sine qua non* of music making. In taking this position I do not attempt to refute its adversaries (among many others, John McTaggart and "new" tenseless theorists of time); nor do I explicitly invoke the proponents of time's reality for support (save occasional references to William James, Henri Bergson, and Milič Čapek). An attempt to ground this theory of musical meter in a general theory of time or process, while clearly desirable, would far exceed the bounds of this study. I do, however, begin part II with a broad inquiry into durational quantity conceived as process. In view of the novelty of such an approach to questions of musical rhythm, chapter 6 may at first present some difficulties to the reader, especially since it will not be clear at this point exactly how the concepts introduced here are to be related to concrete musical situations. However, since these concepts are developed throughout the study, a patient reading should be rewarded with increased comprehension as the argument proceeds through the remaining chapters.

Chapter 7 introduces the central analytic concept of the book—metrical or durational "projection"—and it is here that my debt to Whitehead's work is most pronounced. Although I do not engage Whitehead's elaborate philosophical distinctions and terminology in my questions concerning measured duration, I do freely adapt some of his central insights to the very specific problem of musical meter. As in chapter 6, the concepts and terms I use in this attempt to understand the phenomenon of meter have little resonance in the language of current theory. Although it might have been possible to frame some of these concepts in more familiar phenomenological, semiotic, or information processing terms, I have chosen a less narrowly specialized vocabulary, in part, to avoid some of the prejudices of these new sciences—the unabashedly mechanistic character of information processing models, the transcendental and idealistic bias of classical phenomenology, and the characteristically atemporal perspective of semiology. Though perhaps quaint by current standards, the vocabulary and the manner of speech I use in theoretical reflection throughout this study aim to escape or at least to blur prevailing oppositions of mind and body, feeling and thinking, culture and aesthetic experience. These oppositions have not proved so productive for our understanding of music that we need to limit our thought by presupposing them.

After a brief return to the theories of Friedrich Neumann and

Moritz Hauptmann in light of the theory of projection, chapter 9 embarks on what an especially perceptive (and anonymous) reviewer of this book in manuscript called a "retooling" of metrical theory on the basis of what in chapters 6 and 7 emerged as a radical departure from conventional views of meter. Here the agenda is set to a large extent by the traditional division of topics pertaining to meter. This chapter ends with a projective account of the bifurcation of meter into duple and triple types.

Chapter 10 initiates a turn to detailed discussions of properly musical examples. This trend will culminate in a fairly extensive analysis of metrical issues in the first movement of Beethoven's First Symphony (chapter 13) and in detailed analyses of pieces that belong to repertories less favored by theorists of rhythm and meter (chapter 14). The final two chapters open our inquiry, first to a consideration of musics that would escape the hold of metrical determination, and then to more general questions that point to broader applications of the concepts and observations that have guided the course of this essay.

Since the usefulness of the concept of projection for an understanding of meter is inseparable from its effectiveness as an analytic tool, I would like to close this preface with a few comments on the analytic aspect of the present theory and its notational conventions. In designating metrical primitives and their graphic representations, I have aimed for simplicity. The primary distinction is that of *beginning* (symbolized by a vertical line, |) and *continuation* (symbolized by a slanted line, \ or /). Although this topic is not broached until chapter 9, I should point out even here that the distinction of beginning and continuation must not be confused with that of strong and weak beat. Among continuations, I further distinguish among those that are anacrustic (/), those that are arsic or non-anacrustic (\) and those that, in the case of triple or unequal measure, are subject to *deferral* (- \ or - /). Finally, there is a symbol for the reinterpretation of metrical function (\ $\rightarrow$ | or | $\rightarrow$ \) and a symbol for metrical *hiatus* (||) or a momentary dissolution of the projective field. This group of symbols always appears above the staff. Below the staff are shown more specifically projective symbols—pairings of continuous and broken lines that indicate the immediate inheritance of durational complexes accepted or rejected in the new event.

It must be said that these symbols are very crude devices for pointing to extremely subtle processes that, although vividly registered in hearing, cannot be captured in a graphic representation. Because there are relatively few symbols and because even a brief passage of modestly complex music will present many possibilities for interpretation, an effective analytic use of these notational devices will require a keen aural sensibility exercised in many careful and critical hearings, along with a speculative musical imagination that would attempt to discover some order and function in the ear's judgments. These are, of course, requirements for the use of any analytic technique that recognizes the complexity of musical experience and its openness to interpretation.

I would stress the subtlety of projective analysis here because meter is not generally accorded the value, the variety, or the intricacy of harmonic/contrapuntal relations. It is a central tenet of the theory presented in this book that the metrical is inextricably tied to all those aspects of music that together form the elusive and endlessly fascinating creature we call "rhythm." Because meter is here defined as a creative process in which the emerging definiteness or particularity of duration is shaped by a great range of qualitative and quantitative distinctions, we will have no reason to oppose meter to other domains or to rhythm. Nor will we have any reason to regard meter as a primitive component of music and an ancillary factor in musical analysis. Indeed, from the perspective of the present study, the contribution of meter must be understood as crucial both for our active engagement with music and for our analysis of this engagement.

If we are to acknowledge the complexity and creativity of metrical process, we must also acknowledge a host of analytic problems—problems, for example, of subjectivity, representation, introspective evidence, ambiguity, and the openness of interpretation. We must ask whose experience is being described; what connection there might be between the abstractions of analysis and the full particularity of hearing; whether we can trust in some commonality of musical experience, and, if so, how we might find evidence of such commonality. Given the history of analytic disputes concerning rhythmic/metric interpretation, prospects for agreement or even productive debate may seem dim. However, I believe that the cause of most disagreements lies not in radically incompatible perceptions but in incompatible theories and in concepts that are not clearly connected to real distinctions in hearing.

The theory presented here is, among other things, an attempt to provide a language in which musical perceptions could be reported, compared, and evaluated and, moreover, a language in which attendant issues of musical communication and interpretation could be productively engaged. The success of this enterprise will be judged, in part, on the basis of a sympathetic testing of the various analyses I offer. In many respects this is the most demanding task asked of the reader of this book. Repeated, self-critical hearings will be required, as will be some openness to experimentation. In view of the complexity and creativity of meter and in view, too, of the limitations of analytic description, the reader may be drawn to somewhat different conclusions from those offered here. Nevertheless, in most cases such discrepancies will not likely be so wide that a projective perspective could not accommodate both interpretations and provide some understanding of their divergence (assuming, again, that there is an agreement to focus our attention on feelings of durational *quantity* rather than on accent). Of course, whatever positive value the present theory might have will lie in its usefulness for understanding music not considered in this study and, more generally, for addressing relevant questions that have not been considered here or that have been considered only superficially.

Whether or not my particular solutions are found compelling, I would hope that the theoretical and analytic work presented here might at least open possibilities for approaching problems of musical rhythm from the perspective of time and process. If it can be granted that metrical processes are as various and richly differentiated as this study would indicate and as intimately connected to broad issues of musical rhythm and form, there will be much more we shall want to know about meter, in general and in particular.

Princeton, New Jersey   C. F. H.
June 1996

Acknowledgments

Among the many people whose wisdom and generosity I have relied on in completing this study, my deepest thanks go to my wife, Olga, and daughter, Kate, to whom this book is lovingly dedicated. I am especially grateful also to my colleagues in the music department at the University of Pennsylvania for providing an extraordinarily stimulating and supportive environment for research and teaching. In particular, I am indebted to Eugene Narmour for his careful reading and judicious criticism of the entire manuscript in an early draft and Eugene Wolf for his help with an early draft of part I. The clarity of my exposition in chapter 9 has been greatly improved as a result of Matthew Butterfield's keen observations, and the entire book has benefited from recommendations made by the three anonymous readers chosen by Oxford University Press to review the manuscript. For generous financial assistance with production costs, I gratefully acknowledge the Research Foundation of The University of Pennsylvania. Last but not least, my thanks go to Maribeth Payne, not only for her help in bringing this work into print but also for her long-standing commitment to issues of time and rhythm in music.

Contents

PART I

METER AND RHYTHM OPPOSED   1

ONE

General Characterization of the Opposition   3

Periodicity and the Denial of Tense   6
Rhythmic Experience   10
Period versus Pattern; Metrical Accent versus
  Rhythmic Accent   13

TWO

Two Eighteenth-Century Views   22

THREE

Evaluations of Rhythm and Meter   34

FOUR

Distinctions of Rhythm and Meter in Three Influential
  American Studies   48

FIVE

Discontinuity of Number and Continuity of Tonal
  "Motion"   59

PART II
A THEORY OF METER AS PROCESS   65

SIX
Preliminary Definitions   67

Beginning, End, and Duration   69
"Now"   76
Durational Determinacy   78

SEVEN
Meter as Projection   84

"Projection" Defined   84
Projection and Prediction   91

EIGHT
Precedents for a Theory of Projection   96

NINE
Some Traditional Questions of Meter Approached from
   the Perspective of Projective Process   103

Accent   103
Division   107
Hierarchy   115
Anacrusis   119
Pulse and Beat   129
Metrical Types — Equal/Unequal   130

TEN
Metrical Particularity   148

Particularity and Reproduction   149
Two Examples   154

ELEVEN
Obstacles to a View of Meter as Process   168

Meter as Habit   168
"Large-Scale" Meter as Container (Hypermeter)   174

TWELVE

The Limits of Meter   183

The Durational "Extent" of Projection   *183*
The Efficacy of Meter   *197*
Some Small Examples   *201*

THIRTEEN

Overlapping, End as Aim, Projective Types   210

Overlapping   *211*
End as Aim   *219*
Projective Types   *225*

FOURTEEN

Problems of Meter in Early-Seventeenth-Century and
   Twentieth-Century Music   237

Monteverdi, "Oimé, se tanto amate" (First Phase)   *237*
Schütz, "Adjuro vos, filiae Jerusalem"   *243*
Webern, Quartet, op. 22   *257*
Babbitt, Du   *275*

FIFTEEN

Toward a Music of Durational Indeterminacy   282

SIXTEEN

The Spatialization of Time and the Eternal
   "Now Moment"   296

References   305

Index   308

PART I

Meter and Rhythm Opposed

Wer will was Lebendigs erkennen und
  beschreiben,
Sucht erst den Geist herauszutreiben,
Dann hat er die Teile in seiner Hand,
Fehlt leider nur das geistige Band.

—Mephistopheles, *Faust*, Part I

CHAPTER ONE

General Character of the Opposition

Of all the things we call rhythmic, music is surely one of the very best examples. Everything the word "rhythm" implies can be found in music. Among the attributes of rhythm we might include continuity or flow, articulation, regularity, proportion, repetition, pattern, alluring form or shape, expressive gesture, animation, and motion (or at least the semblance of motion). Indeed, so intimate is the connection of the rhythmic and the musical, we could perhaps most concisely and ecumenically define music as the rhythmization of sound (thus, the "musicality" of speech or verse). Nevertheless, rhythm is often regarded as one of the most problematic and least understood aspects of music.

If we were to restrict the preceding list of attributes to those that are susceptible to calibration and measurement, it might be said that music theory presents us with a reasonably clear understanding of rhythm. Thus restricted, rhythm is identified with meter, durational pattern, or durational proportion. However, when we speak of rhythm, we cannot easily dismiss other attributes that in one way or another haunt most discussions of musical rhythm and surreptitiously work to foment disagreement about the things we *can* measure.

If we restrict musical rhythm to meter, pattern, and proportion, we feel that something essential has been left out of account. And yet,

how shall we account for those attributes of rhythm that point to the particularity and spontaneity of aesthetic experience as it is happening? To take measurements or to analyze and compare patterns we must arrest the flow of music and seek quantitative representations of musical events. But music as experienced is never so arrested and is not, I will argue, an expression of numerical quantity. To the extent we find it comprehensible, music is organized; but this is an organization that is communicated in process and cannot be captured or held fast. What we can hold onto are spatial representations (scores, diagrams, time lines) and concepts or ideas of order—fixed pattern, invariance, transformation, hierarchy, regularity, symmetry, and proportion. Certainly such ideas can usefully be drawn from musical organization presented as something completed and fully formed. However, a piece of music or any of its parts, while it is going on, is incomplete and not fully determinate—while it is going on, it is open, indeterminate, and in the process of becoming a piece of music or a part of that piece.

This tension between the fixity of what can be grasped as order in abstraction and the fluidity of a felt order in experience arises whenever we attempt to submit an aesthetic experience to analysis. We can to some extent allay this tension by referring analysis to an aesthetic object, a piece of music that is itself structured. Structure is "in" the piece, fully formed and awaiting inspection. But in the analysis of rhythm we cannot so easily ignore the course of events as they emerge for us in a particular experience of "this" piece. To the extent that it suggests process rather than product, dynamic becoming rather than static being, a *fait accomplissant* rather than a *fait accompli* (to use Bergson's distinction), rhythm stands as a reminder of the reality of temporal passage. And it is for this reason that rhythm remains such a problematic concept for music theory and analysis. Neither our technical vocabulary nor our habits of thought prepare us to engage the questions of temporality implicit in the notion of rhythm, or rather in the notion of rhythm most broadly conceived. To make matters worse, in its broad range of applications the word "rhythm" seems to contain incompatible or even contradictory meanings that can exacerbate the problematic opposition of structure and process.

Central to our understanding of rhythm is the notion of regular repetition. Any phenomenon that exhibits periodicity can be called rhythmic, regardless of whether evidence of this periodicity is accessible to our sense perception. We speak of the rhythm of a ticking clock, the rhythm of the seasons, and the rhythm of birth and death. Rhythmic also are the procession of Vedic *Kalpas* and the oscillations of a cesium atom. Similarly, when we speak of the rhythm of work there is an implication of regularly repeated activity or routine. To many, rhythm in music is above all else the repetition of pulse or beat (what the schooled musician is inclined to call meter). At the same time, we can use the word rhythm to characterize phenomena in which periodicity is not apparent: a fluid gesture of the hand, a still life, the course of a narrative, the "shape" of a musical phrase. Such applications necessarily rely on human sensory perception and may therefore be called "aesthetic" (from *aisthanesthai*, to sense or feel, related to *aiō*—or Latin *audio*—"I hear,"). In contrast to the first meaning of "rhythm," which may be ascribed to a phenomenon solely on the basis of periodicity, this second meaning relies on aesthetic judgment and admits of degrees. As lexicographers confirm, this latter usage is less com-

mon than the former, but it is not in any sense metaphorical.

If we can detect a split or bifurcation in the meaning of "rhythm" here, it should be borne in mind that the word holds these meanings together in a complex union—regularity or periodicity can be a highly valued characteristic of rhythm in our "aesthetic" sense. However, we can easily bring these various connotations into sharper contrast by considering the attributes of rhythm in isolation from one another. To polarize these attributes we could say that rhythm means, on the one hand, lawfulness, regularity, and measure and, on the other hand, expressive or compelling motion, gesture, or shape. Rhythm can imply regularity, or spontaneity; an objective property that can be abstracted and measured, or something ineffable that can only be experienced; an order that is generalizable and, in principle, repeatable, or an order that is particular and unrepeatable.

In the study of music, such dichotomies have become institutionalized in the opposition of rhythm and meter. In this opposition, regular repetition, a hallmark of rhythm in common parlance, is detached from rhythm. Such repetition, conceived as a system of periodicities, provides the "measure of time" for rhythmic activity—a temporal grid for the timing of musical events or a scaffolding for the construction of the genuinely rhythmic edifice of music. In this way, meter can be conceived as a more or less independent structure that rhythm uses for its own ends. Rhythm freely plays with or even against meter. Although meter as regularity, repetition, and equality is generalizable, mechanical, expressively neutral, and itself largely devoid of character, rhythm can use meter to create its own particularity and expressivity. From this description, the distinction between meter and rhythm might be regarded as the distinction between abstract and concrete. However, we understand meter to be something no less palpable than is rhythm, and it is generally claimed, explicitly or implicitly, that we hear both meter and rhythm and their interaction.

It is in the opposition of meter and rhythm that we encounter most poignantly the opposition of law versus freedom, mechanical versus organic, general versus particular, or constant repetition of the same versus spontaneous creation of the ever new. And in such oppositions meter is usually denigrated. We speak of rhythmic freedom and the tyranny of the bar. We can disparage a performance as being too metrical, but it would make no sense to say that a performance is too rhythmic. When we are taught to read music we must first master counting, but if we continue counting we shall never play rhythmically. Oddly, meter is regarded as necessary or at least useful for rhythm and yet opposed to rhythm. In its alterity meter can come to be seen as nonrhythmic or even antirhythmic or, at best, inauthentically or not fully rhythmic. And yet, as means to an end or as foundation or basis, however primitive, meter should have no negative connotations. That such a useful and productive aspect of music should be regarded with suspicion, I think, has to do with our inability to satisfactorily connect meter and rhythm, for it is not at all clear how rhythm uses meter or in what sense meter can be a foundation for rhythm. If, in fact, meter is an aspect of rhythm, there should be no opposition and no contradiction.

This disjunction of meter and rhythm arises less from a disjunction within musical experience than from the terms we customarily employ in the definition of meter. Thus, while I submit that there is nothing at all abstract about our experience of meter, I shall argue that our concepts of meter, although useful in many ways, detract from the temporal nature of those feelings we call metrical and that, as a result, our concept of meter comes to be separated from our intuitions of rhythm as something fully temporal and processive.

Certainly, the intricate play of durational repetition that we call meter is only one among many ingredients of musical rhythm. It is, however, a central feature of most musics and that aspect of music that would seem most deeply involved in music's rhythmic and temporal nature. Indeed, so crucial is the repetition of durational quantity for our musical experience, the layman may well call this phenomenon rhythm pure and simple. In this, the layman unfamiliar with the dichotomy of meter and rhythm may have more wisdom than the schooled musician, whose introduction to this dichotomy usually takes place at a tender age with the demands of learning to read music.

In our attempts to master the skills required of metrical notation we may indeed come to think of meter as a matter of counting or as a grid for the correct disposition of durations. In the music we are taught to read, a meter (or time) signature stands at the beginning of each piece as a rule that will determine the order of pulses and their subdivision. Each bar will have a fixed number of pulses, which may be joined and divided in prescribed ways without losing their identity as pulses. While bars may vary in the durations they contain, each bar is metrically identical to all the others. Indeed, such homogeneity has been regarded as an essential characteristic of meter and that characteristic which most clearly distinguishes meter from rhythm. The "and of two," for instance, is understood to be the same in each and every bar. It is the same "place," and throughout the piece we continually return to this place—in fact, it would appear that we return to or at least pass through this place even if it is not articulated with an attack. There is, to be sure, heterogeneity among the various "levels" of regular repetition (bar, beat, and subdivisions of the beat). And such heterogeneity can be viewed as the result of qualitative distinctions of accent. Nevertheless, this hierarchical order is itself fixed; if *the* meter does not change, this order is completely homogeneous. Viewed in this way, meter, like a clock, runs unperturbed, continually and uniformly measuring a time in which a variety of events may occur—the genuinely rhythmic events that occupy the time meter measures off. And with this image it is difficult to avoid the implication of a rigid determinism. Once set in motion, meter can seem to run autonomously, driven by its own internal law and fated from the beginning to reproduce its preordained set of time divisions.

Now, it must be granted that in our elementary training we do not reflect on the issue of homogeneity or on what metrical homogeneity must mean for our conception of musical rhythm and time in general. But it must also be granted that the practice and pedagogy of metrical notation are not detached from theory. Since we have little reason to reflect on the conceptual framework we accept in learning to read, with long familiarity we can come to accept certain customary notions of meter and rhythm simply as matters of fact. Such notions may then enter our thought quite tacitly when we turn to speculate about the nature of meter and rhythm. Indeed, I would argue that all our systematic theories of meter draw upon a conceptual framework grounded in the technology of metric notation. Moreover, I would argue that the assumptions of homogeneity and determinism that derive at least in part from notational practice (and in part from more general assumptions concerning time) are responsible for the opposition of meter and rhythm.

In part II of this study I will present a theory in which meter is treated as an aspect of rhythm that is characterized by the creativity, spontaneity, and particularity that we often ascribe to rhythm in opposition to meter. This undertaking will involve a radical reinterpretation of many of the terms of traditional metric theory and an explicit account of some fundamental categories that are undefined in most theories of rhythm and meter. But before offering a "rhythmic" theory of meter, I would like to explore some features of this opposition in more detail, in order to better understand the separation of meter and rhythm and the tendency to regard meter problematically as a central feature of rhythm but not itself fully rhythmic. I shall begin at the most general level by briefly exploring some of the temporal implications contained in our ideas of periodicity and rhythm. My contention here is that in conceiving of musical meter as periodicity, we import from scientific theory ideas of time that are incompatible with our intuitions of rhythm as a sensible or aesthetic category. The word "rhythm" speaks to us, however obscurely, of a time that is not other than the particular course of an event that we follow with interest—a time that can be neither predicted nor recaptured, a time articulated not by points or segments but by the emergence of felt events. It will be by interpreting meter or the repetition of durational quantity as such an aesthetic category that I will later attempt to treat meter as an integral part of rhythm.

Following this general discussion of rhythm and periodicity, I shall turn to more specific questions of musical rhythm and meter and, finally, to the speculations of several modern music theorists.

Periodicity and the Denial of Tense

If there are oppositions or contradictions implicit in the notion of rhythm, they are not very sharply drawn in our everyday uses of the word. In most contexts, "rhythm" is not an especially problematic word. It is only in the theory and analysis of music (and, to a lesser extent, in theories of poetic meter) that the oppositions I have sketched here are made explicit in the distinction of rhythm and meter. In more general parlance we have little reason to make such distinctions. Although repetition or regular recurrence is usually taken to be the central feature of rhythm, it is not assimilated to number or to the determinism of regularity as rule or law. By "rhythm" we generally understand some definite movement or process characterized by more or less regular repetition and not the measurement of this regularity or the regularity per se, which has been abstracted from movement or process and represented as numerical quantity. For these latter concerns we turn to the more technical term "periodicity." Thus, we calculate the periodic motions of planets or the periodicity of atomic oscillations rather than the rhythms of planets or atoms. Certainly, we can speak of planetary and atomic rhythms, but such expressions have a nontechnical, almost figurative ring. It is only in biological science that "rhythm" has been taken as a technical term to refer to the often labile periodicities of living organisms. If, as I hope to show, "rhythm" and "periodicity" interpret notions of repetition and temporality quite differently, this difference is not a source of conflict, simply because the two terms belong to realms of discourse that we ordinarily have no reason to attempt to reconcile. Outside of music, we do not regard rhythm as something over against regularity—it is not something superimposed on periodicity, something in need of periodicity for its rationalization, or something that asserts itself in its play against periodicity. What is rhythmic is ordered and therefore comprehensible, but this is an order that cannot be abstracted from the thing or event.

In music theoretical discourse, periodicity and rhythm have been very sharply distinguished. Here periodicity as meter is brought into conflict with rhythm and is characteristically denigrated as mechanical and inartistic. In this conflict two very different interpretations of temporality are placed in opposition and evaluated. To the extent meter is devalued vis-à-vis rhythm, the concept of rhythm may be understood as an implicit criticism of periodicity and the temporal presuppositions upon which the idea of periodicity is based.

The notion of time meter evokes is that of classical scientific doctrine—a homogeneous, evenly flowing time that serves as a receptacle for events while remaining unaffected by the events it comes to contain. It is a conception of time modeled on number, an infinitely divisible continuum composed of (or decomposable into) durationless instants—temporal counterparts of the extensionless points of mathematical space.[1] This construction of time has so permeated our language and habits of thought that many of its tenets seem unquestionable. Present, past, and future are readily pictured as locations on a "time line." "Now" as an absolute present seems necessarily to be a durationless instant. We speak of a "span," an "amount," a "point" of time, of events happening "in" time, "at a certain moment" of time, "during the same period" of time. As commonsensical as such expressions are, it should be remembered that the constructions that have given rise to them have also led to doctrines of rigid determinism in the physical sciences and to debates concerning the reversibility of time and even the reality of time or temporal passage—notions that could hardly be more remote from human experience.

If rhythm evokes an understanding of time different from that of periodicity or meter, this understanding seems quite vaguely defined. There is no doctrine or theory of time that rhythm would offer in place of the "mathematical" time of meter. Indeed, so pervasive is the notion of time as a container for events (or a metric of their change), we may have no other way of imagining or *visualizing* time. Rhythm focuses our attention, not on time as a substrate or medium for events, but on the events themselves in their particularity, creativity, and spontaneity. To speak of rhythm is to speak of the rhythm of something—a characteristic gesture or shape that makes this something special. Moreover, it is to raise the question, special for whom? Rhythm, in our aesthetic sense, seems to refer to a time of subjectivity and human experience—a world apart from the objective, "absolute" time of Newtonian physics (but perhaps not so far apart from quantum physics). Again, periodicity seems to be a matter of fact, not, like rhythm, a matter of judgment. Nor is the fact of periodicity in any way dependent upon an observer. And yet, for all the subjectivity and vagueness that the idea of rhythm seems to present, it may serve as a reminder of the real complexity of musical experience and perhaps also as a reminder of the inadequacy of our conception of temporality.

The great value that we attach to rhythm in music, coupled with a customary devaluation of meter as periodicity, is not, I think, a celebration of the irrational and vague and a debasement of

---

1. In my discussion of periodicity I will focus on the "absolute" view of time, or the notion that time itself flows and that events occur *in* time. On the "relational" view, it is not time that flows, but events or occurrences that "flow" (or at least succeed one another) *at* markings that we call "times." These two views admit of a variety of interpretations, and in many practices (for example, the practice of music theory), features of the two are often mixed. For these reasons, I do not think it appropriate here to undertake an analysis of this dichotomy. Suffice it to say that the relational view does not satisfactorily account for the equality of duration as a repetition of the same absolute quantity. Although the relational interpretation of time has played an important role in modern scientific doctrine, it has received its clearest formulations in Idealist philosophies where time is regarded as a form of appearance. Something resembling this interpretation

can be seen to underlie the elimination of real temporal passage in many structuralist models. For an incisive analysis and criticism of the relational view, see Irwin C. Lieb's *Past, Present, and Future* (1991), pp. 19–26. Of the many critical discussions of concepts of time in Western scientific doctrine, Milič Čapek's *The Philosophical Impact of Contemporary Physics* (1961) and G. J. Whitrow's *The Natural Philosophy of Time* (1961) are perhaps the most thorough and, from this writer's point of view, the most trenchant. From the novel perspectives offered by relativity and quantum physics, Čapek argues for a reinterpretation of time consonant with recent "process" philosophy. Whitrow's much broader study summarizes thinking about time in many scientific disciplines and contains useful accounts of a variety of "absolute" and "relational" views. Both Čapek and Whitrow argue forcefully for the reality of time and tense.

the clear and distinct. Rather, I would suggest that our valuation expresses an intuitive mistrust of periodicity as an abstraction. That what we call meter has come to be mistrusted is an unfortunate consequence of the power of this abstraction. In order to better understand the opposition of meter and rhythm and to lay some groundwork for a rehabilitation of meter, I would like to return to the issues of homogeneity and determinism and explore some of the temporal implications of the concept of periodicity. Although this exploration will prolong the generality of our discussion, it will, I hope, help clarify some of the points made above and provide us with a framework in which to reevaluate the relation of meter and rhythm.

It is by conceiving of meter as the regular recurrence of time span that meter is assimilated to periodicity. Here it may be well to remember the origin of "regularity" in *regere*, to guide or direct by command. The exercise of rule is necessarily temporal, but the rule itself can be imagined as something immune from time and becoming. For as long as there is rule, rule is the same—an atemporal law that, itself fixed, directs becoming. The regularity of cycle is the recurrence of a definite amount of time; it is the return of the same time span over and over again without regard to qualitative differences among returns and without regard to the number of repetitions. This single quantity, numerically conceived, is thus elevated to the status of rule. The notion of a "return of the same," however, seems quite paradoxical in that "return" implies multiplicity and "same" implies identity or unity. This ultimately mathematical dialectic of unity and multiplicity is here transferred to the temporal domain as a merging of permanence and change. But what can it mean in a truly temporal sense to say that the same is repeated?

What is "the same" in a repeated thing or event is presumably some feature abstracted from the thing or event that can be identified in all those individuals we call repetitions. In the case of cyclic repetition, what is abstracted is duration conceived as "time span"—the regularity of the cycle is the repetition of identical time spans. Such abstraction seems harmless enough until it is remembered how many decisions have already been made in the reduction of duration to time

span: among others, the decision that durational quantity is to be understood only as numerical quantity, measured from durationless instant to durationless instant, preserved from passage by numerical representation, divisible into selfsame units; and the decision that time is to be conceived as a homogeneous medium, continuous because infinitely divisible, independent from the actual events it is to contain. These ideas have far-reaching consequences for music theory and have played a crucial role in definitions of meter and rhythm. However, it must be said that these concepts of duration and time, although they have been extraordinarily productive for the physical sciences, have not been adequate to the questions posed by music—otherwise, there would be less disagreement surrounding the topics of rhythm and meter.

If unity or what is taken as "the same" here is seen as an abstraction that is not beyond reproach, it may be possible to find other and perhaps richer and more fruitful ways of regarding musical duration and time. If, however, "the same" is taken as essential to what duration and time are, unity will point toward an essentially static homogeneity and determinism in which multiplicity can seem accidental or even illusory. In the case of meter, the multiplicity of repetition has rarely been seen as illusory. Nevertheless, the novelty, particularity, and indeterminacy that might be granted to the process of repetition have been denied in deference to the return of the same. The homogeneity of cycle has been ascribed to meter as its essential attribute whether meter has been defined as the periodicity of bar or tactus, as pulse grouped by accent to form bars, or as a hierarchical coordination of cycles.

It is true that, since cycle is also multiplicity, cycles must be distinguished as individuals and marked as terms in an order of succession. But *the* cycle itself, as rule, is autonomous and logically precedes any such marking. While cycles must be externally differentiated in order to be *returns* of the same, this differentiation does not deny the homogeneity of the series. Thus, we speak of *the* meter of a piece as something given in advance that need not itself be subject to change during the course of the piece. The homogeneity of periodic repetition is also reflected in our use of the term "cycle," which can mean either a single period or the complete set of repetitions.

Certainly, cycles may be internally heterogeneous; that is, individual cycles may have different "contents"—successive bars, for example, may contain different arrangements of durations (often called "rhythms"), tones, contours, et cetera. But it is the homogeneity of returns that makes them cycles—their heterogeneity has no bearing on the repetition of identical time spans. If the period is reproduced, the law of cycle is fulfilled, regardless of whether there are qualitative distinctions among the returns. If we take this denial of qualitative difference seriously, we might even regard the *repetition* of identical time spans as mere appearance. Thus, in very many cultures the cycle or circle is treated as a symbol of eternity. In Western technological-scientific culture, cycle has lost this traditional, symbolic meaning; but as I shall argue, a mathematical concept of time with its concomitant homogeneity and determinism is, nevertheless, used by us to put time out of account in our attempts to gain control over events.

Where heterogeneity or difference cannot be denied is in the constitution of the individual period prior to its repetition (in this case, logically and temporally prior). A cycle must be differentiated internally in order to mark a duration that can be equal to the duration of another instance of the cycle. Indeed, there can be no return to the same place or state unless there is a departure into what is *not* this place or state. This fixed place as a point of beginning defines the cycle, and the span or duration of the cycle is filled with nonbeginning—a continuous passage that is terminated by a new beginning (a point that must be, at the same time, the end of the old cycle). If this continuous passage is regarded as the passage of time, it will be *the flow of time* that provides difference. And yet this flow itself has been conceived as absolutely homogeneous and essentially independent from the things whose fate it is to happen in time or to be measured by time. Moreover, if there are regularities or rules that (pre)ordain the location of events in time, the direction of passage can come to be seen as a mere formality, and the differentiation provided by the flow of time can be regarded as a sort of enduring space in which

events are being, have been, and necessarily will be located (such distinctions of tense being relativized to mere differences of perspective).

Although cyclic repetition as measure has been seen as paradigmatically temporal, there is a sense in which it annihilates time, or at least time's arrow. Since the cycle is always the same, the future (any future) is predetermined, and the present phase can, in principle, be detached from all past repetitions. In fact, all phases can be equally "present" for thought. If we know the cycle's law or periodicity, we can predict any future phase and reconstruct any past phase, and in this way we can instantly comprehend past and future. Thus, if in thought we have access to one repetition, we have access to all, and can refer to any phase in isolation from all the rest. The possibility of regarding all phases as co-present (in this case, timelessly co-present) arises from the homogeneity of cyclic repetition. Since repetitions are all the same, there is nothing to distinguish the various returns except for their *order of succession*, which is assimilated to *numerical* succession. But here it must be remembered that numerical succession is not equivalent to temporal succession.

In its infinite divisibility and infinite multiplicity, number is given all at once. Any number, any numerical relationship, implies the whole of number and the infinite, systematic totality of all relationships. This whole is instantaneous. Although we may count sequentially, this temporal and rhythmic act may be thought to be based upon an order that does not and has not become, but which has existed for all eternity. By transferring the concept of number to time, we exorcise becoming, transition, and indeterminacy and replace them with a static, instantaneous being. In this way we can gain control over time—the past is never truly lost, and the uncertainty of the future can be dispelled by the operation of addition applied to the variable t. For the purpose of analyzing temporal phenomena, this concept of time is useful in providing us with a changeless standpoint for describing change. Although things change in time, time itself remains fixed. As Newton states:

> Absolute, True, and Mathematical Time, of itself, and from its own nature flows equably without regard to anything external, and by another name is called Duration.

The True, or equable progress, of Absolute time is liable to no change.

As the order of the parts of time is immutable, so also is the order of the parts of Space.... For times and spaces are, as it were, the Places as well of themselves as of all other things. All things are placed in Time as to order of Succession; and in Space as to order of Situation. (Newton 1729/ 1968, pp. 9, 11, 12)[2]

Absolute time thus presents us with the opportunity to view process as a fait accompli, its phases fixed in an immutable order and available for synoptic inspection, like the notes of a score. Since all the parts or phases are discrete units, precisely located on a single time line itself infinitely divisible, we can place the present at any point along the line. Past and future are relations that can be variously assigned to parts of a whole that already is. The continuity of the whole rests on the continuity of the time line composed, paradoxically, by the adjacency of successive absolutely discrete, but durationless, instants.

This collapsing of past, present, and future brings temporal flux under our control—we can thereby move freely along the "time line," isolating any position we choose. Time becomes comprehensible and manageable if we can abstract it from the continuous becoming of events that take place "in" time and, in effect, regard time as a sort of space—an enduring or persisting order for the dating and coordination of discrete events.

Even though the concept of a mathematical "flow" of time is not what we usually mean by rhythmic flow, the two are often implicitly conflated in music theory. Any discussion of rhythm and meter in music will involve decisions concerning the nature of time, succession, duration, and continuity—topics that are usually con-

ceived in classical scientific terms. Moreover, an analysis of meter in which meter is conceived as cyclic repetition will explicitly invoke the discontinuity of number and will result in the representation of rhythm as a systematic whole of coordinated periodicities in which all the parts are ultimately fixed in a scheme of changeless relationships.

Rhythmic Experience

Although cyclic repetition or regular recurrence is usually thought to have been implied in the meaning of the Greek *rhuthmos* (from *rhein* "to flow"), as, presumably, in the periodic motion of waves), the association of rhythm with periodic motion, measurement, and number seems to have been accomplished by the conceptual innovations of Plato, who radically altered the meaning of *rhuthmos* that had prevailed from the early Ionian period until the mid-fifth century. Emile Benveniste describes Plato's contribution to the subsequent understanding of the term as follows:

His innovation was in applying it [*rhuthmos*] to the *form of movement* which the human body makes in dancing and the arrangement of figures into which this movement is resolved. The decisive circumstance is there, in the notion of a corporal *rhuthmos* associated with *metron* and bound by the law of numbers: this "form" is from then on determined by a "measure" and numerically regulated. Here is the new sense of *rhuthmos*: in Plato, "arrangement" (the original sense of the word) is constituted by an ordered sequence of slow and rapid movements, just as "harmony" results from the alternation of high and low. And it is the order in movement, the entire process of the harmonious arrangement of bodily movements combined with meter, which has since been called "rhythm". We may then speak of the "rhythm" of

---

2. For an analysis and critique of Newton's (and Galileo's) conception of time, see Edwin Arthur Burtt's *The Metaphysical Foundations of Modern Science* (1959), chapters 3 and 7. For a discussion of Newton's characterization of time as "flowing equably without regard to anything external," see especially pp. 261–262 (or Burtt 1954, pp. 263–264). This latter, masterfully compressed summary of Newton's thought is highly relevant for many of our present-day intuitions concerning the na-

ture of time. Burtt does not, however, discuss in this passage a very practical reason for Newton's conception of an absolute time—the need to provide an ideal *measure* for change. As Whitrow (1961) explains, "Newton regarded the moments of absolute time as forming a continuous sequence like that of the real numbers and believed that the rate at which these moments succeed each other is a variable which is independent of all particular events and processes"(1961, p. 35).

a dance, of a step, of a song, of a speech, of work, of everything which presupposes a continuous activity broken by meter into alternating intervals. (Benveniste 1971, p. 287) [3]

According to Benveniste, the meaning of *rhuthmos* that Plato's specialized definition to some extent displaced involved the notion of "form," but not form as something fixed and immutable, susceptible to generalization, or as an arrangement that arises from regularity or repetition. *Rhuthmos* does appear to be related to the verb *rhein* "to flow," but *rhein* could not refer to the regular, periodic motion of waves—the sea was not said to flow, and *rhuthmos* was not used to describe the motion of waves. Benveniste cites many examples in the use of *rhuthmos* that imply the "fixity" of a spatial, visual arrangement or of proportion: among others, the form or shape of a letter of the alphabet, the proportion that is the quality of a fine cuirass, and the balance between opulence and poverty. However, he maintains that this sense of form is neither abstract nor static. For example, the "rhythm" of a letter of the alphabet refers to the distinctive shape of the letter, the particular way the strokes are made. (And I would suggest that the gestural quality of a letter is likely to have been more strongly felt by the Greeks than it would be by inhabitants of a print culture.) This sense of shape is rhythmic, in contrast to other "formal" properties: the order of the letters of the alphabet or their relative positions. Human character, disposition, and mood at any moment are all characterized by *rhuthmos*, as is the present form of a constitution or the formation of an opinion. Common to all the examples Benveniste cites is the notion of form "understood as the distinctive form, the characteristic arrangement of the parts in a whole" (p. 283). And while this notion allows for similarity of form or resemblance, form so conceived is irreducible—it inheres in the individual as a mark of its particularity.

Although *rhuthmos* can refer to spatial configurations and states, a sense of flux is never entirely absent:

> *Rhuthmos*, according to the contexts in which it is given, designates the form in the instant that it is assumed by what is moving, mobile and fluid, the form of that which does not have an organic consistency; it fits the pattern of a fluid element, of a letter arbitrarily shaped, or a robe which one arranges at one's will, of a particular state of character or mood. It is the form as improvised, momentary, changeable....
>
> Thus *rhuthmos*, meaning literally 'the particular manner of flowing', describes 'dispositions' or 'configurations' without fixity or natural necessity and arising from an arrangement which is always subject to change. (Benveniste 1971, pp. 285–286)

Although I cannot speculate on the possibility that some sense of the archaic *rhuthmos* might have clung to the word "rhythm" as it has been passed along to us, I do believe there are features of the archaic meaning that, for whatever reason, resemble intuitions expressed in our use of the word in senses that cannot be reduced to cyclic repetition. These meanings do not point to measurement or to a generalized regularity, but rather to an aesthetic judgment—that is, to something felt or sensed in an aural or visual perception and valued as interesting and attractive. Indicating admiration and approval, we call many things rhythmic: for example, a performed piece of music (whether metrical or not), a dance, a recited poem or simply speech, a person's graceful carriage, a stalking animal, the fluid gesture of a pitcher's windup and throw, a baseball game, a sculpture, a painting, a flower arrangement. If approval is withdrawn, we may in some cases say that these events or objects are characterized by bad or uninteresting rhythm. But we are more often inclined to say that they are not rhythmic. The differences among putatively rhythmic phenomena are considerable—some involve what we might call "periodic" motion, others nonperiodic motion, and others no motion at all; some are more prototypical

---

3. In his dissertation "*Rhuthmos*: A History of Its Connotations" (1972), Robert Christopher Ross provides a much more detailed discussion of the meanings of *rhuthmos*. Although Ross does not find such a sharp discontinuity of meaning initiated by Plato (and doubts the etymological link to *rhein*), his account is otherwise largely in agreement with Benveniste's analysis.

than others (thus, a dance seems in many respects a better example of the rhythmic than is a flower arrangement). Nevertheless, the value attached to the appellation "rhythmic" in all of these cases points to a common perceptual attribute. Something in each case attracts and holds our attention. We follow the event or observe the object with interest. Rhythm in this sense implies participation and sympathy. We are drawn into the object or event in order to experience "its" rhythm. As something experienced, rhythm shares the irreducibility and the unrepeatability of experience.

Although the rhythm of an event is but one of many properties we might ascribe to the event, we cannot abstract rhythm from the wholeness of the event or from the event's particularity. The rhythm of the pitcher's gesture is not separable from the pitcher in this act, and this felt gesture will never be precisely reproduced. Nor is it precisely "reproduced" in the perceptions of thousands of spectators, each of whom feels the rhythm differently according to his or her mood, attentiveness, and own countless physical, gestural experiences. When it is past, the rhythmic event cannot be again made present. Whatever being it has rests in the uses memory will make of it in the formation of novel experience; thus, for example, this throw may color our experience of the next throw. But since these uses are various, there is no real fixity in what the past event holds for present experience—it will become whatever is made of it. Rhythm is in this way evanescent: it can be "grasped" but not held fast.

As an aspect of experience, the rhythmic is not captured by analysis and measurement. We can set up a mechanism—for example, a clock—to mark whatever articulations we deem rhythmically salient and record these articulations as successive instants, but we will not have preserved a rhythmic experience for analysis. Instead, through our acts of calibration, measurement, and analysis we will have created a new experience (perhaps rhythmic in its own right). Our attempts at analysis put time out of account in that we must copy a past event into a timeless present that will allow us to observe its structure at our leisure. The structure itself is also timeless in that all its elements and relations must be si-

multaneously present and differentiated temporally only by order of succession, an order that is fixed from beginning to end.

But by calling something rhythmic we mean that it is not fixed—it is dynamic as opposed to static; fleeting as opposed to permanent. A block of wood is not rhythmic unless we closely observe its grain and find the shape of the markings interesting. Of course, the grain is as permanent as the block itself—we can return to the block later and expect to find the markings unchanged. But what we cannot return to is our experience of rhythm as we attend to the markings. That we can call apparently static arrangements properly, and not metaphorically, rhythmic shows how closely linked rhythm is to immediate experience. A painting seems to be presented all at once, and whatever rhythm the painting has would seem to be fixed at any instant and in this sense timeless. But our perception of the painting's rhythm is not less temporal than our perception of a dance. It takes time to observe the painting, and this observing is a rhythmic act. If there is a sense in which the painting itself is inherently rhythmic, it is that the painting as an object holds potentialities for rhythmic experiences. Our perception of its rhythm is real, not illusory—the painting is rhythmic, not "as if" rhythmic. What we are inclined to regard as illusory (or as metaphorical in ascription) is motion—the painting is rhythmic, as if in motion. Certainly, we may move about as we view the painting—our head and eyes will move involuntarily (and if we were aware of these motions we might call them rhythmic also)—but none of these motions corresponds to the rhythm that we see in the painting. We may see traces of the painter's motions or, in the case of the wood grain, traces of a tree's growth, but we do not see these motions. Although nothing moves, there is process—that of our attention to an object that, although itself immobile, can evoke innumerable aesthetic experiences. To feel rhythm and the semblance of motion in a visual arrangement requires that we become actively engaged in making sense of it. If we cannot make sense of it, if the object remains incomprehensible, we are not inclined to call it rhythmic.

Rhythm in this sense necessarily involves

time, but not, I will argue, the homogeneous time of classical Galilean-Newtonian physics—a time "equably flowing," which passively receives contents. The time of aesthetic experience is characterized by dynamic becoming rather than static being, by novelty rather than return of the same, and by the indeterminacy of the future as potentiality rather than the determinacy of a fixed arrangement. If in music the repetition of equal durations as meter is judged as an especially compelling factor in our experiences of rhythm, it is not because meter presents a predetermined order for the constraint of a heterogeneous content we call rhythm.

In view of the various connotations of the word, it must be said that "rhythm" implies a play of determinacy and indeterminacy or of "law" and "freedom," but if we identify meter with law and rhythm with freedom, such a dialectic will be removed from rhythm itself, and we shall be unable to speak of a nonmetrical rhythm or of meter as something that is itself rhythmic. Later I will suggest that such a play of rhythm could be conceived as the play of the past as determined and the present as undetermined or, rather, in the process of becoming determined in a continuous realization of more or less definite potentials. From this perspective, meter is not opposed to rhythm—it, too, involves the determinacy of what is complete and the indeterminacy of what is on the way to completion.

At this point in the argument, however, it will be helpful to connect some of these general observations to more specific questions of musical meter and rhythm. In the following section we will examine some customary distinctions between rhythm and meter in light of the more general distinctions we have developed thus far.

Period versus Pattern; Metrical Accent versus Rhythmic Accent

The chief obstacle to conceiving of meter as rhythm lies in meter's apparent determinacy and homogeneity. Thus, it can be argued that a piece notated in 3/4 constantly repeats triple measure. Each measure will then be regarded as an instance of a type that itself is determined from the outset. As representatives of the type, all instances are identical and are distinguishable only by count or location within a succession of measures that compose the piece (or within some part of the piece that we identify as a unit). Certainly, in their content, these measures are not all the same, but variability of content can have no bearing on the meter as long as metrical type is perpetuated.

Conceived in this way, the measure, like the time it measures, becomes a receptacle—a container for events. And like time, the duration of the measure is a potential for division (in some accounts, likewise, a potential for infinite division). Of course, unlike time, the measure is itself an event—the measure happens *in* time. But measure can also be regarded as a medium for properly rhythmic events and as a more or less autonomous principle of articulation—an atomic unit for the measurement of a musical time diversified by an actual musical content. And to the extent measure is regarded as a medium for rhythm and conceived as a selfsame unit of measurement, the measure will share something of the homogeneity, the autonomy, and the immateriality of time itself (time, that is, in its "mathematical" conception).

If the particular or unique patterning of measures, or rather their content, is taken as rhythmic rather than metrical differentiation, meter may be regarded as the foundation or basis for rhythm. But such a basis will be abstract or ideal—either a matrix of possibilities from which rhythm chooses an actual shape or an underlying form to which the particularity of rhythm can be reduced. We are thus presented with this conundrum: that the repetition of durational quantity—arguably, one of the most palpable, even visceral, aspects of musical art—when viewed theoretically seems to recede from the immediate deliverance of the ear to become a form or a principle of organization.

Before we consider the ways in which this dilemma has been treated in the work of several theorists, it will be helpful to examine some general features of the opposition of meter and rhythm as they appear in distinctions that are customarily made between meter and rhythmic "pattern" and between metric and rhythmic accent.

If the defining characteristic of meter is the

EXAMPLE 1.1   Meter as a system of coordinated periodicities versus rhythm as variegated pattern

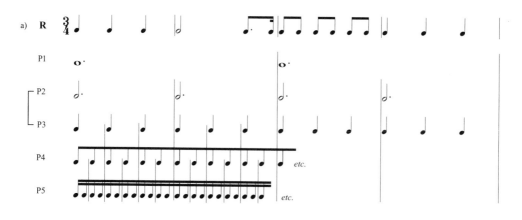

continuous succession of equal durations, rhythm, by contrast, may be characterized by inequality and defined as a succession of various durations. In this very narrow definition of rhythm, there will be no conflict between rhythm and meter if the series of various durations are seen as multiples or as equal divisions of a metrical pulse. (For the time being, we will ignore the question of accent.) In fact, rhythm's various durations could be viewed as products of the properly metrical operations of multiplication and division.

Thus, in example 1.1a we could regard the dotted eighth note in bar 2, for instance, as a multiplication (times 3) of a "submetrical" (sixteenth-note) division of the beat. Or we might imagine that the several pulse "levels" or "strata" shown in the example as P1, P2, P3, P4, and P5 provide a set of coordinated periodicities that can be sampled by the actual rhythm. Incidentally, if there were "irregularities" (as there often are in music) in the coordination of periodicities at lev-

els P1, P4, and P5, we could still avoid speaking of conflict if we were to privilege P2 and P3 as properly metrical (in accordance with the signature 3/4) and demote the other levels to the status of the "hypermetrical" and "submetrical."

If there is no conflict here, the distinction between meter and rhythm would seem to turn instead on the contrast between law and freedom or abstract and concrete. The (ruling) meter, 3/4, prescribes a succession of three-beat units, *potentially* joined or divided in a variety of ways. The *actual* patterns, though made possible by meter, are freely chosen—and this choice is not determined by meter. Too, it would appear that none of the metrical levels shown beneath the rhythm in example 1.1a is to be understood as a succession of actual sounding durations. Although the first bar of P3, like the first bar of the rhythm (R), represents three beats, these two representations have very different meanings. If meter were to be conceived as the grouping of equal sounding durations, bar 1 of R would itself be meter or, at least, indistinguishable from meter. We would then have to say that only in bars 2 and 3 (or perhaps only in bar 2 if we take P4 into account) is there pure rhythm or rhythm as something more than or different from meter. Certainly, this is not the way we customarily view rhythm. It will, I think, be generally agreed that all of R is rhythm, that bars 1 and 4 are not less rhythmic than bar 2, and that if P3 were to be actually performed this, too, would be a representation of rhythm. Thus, if in example 1.1 there is a distinction between meter and rhythm, then meter, unlike rhythm, must not be a sensible phenomenon.

A similar conclusion emerges if we consider the possibility of isolating one or the other component. If rhythm in the sense we are now considering is metrically organized, its particularity derives, at least to some extent, from the order that meter imparts to it. For example, we cannot hear rhythm R apart from meter. If there were a change of meter, as in example 1.1b, the rhythm (R') would not remain the same. (At least, this is the way most musicians, I think, would speak of rhythm here.) On the other hand, meter can be conceived apart from rhythm, as "general" can be conceived apart from "specific" or "universal" from "particular." Thus, rhythm may change while meter remains the same, as, for instance, in example 1.1a, where bars 1 and 2 differ in rhythm but not in meter. Meter would thus appear to be very remote from the materiality of rhythm—a form of order as distinct from the substance it informs.

Meter is customarily defined not only by durational quantity but also by accent—regular alternations of strong and weak or thetic and arsic beats. With this qualitative addition there is the possibility for a conflict of meter and rhythm if

the metrical distinctions of strong and weak are not coordinated with forms of accent that can be regarded as "rhythmic." Again, let us say that the arrangements of actual sounding durations represented in example 1.2 are rhythms, as distinct from the meter that informs them. But here rhythm is further distinguished from meter by conflicts of accent.

In example 1.2a the metrically weak second beat receives a dynamic or "stress" accent. In example 1.2b the second beat receives an agogic accent, and the metrically stronger third beat is suppressed.

To enter into conflict, meter and rhythm must share some common ground. The qualitative category of accent can provide this shared character and bring meter into the concrete, sensible realm of rhythm. Even the means of accentuation are shared—all the forms of accent (dynamic, agogic, tonal, etc.) that effect rhythmic accent can function to reinforce or intensify metrical accent. However, the means must be distinguished here from the ends. Metrical and rhythmic accent must be different in kind; otherwise rhythm, in this sense, would be distinct from meter only when its accents are not coordinated with those of meter (and we would be presented with the same sort of problem we encountered above with respect to durations). If the two kinds of accent are fundamentally different, meter and rhythm are always distinct. We could imagine this difference giving rise to a variety of interactions, ranging from the extreme of tedious, metronomic coordination, in which there is little or no conflict, to that of anarchic disjunction, in which rhythm could threaten to destroy meter.

If rhythmic and metrical accent are essentially distinct, how shall we characterize the difference? Again, we might say that metrical accent is

EXAMPLE 1.2   Conflicts of metrical accent and rhythmic accent

fixed and rhythmic accent is free.[4] The fixity of metrical accent can be conceived in two quite different ways. Metrical accent can be fixed once and for all by the meter signature, which prescribes, at least on the bar level, a homogeneous order of accents. Not only is a metrical type prescribed for the piece, but also each bar will have an order of metrical accent identical to every other bar under the rule of the signature. Downbeats of bars may be variously accented in relation to some larger metrical formation, but the internal order of all bars (or any unit we regard as metrical) is the same. And this is true not only of a single piece—any measure of three beats, for example, is in its structure of metrical accent identical to any other measure of three beats. Or, from a less global and schematic perspective, we may equate the fixity of metrical accent with the fixity of habit. Thus, it is often maintained that a meter, having once been established, will tend to perpetuate itself even against the influence of conflicting rhythmic accent. In either case, rhythmic accent, by contrast, seems more mercurial. Since rhythmic accent is heterogeneous, there is no rule that would prescribe the order or formation of such accent. Again, rhythm, in contrast to meter, is characterized by novelty and spontaneity. It might be argued that rhythm, like meter, is fixed and determined in advance by virtue of being previously composed and precisely notated. To argue in this way, however, would be to ignore the temporality (and variabilty) of performance and the interpretive creativity that rhythmic accent draws upon for its particularity.

Because rhythmic accent is so clearly a qualitative distinction, its definition can remove rhythm even further from the quantitative regularity of meter. Rhythm can now be released from the confines of durational pattern and even from determinate durational quantity and characterized in terms of motion, energy, tension, and relaxation. Such categories speak of process

rather than time span, of what goes on "in" time and the character of this going on instead of arrangements of durational quantities abstracted from their "contents." In this broadening of the concept of rhythm, it is possible to abandon durational "pattern" as the central characteristic of rhythm. And with this turn it becomes less pressing to attempt to relate rhythm to the essentially quantitative order of meter. The problem now is to relate the two qualitative categories of accent. This task has been undertaken by numerous theorists, and their various solutions need not be reviewed here. More pertinent to this stage of my argument is a discussion of some of the difficulties raised by the attempt to wed the qualitative category of accent to the concept of meter.

If the qualitative distinction of accent functions to mark the initiation of cycles, this marking itself must be conceived as durationless. A durationless accent comports very well with the timelessness and infinite divisibility of number, and with the conclusion that meter in itself is impalpable, being a container for or measurement of the sounding rhythmic event. In the following passage from *The Time of Music*, Jonathan Kramer draws what I believe are some unavoidable conclusions from the customary views of rhythm and meter just outlined. Here Kramer adopts David Epstein's distinction between beat and pulse:

> Beats are timepoints. The temporal continuum of most traditional music consists of a series of more or less evenly spaced beats: the meter of the music. Pulses, however, are flexible, and they are rhythmic. . . . A pulse is literally heard, not intuited the way a beat is. Pulse is susceptible to rhythmic accent, while metric accents are applied to beats.
>
> Not only are metric and rhythmic accents different phenomena but also they are applied to different kinds of musical events. The two may or may not coincide, but they are conceptually—and *experientially*—distinct. A pulse is an event in the

---

4. This interpretation, which emerged in nineteenth-century theories of accent, is expressed by Mathis Lussy, for example, as a contrast between instinct and understanding: "Measures and rhythms constitute two separate domains. Indeed, they arise from the same principle: they are sons of one father—the division of time; and they have one and the same mother—the necessity of ictus or accented tones to become comprehensible to us. However, the measure has remained in the realm of instinct—it has the power to transmit to our ear merely the conception of a mechanical, regular division of time. Rhythm has risen to a higher calling—it has attained the spheres of understanding, in which it reveals the form of a comprehensible unity" (1885/1966, pp. 147–148).

music, interpreted by a performer and directly heard by a listener. It occurs *at* a timepoint. A beat, on the other hand, *is* a timepoint rather than a duration in time. . . . Beats acquire significance because of where they occur within their metric hierarchy. The significance of pulses, by contrast, is not created by their location along the temporal continuum but rather by their rhythmic context.

Performers and listeners use the information in a composition to understand where beats fall and how strongly accented they are, but we do not literally *hear* beats. We experience them, we feel them, and we extrapolate them—by means of mental processing of information. But we cannot hear something that is a timepoint, that has no duration. We react physically and emotionally to meter, but we do not literally sense it with our eardrums. (Kramer 1988, p. 97)

These conclusions notwithstanding, it remains a mystery how a qualitative distinction of accent can be without duration—a distinction that somehow touches our sensibility to the extent that it is capable of actually conflicting with rhythmic accent. Certainly, meter is not perceived directly or immediately—we have no sense organ for meter—but must not the same be said of our perception of rhythm? Indeed, if we consider the sophistication required to perceive rhythmic distinctions, particularly those fine discriminations of tonal or cadential "weighting" so valued as rhythmic in many theories, it could be argued that meter (as a relatively primitive, less acculturated discrimination) involves less interpretation, less construction, than rhythm. In any case, if we are to construct meter or to "extrapolate" metrical accents, we will need some aural cues that are not nothing. Furthermore, because of the dubious perceptual and ontological status of the durationless metrical accent, it is not at all clear whether accent is the cause of meter or a result of meter's autonomous regularity—whether accent is the means by which periodicities are hierarchically coordinated or simply an epiphenomenal result of their coordination.

Carl Schachter voices the puzzlement felt by many musicians who have considered this issue:

A point in time can never receive an emphasis; only an event that occurs at that point can. The metrical accent, therefore, always colors the event—tone, harmony, occasionally even silence—that falls on the favored point. Conceptually the accent is localized at the boundary point, but the accent as embodied in the compositional event must shade off through time. This bears directly on one of the most obvious aspects of metrical organization: the emphasis on beginnings. The accent occurs on the boundary between two time spans, an old one and a new one. If only because of its novelty, the beginning of the new span attracts more attention than the end of the old one, and the emphasis accrues to the event that the new span brings to the listener. (Schachter 1987, p. 6)

Schachter rightly points to the conceptual and visual character of the "point in time." It is precisely because we conceive of succession spatially—a "boundary between two spans"—that we must conceive of accent (and beginning) as a point without duration. The first few sentences of this quotation very thoughtfully expose several of the problems that arise from this metaphor. A point in time, since it is purely conceptual and is nothing to be experienced, cannot receive an emphasis, whereas an event can indeed be emphasized or accented. However, an event cannot occur at a point of time—nothing can *occur* at a durationless instant. Nor can an event's accentuation fall on such a point if we regard an event as a temporal whole. If accent qualifies or "colors" the event (and the duration of the event) to which it pertains, then the accent cannot be abstracted from the event as a time point. This initial time point does not belong to the event or to duration; it is not, as Schachter says, "embodied" in the event. Instead, it belongs to time, or rather to a mathematical time which flows independently from the events that take place in time or which functions as a metric for (a perhaps illusory) change. Furthermore, it should be remembered that the mathematical continuity of this "flow" is at bottom nothing but *infinite* discontinuity. The number 1 does not, in fact, "shade off" into 2; 1 and 2 are discrete quantities, and between 1 and 2 lie an infinity of real numbers.

This distinction between duration and numerical quantity as it pertains to the concept of metrical accent has been very explicitly drawn by Andrew W. Imbrie:

Rhythm is the patterning or proportional arrangement of sounds and silences with respect to their durations, while meter is the measurement of the distances between points of time. Distance and duration are not synonymous: the former is the measure of the latter. (Compare the spatial distance between two points in geometry with an actual line drawn between or through them.)

Meter acts as a conservative force. It is the principle that attempts to reduce to "law and order" the protean rhythmic complexities of the musical surface. It is the frame of reference by which we try to measure and judge the relative values of the changes taking place in the music. (Imbrie 1973, pp. 53–54)

And, although he does not argue explicitly from the notion of time point, William Benjamin reaches a similar conclusion: that "as a way of structuring music's time which is essentially independent of music's events, [meter] allows us to characterize those events as to where they happen and not merely to what they are in sonic terms" (1984, p. 412).

In chapter 6 of the present study I will attempt to develop an alternative to the notion of a durationless instant of beginning (and ending) and a redefinition of temporal succession that would place continuity and discontinuity in less stark opposition. Here we need only consider why the notion of a purely metrical accent should lead us inevitably to the paradoxes of a durationless instant of accent. Again, I would argue that this problem arises, at least in part, because of the incompatibility of qualitative and numerical-quantitative categories.

As primitives of modern accentual theories of meter we may identify two states or *values*—accented and unaccented or strong and weak—and three (numerical) *positions*: first, second, and third. All first beats are accented as first beats (and metrically identical as first beats); indeed, "first position" and "accent" may be regarded as interchangeable expressions. Second and third beats are unaccented (and metrically identical as second and third beats) in duple and triple meters respectively. Fixed for each level, metrical accent is variable only in terms of higher or lower metrical order as an alteration of the relative position of a beat. For example, the point of accent for the second quarter-note beat of a bar

of 3/4, though weak for the bar by virtue of being second, is strong as, say, the first of two eighth-note beats (strong, that is, by virtue of being a first). Thus, in example 1.3a all firsts—all alphas and A's—are strong; but from the perspective of a "higher" level (level 1, beta^1) the point r of a strong first on a "lower" level (level 2, beat A^2) can be viewed as the point of a weak second. Conversely, all seconds are weak, though from a lower level any point marked as weak can be viewed as strong.

Notice in example 1.3a that although beta^1 is weak and alpha^1 is strong, B^2 on level 2, which is positioned within the second time span of level 1, is not weaker than B^1 of level 2, which is positioned within the first time span of level 1. Or, in example 1.3b, notice that b^1 is the weakest beat, though b^1 marks a duration that lies within that marked by the strongest beat, alpha^1. These observations demonstrate the fact that time-span does not itself bear the distinction strong/weak. Thus, metrical accent cannot occupy a span of time. Because metrical accents are not "in" the durations they mark, levels of accent are, as it were, "transparent" to one another; there is a hierarchy of span or extent (i.e., the time span from beat a^1 to b^1 is contained within the time-span interval A^1–B^1), but qualitative differences of accent are not transferred from one level to another (b^1 is not contained within the "strength" of A^1). We might say that the lower level or "smaller" qualitative determinations are thus ignorant of higher level interpretations—that higher levels of interpretation communicate nothing to the lower levels of the hierarchy. Again, this sort of metrical hierarchy represents a coordination of periodicities in which the externality and homogeneity of repetition are preserved from level to level.

If metrical accent is external to the duration it marks, it must be asked whether this sort of accent is, in fact, a qualitative distinction or purely a creature of measurement. The latter explanation accords much better with those features of metrical accent we have observed thus far. From this perspective, the beats marked "weak" in example 1.3 may be construed simply as labels for points that divide in (two or three) equal parts the interval from strong beat to strong beat on any level. Since the interval is

EXAMPLE 1.3   Metrical accent interpreted as a durationless instant

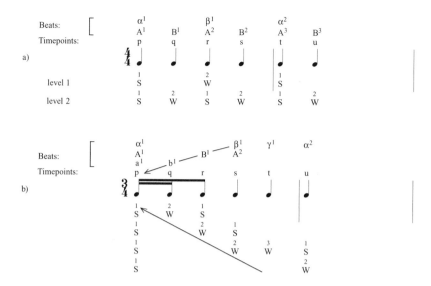

given for division (i.e., there must be an interval "before" that interval can be divided), strong beats logically precede their dividing weak beats. Since the operation of division produces intervals, this operation can then be applied to the products. Thus, in example 1.3a "beta¹" labels a point of division, and "A²" labels this same point as a boundary of an interval that itself can be divided (and is here shown divided by B²). As example 1.3b indicates, there are an infinite number of positions to the right of an accent that can mark an unaccented second beat. In the example, division has been carried as far as beat b¹. Since we could continue performing the operation of division through an infinite number of steps, it is clear that there are an infinite number of possible accented beats that are located at point p and that p itself must be durationless. There are an infinite number of beats because there are an infinite number of *measurements* that can be taken from point p. The point p is durationless because we measure from zero. Here, in saying that alpha¹ is the strongest beat we mean that alpha¹ marks a boundary of the largest span that is given prior to division or, perhaps more accurately, that alpha¹ is the point from which we measure this largest span.

Viewed in this way, metrical accent is assimilated to numerical quantity. The purpose of ac-

cent, then, is to provide a set of points from which measurements can be taken. The hierarchical arrangement of such points taken as a whole is meter. So understood, meter (no less than the points that constitute meter) marks durations but is external to the durations it marks—just as the preceding quotations from Imbrie and Benjamin claim. A result of this numerical interpretation of metrical accent is a radical separation of meter and rhythm. Unlike the durationless accent of meter, rhythmic accent actually *occurs* in time and through duration. In this case, there can be no genuine conflict of meter and rhythm—no conflict between the measuring and the thing that is measured —but neither can there be any intercourse. Rhythm and meter now can be treated as separate musical factors and analyzed in isolation from one another.

One effect of this separation is, again, to free the definition of rhythm from the categorical limitations of durational quantity and to open rhythm to questions of process and to qualitative and affective categories such as gesture, movement, impulse, tension, and relaxation. Unfortunately, these categories remain ill-defined, with the result that, compared to analyses of meter, "rhythmic" analyses are generally vague, unsystematic, and open to dispute. Analyses of meter pure and simple are characteristically less problematic and (questions of "hypermeasure" aside) less controversial—they are for this reason also perhaps less interesting. Although rhythm as process and "motion" would seem to take into account questions of music's temporality that are ignored in metrical analyses, our concept of rhythm can only suffer from the abstraction of durational quantity and the repetition of durational quantities that we call meter. Likewise, our concepts of musical duration and meter must be impoverished if process and becoming are eliminated and time is reduced to point and line.

In the foregoing sketch I have presented the opposition of rhythm and meter as a contrast of (1) rhythm as variegated pattern and meter as periodic repetition and (2) rhythmic and metric accent or, more broadly, rhythm as event and meter as a measurement of the duration of that event. These oppositions are sufficiently commonplace that it has not been necessary to invoke the work of specific theorists except to document the most radical interpretation of metrical accent as durationless (though, as I have attempted to show in example 1.3, such an interpretation is implicit in conventional representations of meter). In one form or another, these two interpretations can be found in most current writing on rhythm and meter. Although these interpretations need not be seen as incompatible, there has been a tendency in more systematic treatments to posit one or the other as fundamental. (For example, as we shall see later, Cooper and Meyer favor the first and Lerdahl and Jackendoff the second.)

The preceding, necessarily simplified, account has given no indication of the richly imaginative speculations through which these contrasts have been elaborated in recent theoretical writing. Nor has an identification of these two views indicated the great variety of contrasts that have been generated by differing concepts of rhythm and meter. Although the following three chapters will not entirely remedy either of these shortcomings, they will provide us an opportunity to sample a variety of opinion and to examine in more detail the problems posed to music theory by an opposition of meter and rhythm. These problems, both in their origins and in their implications, bespeak concerns that extend well beyond the merely technical. At issue are questions of determinacy and indeterminacy, law and freedom; homogeneity and heterogeneity, unity and multiplicity; and structure and process, order as a fixed arrangement of parts and relations and order as the emergence of dynamic, novel "wholes." Such questions, whether or not they are explicitly addressed, color our speculations concerning musical rhythm. If we can never entirely escape questions of temporality, we may, nevertheless, lose sight of their importance in our effort to find solutions to specifically music-technical problems—in the case of meter, problems posed as much by traditional theoretical vocabulary and notational practice as by facts of musical experience. Certainly, a focus on the special features of musical practice is necessary if music theory is not to lose sight of its object; but unless our focus is too narrow, the special insights music offers will be connected to a larger world and more general questions, and it is not unreasonable to suppose that such insights might serve to make that larger world and those more general questions more intelligible. As a time art par excellence, music surely must hold important clues for our understanding of human temporal experience and perhaps even for our understanding of time in general.

In view of music's inescapably rhythmic and temporal nature, it is not surprising that musical analysis should bring into especially sharp relief oppositions embedded in the concept of a *rhuthmos* regulated by *metron*. A comprehensive review of the rhythm/meter dichotomy or even a detailed analysis of one of its historical episodes is neither within the scope of this study nor its aim. However, since the aim of our study is to overcome this dichotomy and offer a new theory of meter, it will be helpful to review a variety of positions that have been taken on this issue. This exercise will, I hope, demonstrate the urgency of the problem and place the present study in the context of a long line of attempts to account for music's powerful but strangely problematic repetition of durational quantity.

From the wealth of postwar American studies, I have chosen to examine the three most widely read—those by Cooper and Meyer, Cone, and Lerdahl and Jackendoff. Several other excellent studies might have served equally well, but these three, by virtue of their popularity, may be taken as more representative of recent opinion. To provide a broader context for our reading of current theory, I have selected a group of (predominantly German) writers from the mid-nineteenth to the mid-twentieth centuries. It was during this period that rhythm and meter came to be most explicitly and sharply opposed and that the temporal and "metaphysical" ramifications of this opposition came to be most keenly felt. Here my selection of authors may seem most arbitrary. I have included some lesser-known theorists and some peripheral figures in an attempt to present a wide range of opinion. Among the viewpoints we will consider in this chapter, only those of Hauptmann, Riemann, Neumann, and Georgiades will be reviewed in any detail. (In chapter 8 we will examine the theories of Hauptmann and Neumann more closely.)

I shall begin my survey with the eighteenth century. Here the choice has been relatively easy. The modern pulse theory that emerged midcentury (and that in one form or another survives today) was most systematically formulated by Heinrich Christoph Koch in 1787. Koch's work is especially interesting in its characterization of the psychological mechanisms that give rise to our rhythmic-metrical experi-ence. Koch does not explicitly oppose meter and rhythm, in part because he conceives of metrical grouping as a creative and spontaneous process of our imaginative faculties. Nevertheless, what we would call "meter" and "rhythm" are opposed implicitly in Koch's theory as an opposition of unity and multiplicity or as the givenness and fixity of pulse against the creative activity of grouping.

To appreciate the novelty (and perhaps also the peculiarity) of a pulse theory that is nowadays all but taken for granted, we will begin with the work of Johann Mattheson, whose writings precede those of Koch by a half-century and retain traces of a mensural perspective that was soon to be displaced by new theories of accent. In his thought about rhythm, as in so many aspects of his theoretical work, Mattheson is at once eccentric and central, conservative and farsighted. For Mattheson it is the measure that is given as a fixed and in some sense ever-present span of time. What is remarkable in Mattheson's account is his sensitivity to the dilemma such a concept poses for music and his attempt to reconcile measure as number and regulator with measure as the site of musical "motion" and feeling.

Two Eighteenth-Century Views

In *Der vollkommene Capellmeister* (1739) Johann Mattheson systematically develops the concept of *die Rhythmik* as a means of uniting meter as the division or measuring of time and rhythm as the particular course this measuring takes in melody. To understand this concept it will be necessary to explore Mattheson's subtle and, from a twentieth-century perspective, quite unfamiliar terminological distinctions. In his attempt to reconcile what we might think of as rhythm and meter, Mattheson is not concerned with the distinction between measure and "rhythmic pattern" (and certainly not the distinction between metrical and rhythmic accent), but rather with the distinction between *mensuration* and *movement* (*Bewegung*) and their mysterious union in *Rhythmik*.

Mensuration is accomplished most generally by the *Zeitmaß* conceived as a single, repeated beat that regulates musical time, and more particularly by the *Takte*—those individual manifestations of *Zeitmaß* that serve as containers for an endless variety of patterns or tone feet (*rhythmi*) analogous to the poetic feet of classical versification. *Rhythmik* is the joining of all the tone feet in a melodic whole and also the joining of all measures (*Takte*) in a unity that these measures themselves regulate as manifestations of *Zeitmaß*. To grasp this concept it must first be understood

that *Takt* does not correspond to our modern notion of measure or bar.

The *Takt* itself is divisible but undivided. All measures, of whatever *Taktart* and of whatever content, consist of only two phases—arsis and thesis, "ebb" and "flow"—and are to be beaten with two (equal or unequal) strokes of the hand. But Mattheson insists that this actual beating is only an outward sign for an ebb and flow that cannot be reduced to a division of pulses. An especially forceful assertion of the divisibility but intrinsic undividedness of the measure can be found in the fifth lesson of the *Kleine General-Baß-Schule*:

> Someone said, and published it, too, throughout the world: *The measure [Takt] is nothing but a raising and lowering of the hand.* What a lovely idea this must give to those who would like to know what sort of thing the measure is! . . .
>
> In my modest opinion, the beginner would be better informed and less confused if one said to him frankly what is stated in this important Fifth Lesson (and these words should be printed elsewhere a hundred times): *That the measure is a genuine measuring-off of time* by means of which each and every melody is supported in its fundamental motion and in a generally even progress according to the slowness or fastness of its parts . . .
>
> The best comparison whereby the nature and

significance of the measure might be seen, heard and *felt* [here Mattheson inserts the following footnote: "*Tactus* means nothing other than a *feeling* in which all meaning subsists"] is that with a great striking-clock, whose plumb-line carries a steady, even stroke and through which the minutes, seconds, and the canonical hours are kept exactly according to the time-measures. In this comparison it should be noted that the measures of the clockwork lie only in equal relationship to the fundamental stroke, whereas the musical measure not only itself can be unequal but can also have quite diverse members and articulations. (Mattheson 1735/1980, pp. 92–93)

The rhythmic comprises not only the measuring of time, but also, and with equal importance, the "movement" this measuring achieves in melody:

> Rhythmic is accordingly a measuring and orderly disposition of time and movement in the melodic science, how slow or fast such is to be. . . . In other words it is, in the common parlance, the tempo and beat which derive from the sense of feeling (*a tactu* [from or according to the tactus or measure]).
>
> For no melody has the power to arouse a true affection or a real *feeling* in us, if the rhythmic does not regulate all movement of the tone-feet to such an extent that they achieve a certain pleasing relationship with and against one another. (Mattheson 1739/1981, p. 364)

Movement (*Bewegung*) concerns tempo, but our notion of tempo as "rate of speed" does not, I think, capture Mattheson's meaning. Movement concerns the character or expression that emerges from proper tempo, indicated, as Mattheson suggests, by markings such as "*affettuoso, con discrezione, con spirito*, and the like." However, movement is not reducible to a type. These markings are only crude indications for an expression that is itself the mark of individuality and particularity. Although mensuration and movement are presented as the two aspects of the rhythmic, Mattheson in a remarkable dialetical turn refers to these aspects as the two classifications of *Zeitmaße* or "time measure." Thus, the rhythmic is not opposed to time measure but functions as a concept that brings to light the dual nature of time measures in an actual composition. Of these two components of time measures—mensuration and movement—the first "concerns the usual mathematical classifications; though through the other one the hearing prescribes certain extraordinary rules, according to the requirements of the affections, which do not always correspond with mathematical propriety but look more towards good taste" (Mattheson 1739/1981, p. 365):

> The above-mentioned arithmetic or mathematical part of the rhythmic, namely mensuration, could be illustrated and learned quite well. . . .
>
> However, the second and more spiritual thing, since the former is more physical, I mean *Movement*, can hardly be contained in precepts and prohibitions: because such depends principally upon the feeling and emotion of each composer, and secondarily upon good execution, or the sensitive expression of the singer and player.
>
> Those who would want to remedy such a difficulty with many expletives miss the mark. Everything *allegro, grave, lento, adagio, vivace*, and however the list reads further, indeed indicates things which pertain to time-measures; however, they produce no change in the thing.
>
> Here each one must probe and feel in his own soul, his heart: since according to the state of these our composing, singing, and playing to a certain degree will obtain an extraordinary movement which otherwise neither the actual mensuration, in and of itself, nor even the *perceptible* slowing or accelerating of it, much less the notes' own value, can impart; but which stems from an *imperceptible* impetus. One indeed observes the effect, but does not know how it happens. (Mattheson 1739/1981, pp. 366–367)

To conclude his discussion of the rhythmic in *Zeitmaß*, Mattheson refers to Jean Rousseau's attempt to define the relationship of mensuration and movement:

> *What is the difference between mensuration and movement?* Answer: mensuration is a means; its aim however is movement. Now just as one must distinguish between the means itself and the end whence the means leads: thus there is also a difference between mensuration and movement. And as the voice or song must be led by mensuration, thus mensuration itself is led and animated by movement.
>
> Hence, with one sort of mensuration the movement often turns out quite differently: for it

is sometimes more lively, sometimes more languid, according to the various passions which one is to express.

Thus it is insufficient for the performance of a piece of music for one to know well how to strike and maintain the mensuration according to the prescribed signs; but the director must as it were guess the meaning of the composer: that is, he must feel the various impulses which the piece is supposed to express....

Here many a person might perhaps want to know: how is the true *Movement* of a musical piece to be discerned? Yet such knowledge *transcends all words* which could be used: it is the highest perfection of music, and can be attained only through considerable experience and great gifts.

Now whoever listens to a piece which is performed by different persons, today here, tomorrow there, if the last were to achieve the true *Movement* but the former were to miss it, can easily say which of the two would be correct. (Mattheson 1739/1981, p. 368) [Jean Rousseau, *Methode claire, certaine et facile pour apprendre a chanter la Musique*, Paris, 1678, p. 86]

To close the topic, Mattheson writes: "This much is Rousseau, and so much for now on the extrinsic and intrinsic character of time-measures: particularly since the last can not be captured by the pen."

I have quoted Mattheson and Rousseau at some length because we find in this writing a frank acknowledgment of an aspect of measured rhythm that resists analysis and quantification—something spontaneously produced and judged attractive or expressive in performance. What is remarkable in this account is the attempt to unite these aspects of the rhythmic within the concept of *Zeitmaß*. Thus, Mattheson speaks of the "intrinsic" and "extrinsic" character not of *Rhythmik*, but of time measure (*Zeitmaß*). This ingenious union is, however, quite problematic. Apart from the difficulty of reconciling a fully describable means with an ineffable end, there is the difficulty of reconciling movement, animation, and the particularity of musical expression with the clocklike regularity of *Zeitmaß*, which as the measure of time and the receptacle of musical content proceeds with full autonomy and homogeneity. Wilhelm Seidel eloquently describes the spacelike character of Mattheson's concept of *Zeitmaß*:

Mattheson's measure does not define the particular character of musical motion which it comprehends; it does not determine the accentual order and does not designate the mechanical motions of conducting. What is it then? It is a *measure of time*. To take up Walter's metaphor, it is like a yardstick, which is laid out against time. A determinate measure articulates the continuous progress of time into constant, equal time-spans. It gives to time the appearance of spatiality. Thus, it is of no importance whether this division is carried out physically or in the imagination, "only in the mind" as Walter says. The measure measures off the open space in which a composition comes to be realized. Any number of spaces may be cut out of the flow of time; however, their measure—the measure—is always the same. Only on paper does measure follow measure—in sounding, the composition stands under the law of *one* measure. The law-giving compulsion of the measure is expressed in the metaphors used to describe its effect. Mattheson speaks of the authority of measure, music as governed by measure. Janowka compares the measure to the town clock "according to which everything is customarily regulated and directed." Just as the tower clock establishes a manifest system for the ordering of activity (one thinks perhaps of the schedule of religious and secular events for a town in preindustrial times, of the church services, the closing of the town gates, of the night watch crying the hours), similarly, the measure determines what can happen in the music during the time it is in force. And just as little as the time ordering of a clock itself describes what actually happens during its durations does the measure describe what is accomplished musically during its time ordering. (Seidel 1975, pp. 55–56)

That the temporal can be assimilated to the spatial in this way I attribute to the "givenness" of Mattheson's *Takt* as cyclic return (as *Zeitmaß*). Certainly, measure succeeds measure, and within each measure there is the "passage of time"; but this succession and this passage are easily removed from becoming, and in the return of "the" measure (*Zeitmaß*) as ever-present it is possible to conceive of static being and to conceive of passage, transition, and becoming as illusory. Seidel, in fact, argues for such a conception and, moreover, for such an experience of measured music:

Music thus turns away from the observation of the continual passing away of time. Music, while it is going on, leads to a forgetting of time and, for anyone who is affected by it, seizes a consciousness of the transitory. I would like to venture the hypothesis that the musical event can accomplish this because it does not display itself in an open time. It does not play itself out in boundlessness, does not advance into uncertainty and obscurity, but rather divides a time span that is marked off a priori. One has the security and the satisfaction of knowing beforehand, not everything, but at least the dimensions of becoming. As Mattheson says, "everyone enjoys knowing in advance and judging."

Temporal then is only the space in which the musical event completes itself, and not this space itself. For the empirical motion of music brings to consciousness only indirectly and brokenly the temporality of the space which *Takt* measures off. That is to say, time is not music's object; music neither grasps, alters, nor interprets time. It has time only as a space for observation. The fact that the measure, a measurement given once and for all, is in principle unalterable clearly reveals the statics of the system. One could say, rather subtly: this music has no temporal structure. It makes timelessness actual. It gives the human beings who play and hear it the illusion of an escape from time and transitoriness. Therein perhaps arises that happiness which music brings: it is a foretaste of eternal joy. (Seidel 1975, pp. 56–57)

This is a fond thought and one that doubtless inspired Mattheson in his formulation of the concept of measure as *Zeitmaß*. It is also a thought that places meter in opposition to the temporality of a more worldly experience of musical rhythm. If *Takt* is an image of eternity, how can it also be a vehicle or means for *Bewegung*, and how can *Bewegung* be the "intrinsic" and "more spiritual" part of a *Zeitmaß* for which mensuration is "extrinsic"?

Since Mattheson's understanding of meter is so different from our own, we may gain some perspective on what is novel in later theories by briefly reviewing his notion of *Takt*. Mattheson's conception of meter is based on traditional mensural theory, in which *Takt* is understood as tactus—a single "beat" conducted with two strokes of the hand, whether equal (what we call "duple") or unequal (what we call "triple"). In this understanding, division takes place within the measure, but division does not constitute the measure. The measure as *Zeitmaß* is given for di-

vision, and its givenness precedes its division. The distinction of arsis and thesis as ebb and flow is also part of the givenness of the measure, but this distinction does not itself arise from a process of division. And as our first quotation from the *Kleine General-Baß-Schule* indicates, Mattheson strenuously argues against the reduction of measure to an actual or imagined "beating" of equal parts. In *Der vollkommene Capellmeister* Mattheson writes:

> Now since it was soon found that upbeat and downbeat could not always be related as equal, there arose from this observation the classifications of equal and unequal measure; and these two are the only true principles of the rhythmic or time-measure. From ignorance of these basic doctrines, as natural as they are easy and simple, more errors arise than one might suppose. Again, namely a disregard of the first principle by those who would look for four parts in an equal measure and three parts in an unequal measure, whereby they give rise to nothing but confusion. (Mattheson 1739/1981, pp. 365–366)

The divisions that concern Mattheson are not the accented and unaccented *Taktteile* of later theorists, but the patterns (*Rhythmi* or *Klang-Füße*) that can be contained in a *Takt*. These patterns are types and so are repeatable. And although he lists twenty-six types corresponding to the categories of traditional poetic feet, Mattheson acknowledges that music can employ a virtually unlimited number of types. In the examples he gives, the integrity of the measure as receptacle is retained by permitting *Klang-Füße* to occur only within a bar and not across bars. There is one exception—the first epitritus (short–long–long–long), which is illustrated as beginning with an eighth-note anacrusis. The inconsistency here seems to arise from the difficulty of realizing this pattern within a single bar without creating a composite of iamb and spondee.

In his discussion of rhythmopoeia, Mattheson does not attempt to relate patterns to the organization of beats in the measure except to distinguish among the *Klang-Füße* those appropriate for equal or unequal measures. The closest Mattheson comes to relating pattern to pulse is

EXAMPLE 2.1   Johann Mattheson, *Der vollkommene Capellmeister*, part 2, chapter 6, figure 5. Illustration of dactyl (long-short-short).

in his discussion of the dactyl. Two forms of the dactyl (long–short–short) are illustrated in our example 2.1.

In the second form "the length and shortness of sounds vary as much in their proportion as 3, 2, 1: whereby the last or third in the measure, though it seems to be twice as long according to its external aspect as the middle one, is nevertheless just as short in its intrinsic value because of the upbeat of the measure" (Mattheson 1739/ 1981, p. 355). Thus, within *Klang-Füße* neither shorts nor longs are required to present equal durations or equal divisions. For example, the second paeon (short–long–short–short) is represented by a bar containing the succession quarter-half-eighth-eighth. Nor is the distinction "long versus short" related to accent. A short may appear on what we call the accented part of the measure, or a long may appear on an unaccented part. In all the examples, only the actual sounding durations of tones are considered—a long or a short is never composed of more than one note.

Mattheson's understanding of meter was soon to be replaced by a conception of the measure in which the givenness of *Zeitmaß* is transferred to that of pulses which compose the measure. This idea of meter, which has with relatively little alteration been carried into present-day metrical theory, is based on the notion of a constant train of isochronous pulses grouped by accent to form measures. The most thorough eighteenth-century exposition of this theory is found in Heinrich Christoph Koch's *Versuch einer Anleitung zur Composition*, and it is Koch to whom I will turn for an account of measure as the grouping of like durations. The new theory arose perhaps in part in response to the proliferation of meter signatures, whose variety is largely suppressed in Mattheson's conservative reduction to *Zeitmaß*. But its lineaments clearly reflect an assimi-

lation of classical aesthetics in the dialectic of multiplicity and unity and the more narrowly "empirical-psychological" interpretation of their play in aesthetic experience.

With the new view of meter as a unity of isochronous pulse units related to one another through the operations of multiplication and division, it became possible to conceive of a properly mathematical order of duration. As Ernst Cassirer writes:

> The aesthetic "unity in diversity" of classical theory is modeled after this mathematical unity in multiplicity [i.e., to understand and *deduce* multiplicity from a general law]. . . . In the realm of art the spirit of classicism is not interested in the negation of multiplicity, but in shaping it, in controlling and restricting it. (Cassirer 1951, p. 289)

It was Johann-Georg Sulzer who first articulated the aesthetic foundation of a pulse theory of meter that was taking shape, even as Mattheson was endeavoring to hold on to the older mensural perspective. Wilhelm Seidel's book includes an extensive and penetrating account of Sulzer's innovation, and I return to Seidel for a glance toward Sulzer's discussion of unity and multiplicity and the relation of these categories to meter:

> [Sulzer] writes that rhythm is at bottom nothing other "than a periodic arrangement of a series of homogeneous things whereby the uniformity of these same things is united with diversity; so that a continuous sensation, which would otherwise have been completely homogeneous (same-sounding), obtains, through rhythmic divisions, change and variety" [Sulzer 1792, vol. II, p. 96]. This is Sulzer's version of the Greek formula—rhythm is the order of movement [i.e., the Platonic order of *Metron*, as we have seen in chapter 1]. . . .
>
> Uniformity designates "the identity of form across all the parts which belong to a single ob-

ject", and is to this extent a formal category. "It is", writes Sulzer, "the basis of unity; for many things, laid next to one another or following upon one another, whose disposition or order is determined according to a single form or a single rule, can, with the support of this form, be held together in a single concept, and to this extent constitute One thing" [Sulzer 1792, p. 21]. (Seidel 1975, pp. 92–93)

Koch, on the other hand, is not especially concerned with the unity of *Takte* and *Taktteile* as a "formal category," but rather with the process through which the many become one. Rather than of *Zeitmaß*, Koch speaks of *Zeitraum*—a determinate duration that is inherently undifferentiated, lacking any distinction of arsis and thesis. A *Zeitraum* (represented by Koch as a whole note with no signature) becomes a measure only if it is given content and organized as a grouping of constituent pulses. But, in fact, Koch makes little use of the concept of *Zeitraum*. In his analysis, measures are not formed from the division of a given whole; they are created synthetically by the addition of pulses (or, more generally, the multiplication of pulse). Koch makes no attempt to explain how these equal pulses emerge or why the measure should be based upon a series of equal units that, as he shows, may in some cases be implicit rather than actually sounded. Like Mattheson's *Takte*, Koch's *Taktteile* are simply given. However, for Koch the *Takt* is not simply given. A series of pulses can give rise to a variety of measures. The selection of a particular metrical interpretation can be accomplished through the notational devices of bar line and signature, but the basis for this interpretation lies in our capacity for grouping like objects.

In the second part of volume 2 of the *Versuch*, Koch observes that given a series of six pulses, we will spontaneously group these sounds in one way or another, and that in any succession of equal durations we have no choice but to hear the articulation of composite units composed of two or three pulses. Such a grouping serves comprehension by establishing a particular relationship of quantity among the members of the series—"eine gewisse Verhältniß, eine gewisse Anzahl." Although he leaves it to the reader ultimately to decide whether our "subjective group-ing" of pulse arises from an acquired feeling of measure or from an innate disposition to group like objects, Koch prefers the latter account. If such grouping is innate, we will find the basis of meter in the nature of our sense perception and our power of imagination or "representation" ("in der Natur unserer Sinnen und unserer Vorstellungskraft" [Koch 1787/1969, p. 278]).

Koch describes in considerable detail how these natural capacities operate in an attempt to explain the essential properties of meter, "nicht allein die Ursache des Daseins, sondern auch zugleich die wesentlichen Eigenschaften des Taktes" (p. 282). In order to bring a series of like objects into a "particular relationship," we will spontaneously seek an articulation and create an articulation if none is actually given to us. Koch calls these articulations *Ruhepunkte des Geistes* or *Ruhepunkte der Vorstellung*:

> If several objects of one and the same species and type act upon our feeling in such a manner that from their particular combination our imagination cannot extract a resting point in order to draw a distinction among them, we are then required to ourselves imagine such *Ruhepunkte der Vorstellung*, through which we are enabled to draw distinctions among them and reflect upon them (Koch 1787/1969, p. 278)

Koch's *Ruhepunkt* is not an actual pause that alters a duration. It could be conceived as a resting place of our attention, but even this description is somewhat misleading if it is not understood that this resting place is also an active gathering together of pulses as a unity. In this unification the note marked by the *Ruhepunkt* takes on a special prominence by becoming intrinsically "longer" than the following pulses—it is distinguished by "ein gewisses Gewicht, ein gewisses Nachdruck, mehr innern Wert." In the example Koch gives of a series of dynamically undifferentiated tones, the hearer will perceive emphases created by *Ruhepunkte* alone; that is, the distinction of intrinsically "long" and "short" is the work of our powers of representation (*Vorstellungskräfte*). Thus, Koch offers the following analysis of a hearing that would result from a metrical interpretation of a succession of six quarter notes:

If the imagination of someone who would sing or play these six tones brings together with the first of these tones only a second tone so that a resting place of the imagination arises on the third note, they will perform the passage as the following figure illustrates:

fig. 1.

(Koch 1787/1969, p. 280)

On the other hand, the hearer will sense two groups of three tones each, "if the imagination draws the first of these notes together with the next two tones so that the next resting place of the imagination, and consequently the next manifest emphasis, fall to the fourth note" (p. 281). Koch also allows for the possibility of hearing the first note as anacrusis in equal or unequal time (duple or triple meter) if the imagination is not drawn to the first note, "which merely stands apart, that is, has no similar tone preceding it, and thus in itself can be more easily overlooked than the remaining tones" (p. 281).

The function of notation is to specify precisely where the *Ruhepunkte* are to occur. Much of Koch's discussion of meter is aimed at showing the student of composition how best to express the proper groupings of musical events through metric notation. The notational device that indicates the *Ruhepunkt* and the quantitative order of pulses unified as a group is the barred measure. For Koch the properly notated measure alone is province of the *Ruhepunkt*, and through the agency of *Ruhepunkt* the measure, whether equal or unequal, comprises two durationally determinate *parts* (not "phases" as in Mattheson's account)—the "essential parts," thesis and arsis, marked by downbeat and upbeat:

> Should different notes of the same species, or different tones of the same duration, become bound together in one measure, so must the quantity of these notes or tones become united under a single perspective, that is, the first of these tones must comprise the *Ruhepunkt der Vorstellung* or point of division [*Abteilungspunkt*—the *point* that initiates the division or *unit*]. And because this

tone as the tone of division [*Abteilungston*] contains a certain emphasis in the imagination which is passed on to the performance, this first note or first tone of the measure is intrinsically long. This intrinsically long tone thus constitutes the first essential part of the measure. The second note or (if the imagination unites to the first and second a third note) the second and third are comprehended under the division point of the first note, that is, they are united with the first under a single perspective. And because no point of division is given to these following notes, they are intrinsically short, that is, there is a degradation from the emphasis that marks these tones. And this intrinsically short tone (or, if the imagination unites these to a third tone, the intrinsically short pair of tones) constitutes the second essential part of the measure. (Koch 1787/1969, pp. 282–283)

These two essential parts are the *Taktteile* (*gute* and *schlechte*). Again, in distinction from Mattheson, these divisions emerge as parts through a process of synthesis uniting equal pulses that are "given" and thus (logically) precede the measure. Since the measure is formed synthetically from the perspective of a first beat as *Taktteil*, Koch can allow the second *Taktteil* in unequal measure to fall on either the second or third pulse unit.

Thus, if in 3/4 a half note is followed by a quarter, the half note will constitute the first (*guter*) *Taktteil*, because the half note unites the first two "primary notes" (*Hauptnoten*) of the measure. For this reason the half note will be both intrinsically long and extrinsically long. If a quarter is followed by a half, the half note, although extrinsically long, will constitute the second (*schlechter*) *Taktteil*, since it comprises two intrinsically short notes under the perspective of the first (see Koch pp. 316–317). However, the asymmetry of "triple" meter creates some confusion of terms. In equal measure Koch most often calls the "primary beats" of the bar *Taktteile*, but in unequal measure the beats must be called *Hauptteile*. Also, the essential binary division of *Taktteile* leads Koch to regard the signature C as a composite of two measures or a *zusammengesezte Taktart* (and, in this case, the bar does not indicate the measure).

Koch's synthetic perspective would seem to permit a consistently hierarchical approach to

EXAMPLE 2.2   Heinrich Christoph Koch, *Versuch einer Anleitung zur Composition*, vol. 2, figures on p. 301.

EXAMPLE 2.3   Heinrich Christoph Koch, *Versuch einer Anleitung zur Composition*, vol. 2, figures on p. 302–303.

problems of uniting measures as constituents of larger units and accounting for subdivisions within a measure. The process whereby *Taktteile* (or *Hauptteile*) are produced as constituents of the measure is to some extent replicated in the smaller division of the measure. For example, in a measure of 2/2 where the signature indicates the half note as *Taktteil*, Koch identifies quarter notes (or triplet quarters) as *Taktglieder* and the division of the *Taktglied* into eighths (or triplet eighths) as *Taktnoten*. Both of these divisions are, like the *Taktteile*, distinguished as intrinsically long or short. However, the multiplicity of *Taktglieder* or *Taktnoten* is not of the same nature as the multiplicity of *Taktteile*. The *Taktteile* arise from the unification of given pulses, and the measure results as the product of their synthesis. The *Taktglieder*, on the other hand, arise as divisions of the given pulses—they do not precede or constitute these pulses. What we would call "submetrical" divisions are united under the perspective of an *Abtheilungspunkt*—the articulation of one of the *Taktteile*—but in themselves these smaller values are not united under the perspective of a *Ruhepunkt*. The unifying perspective of *Ruhepunkt* is reserved exclusively for the formation of a true measure—the *Takt*. Thus *Taktteile* represent a privileged class of equal, periodic durations. And Koch warns the composer against confusing this primary level of articulation with other levels. Such a confusion is illustrated in the two sets of phrases reproduced as our examples 2.2a, b and 2.3a, b.

In the first case, what is in fact a *Taktteil* is falsely represented in the notation as a *Taktglied*

(and corrected to four bars in 2.2b). In the second case, what is in fact a *Taktglied* is represented as a *Taktteil* (in 2/4). In connection with the second set of examples, Koch explains that the first barring is incorrect in that it implies an uneven seven-measure phrase length when, in fact, the phrase is an even four-bar length. The point Koch wishes to make with such examples is that proper notation calls for "a knowledge of the constitution of the extent and the conclusion of the parts of a melody" ("die Kenntniß von der Beschaffenheit des Umfangs und der Endigung der Theile der Melodie," p. 307).

At the "suprametrical" level Koch also speaks of *Ruhepunkte* in the articulation of phrases of various lengths, but such unities of measures are not themselves metrical. The measures of a phrase are not "united under a single perspective" initiated in the *Ruhepunkt*, and the first measure of the phrase is not intrinsically long. *Ruhepunkt* now refers to closure or the completion of a unit—a "punctuation" that is a point of articulation and *division* rather than a moment of gathering together. Thus Koch writes: "that place where a resting point is shown in the melody, that is, the place where one section of the melody can be separated from the following one, is called a *caesura* (cutting)" (Koch 1983, p.

19).[1] In the discussion of phrase construction there is now a separation of grouping or unification and the articulation that would mark the group or unit:

> If we consider the various sections in musical works which compose their periods, then two main classifications are found through which they distinguish themselves as divisions of the whole. The first is the type of their endings, or that which characterizes the resting points in the material aspect of the art. The second is the length of these sections, together with a certain proportion or relation between them which can be found in the number of their measures once they have been reduced to their essential components. [Note that Koch speaks of reduction here rather than of composition or synthesis.]
>
> The endings of these sections are certain formulas, which let us clearly recognize the more or less noticeable resting points. . . . We shall call this *melodic punctuation.*
>
> The length of these melodic sections, on the other hand, and the proportion or relationship which they have amongst themselves with regard to the number of measures will be called *rhythm.* (Koch 1983, pp. 1–2)

Koch quite properly titles his essay on rhythm in the second part of volume 2 of the *Versuch* "the Mechanical Rules of Melody." The preceding section on meter he titles "On the Nature of Measure in General," and here, as we have seen, his approach is quite speculative. Koch's concept of a *Ruhepunkt des Geistes* (corresponding more or less to our notion of "metrical accent") represents an attempt to describe meter as a creative act of attention, not bound by law, but arising from the exercise of our cognitive or imaginative powers. Nevertheless, by grounding meter in the presentation of a string of equal pulses that must be given as objects (*Gegenstände*) for the imagination to unify, Koch has bound the imagination to a prior and homogeneous order that cannot but appear autonomous and mechanical. Even where they are not

sounded, the pulses that become meter's *Hauptteile* proceed in an essentially predetermined "motion" as measure follows measure:

> Here [in musical composition] there emerges among notes of the same type, in addition, a special attribute—namely, the equality of motion. Since already with the first number of notes which one unites under a single perspective there must simultaneously be perceived a definite motion of this group of notes, if it should be presented to hearing; therefore the number and motion of these notes of the same type which one unites in the first perspective, that is, in the first measure, will determine the number and motion of the same notes in all succeeding measures. And the identity of number and motion in these same measures fully confirms the necessary unity which must characterize the parts of a whole. (Koch 1787/ 1969, pp. 285–286)

This thought is echoed in that of Sulzer, who more explicitly transfers an intuition of the unity of measures as measure to the imagination:

> In a composition that indeed has one sort of measure, by taking in only the first measure one can then beat the proper time for the entire piece. Thus, uniformity facilitates the conception [*Vorstellung*] of a single object composed of many parts, and makes it possible for one to see or to know this object (at least in regard to a single property) at one time. (Sulzer 1792, II, p. 21)

In this thought, the unity of measure is a predetermined and determining order that finds its temporal expression in the multiplicity of measures. By not postulating a true hierarchy of beats, Koch restricts the range of metrical unification and leaves open the determination of metrical or submetrical pattern (Mattheson's *Rhythmi* and what Koch calls *Metrum*) and the determination of "phrase structure" (what Koch calls *Rhythmus*). Nevertheless, whatever form pattern and phrase (*Metrum* and *Rhythmus*) take

---

1. This confusion of terms wherein *Ruhepunkt* refers both to the unification of the bar created by a metrical beginning and to the articulation and segregation of phrases by means of a cadential gesture corresponds in

many respects to the ambiguities later theorists will encounter in drawing a distinction between "metrical accent" as an accent of beginning and the "tonal accent" of cadence as end accent.

will be organized by the proportion and quantity of *Takte* (without which there can be neither *Metrum* nor *Rhythmus*). The new *Bewegung* is not, like Mattheson's and Rousseau's, ineffable; it is the repetition of an order that can be grasped at once in the form of the ruling measure.

That Koch's *Ruhepunkt* can become, outside the measure, merely a point of articulation and that, even within the measure, the *Ruhepunkt* as an agent for a process of integration can result in a *Takt* that is repeated as the same indicate the difficulty of any attempt to submit temporal experience to analysis. It would seem that in our attempts to name and thus to hold onto the "parts" of rhythm we must remain silent before transition, process, or flow (if, indeed, we are even willing to acknowledge the reality of such categories). Although Koch's intuition of a *Ruhepunkt des Geistes* begins with an acknowledgment of the ongoing activity (and indeterminacy) of metrical grouping, the concept ultimately serves as a psychological mechanism by means of which we can abstract parts from the flow of melody. Even William James, who argued so strongly for the stream of consciousness (and against the "knife-edge" of an instantaneous present), distinguishes in this stream between "substantive" and "transitive" parts, or "places of rest" and "places of flight." While I do not suggest that Koch's *Ruhepunkte* (in the two forms: beginning and ending) are equivalent to James's "resting places," I do believe that there is some similarity in these concepts. And I would like to quote from James's discussion of this issue—a discussion that contains some valuable

insights into the problems of segmenting a rhythmic whole. Thus James writes:

> Like a bird's life, it [the stream of our consciousness] seems to be made of an alternation of flights and perchings. The rhythm of language expresses this, where every thought is expressed in a sentence, and every sentence closed by a period. The resting-places are usually occupied by sensorial imaginations of some sort, whose peculiarity is that they can be held before the mind for an indefinite time, and contemplated without changing; the places of flight are filled with thoughts of relations, static or dynamic, that for the most part obtain between the matters contemplated in the periods of comparative rest. *Let us call the resting-places the 'substantive parts,' and the places of flight the 'transitive parts,' of the stream of thought.* It then appears that the main end of our thinking is at all times the attainment of some other substantive part than the one from which we have just been dislodged. And we may say that the main use of the transitive parts is to lead us from one substantive conclusion to another. (James 1890/1981, pp. 236–237)

James's distinction between places of rest and places of flight is not intended to introduce discontinuity into consciousness. His purpose in making this distinction seems, rather, to draw attention to the reality of feelings of relation and transition strenuously denied by traditional empiricism. For James, there can be no discontinuity in perception.[2] Nevertheless, that James calls the places of rest "substantive" points to a tendency to regard the parts of a rhythmic whole as static, fixed images or objects (Koch's *Gegen-*

---

2. Since the issue of temporal continuity is central to the present discussion, I shall quote James on this topic, from a passage that, tellingly, takes aural experience for its primary example: "Consciousness, then, does not appear to itself chopped up in bits. . . . It is nothing jointed; it flows. . . . But now there appears, even within the limits of the same self, and between thoughts all of which alike have this same sense of belonging together, a kind of jointing and separateness among the parts, of which this statement seems to take no account. I refer to the breaks that are produced by sudden *contrasts in the quality* of the successive segments of the stream of thought. . . . Does not a loud explosion rend the consciousness upon which it abruptly breaks, in twain? Does not every sudden shock, appearance of a new object, or change in a sensa-

tion, create a real interruption, sensibly felt as such, which cuts the conscious stream across at the moment at which it appears? . . . This objection is based partly on a confusion and partly on a superficial introspective view. The confusion is between the thought of the things themselves, taken as subjective facts, and the things of which they are aware. It is natural to make this confusion, but easy to avoid it when once put on one's guard. The things are discrete and discontinuous; they do pass before us in a train or chain, making often explosive appearances and rending each other in twain. But their comings and goings and contrasts no more break the flow of the thought that thinks them than they break the time and the space in which they lie. A silence may be broken by a thunder clap, and we may be so stunned and *stände*, Sulzer's *Sachen*) that "can be held before the mind for an indefinite time, and contemplated without changing." In this way, the parts can be imagined to have the permanence that we impute to physical objects—time passes, but objects remain unchanged. From this thought it is not a great leap to imagine that we can return to these objects at any time or, more generally, that there can be a return of the same. This was certainly not James's conclusion:

> ...I wish to lay stress on this, that *no state once gone can recur and be identical with what it was before.* . . . there *is no proof that the same bodily sensation is ever got by us twice. What is got twice is the same OB-JECT.* We hear the same *note* over and over again; we see the same *quality* of green, or smell the same objective perfume, or experience the same *species* of pain. The realities, concrete and abstract, physical and ideal, whose permanent existence we believe in, seem to be constantly coming up again before our thought, and lead us, in our carelessness, to suppose that our 'ideas' of them are the same ideas. . . . *A permanently existing 'idea' or 'Vorstellung' which makes its appearance before the floodlights of consciousness at periodical intervals, is as mythological an entity as the Jack of Spades.* What makes it convenient to use the mythological formulas is the whole organization of speech . . . What wonder, then, that the thought is most easily conceived under the law of the thing whose name it bears! . . . If one part of the thing have appeared in the same thing or in other things on former occasions, why then we must be having even now the very same 'idea' of that part which was there on those occasions. (James 1890/1981, pp. 224, 225, 230)

For Matteson, particular feelings of transition or "movement" are essential ingredients of the time measures that comprehend them. However, Matteson could not reconcile the fluidity of such feelings with the objective, "substantive," and ultimately static character of the time spans that house them. Nor could he reconcile the lawfulness of periodicity with the ineffability of a motion that "can hardly be contained in precepts and prohibitions." Matteson's eighteenth-century successors were little concerned with these problems. Once meter is defined as the multiplication of a selfsame pulse marked by accent (but otherwise characterless), a metrical repetition can introduce no change. If there is to be a properly "metrical" motion, it will, as Koch points out, describe the order and number of pulses permissible for one of the metrical types represented by our time signatures. But unlike Matteson's *Bewegung*, such a motion is to be regarded as fully determinate and fixed, a "single object" (as Sulzer writes), each individual instance of which can be "conceived under the law of the thing whose name it bears."

Although Koch's highly suggestive psychology of meter has had little influence on subsequent musical thought, the late-eighteenth-century understanding of measure that his writing expresses with exceptional precision has been little altered (though, as we shall see in the next chapter, there have been some notable attempts to escape its deterministic character). In most current accounts the measure remains an accentual grouping of a train of pulses themselves divisible into smaller pulse units. And where the operation of *Vorstellung* is reduced to the assigning of markers or points of articulation, and where a continuous metrical hierarchy is conceived as the interaction of homogeneous pulse strata, the autonomous, abstract, and me-

---

confused for a moment by the shock as to give no instant account to ourselves of what has happened. But that very confusion is a mental state, and a state that passes us straight over from the silence to the sound. The transition between the thought of one object and the thought of another is no more a break in the *thought* than a joint in a bamboo is a break in the wood. It is a part of the *consciousness* as much as the joint is a part of the *bamboo*. The superficial introspective view is the overlooking, even when the things are contrasted with each other most violently, of the large amount of affinity that may still remain between the thoughts by whose means they are

cognized. Into the awareness of the thunder itself the awareness of the previous silence creeps and continues; for what we hear when the thunder crashes is not thunder *pure*, but thunder-breaking-upon-silence-and-contrasting-with-it. Our feeling of the same objective thunder, coming in this way, is quite different from what it would be were the thunder a continuation of previous thunder. The thunder itself we believe to abolish and exclude the silence; but the *feeling* of the thunder is also a feeling of the silence as just gone ..." (James 1890/1981, pp. 233–234).

chanical character of meter will be easily placed in opposition to the freedom and spontaneity of rhythm. In this opposition rhythm may be conceived as variegated pattern, perhaps in itself irrational, requiring the constraint of meter to give it form. Or rhythm may be conceived as form itself, regarded either as the static edifice of music or as a dynamic, energetic shaping of musical experience. Regarded positively, meter gives rhythm *ratio* and comprehensibility, or meter provides the scaffolding for the construction of rhythm (but a scaffolding that is, most problem-atically, not taken away when the building is complete!). Negatively, meter is the "primitive" in music—the "beat" whose constraint and aesthetic limitations are surpassed in a mature art. Or if meter is not of low artistic rank, it may be of low rank structurally, either by contributing to form only on the "small scale" and thus being powerless (especially compared with tone) to act globally in the formation of the whole, or by being merely a container to be filled with genuine musical content. The following is a small sampling of opinion.

THREE

Evaluations of Rhythm and Meter

To begin with a relatively neutral assessment, we may turn first to the thought of Alfred Lorenz. Like Edward T. Cone, with whose opinion we shall begin the following chapter, Lorenz can avoid a conflict by assimilating both meter and rhythm to form and by referring the difference between regularity and irregularity (or, as Lorenz puts it, "rational" and "irrational") to a difference of time scale. In equating form and rhythm, Lorenz designates meter as *rationale Rhythmik*, one means of rhythmic formation among many (the others he lists are melodic, harmonic, dynamic "elements," and timbre). For Lorenz, the function of musical form is to articulate and make comprehensible spans of time that serve as receptacles for a dynamic musical substance. But since he does not sharply oppose form and substance, Lorenz does not denigrate meter as an intrinsically empty or passive container for a properly musical content. Meter is, nevertheless, limited in its effectiveness by our ability to perceive definite durational quantity. Where such limits are exceeded, our feeling of duration must give way to the less regular and less definite temporal spans created by the articulations of the tonal phrase. But here, too, there is no opposition. For Lorenz, the rational "pulse" of meter is organically harmonized with the intelligible "breath" of large-scale rhythm:

The question of musical form belongs to the domain of rhythm. Form is recognized in the plastic arts through spatial symmetry and in music, which takes place in the medium of time, through the perception of temporal articulations. The simple alternation of strong and weak, which forms the essence of the rhythmic, is raised to a feeling of form when this is carried to a higher order by two, three, or more gradations of accent. These accents, if they quickly succeed one another, must stand in a rational relationship to one another, like the human pulse. The longer the time which passes between them, the more irrational they can appear, since our memory for duration is imperfect. Thus, actual time-length alone is incapable of providing a clear focus for articulation. Another musical occurrence forms a rhythm which, temporally, need not always be completely rational. This we can compare to the human breath, which according to the inward agitation of the breather can vary greatly in length and nevertheless show an intelligible coursing of life. (Lorenz 1924/1966, p. 13)

Moritz Hauptmann also identifies the metrical with the rational but insists upon a strict separation between meter and rhythm in which rhythm itself is viewed as irrational. For Hauptmann, meter is not an aspect of rhythm but an autonomous phenomenon that brings order, comprehensibility, and aesthetic value to rhythm. Hauptmann's analysis of meter is in its fundamental conception little indebted to traditional theories and has remained something of a curiosity. (We will return to Hauptmann's concept of metrical formation in chapter 8 for a more detailed account of his innovation.) Hauptmann's meter does not concern given durational "units" that are divided or multiplied. Instead, meter is a process whereby duration is created, a process grounded in an innate perceptual disposition for measure. Without this creation of determinate, comprehensible duration there can be no properly aesthetic rhythm. Meter is order and regularity, but since it is also a creative, "organic" process and in no sense "automatic" or mechanical, it can be viewed in an entirely positive light:

> We shall call the constant measure according to which the measurement of time is carried out, *meter*; the kind of motion in this measure, *rhythm*. . . . Motion in the measure, which in itself can be of endless multiplicity, will, as measured, find its intelligibility only in regulation, an intelligibility that results from its metrical conception.

> In its rhythmically agitated progress music can by no means do without metrically regulated support. The rhythmic phrase finds its artistic meaning first of all in meter. . . . However, with many productions of newer and newest music, in deviations from directly intelligible metrical regularity we are not always led to an artistic interweaving of the texture; more often it is rather a tangle in which the composer himself has not arrived at a metrically clear perception and must now leave it for us to feel this lack of clarity. (Hauptmann 1873, pp. 211, 296)

And although meter itself has no aesthetic value apart from rhythm, it is now rhythm that is viewed with circumspection. Not only is there an inherent formlessness in rhythm per se (which need not be ordered metrically to be rhythm), but also there is a conceptual wholeness that rhythm lacks by virtue of its multiplicity and particularity. To clarify the terms used in the following quotation, I should explain that Hauptmann allies meter and harmony as organizing, determinative forces for music and opposes these to rhythm and melody, to which order must be given. These two sets of processes interact to create a "concrete unity"—a musical product:

The melodic-rhythmic, however, does not admit of an abstract, systematic conception in manner and in execution like that of the harmonic-metric. With the former, in the endless multiplicity of possible phenomena, we can speak only of what is most general or of what is most particular. With the latter the particular is comprehended in the general, and from the whole the explanation of every individual can be deduced. (Hauptman 1873, p. 353)

The systematic deficiencies of rhythm are, of course, tied to its intrinsically anarchic nature; and while others have viewed meter as "primitive" and inartistic, for Hauptmann it is rhythm that poses the greater threat to the art of music. For an analysis of Hauptmann's conception of rhythm and its temporal character, I will turn again to the observations of Wilhelm Seidel (based, in part, on Hauptmann's letters to Franz Hauser):

> Hauptmann considers rhythm incomprehensible, ephemeral, and in itself inartistic. He indeed senses its naturalness, but he is not able to comprehend its motions in the signification of the formula to which he entrusts his theoretical reflection. Rhythms are incomprehensible because they are formless. In the infinite realm of human experience they make the infinite sensible. Hauptmann thinks of them as violent, raw emotion. They unfold and exhaust themselves freely, know only of proliferation without reflection, that is: unknown to them is the ordering and form-giving relation of the present to what is past and what is to come. They lose themselves in the moment and are incapable of forming something that could last beyond the moment. For this reason they lead away from art, they are inimical to art, arbitrary, and prosaic. Real suffering is without aesthetic interest. (Seidel 1975, pp. 151–152)

For Hugo Riemann, it is only *reales Leiden* or at least the dynamics of real, unfettered musical motion that is of aesthetic interest, and not an abstract *Zeitmaß* imagined as the regularity of equal divisions divorced from content. In his attempt to reconcile rhythm and meter, Riemann begins not with Plato, but with the temporal relativism of Aristoxenos:

> "Time is not, after all, itself divided; rather, for the articulation of the lapsing of time there is required a materially perceptible Other to carry out

this articulation." . . . [This fundamental assertion of Aristoxenos] finally condemns to death all attempts to propose as the basis for a vital and productive theory of rhythm bare schemata for the division of time into fragmentary elements of equal duration. H. Lotze himself did not make clear the full significance of Aristoxenos' fundamental dictum when he ascribed only to equal time segments a negative character, that they "strain and torment as immediately reiterated stimuli". *Equal time segments have no effect at all apart from something that occurs in them and that itself first makes the passage of time an object for sensible perception*; rather, the strain and torture of "equal time segments" can only be the effect of things that happen in time which through their homogeneity and unattractiveness engender monotony and boredom. . . . It is a false inference however to assume that the meager interest awakened by this unmodulated reiteration should be a characteristic of time division itself. The fallacy is not avoided but is, instead, magnified if one attempts to elevate uniformity and offer greater interest through the regular alternation of strong and weak beats; for even in this case there is demonstrated a removal from the rich activity within the marked time segments itself without testing the impressions produced by this content and without seeking in this content the essence of rhythm. (Riemann 1903, pp. 1–2)

Time division is accomplished by the *Grundmaß* or beat, a "medium-sized duration" (*Mittelmaß*) that corresponds approximately to the human pulse but which can vary between 60 and 120 cycles per minute. As given in a piece of music, the *Grundmaß* is absolute, but it is only in abstraction that it can be regarded as a self-sufficient object. Although Riemann cannot deny the periodic repetitions of the *Grundmaß* or of larger time divisions created by "the regular alterations of strong and weak beats," he repeatedly casts doubt on the perceptual reality of such division and the "spans of time" they would mark off. In musical art we are called upon to hear the periodicity of the *contents* of duration (primarily tonal contents and their motions), not the repetition of duration itself:

[If we ask] what role can fall to stringently closed time division in the aesthetic analysis of our appreciation of musical art, the answer must run as follows: that the realization and marking of such a division of time gives rise to the *comparison of the con-*

tents delimited by this division, that what happens within the time divisions thus marked will first be outwardly stamped with a fixed periodicity which stimulates the search for a real periodicity in the organically structured tonal motions themselves. For this reason it is quite useless to wish to make an attempt to ground the reality of rhythm in uninteresting markings of time division, as by drumbeats, for example. . . . In this sense rhythm is thus not only a principle that produces unity in the multiplicity of phenomena, but it is at the same time that which makes this unity *perceptible*—a positive achievement, a support for the spiritual activity that requires such unity in the satisfaction of its demands, which indeed is the claim that is laid upon artistic appreciation. (Riemann 1900, pp. 134–135)

For Hauptmann, too, meter without rhythm is of no aesthetic interest, but it is real, not abstract. The measure as such is empty of properly rhythmic content, but it is not a passive container for rhythm or for duration. Measure here is conceived as *measuring*—a process through which sensible duration is created. The repetition of equal durations is for Hauptmann not a given but a continuous activity and, thus, in itself "a positive achievement." Riemann, on the other hand, takes the traditional view that the pulse train is given. It is for this reason that Riemann finds the *Grundmaß* so problematic in his attempt to break away from a mechanistic conception of rhythm. At every stage in his analysis Riemann explicitly or implicitly invokes the *Grundmaß* as homogeneous return, and yet this *Einheitsmaß* is itself something abstract that becomes real only when it is given rhythmic content:

What the *Grundmaß* is in each particular case does not result, as we have previously emphasized, from the abstract, absolute *Mittelmaß*, but results instead from the concrete melody itself. The actual counts of time (felt beats, rhythmic *Grundzeiten*) under all circumstances win their first real existence through their content. (Riemann 1903, p. 8)

Although Riemann retains the traditional conception of measure as a homogeneous return of the same, he attempts to overlay this conception with a new dynamic or organic interpretation in which *motion* can take the place of periodicity as the defining characteristic of the measure. Riemann's new *Takt* is not contained within bar lines and is not expressed in equal division. It is *Taktmotiv*—a "measure" from which rhythmic content cannot be abstracted. Distinctions of strong and weak do not function to segment the pulse train into bars; rather, they create *motion* (thus the word *Motiv*; cf. Riemann 1900, p. 157)—motion toward or away from. Motion away from leads to repose and the cessation of motion. Thus, the moment that marks the cessation of one motive and the beginning of another Riemann calls "dead" (Riemann 1903, pp. 14–15). It is the gesture of moving toward that characterizes the dynamic of the motive, and thus Riemann defines *Taktmotiv* as quintessentially anacrustic. In its basic form, the *Taktmotiv* consists of two elements: an unaccented first part (*Aufstellung, proposta*) and an accented second (*Beantwortung, riposta*). In view of the novelty and eccentricity of this interpretation of measure, Riemann offers suprisingly little explanation for the absolute priority he accords anacrusis. He does, however, offer extensive criticism of traditional theories, and I suspect that a central motive in Riemann's definition of *Taktmotiv* is an attempt to break the bar and to free rhythm from the homogeneity and regularity of measure. Although Riemann cannot deny *Grundmaß*, he suppresses it in a *Takt* that is self-ruled through the dynamics of motion and not ruled by an underlying periodicity.

Before leaving Riemann, I would like to consider very briefly his notion of hierarchy, for it is the "Zusammenschluß von Einzelmotiven zu größeren Formen, also das musikalischen Periodenbau" that Riemann calls "meter" (*Metrik*) (1903, p. 18). *Taktmotiv* is not based on durational equality; it is an essentially qualitative and not a quantitative order. In its primitive, characteristic form, *Taktmotiv* is represented by a short upbeat followed by a longer downbeat and finds its clearest expression in triple or unequal measure. However, in the compositions of *Taktmotiven* that form the entities of *Taktgruppe, Vordersatz*, and *Periode*, equality of duration is a necessary condition, and the hierarchy can proceed only by powers of two. It may happen that metrical units are not actually composed of two-, four-, or eight-measure constituents, but such irregular formations are regarded as derived from

an underlying regularity. Although Riemann does not reconcile this difference between small- and large-scale "rhythm," he applies a similar concept of accentuation. And by focusing on *accent* rather than on *equality,* Riemann can downplay the roles of quantity, regularity, and abstraction in his concept of the *Metrik*—features that would seem to underlie the symmetry of the eight-measure period as a *normatives Grundschema*.

Whether in the *Taktmotiv* or in the period, it is motion toward conclusion that unites, and it is the end or goal of this motion that receives weight or accent. Such unification arises from a "synthetische Thätigkeit der Phantasie" (Riemann 1900, p. 165). This process of synthesis that occurs in both the large and small dimensions is described as the unity of perception and memory. Again Riemann draws on the thought of Aristoxenos: "On two things rests the comprehension of music: on perception and memory. To perceive, one must hold on to becoming, and in memory retain what has become. Else it is impossible to follow an unfolding of music" (p. 138). The symmetry of the eight-measure *Grundschema* is thus conceived not as a product of equal time divisions but as a process of unification whereby a first is united in memory with a second to form a greater event. And since it is the second that completes the event and is the occasion for a memory of the first, the second receives greater weight and a "besonderen ästhetischen Wert" (p. 141).

In the conclusion to *Musikalische Rhythmik und Metrik*, Riemann summarizes what is indeed a "guiding principle" for his theoretical reflection:

> This guiding principle has been nothing other than the continual distinction of *statement* and *answer*, "proposta" and "risposta", and thus of a *first* and of a *second* that stands in relation to the first as a completion, the distinction of *weak* and *strong* as *metrical quality* in musical structures of the most diverse dimension—structures which undergo quite definite aesthetic valuations: first as contents of temporal units and then as simple and compound divisions that, by virtue of our physical constitution, are presented to us directly by nature (though they are variable within moderate limits), and then further as contents of higher-level units formed by their combination into easily scanned groups. (Riemann 1903, p. 305)

Thus, by shifting his discourse from "time values" to a qualitative, aesthetic "valuation" of measured durations, Riemann effectively dismisses meter as numerical quantity. The distinction accented/unaccented has been removed from the realm of periodicity and now characterizes phases of a properly rhythmic motion.

Although his work bears many similarities to that of Riemann and Hauptmann, Friedrich Neumann proposes a much starker separation of meter (as numerical quantity) and rhythm (as a form of attention). It is not meter that Riemann denigrates, but only his predecessors' schematization; and it might be said that Riemann attempts to save meter by rhythmicizing it. For Neumann the distinction between meter and rhythm is, as it was for Hauptmann, categorical. But whereas Hauptmann's sympathies lie with meter as a fully sensible, form-generating process, Neumann with equal fervor takes up the banner of rhythm. Rhythm and meter become for Neumann separate worlds—rhythm, the deep, holistic world of human time-consciousness blending seamlessly into the "timelessness" of the unconscious; and meter, the shallow, merely intellectual world of reckoning with durations as quantities. So incommensurate are the range and "contents" of these worlds, we can hardly speak here of an opposition. In the experience of music (and, one must assume, in many domains of human experience), these two worlds conspire without conflict to produce the totality of that experience. But although there is no conflict, there is a clear distinction of priority. The wholeness of rhythm as a sort of Husserlian "time-consciousness" precedes and forms the ground for any counting or comparison of durational quantities. In music meter is joined to rhythm, but this addition does not give order or form to rhythm—rhythm is in it-self already fully organized in its own terms. Neither does meter owe its distinctive quantitative order to rhythm. And yet, as an addition or supplement, meter is inconceivable in any concrete instance apart from its grounding in rhythm and for this reason remains for Neumann something of an abstaction linked to the abstraction of mathematics.

Neumann characterizes meter (*Zeitmaß*) as "quantitative/outer time"—time viewed in relation to space (or, rather, an abstract, geometric construction of space). From this perspective, time is measured by the distance between durationless instants—time points. This measuring permits us to compare genuinely numerical time quantities. Rhythm (*Zeitgestalt*), on the other hand, is "qualitative/inner time"—time viewed from the standpoint of being and becoming, past and future, and memory and anticipation (i.e., time as *lived*)[1]:

> Owing to this close connection to space, we will call quantitative time also *outer time*. Qualitative time, on the other hand, obviously belongs to the living organism, and thus we will also call it *inner time*. In this way, outer and inner time are to be understood as *forces*, both of which are present and manifested in any real time. (Neumann 1959, p. 21)

It might be said that the difference between meter and rhythm is the difference between time *span* and time as *Spannung* (or *Spannung/Entspannung*). Rhythm gives us the continuity of an event experienced as a whole. Meter gives us the continuity of number (or, rather, the continuity of a mathematics that unites discrete quantities under a system of operations—as I have argued, *a* number, *a* time point, is pure discontinuity):

> The metrical is based upon the capacity for *time comparison*, and further on the ability to compre-

---

1. If meter is time viewed spatially as quantitative extent, this view does not for Neumann exhaust the meaning of space (or of time). Just as he opposes *Zeitgestalt* to a metrical (arithmetic) division of time, Neumann opposes *Raumgestalt* to geometric space. It is again in *motion* (*Bewegung*) that time and space are united as "rhythmic" categories—here a temporalization of space wherein rhythm is made visible. Moreover, the rhythmization of motion is a fact of life, not of lifeless matter. As Neumann writes:

"Motion, however, in the sense of the spatialization of the *Zeitgestalt* belongs above all to the reality of the living and therefore is not to be understood exclusively in physical terms. Just as the *Zeitgestalt* has unity, so too shaped motion in space is in itself closed, that is, it is an undivided *motion-process*. It leads finally to a *Raumgestalt* in which the shaped motion leaves behind it, as it were, an indelible, visible trace. *Raumgestalt* is in principle something other than the geometrical figure" (Neumann 1959, p. 12).

hend any sort of quantitative temporal relation. The object of the metrical is time as directly given quantity. The method for taking measure of the metrical can accordingly be learned only from the general study of quantity or mathematics. The simplest mathematical operation is counting, and this generates at once the integer series as the basic material of mathematics. It is by virtue of the ability for time comparison that we can count in *uniform tempo*, and in this way there arises already a metrical structure, or as we might more briefly say, a *meter*. (Neumann 1959, p. 24)

One of the more remarkable features of Neumann's analysis is his generalization of meter. Here we find no talk of a *given* pulse train—that reification of meter which in the form of *Grundzeiten* so bedeviled Riemann. Neumann avoids such reification by presenting meter as our ability to measure or compare (together with real opportunties for measurement). Notice that the metrical is said to comprise *any sort* of measurement or comparison of durational quantity. Thus, Neumann characterizes as metrical a succession of pulses, undifferentiated by accent, and, moreover, allows us to speak of meter even in the absence of regularity or periodicity:

> We designate as *flexible* or *inexact* meter a series of beats in which there can no longer be found a common metrical unit or time-beat to which they might be related. Indeed, a time-comparison will continue to be made here also, but the ear will find between two immediately successive beats no, or rather no exact, metrical relation and will simply determine whether a beat is longer or shorter than the preceding beat. (Neumann 1959, p. 27)

Such cases are deemed metrical because they, too, involve measuring, or the comparison of durational quantity, and the basic "operation" of counting. The remaining operations Neumann posits are addition, multiplication, exponentiation, and division. Subtraction is excluded because time does not flow backward. (Like many theorists, Neumann does not consider this problem in connection with division.)

Rhythm, on the other hand, knows nothing of such measurement. It is a *shaping* of time into concrete units of experience filled with memory and expectation. This shaping involves two psy-

chological or cognitive components: (1) the act of "attentiveness" (*Aufmerkung*), by which we recognize points of discontinuity—*Zeitpunkte*—and divide time into discrete intervals; and (2) the "immediate power of comprehension" (*unmittelbare Fassungskraft*) that binds together these successive, atomic *Aufmerkungen* and their articulated limits in the unity of immediate memory (*die unmittelbare Gedächtniseinheit*). Neumann designates as "*rhythmic qualities*" the dynamic continuities of memory, expectation, and the fulfillment of expectation or completion (*Erfüllung*). These qualities function to transform the abstractions of point and line segment into the dynamic, organic realm of human experience. In the following two passages Neumann contrasts first *Zeitmaß* and *Zeitgestalt* and then the species of temporality ("outer" and "inner") upon which each of these is based:

> The fundamental concept of the rhythmic is the Zeitgestalt as a whole composed of temporal qualities. At the beginning of the metrical stands the time-count, and the first operation that is undertaken with the time-count is the unspecified reproduction of the same. In opposition to this, the fundamental unit of the rhythmic is the whole of the Zeitgestalt, and this whole is to be conceived as a unitary, inclusive whole. The operation which leads from wholeness and unity to the multiplicity of parts is *division*; and the capacity for time-comparison within a continuous, boundless series in the metrical corresponds in the rhythmic to the capacity to conceive of temporal lengths as filled with complementary rhythmic qualities [above all, recollection and expectation] as parts of a closed temporal whole.

> We have labeled as outer time the continuous [i.e., mathematically "continuous"], quantitatively exact time. Inner time, on the other hand, is filled with rhythmic qualities; whether expanded or contracted it is metrically unfocused. Rhythmic time we must moreover think of as intermittent, spontaneous; it is *composed* time. Outer and inner time, however, are not to be dissociated from one another. To some extent, inner time is *placed into* outer time. Inner time emerges from timelessness; outer time is removed at the farthest possible distance from timelessness. Inner time *unites* timelessness with outer time. Neither inner time nor outer time is thus in itself actual [*wirklich*]; rather, in what is actual both are there from the beginning where

the inner is *placed* in the outer, and *through* this placing inner and outer time are for the first time actual. (Neumann 1959, pp. 29, 93–94)

Rhythm and meter are *real* from the beginning, but they are *actual* (*wirklich*) only when they act; indeed, they must act at the same time—the time in which we experience them together in musical performance. Moreover, Neumann does not deny that the durations produced by a hierarchy of periodicities and marked by metrical accent are also given to rhythm for its particular acts of integration that produce an expressive, temporal whole. But in this point of contact between the rhythmic and the metrical it is rhythm that again is privileged as the agent that selects which metrical *possibilities* are to be actualized:

> The metrical *makes possible*, after all, the concept of temporal quantitative relations; the rhythmic, on the other hand, explores which of these possibilities are musically useful, or, if I may be allowed to say so, *actual*. Its key concept is that of the *fitting measure*—thus we will call quite generally the grouping of quantities which can be assimilated to a qualitative wholeness. (Neumann 1959, p. 30)

If metrical accents are merely time-points for the segmentation of spans of pure durational quantity, how then shall we conceive of the rhythmic accents that are felt as dynamic qualities that spread through felt durations, continuously uniting diverse sensations as components of a properly rhythmic whole? Neumann's solution to this problem is one of the more ingenous aspects of his theory. In the question of accent and duration (or "length"), rhythm and meter are again separated, but not opposed. In chapter 8 of the present study I will discuss in more detail the basis upon which Neumann constructs a theory of rhythmic accent or "weight." Suffice it for now to say that accent in the *Zeitgestalt* arises from the workings of "the immediate power of comprehension" (the durational "extension" of a point of beginning aimed at the unification of two or more events) and from the unifying processes of recollection and anticipation. At any "level," when two or more events are joined in a temporal whole, memory and anticipation can create a distinction of *weight*. Strongly reminiscent of Riemann's "guiding principle," Neu-

mann's prototypical rhythmic phenomenon is the "rhythmic pair," a union of two events that *as a whole* is characterized by equilibrium (*Gleichgewicht*). This essential equilibrium can, however, be disturbed in countless ways by any factors that direct our attention toward one or another part. Most generally, it is (contra Riemann) beginning and not end that has weight. The movement from beginning to end is a movement from the clear to the diffuse, from attentiveness to inattentiveness. The point of beginning "belongs to the *being* of the phenomenon"; "the end of a phenomenon belongs to *non-being*" (p. 16). It is the "immediate power of comprehension" that binds beginnings and that extends beginning into a duration begun; and, thus extended, beginning can bear weight. However, if beginning is strongly directed toward the future (*steigend*), as in the case of an upbeat, it will not have weight. Anticipation or openness to the future detracts from weight. If the beginning does have weight, the gesture is one of "falling," and in this case recollection is paramount—anticipation is here anticipation of an end that preserves the beginning in memory. Thus, it is the "rhythmic qualities" of recollection and anticipation that determine weight. Furthermore, this distinction of weight is not relative; there are not gradations of weight as there are gradations of metrical accent:

> From this perspective one can divide the parts into strong and weak and say in general that in the stronger parts recollection and immediate comprehension predominate, and in the weaker parts, expectation. An important consequence emerges in this connection. In the metrical the difference between stressed and unstressed parts is a *graduated* one, i.e., even the unstressed part has a certain stress, if, nevertheless, a weaker one. However, in the rhythmic, which looks toward content, stressed and unstressed parts *are set in logical opposition*—the unstressed point to the future, the stressed to the past. (Neumann 1959, p. 39)

In his discussion of rhythmic weight, Neumann speaks of "regular lengths," and his examples are notated with bar lines and meter signatures. But the regular lengths of rhythm are not those of meter. The simplest case of regular length is again encountered in the *rhythmic pair*, a rhythmic but not yet a metrical union of two equal lengths. First comes the rhythmic pair, and only afterward metrical accent. Moreover, this relation of before and after is also the relation of background and foreground (in a vaguely Schenkerian sense). Deep in the background lies the balance of the rhythmic pair. Prior to the metrical differentiation of the foreground, the pair in both small and large ensures the wholeness and essential undividedness of the *Zeitgestalt*:

> Now if the temporal whole here appears as a regular length, it is to be distinguished in this regard in its very essence from the *metrical* concept of regular length that we have developed above. There the regular length was characterized as a single large measure with manifold graduated accents of various degrees of strength. Here both segments of the pair are to be understood above all as being in rhythmic *equilibrium*, and this equilibrium is transferred to all levels. In all the diverse motion and suspense of rhythmic energies the form-world of the pair remains virtually *not at all* differentiated. This does not exclude the possibility that in the further structuring of the individual segments the customary meters and with them differences of metrical weight can appear. However, as we have said, at the background structural levels the impression of equilibrium dominates. (Neumann 1959, p. 37)

There is no conflict between metrical stress and rhythmic weight or between the regularities proper to meter and those proper to rhythm. But this lack of conflict, rather than indicating a union of meter and rhythm, points instead to their essential separation. Metrical accent and rhythmic weight can, and often do, correspond in one and the same time point (selected by our attention), but there is no interaction—neither can, in principle, affect the other. To say simply that this is a polarity is to beg the question of the "actual" formation of a musical experience. If there is, in fact, *Steigerung* or *Aufhebung*, Neumann does not characterize the process or the product. Although Neumann does not deny the general efficacy of meter for *das Wirkliche*, his sentiments clearly lie with rhythm and against meter. And in many passages the polarity of meter and rhythm is presented as the opposition of mechanical and organic (physics versus biology), conceptual and experiential, general and

particular, or abstract and concrete. For example, Neumann compares meter to "pure harmony" or the *conceptual possibilities* for any actual harmonic organization:

> Similar to the way in which pure harmony is related to a fully worked out theory of harmonic structure is the metrical related to the rhythmic: just as these manifold possibilities for meters and other metrical combinations are unfolded, so likewise is asserted the manifold possibilities for tonal systems, individual sonorities, etc. In crossing over from these possibilities to the musical realities, however, a selection will be made from the perspective of the highest manifestation of the *Zeitgestalt* in the tonal succession. (Neumann 1959, pp. 133–134)

Quite in line with Neumann's thinking is the following statement from August Halm (quoted by Neumann): "The measure is a natural temporal *order*, so to speak, an autonomous, self-ordering of time . . . ; rhythm is an artistic *orderedness*; the measure is the schematic *form* of our time perception—rhythm, *that which is formed*. It is temporal shape" (Halm 1926, p. 98; Neumann 1959, p. 18). This much is quoted by Neumann. However, since Halm's immediately preceding discussion touches on many of the issues we have considered above, I would like to expand the quotation:

> We see the rhythmic therefore as a free, non-schematic arrangement of longs and shorts, i.e., not as a display of time values but rather as a *utilization* of long and short—an (artistic) process in which these time values are used, just as the differences of high and low are productive for the melodic (to be sure, in connection with the rhythmic).
>   . . . the measure is endless (i.e., it desires, by its nature, to be unending, for its purpose is to again and again attach itself to its predecessors); rhythm is finite, it lives in rhythmic figures, i.e., in commenced and concluded motives and themes. The measure affords two possibilities, namely, either equal or unequal; i.e., as equal measure it is divided into four or two parts, as unequal it is divided into three parts; each of these types is simple. Rhythm, on the other hand, is multiple, and, indeed, multiple not only because in each individual rhythm there is a more or less intense variation of longs and shorts but also because there is a perhaps incalculable

number of different rhythms, i.e., rhythm as possibility, as principle is probably indefinitely manifold, or actually infinitely manifold. Measure is a (spiritual) constraining force of nature; rhythm is our free acting and feeling. (Halm 1926, pp. 88–89)

Such a line of thought can lead to a still more radical separation of rhythm and meter, as in the following opinion expressed by Fritz Kuba:

Rhythm is the sensibly perceived articulation of time; in this sense, that which is really heard! Measure is the conceptual articulation of time; in this sense, that which is really planned or understood! . . . The accession of the merely sensibly perceived to larger complexes, that is, the possibility of perceiving such larger passages as unities does not, even with the assistance of pure sensibility, warrant the attempt to see in this the workings of a *metrical* unity. For the metrical can serve as a meaningful reference only for the abstract brain function of counting, and we must reserve the concept of meter for this abstract functioning since we are, moreover, not in the position, as would be required, to arrive at a general understanding of that abstract function and to clearly designate it. (Kuba 1948, pp. 7–8, quoted in Henneberg 1974, p. 94)

If meter as time measure does indeed seem abstract, it must be said that as felt "beat," meter hardly places us in the world of concepts. In the enjoyment of measured activity, the beat is vividly felt not as a monotonous return but as a vehicle that pushes us forward into fresh experience. In his *Arbeit und Rhythmus*, Karl Bücher finds no need to make a distinction between rhythm and meter. For Bücher the regularity of rhythm is itself of aesthetic value. Rhythm here is measured rhythm,

the ordered articulation of motions in their temporal progress. Rhythm arises from the organic nature of man. In all the natural activities of the animal body rhythm appears as the ruling element governing the most economical use of energies. The trotting horse and the laden camel move just as rhythmically as the rowing oarsman and the hammering smith. Rhythm awakens feelings of joy. It is not merely an easing of toil, but rather also one of the sources of aesthetic pleasure and that element of art for which all men, regardless of differences of custom, have an inherent feeling. Through rhythm it seems in the early days of

mankind that the principle of economy comes into play instinctively, a principle which bids us, enables us to strive for the greatest possible activity and enjoyment with the least possible sacrifice of vitality and spirit. (Bücher 1924, pp. 434–435)

If this pleasure is instinctive, it is not, for Bücher, "primitive." And he suggests that in new routines of work, directed by the peculiar regularities of machines, we may lose supremely valuable connections between work, art, and play.

For an opinion that meter as something universal and "natural" is therefore not fully "artistic" but, rather, a primitive component of art, one may turn to Ernst Toch's discussion of form. Although in the following passage Toch speaks of an artistic contrast that would seem to distinguish meter from pulse, this properly "artistic" contrast of tension and relaxation is, in fact, the work of tone and does not imply a ratio of equal durations:

Time rolls on uniformly, uninterruptedly, unceasingly. Units add to units, to form bigger units unceasingly. Seconds accumulate to minutes, to hours, to days, weeks, months, years, decades, centuries. At the bottom of time operates a monotonous rhythm, mirrored in our own being by the beat of our heart, the pulsation of our bloodstream.

This regularly reiterant rhythm forms, as it were, a bottommost stratum of which we become conscious only at rare intervals.

Above this nethermost stratum lies and works another stratum: the periodic alternation of contrast.

While seconds, minutes, hours roll on in constant equality, at the same time there is a constant alternation of day and night, winter and summer, high tide and low tide. While the fundamental rhythm of pulsation accompanies us continuously, at the same time we alternate in exhalation and inhalation, in the consciousness of being awake and the unconsciousness of sleep.

It is the interplay of these two elementary forces that builds and feeds the skeleton of music. Primitive music may be satisfied with the basic element, the rhythm. The reiteration of a definite rhythmical pattern, produced mainly, if not solely, by percussion instruments, will create a certain stirring effect. Inspired by bodily movements, and inspiring bodily movements, like marching or dancing, it may be protracted at random, may give suitable support to such performances, may create certain moods and even a kind of primitive mental ecstasy. But it will never create *musical form*, no matter how complicated, intricate and refined such rhythmical patterns may be. For that, the second element has to be added: the element of *contrast*, of black and white, of light and shade, of *tension and relaxation*. It is the right distribution of light and shade, or of tension and relaxation, that is formative in every art, in music as well as in painting, sculpture, architecture, poetry. (Toch 1977, pp. 155–156)

At the opposite extreme from Toch, Thrasybulos Georgiades argues that it is precisely meter, newly conceived as a relatively autonomous "concept" or *Taktbegriff*, that is the hallmark of High Classical style. In a radical departure from eighteenth- and nineteenth-century perspectives on meter, Georgiades suggest a way of saving the measure from regularity and homogeneity. The measure is still a container independent from the musical material that it will house. But the particularity of that material can break measure from measure, and so broken, the measure, rather than being a return of the same, can emerge as an unpredictable moment that, cut off from the past, places us in an absolute now. Since Georgiades explicitly addresses questions of continuity and discontinuity, temporality, law and freedom, structural determinacy, and experience, I would like to review some of the main points of his argument. Although Georgiades' ideas may seem eccentric, they are generally compatible with notions of time that have gained currency in discussions of postwar avant-garde music.

Georgiades argues that the new style that came to full maturity in the 1780s developed a radically new concept of measure as a means of creating for music a genuine feeling of the "theatrical," a *Theaterwirklichkeit* that has now displaced the pre-Classical "epic" reality. The essential characteristic of the theatrical is discontinuity—a concentration on the "here and now" cut off from a determining, causal past and a determined future.[2] It is also a discontinuity of the

observer and the observed, of subject and object. (And as Geordiades later implies, this Classical disjunction leads to estrangement and alienation in the twentieth century.) The theatrical is for Georgiades a moment of "intellectual history" linked to eighteenth-century empiricism and scientific method (perhaps as "theater" and "theory" are etymologically linked through *theorein*—to look at). The expression of the theatrical is *das Vorführen*, both in the sense of a theatrical "production" and in the sense of a scientific "demonstration"—that is, an act of proving or making evident, an exhibition of an event in which its workings are manifested, as fully "present,"

> ... a demonstration which may be understood as a succession of the Here-and-Now. When I observe characters acting before me, in my presence, so do I understand this event as an other placed in opposition to me. It is something real but something that is not, however, congruent with my own reality. ... With theatrical reality [*Theaterwirklichkeit*] an otherness is created ad hoc and accordingly composed in whatever way the author deems useful. Theater is, as it were, an experimental laboratory. The aim is, at any given time, to come up with a useful arrangement of the experiment which is necessary in order to be able to demonstrate an event as present, that is to say, to produce the event as theatrical reality, i.e., as something discontinuous.

What now enables Mozart's musical language to bring about the demonstration? We must look for the answer in the new meaning that the Viennese classicists gave to the measure. The new conception of the measure occurs in that moment wherein the musical language is transformed to become the legitimate sensible representative of theatrical reality, both in regard to its discontinuity and to its presentational design. The new handling of the measure allows for the composition to be, like a physical experiment, planned out in whatever way is useful for a demonstration of the event to be observed.

> ... the measure is to be understood as an autonomous quantity and independent from its fill-

---

2. The theatrical here is not to be confused with the operatic. Georgiades finds the "purest" examples of the composition of discontinuity in instrumental music, and in the instrumental music of Haydn rather than that of Mozart.

ing-out through the sounding material. It elapses at a uniform rate and guarantees unity. In opposition to the measure, the filling-out with tones will be treated as a likewise autonomous but variable, changing quantity; also, both of these can be displaced with respect to one another. Through the possibility for transformation, as it is tested by us in the experiment, we come to know their new autonomy. The spiritual measure of the classicists is the analysis of what up until this time had been a presumed unity of rhythmic-tonal shape into two autonomous quantities, separated in their manipulation. (Georgiades 1953, pp. 50, 53–54)

Whereas Riemann attempted to wed meter to a rhythmic content, Georgiades conceives of a *leeres Takt*, a measure emptied of all content. And although Georgiades in the preceding quotation speaks of metrical uniformity, he insists that the Classical measure, freed from content and in essence discontinuous, is itself the site of an *absolute presence*. Georgiades conceives of the "pre-Classical" as a relatively homogeneous realm of feeling wherein tone and time are coordinated, rather like the voices of the old polyphony. What is novel, and perhaps tragic, in the late-eighteenth-century Viennese world of form is the radical separation of form and content—a world in which the "otherness" (read *individuality*) of content breaks free from the restraint of form. *Takt* no longer measures the temporal passage of a rhythmic content. Rather, content explodes in a diversity of character that exceeds measure. The measure, on the other hand, released from its Matthesonian function of eternally housing an infinite variety of rhythmic contents, is now free to pursue an independent course that will lead, ultimately, to an intuition of "absolute" time. In order to save the measure from the determinism of a repetition of the same, Georgiades conceives of each measure as autonomous, existing for itself alone, undetermined, present simultaneously with other measures in a "polyphony" of unconditioned, self-willed moments.

The Classical phrase (*Satz*) is, like the measure, an autonomous constituent. But unlike the empty measure, which is conceived as pure durational quantity (i.e., filled with "time"), the phrase is a closed entity already filled with content, a *fester Körper*. For Georgiades there is no hierarchy—phrase and measure are incommensurate:

If one endeavors correctly to understand the [Classical] phrase-structure one has no choice but to ascertain the highly original manner in which it is structured: nothing continuous, each member is in itself compact—for itself closed, a solid body, heterogeneous with the other members; the succession, broken by fits and starts, for itself inexplicable. . . . The symmetry [of Classical phrase construction] is, one might say, a sort of straw man. The guiding spirit is the new and specifically Classical concept of the *measure*. This new concept of measure can be designated as a correlate and a reciprocal concept to the concept of the "solid body" for the Classical phrase. . . . With the Classicists the solid, compact figures indeed appear of their own accord; they capture their position and maintain it whether they be in conflict with the measure or in coordination with the measure. The combined effect of these two elements is what above all determines the countenance of the properly Classical. (Georgiades 1951, pp. 85–86)

In Georgiades' vision, measures and phrases emerge as particular, self-enclosed expressions of the here and now. Their multiplicity creates a new, discontinuous "polyphony" of moments freely combined, overlapped, and contrasted in character, in metrical weight, and in length—active and interactive like the characters of a drama.

In such a compositional technique there emerges the impression of a pure, inexplicable freedom: shapes which flare up out of the void; unprecedented in their autonomy, fully plastic, graspable with the hands, accepting their place in space, unconcerned with their neighbors. . . . Whereas with polyphony we thus confront undivided lines advancing through the piece, we stand here before singular, closed shapes that lead their own, metrically individual lives; before individual "solid bodies" that assert themselves in the simultaneity of their co-existence. Thus, there arises here what we may, for good reason, call "polymeter." (Georgiades 1951, p. 95)

If phrase as *fester Körper* and measure as *leere Takt* are for themselves independent objects, they nevertheless represent an essential component or pole of unity and wholeness. They constitute the sensuous foreground that is organized by and that itself gives shape to the constructive background. The latter is a structural, *harmonic* background or "scaffolding"—"prerhythmic," "premetric," a "uniform-gray foundation" that is given a definite shape by the rhythmic-metric foreground. The succession of tonal cadences is "like a sea of harmony, a homogeneous ground, a coursing, undifferentiated undercurrent" (Georgiades 1951, p. 92). Indeed, one of the more remarkable features of Georgiades' opposition of foreground and background is its inversion of the customary opposition of the contributions of tone and meter to rhythm, where tonal relations are generally regarded as dynamic, unfettered agents of musical motion and meter is regarded as *Gerüst*—a more or less automatic, mechanical (uniform-gray) regulator of motion vivified by tone:

The foreground is freely animated, as if here the naked forces of nature held sway. However, in animation it thereby draws its legitimacy from an invisible background. (This separation is not without analogy to the distinction between measure on the one hand and the solid shapes on the other.) Thus emerges a tension, an enlivening interaction between the scaffolding and the sensible, rhythmic-melodic-textural shaping of the foreground—on the one hand, a constructive principle; on the other, embodied characters created through music and placed on the stage. In the customary way of thinking, however, one identifies the foreground simply with the composition. In this way, one views the work merely as a naturalistic form. Thus, characteristically, one supposes that the framework of the composition is understood simply through an identification of periods, concatenations of phrases, overlappings, and so forth; in reality, however, this sort of analysis does not even correctly understand the foreground. It ignores the living source of the Classical phrase, the fact that several metrical structures can endure simultaneously as co-present. . . . This analysis awakens the false idea that a phrase must become effaced when another takes its place, since at any given moment only *one* metrical order is admitted as being operative. . . . This method thus comprehends neither the polymetric phenomenon nor the relation of this phenomenon to the background. (Georgiades 1951, pp. 95–96)

However, this characterization of the foreground does not touch on the "prerhythmic" meaning of measure itself—the *leere Takt* that precedes the "shaping of the foreground." In this sense, measure is indeed abstract and, for Georgiades, an abstraction that reflects the new conceptual world of the late eighteenth century. In a remarkable conflation of musical style and metaphysics, Georgiades maintains that the new "Classical," Kantian *concept* of time is itself concretized or embodied in the actual music of the period—in the mature works of Haydn and Mozart:

From the perspective of compositional technique . . . the empty measure, independent from its rhythmic filling-out, is manipulated by the Classical masters as an individual substance [*Wesenheit*]. It has come to be an autonomous factor in composition. One might almost say: A musical idea can be composed of an empty measure, solely from the concept of "measure". This measure, freed from any material, now has the power to hold the heterogeneous members together, precisely because nothing material is to be found in the measure itself that could be set in conflict with it. (Georgiades 1951, p. 86)

It functions as a pure system of relationships which creates unity only in the mind's eye. This represents, however, the ultimate abstraction possible within a craft: to operate with a factor which has become pure form (in Kant's meaning), which has rid itself completely of substance [*Materie*]. We are reminded that the same year, 1781, which marks the beginning of the mature classical period (Haydn's quartets op. 33 and Mozart's *Abduction from the Seraglio*) also brought the Kantian pure forms of perception, i.e., space and time; and it seems reasonable to appeal to the concept of absolute time and that of absolute measure [*Taktbegriff*] as parallel turning points in the intellectual-cultural history of Western civilization. . . . The freedom of the Viennese classical masters is the freedom propounded by Kant: it is realized by attaining the last possible point of departure from which meaning in its absolute sense can be grasped. This last foothold is the "*unity of apperception.*" This requires, however, the ultimate exertion of our person, our powers of apperception, our mental activity. The Viennese classical masters pursued conceptualization in the application of musical techniques so far that they reached the outer-most confines of musical possibility. The next instance, from which the work can still be comprehended as autonomously meaningful, is the purely conceptual, which has no analogy in musical substance. One step further, and debilitation of the musical language as autonomous language is the result. (Georgiades 1982, pp. 112–113)

For Georgiades the new, radical discontinuity in which individual measures and measure groups break from the homogeneous train as an unpredictable, unpredetermined multiplicity of fragments, shards (*Splittern, Fetzen*), each with its own, particular *Bewegungsimpuls* (Georgiades 1951, p. 76) contrasts with the continuity of pre-Classical music and reveals a new time-consciousness—a concentration on the "now" and a departure from any intuition (such as Mattheson's) of "eternal return." In the old music there was

> a process of continuous unfolding . . . Past, present and future there form an unbroken whole. Time was not realized as an independent element. The classical format, on the other hand, which corresponds to the attitude of the theater, is discontinuous; in the course of its progress unexpected forces intervene which alter its movement. In classical music *time* can no longer be calculated in advance. We become conscious of it as an independent element. The Viennese classical technique consists in our becoming conscious of time. Temporality forces its way in. Through its emphasis on the here-and-now, that former epic unity has broken apart into present and future. Only Viennese classical music comprehends the consecration of the moment. (Georgiades 1982, p. 113)

But *only* present and indefinite future: the causal past must be exorcised for there to be freedom. In this way, Georgiades has clearly pointed to the central problem of musical meter—the problem of reconciling the determinacy of meter as law with the spontaneity of rhythm as the experience of a novel present. But we must ask whether the renunciation of the past in an absolute "now" (or the renunciation of the future in an "eternal return") in fact corresponds to the temporality of musical experience. And we must ask if this problem can be solved by positing extraordinary temporalities for various styles. Cer-

tainly, styles are particular "worlds" for feeling. But certainly, too, if there is time there is becoming, and if there is becoming there is a present from which a real past and a real future can be distinguished but not separated. I will assert here (and argue in sequel) that the process of becoming is inescapable and that each particular "style" is a world in which becoming is rhythmically shaped.

There may indeed be an "aesthetic arrest" —as Stephen Dedalus says, "an esthetic stasis, an ideal pity or an ideal terror, a stasis called forth, prolonged and at last dissolved by what I call the rhythm of beauty." This is a halt "in the presence of whatsoever is grave and constant in human sufferings," but for Joyce in *A Portrait of the Artist as a Young Man* this is not an arrest of time, an eternal, original present, or an absolute now point—it is a "tragic emotion" wherein we are raised above fear and desire. Least of all is it "a consciousness of time as an independent element." There is, most certainly, a perennial wish to escape from the past—from regret and mourning (memory)— and to escape the uncertainty of the future (or the certainty of the future as death). But such a wish is driven by fear and desire.

Henri Bergson regards the sort of "arrest" that Georgiades (together with Karlheinz Stockhausen) identifies with "the consecration of the moment" as a form of what he calls "diluted" duration—an experience in which the past is no longer "concentrated" in the present. But far from regarding such "timelessness" as a mark of freedom, Bergson argues that such a movement in the direction of extension or spatiality reduces freedom and will and results in a lapse into determinism and passivity. I will return to Bergson's analysis in the conclusion of this study when we turn to questions of rhythmic experience in music from the early postwar years—the time when composers began speaking of a "spatialization" of musical time and a concentration on the moment and when Georgiades presented his idea of the Classical now.

I have argued that the concept of meter as a fixed quantitative-numerical order has the appeal of bringing the vagaries and uncertainties of becoming under our control. And yet, from the opinions we have reviewed in this chapter, it seems, too, that there is a deep mistrust of the law of return that bespeaks a fear of law as compulsion. Georgiades frees meter from law or regularity by severing the measure from past and future, but in doing so he must ignore a central feature of meter—the comparison of durational quantity and the judgment of equality and ratio. Georgiades' meter can become assimilated to the freedom and spontaneity of rhythm only by becoming irrational.

FOUR

Distinctions of Rhythm and Meter in Three Influential American Studies

In the preceding review of opinion concerning the relation of meter and rhythm, I have considered only German-speaking theorists from the mid-nineteenth to the mid-twentieth century, many of whose works touch on problems of temporality. A concern with "philosophical" questions of time became unfashionable after World War II except in the avant-garde's fascination with an absolute now. Neumann's is the last systematic attempt to bring a temporal and vaguely Goethean perspective to questions of musical rhythm (Hauptmann's is the first). And yet, if interest in traditional questions of temporality has waned, interest in problems of rhythm and meter has not. A year after the publication of Neumann's *Die Zeitgestalt* (1959), the appearance of Grosvenor Cooper and Leonard B. Meyer's *The Rhythmic Structure of Music* initiated in the United States an interest in problems of musical rhythm that has resulted in numerous studies. It was followed in 1968 by Edward T. Cone's *Musical Form and Musical Performance*, a parallel but less systematic interpretation of musical form as rhythm. Both studies are indebted to Riemann's work, but they go much further in detaching rhythm from counting.

Like Lorenz, Cone explicitly equates rhythm and form:

> Musical form, as I conceive it, is basically rhythmic. . . . Just as, in a normal musical period, the antecedent phrase stands in some sense as an upbeat to the consequent, so in larger forms one entire section can stand as an upbeat to the next. And if, as I believe, there is a sense in which a phrase can be heard as an upbeat to its own cadence, larger and larger sections can also be so apprehended. A completely unified composition could then constitute a single huge rhythmic impulse, completed at the final cadence. (Cone 1968, pp. 25–26)

Asking how to achieve a "valid and effective performance," Cone answers, "by discovering and making clear the rhythmic life of a composition. If I am right in locating musical form in rhythmic structure, it is the fundamental answer" (p. 31). And again, "valid performance depends primarily on the perception and communication of the rhythmic life of a composition. That is to say, we must first discover the rhythmic shape of a piece—which is what is meant by its form—and then try to make it as clear as possible to our listeners" (pp. 38–39).

In describing the rhythmic shape of music (as form and *per*-formance) Cone uses the language of metrical theory very freely, perhaps because of the kinesthetic, gestural conotations familiar to musicians in terms such as "downbeat," "upbeat," and "anacrusis." However, Cone's upbeats and downbeats are not metrical. They mark, or rather characterize, phases of musical "motion" and not groupings of equal durational units. Motion in this sense might be thought of as the active coherence of a duration. For Cone, this duration is articulated by two such downbeats—one initial and the other cadential, one a moment of departure and the other a moment of arrival. It should be noted here that although Cone uses the expression "point of arrival," it is clear that he conceives of such "points" as moments or *phases* rather than as durationless instants. Beginning and ending are not separated from the motion that begins and ends. Thus, in considering the musical phrase as "a microcosm of the composition" (i.e., the bearer of a process that takes place also on "higher levels"), Cone suggests that "an initial downbeat is marked by a kind of accent that implies a following *dimenuendo*; a cadential downbeat suggests rather the goal of a *crescendo*" (p. 27).

A "large-scale" upbeat is an initial downbeat that relinquishes some of its initial stability by becoming in some sense subordinate to the goal it leads to. "If the cadence, as the goal of the motion, is felt as even stronger than the initial downbeat, then the phrase does indeed become in a sense an expanded upbeat followed by a downbeat, the initial downbeat thereby accepting a reduced role as 'the downbeat of the upbeat'" (p. 27). It is important to note that in Cone's view, the upbeat, as beginning, is not fixed. Rather, the upbeat, although it has a "fixed point" of beginning, *becomes* or emerges as an upbeat during its progress to the cadential goal.

Cone's distinction between rhythm and meter rests, in part, on the observation that meter operates on the small scale of measures and "hypermeasures" (which for Cone rarely exceed two bars) but does not extend to larger units. Thus, the rhythm of a piece of music cannot be regarded simply as an accumulation of measures or as a single measure writ large. Where meter gives way to an essentially different form of rhythmic organization is at the level of phrase:

> The classical phrase has often been analyzed as an alternation of strong and weak measures, on an analogy with strong and weak beats within a measure. In other words, the larger rhythmic structure is treated simply as metric structure on a higher level. Now, I do not deny that such alternation often occurs, especially in the case of short, fast measures; but I insist that on some level this metric principle of parallel balance must give way to a more organic rhythmic principle that supports the melodic and harmonic shape of the phrase and justifies its acceptance as a formal unit. Such a principle must be based on the highly abstract concept of musical energy. (Cone 1968, p. 26)

However, Cone's reluctance to extend meter to the level of phrase and beyond is not based solely on a claim that we do not perceive such extended measures. He also regards the failure of meter to accede to rhythm proper as an inherent shortcoming of meter itself and not simply as a perceptual limitation. Cone argues that "the shortcoming of all attempts to invoke mechanically at higher levels the metrical arrangement of beats in a measure (or of measures within a hypermeasure)" results from the "uniformity" or homogeneity of metrical replications: "The resulting pattern, since it is indefinitely repeatable, fails to support the other aspects of musical form, for it contributes nothing to the progress of the piece toward its goal. This is why meter, as I have suggested, must yield to a more organic rhythmic principle" (p. 40). The metric principle of "parallel balance" or the repeated alternation of strong and weak thus lacks the dynamic continuity of rhythmic motion or "musical energy," a continuity characterized by progress rather than repetition and a continuity that arises from tonal motion.

Cone's often quoted metaphor for musical motion is a thrown ball:

> If I throw a ball and you catch it, the completed action must consist of three parts: the throw, the transit and the catch. There are, so to speak, two fixed points: the initiation of the energy and the goal toward which it is directed; the time and distance between them are spanned by the moving ball. [The qualification "so to speak" is well placed, for fixed points will never lead to motion.] In the same way, the typical musical phrase consists of an initial downbeat (/), a period of motion (⌒), and a point of arrival marked by a cadential downbeat (\ ). (1968, pp. 26–27)

Again, although Cone designates two points and an intervening span, the concept of energy welds the three components into a continuous whole. The energy of the initial impulse extends through the entire duration, and its directedness is realized in the entire completed gesture. Many musicians have found this image compelling, I think, because from it Cone has developed a cogent treatment of rhythm as something distinct from the regularity of meter—an understanding of rhythm that exceeds measurement and homogeneous repetition and that corresponds to our intuition of rhythm as fluid gesture.

In a different way but toward similar ends, Grosvenor Cooper and Leonard Meyer have also argued for a separation of rhythm and meter. In many ways their separation of rhythm and meter seems sharper than Cone's because the distinction does not depend upon scale—rhythm is from the beginning detached from meter. However, I shall argue that, in practice, Cooper and Meyer actually fuse meter and rhythm in order to create a structural hierarchy that extends from the smallest to the largest levels of duration. Their treatment of rhythm is much more detailed, systematic, and comprehensive than Cone's and involves explicit discussion of some basic issues of musical process—continuity, the indeterminacy of events as they are in the process of taking shape, comprehensibility, and the activity of attention. Although Cooper and Meyer also speak of motion, energy, and tension, these terms gain precision in reference to closely described acts of musical hearing. Rhythm is treated as a perceptual activity and is thus regarded as constructive and synthetic. It is not simply a more or less continuous span of motion, but the particular way groupings of events, at all levels of duration, emerge for our attention.

Cooper and Meyer define meter as "the measurement of the number of pulses between more or less regularly recurring accents" (1960, p. 4). Rhythm, on the other hand, is "the way in which one or more unaccented beats are grouped in relation to an accented one" (p. 6). Here "beat" must not be taken too literally—the range of things regarded as rhythmically accented or unaccented extends from submetrical divisions to entire sections of music.

The *way* in which "beats" are grouped is de-

scribed, though not measured, by a small repertory of grouping types. These types represent three fundamental classes of musical events: beginning-accented (trochee, ‾ ˘, or dactyl, ‾ ˘ ˘), middle-accented (amphibrach, ˘ ‾ ˘), and end-accented (iamb, ˘ ‾, or anapest, ˘ ˘ ‾). Beginning- and end-accented events, however, are assigned two types to reflect a fundamental distinction of duple and triple grouping. (Middle-accented events are by definition triple.) There can be only one accented beat or moment in a group because accent is a mark of distinction and thus a unique marking that organizes and defines the group: where there is more than one accent there is more than one group. Reminiscent of Koch's *Ruhepunkt*, "the accented beat is the focal point, the nucleus of the rhythm, around which the unaccented beats are grouped and in relation to which they are heard" (p. 8). Rhythmic accent is a focal point of our attention but, unlike the accent of meter, it does not necessarily mark the beginning of a duration. In fact, Cooper and Meyer, like Cone and Riemann—and for much the same reason—tend to favor end-accented grouping, particularly in the larger durations that require a grouping of groups:

> Beginning groups, simply because they are beginnings, seem to be leading or moving toward a conclusion and therefore expectation is directed toward and emphasizes (accents) the completing groups or units. An antecedent appears to be directed toward the consequent which is its goal. And this goal is stable, focal, and accented in comparison with the motion which precedes it. (Cooper and Meyer 1960, p. 61)

The difference between rhythm and meter may perhaps best be illustrated if we try to give some perceptual reality to what is generally considered to be meter apart from rhythm. For example, 3/4 meter is normally regarded as a grouping of three equal beats or, conversely, as the division of a given duration into three equal parts, in which grouping or division the first part is accented relative to the second and third, thus: 3/4 = ♩ ♩ ♩. But this is already rhythm (a dactyl), and if there is a distinction between rhythm and meter, this cannot also be meter. However, there are factors involved in the description of this metrical "event" that are not included in a description of its rhythm. Rhythm, in Cooper and Meyer's view, says nothing about equality of durations (three *equal* beats) or a "given," quantitatively determinate duration (*divided* into three equal parts, or three beats long). In fact, the example I gave, if it is meant to be played or heard, is not itself meter. It is a measure and, therefore, something concrete, rather than the abstract measurement of 3/4 time that could reside in a countless variety of 3/4 measures. Thus, 3/4 ♩♩♩ is no more 3/4, or necessarily a better example of 3/4, than 3/4 ♩ ♪ ♫. In this way, meter could be regarded as a potentiality for rhythm—a not entirely determinate order that logically precedes rhythmic determination. On several occasions Cooper and Meyer imply something like this:

> Meter is not simply a matter of regularly recurring dynamic intensification. It is a set of proportional relationships, an ordering framework of accents and weak beats within which rhythmic groupings take place. It constitutes the matrix out of which rhythm arises.
>
> Rhythm is independent of meter in the sense that any one of the rhythmic groupings given above [the five grouping types] can occur in any type of metric organization. For instance, an iambic grouping can occur in duple or triple meter. In other words, rhythm can vary within a given metric organization. (Cooper and Meyer 1960, pp. 96, 6)

However, Cooper and Meyer do not pursue this distinction and, in practice, treat meter as something that is no less concrete and determinate than rhythm. The function of meter for rhythm is to supply a special sort of accent. Its function is not, however, to supply quantitatively determinate durational units. For this reason, Cooper and Meyer's rhythmic groupings rarely correspond to bars, and there is no requirement that beats be of equal duration.

Although rhythm is not—and knows nothing of—measurement, it can coincide with equal or measured durations. Thus, a rhythm can coincide with a measure (as in the first example of 3/4 given above); or a rhythm can coincide with a "morphological length,"—that is, a (quantitative) durational unit composed of more than one measure; or a rhythm can coincide with a form, conceived as an arrangement of discrete parts (as in the form AABA). If there is such a correspondence, Cooper and Meyer say that the duration is both a morphological length and a rhythm, or both a form and a rhythm. And if it is both, there is no longer any reason to make a distinction. "Form [or length, or measure], then, may coincide with and *be* a rhythm, or it may not" (p. 147). Although forms or lengths or measures emerge as separate from rhythm only when they conflict with rhythm, they must remain inherently different principles if there is a possibility for conflict. By comparison, measures, lengths, and forms are static, and Cooper and Meyer do not devote much attention to these categories apart from their contrast to rhythm or "movement in music and the issue of this movement in the generalized feeling we call rhythm" (p. 125).

Meter, morphological length, and form are each hierarchical, but unlike the hierarchy of rhythm, these hierarchies are limited—none extends through the entire range of durations, from smallest division to the whole. And since each is a separate principle, they do not compose, as rhythm does, a single hierarchy. Meter extends as far as the measure or hypermeasure (i.e., Cone's hypermeasure—what Cooper and Meyer call a "reduction to measure" or "reducing a measure to the status of a beat," pp. 156–157). Beyond this level, morphological length takes over the function of measurement (thus, four-bar lengths sum to eight- or twelve-bar lengths, etc.). Form occurs at the highest durational levels. It uses lengths, as lengths use measures, but reinterprets them as parts of a pattern of essentially qualitative distinctions (varied repetition, contrast, return—as, for example, in the representation A A' B A).

Although morphological lengths and form can be more easily dispensed with in the analysis of rhythm, meter, since it also presents the distinctions of accent and "unaccent," is more difficult to detach from rhythm. Cooper and Meyer are frequently troubled by the character of this opposition:

> The interaction of rhythm and meter is a complex one. On the one hand, the objective organization of a piece of music—the temporal relationships, melodic and harmonic structure, dynamics, and so forth—creates accents and weak beats (unaccents)

and defines their relationships. And these accents and unaccents, when they occur with some regularity, would seem to specify the meter. In this sense the elements which produce rhythm also produce meter. . . . On the other hand, meter can apparently be independent of rhythm, not only in the sense that it can exist in the absence of any definitive rhythmic organization, but also in the sense that rhythmic organization can conflict with and work against an established meter. Thus, for instance, beats which might become accents (potential accents) or which actually *are* accented may be at odds with the accentual scheme established in the meter. Conversely, beats which for melodic, harmonic, or other reasons would naturally be weak may be forced because of the meter to become accents. While such conflicts of natural rhythmic groups with metric structure constitute disturbances which tend to modify grouping, they need not necessarily result in a change of meter. Rather they may produce either stressed weak beats or forced accentuation. (Cooper and Meyer 1960, p. 88)

The qualification "apparently" in the preceding quotation alerts us to the problematic nature of the opposition. That meter "can exist in the absence of any definitive rhythmic organization" means that meter can be regarded as an abstraction (as we saw previously in the difficulties involved in an attempt to represent 3/4 meter by giving it concrete content). This abstraction, I think, is responsible for the externality of meter as something given or "established" that can "force" the accentuation of "naturally" weak beats.

In practice, however, Cooper and Meyer are loath to call a metrical accent unaccented (or vice versa). The only examples they cite in which such reinterpretation might seem to take place are cases in which there is metrical conflict between simultaneously sounding parts or melody and accompaniment (for example, Debussy's Prelude no. 6, from Book 1, example 166), real metrical ambiguity (Schoenberg's op. 19/1, example 192, or Bruckner's Ninth Symphony, example 108), or a discrepancy between actual and notated meter (the second movement of Mozart's *Jupiter* Symphony, example 105, or the second movement of Beethoven's Eighth Symphony, example 110). In none of these cases is a real (i.e., perceived) metrical ac-

cent converted into a rhythmic "unaccent"—if something is perceived, it cannot be "unperceived" (though we can, of course, come to better understand its function as more context develops). Instead, conflict arises only where accents are unreal or potential. Metrical accents are unreal where they do not, in fact, occur or, equivalently, where they are suppressed. Of course, to say that there is something that does not occur or that is suppressed means that the thing exists in some sense. The reality of meter lies in the accents and groupings it creates. What is not so real is the abstraction that allows us to speak of "it" as a grouping of ideal, equal units that underlie any particular expression of meter. Cooper and Meyer do not generally consider these ideal units as real. For example, a dotted half note initiating a 4/4 measure is treated as one accented duration and not as a composite of accented and unaccented parts, for there is no real accent on the "third beat."

Cooper and Meyer's suggestion of the possibility notwithstanding, I have found in their text only one example in which real metrical accents are shown to conflict with real rhythmic accents, or in which beats "which actually *are* accented may be at odds with the accentual scheme established in the meter." In this case (an analysis of Chopin's Etude op. 10, no. 9, example 134), the rhythmic accent is agogic—the first half of a 6/8 bar, composed of three eighth notes, is weak, followed by a strong beat composed of a quarter and an eighth. Although similar situations abound in the examples, they are not analyzed in this way. Of course, they could in principle be so analyzed, and that such conflicts are not represented might simply be the result of simplifying analytic representations. But it is significant that Cooper and Meyer do not choose to represent such conflicts and are satisfied to allow metrical accents to stand for rhythmic accents. More to the point, these conflicts of metrical accent and rhythmic accent are not to be resolved in favor of rhythmic accent; that is, metrical accent is treated as a type of rhythmic accent (it produces a *rhythmic* grouping), and so the conflict is that between two rhythmic interpretations—not between a metrical and a rhythmic interpretation.

There are examples of "beats which might have become accents (potential accents)" being

EXAMPLE 4.1 Grosvenor Cooper and Leonard B. Meyer, *The Rhythmic Structure of Music*, example 103. Copyright © 1960 by University of Chicago Press. Reprinted by permission.

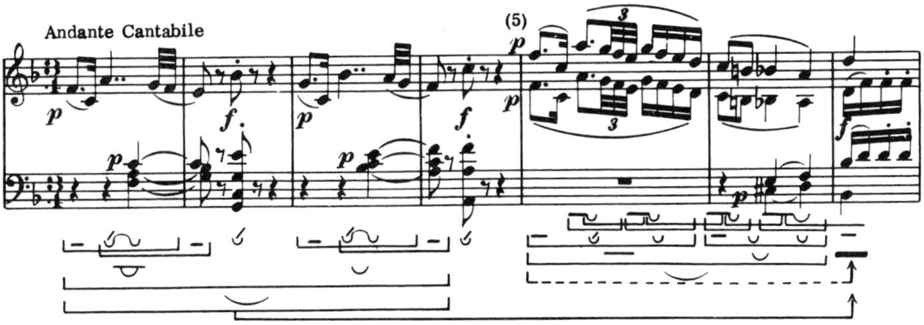

actually unaccented and examples of "beats which for melodic, harmonic, and other reasons would naturally be weak" being "forced because of the meter to become accents." An illustration of this first case is shown in Cooper and Meyer's example 103, the opening of the second movement from the *Jupiter* Symphony (reproduced as our example 4.1).

To translate the analytic symbols: the two interlocked brackets below bars 1 and 2 show two overlapping rhythms—the first beginning-accented (¯˘) and the second end-accented (˘¯); the two shared unaccented beats are "fused" (◡͡◡) as a single unaccented unit that begins with a "stress" (/). The A in measure 1 and the B♭ in measure 2 are regarded as "potential accents [that] are forced to act as weak beats" (pp. 90–91). A and B♭ are stressed (but not accented) and so could conceivably be treated as accented. But they are not. We might say that "the meter" prevents them from being accented, but it would be difficult here to abstract meter from all the factors that create this particular metrical feeling we call 3/4; for example, the tonic F and A in the first measure "moving to" the dominant E and B♭ in the second measure, or the change of bass from F to G, or the contour of the melodic line (the ascending intervals: F–A and E–B♭). Thus, if there is a conflict, it would seem to spread beyond meter per se to arise also "for melodic, harmonic, or other reasons." To argue for the separation of rhythm and meter, Cooper and Meyer must here treat meter as an abstract order that logically precedes and opposes the "natural accentuation" of rhythm.

Syncopation is treated as a special case in which metrical accent conflicts with stress. "The term 'syncopation' refers to a tone which enters where there is no pulse on the primary metrical level (the level on which beats are counted or felt) and where the following beat on the primary metric level is either absent (a rest) or suppressed (tied)" (pp. 99–100). Cooper and Meyer give as an example of syncopation the opening of the Minuet from Mozart's G Minor Symphony (see example 4.2).

The B♭ in bar 1 is marked in their notation as a stressed (/) *unaccented* (˘) beat that initiates a middle-accented (amphibrachic) group composed of three unaccented beats, "fused" as a single component, followed by an accented beat (G) and an unaccented beat (D) in bar 3. Since the B♭ is tied, the metrical accent at the beginning of the second measure is suppressed. The suppression functions to intensify the accent in bar 3 and thus to define the rhythm of the passage as iambic, as is shown at level 2.[1] As Cooper and Meyer write:

1. Incidentally, this is also a case of a morphological length that is not a rhythm: as shown at level 3, the first group is initially assumed to be accented, but with the arrival of the second group it is reinterpreted as unaccented. Presumably, the next phrase will provide the accent that will create an anapestic rhythm on the third level—thus, two morphological lengths are combined (3+3 = 6 measures), but no rhythm is produced.

EXAMPLE 4.2   Grosvenor Cooper and Leonard B. Meyer, *The Rhythmic Struc-ture of Music*, example 116. Copyright © 1960 by University of Chicago Press. Reprinted by permission.

The mind, searching for the focal stability of an accent with reference to which it can group weak beats, places particular stress on the subsequent downbeat. Furthermore, the stronger the potential of the unrealized accent—the stronger it would have been had it not been suppressed—the more effective the syncopation and the more forceful the impulse toward the next accent. (Cooper and Meyer 1960, p. 103)

Of course, the potential of the accent beginning bar 2 is very clearly realized in all the other orchestral parts; otherwise, there might be no syncopation. The conflict here arises because metrical accent both is and isn't. The accent is heard, for otherwise we could not hear syncopation or suppression, but it is not realized in the melody. In this case, meter is not treated as something abstract—as an ideal division or addition of equal durations. There is a palpable metrical accent at the beginning of bar 2. The tied B♭ in bar 2 is said to conflict with meter by not realizing the metrical accent. But the conflict does not result in the establishment of an antimetrical accent. The B♭ in bar 1, although stressed, remains unaccented (˘) in conformity with the meter—if it were to be accented, the conflict would be a metrical conflict and also a rhythmic conflict, not a conflict of rhythm and meter. Note also that there is no conflict here between meter and grouping—Cooper and Meyer do not regard groups that begin with an unaccented beat as conflicting with meter.

I would like to consider one other situation that involves the suppression of metrical accents. In very fluid passages that are not very strongly marked metrically, Cooper and Meyer often dispense with metrical accents, although they do not explicitly call this a conflict of meter and

rhythm. For example, in their analysis of Chopin's Prelude in E♭ Major, shown in example 4.3 (Cooper and Meyer 1960, example 132), the first two bars are viewed as an extended anacrusis to the accented beginning of the third bar.

The rhythm is anapestic. The group begins with an unaccented beat followed by the downbeat of the first bar, which at first seems accented (and is accented in relation only to the preceding beat) but then turns out to be part of a large anacrusis that leads to an accent in bar 3 and its unaccented "afterbeat." Again, there is no conflict between meter and rhythm—at no point does a rhythmic accent occur simultaneously with a metrical "unaccent." There is no displacement or syncopation, and nothing is forced to become what it is not. However, the quarter-note amphibrachic groupings (˘ ¯ ˘) shown in bars 3 and 4 do not appear in the analysis of the first two bars. Such a persistent, homogeneous rhythmic level could have appeared in the analysis, but Cooper and Meyer have chosen not to represent it in order to show the unbrokenness of a motion that leads to a moment of arrival in measure 3. Of course, there are articulations and groupings within the first two measures—eighth-note triplets are grouped in patterns of three (¯ ˘ ˘ or ˘ ¯ ˘) to provide a feeling of pulse, and pulses are grouped (¯ ˘ ˘ or ˘ ¯ ˘) to provide a feeling of triple meter. Certainly, there are grounds for hearing the articulation of two measures—the figure in the right hand in measure 1 is repeated an octave higher in measure 2, and in measure 2 the bass changes pattern and register. However, a conventional metrical analysis (perhaps extended to the level of four-bar hypermeasures), since it rests upon the generality and homogeneity of meter, will

EXAMPLE 4.3   Grosvenor Cooper and Leonard B. Meyer, *The Rhythmic Structure of Music*, example 132. Copyright © 1960 by University of Chicago Press. Reprinted by permission.

not easily capture the particularity of the passage or the expression required of the performer. "The performer cannot afford to play according to the unthinking principle, 'stress the first beat of the bar,' or he will readily fall into a constant subsidiary amphibrach grouping. Chopin, for him, might as well have written as in Example 132b." (See our example 4.3.) The point is well taken. Meter, as usually understood, is the same in both cases, but the effect is radically different. And by suppressing metrical description, Cooper and Meyer are able to describe rhythm as motion, energy, and gesture:

> At the beginning of the piece . . . the anacrusis sails up from the B-flat to the G with a sense of continuous movement through an unobstructed arpeggio and without any minor groupings except for that of the opening B-flat and its anticipation. One might call this anacrusis a lyrical one, or, perhaps, a contemplative one. The feeling which arises from it is rather like that which arises from seeing a speeded-up moving picture of a bud gradually opening into a flower. The tension with which we await the appearance of the full-blown flower is rather like the tension with which we await the reversal of movement (to F and E-flat) in measure 3 of the Prelude; it is a tension of calm rather than one of agitation. . . . The contemplative tension of the initial anacrusis is an essential part of the character of this piece. (Cooper and Meyer 1960, p. 126)

I maintain that the conflict for Cooper and Meyer between rhythm and meter has less to do with a dichotomy within perception than with an incongruity in modes of description, and that this conflict is not fully resolved. Although they define meter as the measurement of pulses,

Cooper and Meyer do not treat meter as measurement or quantity, but as an actual pattern or grouping. From this perspective, the possibility of regarding meter as rhythm might be opened by defining meter as a special sort or aspect of rhythm. Thus, if rhythm is "the way in which one or more unaccented beats are grouped in relation to an accented one," meter could perhaps be defined as the way in which one or more *equal* unaccented beats are grouped in relation to an *initial* accented one. Cooper and Meyer's concept of rhythm, in fact, resembles meter by requiring a single accent to define a group (and by categorizing groups as either duple or triple). In this respect, Cone's separation of meter and rhythm is far more radical. As Cone states, "My analysis thus differs from that of Cooper and Meyer, in its attempt to distinguish three types of 'strong' points: the initial, the terminal, and the medial" (1968, p. 27). Cooper and Meyer attempt to resolve the opposition of meter and rhythm as strict versus free or repetition versus novelty by assimilating meter to rhythm. At the same time, they employ the primitive distinctions of meter—accented and unaccented beats (cohering as a unitary duration)—in order to analyze and describe rhythm. In this way they seek the best of both worlds—the mobility and freedom of rhythm, along with the distinctness and accessibility to analysis of meter. The success of their enterprise depends on achieving a proper balance. If there is too great a disparity between rhythm and meter, we risk being confronted with two theories and two analytic methods for what seems to be a unified musical experience. If there is no disparity, rhythm will likely be assimilated to meter, since meter as cyclic return is eminently analyzable. Moreover, such an assimilation would contradict our intuition (expressed in our use of the word) that rhythm is something more than meter and would make large-scale events inaccessible to rhythmic analysis (assuming that there are durational limits to the action of meter).

The balance Cooper and Meyer achieve is, I think, commendable in many ways. Meter, or at least the effect of meter, is treated as something concrete, genuinely temporal, and unruly. Their analysis, although one might disagree with many details, provides a means of discussing real issues of musical interpretation and "phrasing" and thus has been of considerable interest to performers. And by fusing rhythm and meter, Cooper and Meyer conceive an unbroken rhythmic hierarchy that extends from the smallest to the largest articulations with no change in laws of composition.

However, this balance is precarious and in many ways intensifies the opposition, as I have tried to point out in considering the authors' ambivalence toward the question. Critics of this theory often complain that the homogeneity of the hierarchy represents a confusion rather than a fusion of meter and rhythmic grouping and that the accents and "unaccents" provided on the small scale by metrical distinctions should not be compared to the notions of "accent" and "unaccent" or distinctions of dependency (dominant and subordinate, tension and release, ebb and flow, departure and arrival, etc.) that might be used to characterize the relations of phrases or sections. Fred Lerdahl and Ray Jackendoff, for example, strongly criticize Cooper and Meyer for, among other things, "thoroughly interweav[ing] the properties of, and the analysis of, grouping and meter" (1983, p. 27). This assessment seems fair enough (although it will remain to be seen whether an interweaving of grouping and meter is, in principle, such a bad idea).

For Lerdahl and Jackendoff:

> The basic elements of grouping and meter are fundamentally different: grouping structure consists of *units* organized hierarchically; metrical structure consists of *beats* organized hierarchically. As we turn to the interaction of these two musical dimensions, it is essential not to confuse their respective properties. This admonition is all the

more important because much recent theoretical writing has confused their properties in one way or another. (Lerdahl and Jackendoff 1983, pp. 25–26)

The Rhythmic Structure of Music is then presented as an example of this confusion. And yet, Cooper and Meyer also sharply distinguish grouping or, as they say, *rhythmic* hierarchy from metrical hierarchy (and also from the hierarchies of morphological length and form). However, Cooper and Meyer do not represent the metrical hierarchy in their analyses of rhythm and do not show much interest in it, I suspect because of its abstractness. In fact, little more than a page of their book is devoted to the hierarchical or "architectonic" structure of meter. In this sense, Cooper and Meyer's separation of meter (as measurement and equality) and grouping (as rhythm) is much more radical than Lerdahl and Jackendoff's. The considerable attention Cooper and Meyer devote to meter concerns real accented durations. For Lerdahl and Jackendoff, meter is exclusively measurement and equality, and accent is without duration:

> The term *meter*, after all, implies measuring—and it is difficult to measure something without a fixed interval or distance of measurement. Meter provides the means of such measuring for music; its function is to mark off the musical flow, insofar as possible, into equal time-spans. . . . Fundamental to the idea of meter is the notion of periodic alternation of strong and weak beats . . . For beats to be strong and weak there must exist a *metrical hierarchy*—two or more levels of beats.

> It must be emphasized at the outset that beats, as such, do not have duration. . . . To use a spatial analogy: beats correspond to geometrical points rather than to the lines drawn between them. But, of course, beats occur in time; therefore an interval of time—a duration—takes place between successive beats. For such intervals we use the term *time-span*. In the spatial analogy, time-spans correspond to the spaces between geometric points. Time-spans have duration, then, and beats do not. (Lerdahl and Jackendoff 1983, pp. 19, 18)

Thus, metrical accents are durationless and occur where two or more levels of beats coincide or happen simultaneously. Construed in this

EXAMPLE 4.4   Fred Lerdahl and Ray Jackendoff, *A Generative Theory of Tonal Music*, example 2.14a. Copyright © 1983 by MIT Press. Reprinted by permission.

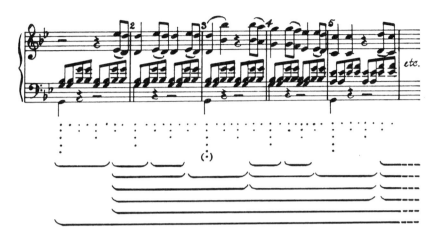

way, meter is indeed problematic for Cooper and Meyer in their attempt to incorporate metrical distinctions in an analysis of rhythm regarded as something intrinsically whole and undivided. For Cooper and Meyer, numerous factors are involved in creating rhythmic articulations, but none of these factors can, even in principle, be isolated from their interaction. For Lerdahl and Jackendoff, however, the abstraction of meter is useful for their attempt to define rhythm as the interaction of discrete components, chief among which are meter and grouping. Thus, in reference to metrical structure and grouping structure (and their analytic representations), Lerdahl and Jackendoff insist that "even though the two structures obviously interact, neither is intrinsically implicated in the other; that is to say they are formally (and visually) separate" (p. 26). This separation is made possible by a temporal distinction—that between continuity and discontinuity. A representation of this distinction can be seen in an analysis of the opening of Mozart's G Minor Symphony, K. 550, reproduced in example 4.4 (Lerdahl and Jackendoff 1983, example 2.14a).

Meter (which consists of beats) *marks* durations, but the marking is without duration; thus, meter is inherently discontinuous and can be represented by dots—durationless points analogous to extensionless geometric points. Groups, on the other hand, *are* durations (durational

"units"), and although they, too, must in some sense be marked by durationless points of beginning and ending, these points mark the beginning and ending of something—that something being inherently continuous and in itself unmeasured; thus, Lerdahl and Jackendoff represent groups by "slurs" or continuous lines. The differences between marking a duration and being a duration—point and line, discontinuity and continuity—serve to fundamentally separate the notions of meter and grouping; meter and grouping can become transparent to one another and can be analyzed as entirely discrete, self-sufficient components.

But, its considerable methodological advantages aside, this interpretation takes from meter something of the mobile character Cooper and Meyer tried (problematically) to impart to it. Meter is no longer explicitly opposed to rhythm as "dead" to "lively" or "law" to "freedom," and yet something of this opposition remains in the separation of meter as that which "mark[s] off the musical flow" from that flow itself. "Motion," "ebb and flow," "tension and relaxation," and "the incessant breathing in and out of music" for Lerdahl and Jackendoff require, above all, pitch relations. Metrical accents may (or may not) help articulate the beginning and end points of a musical motion, but meter does not create this motion. Between two durationless metrical accents there is a "time span," but there

EXAMPLE 4.5   Fred Lerdahl and Ray Jackendoff, *A Generative Theory of Tonal Music*, example 2.18. Copyright © 1983 by MIT Press. Reprinted by permission.

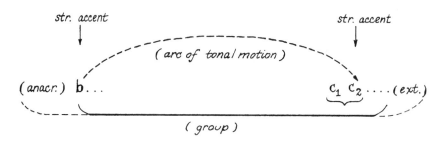

is no musical motion unless pitch events create one. The continuity of motion can, however, be ascribed to groups—primarily, to groups, such as the musical phrase, that are initiated by a "structural beginning" and terminated by a "structural ending" or cadence. A schematic diagram that summarizes the characteristics of the group is given in Lerdahl and Jackendoff's example 2.18 and reproduced as example 4.5.

Adopting Cone's paradigm of the thrown ball, Lerdahl and Jackendoff identify two points (now more literally "points"—as we have seen, Cone was uncomfortable with this term). These points, also durationless, are called "structural accents" and are distinguished from metrical accents, since they are involved in the articulation of groups. The two structural accents do not in any sense measure or even mark the span of the group. They mark attack points of pitch events that function as "points of gravity" or "pillars of tonal organization," and these pitch events do not necessarily correspond to the temporal boundaries of the group. Thus, the beginning structural accent (b) may initiate the group or it may be preceded by an anacrusis that initiates the group; the ending structural accent, since it marks the beginning of the cadential pitch, or the "final cadential element" (c), never marks the end of the group.

Whereas beats mark equal durations and metrical accents delimit time spans, groups encompass time spans and are durations. This difference appears graphically in Lerdahl and Jackendoff's representations of time spans. To indicate time spans in metrical structures, brackets are drawn to connect beats, whereas the slurs used to indicate groups also indicate time spans; that is, the beats, since they are durationless, are not actually parts of the time span, which is a duration. But more significantly, in addition to encompassing a time span, a group—given the proper tonal organization—can also be the bearer of a musical motion. If within the group there is a structural beginning and a structural ending, these two events will create or generate a tonal motion that extends through the entire group. Or as Lerdahl and Jackendoff write, "These events form an arc of tonal motion over the duration of the group" (pp. 30–31). The structural accents are said to "articulate the boundaries of groups at the phrase level and all larger grouping levels," but since the *points* of structural accent do not correspond to the actual boundaries of the group, it must be understood that the arc of tonal motion is not simply a span delimited by two points, but a continuous process that spreads through the whole duration of the group. In Lerdahl and Jackendoff's theory, all the components except for metrical structure can involve motion since they all involve tonal relations (as, for example, in the branchings provided in prolongational reduction that signify tension and relaxation). The exceptional status of meter in this regard stems from a view of meter as something inherently discontinuous, in contrast to both the dynamic continuity of tonal relations and the continuous tonal "substance" that fill the durations delimited by metrical beats. Moreover, tonal organization can have nothing of the (alleged) homogeneity of meter. Tonal differentiation and tonal "motion" arise only from contrast and heterogeneity. And although tonal motion can be charted and described, it cannot be measured as quantity.

FIVE

Discontinuity of Number and Continuity of Tonal "Motion"

The opposition of metrical and tonal organization we have observed in the work of Lerdahl and Jackendoff appears in many current theories of musical rhythm. This disparity arises from conceiving of duration as abstract quantity or "time span" rather than as endurance or the *process* through which something comes to endure. "Motion," "energy," and "tension and relaxation" are ascribed to things that happen "in" time (and not to time itself). Durations, as spans of time, are containers in which things happen and are in themselves empty. As containers, they must be empty in order to receive contents. The sonic contents—tones, for example—actively fill the passive container and can be understood as inherently dynamic and mobile. Points of time or the durations they mark are not mobile but fixed. And if, apart from the tonal contents, there is any process or motion between these points or within the empty container, it can only be the motion of time itself, in which case the container is not in itself truly empty but is filled with time. And yet, the time that would fill such a container is Newtonian, *absolute* time that "flows equably without

relation to anything external"—that is, without any intrinsic relation to the things that occur "in" time. Again, we are confronted with a paradoxical situation—meter, which, as the ordered articulation of "time's flow," seems the most purely temporal of music's components, and which can be felt as one of the most active, energetic, and palpably *rhythmic* of musical properties, can, nevertheless, be treated as a static grid or container for the real motions created by tones and harmonies.

As I have suggested, this difficulty is methodological rather than perceptual and arises from the way we measure musical events. All of the theories I have reviewed engage this problem in one way or another. I have chosen to conclude this preliminary review with a glance toward the metrical theory of Lerdahl and Jackendoff because their treatment of the measure as time quantity is very explicit and clearly focuses our attention on issues of continuity and discontinuity.[1] Although many other theorists do not explicitly evoke the notion of time point, this concept is implicit in any definition of meter as quantitative measurement numerically conceived.

---

1. It is also the only account I know that frankly acknowledges its atemporal perspective. As the authors state in their first chapter, "instead of describing the listener's real-time mental process, we will be concerned only with the final state of his understanding" (Lerdahl and Jackendoff 1983, pp. 3–4).

Abstract duration, conceived as quantitatively determinant time span, is solely the product of measurement; and to take a measurement we must isolate points of initiation and termination. These points, even if they are not represented by numbers, have the properties of numbers, among which is the property of discontinuity. The number 1 does not shade off into 2 or progress to 2—the "interval" between 1 and 2 is not, in fact, continuous but is composed of an infinite multiplicity of necessarily discrete, discontinuous numbers (a fact that, as Zeno showed, is incompatible with the fact of motion). Similarly, time points are discontinuous in that they have no duration and so cannot belong to the durations they mark. And between a first and a second "beat" there must be an infinite number of time points.

Numbers are also autonomous, in the sense that they retain their values regardless of whatever relationships they may enter into. Certainly, numbers are not autonomous in that any number presupposes the totality of number and the systematic relationships of numbers that constitute a mathematics; but as individuals they are not altered by relationships—1 remains 1 whether it is subtracted from 2 or from 3. This autonomy allows numbers to be reproduced as identical—thus, the difference of 1 and 2 is 1, but since 1 = 1, the two 1s are one and the same. Similarly, a durational quantity, whether of beat, measure, or hypermeasure, can be regarded as a unit capable of being reproduced as the same. Thus, otherwise undifferentiated pulses can be understood to be reproduced as autonomous units of measurement (limited in their subdivision only by limitations of aural perception); or if the succession of pulses is articulated by meter, some of these pulses become 1s, and all these 1s can be considered equivalent.

To begin to see how tonal relations can more easily be thought of as dynamic agents of motion, we might—purely as a *Gedankenexperiment* —imagine that pitches also correspond to points. Here we are not concerned with the points of initiation and termination of pitches, but only with the pitches being in some way presented, and as things presented we cannot imagine them to be durationless. Since the precise duration of a pitch has no bearing on its identity as a pitch, points here would represent things of indetermi-

nate duration. The relationship of pitches, what they define or "delimit," is, minimally, an interval. We measure intervals and normally use numbers to do this, but the numbers, of course, have no connection to temporal passage. Also, the traditional nomenclature mixes qualitative and numerical terminology (as in "minor third") and implicitly relates the interval to the organization of a given arrangement of tones we call the diatonic scale. However, this "scale" is heterogeneous and its members or gradations are functionally and qualitatively differentiated, with the result that measurements are not absolute (thus the distinction between "minor third" and "augmented second," both of which may be said to "span" or to "contain" three semitones). We can, of course, make the scale homogeneous and measure intervals using the absolute unit of the semitone (converting both "minor third" and "augmented second" into "pitch interval 3"), thereby effecting a genuine numerical measurement (three times one selfsame semitone). But even so, the semitones used in this sort of measurement do not seem to have the perceptual reality of metrical beats—a measure of 3/4 has three beats because we can, presumably, hear three actual (sounded or imagined) beats in passage. In the case of pitch interval 3, however, we do not hear three actual semitones; the unit of measurement is, instead, a potentiality and, perhaps, even a mere convenience. That is, there *could be* three semitones sounded between the pitches or, equivalently, a whole and a half step. Somewhat similarly, a single duration might be said to last three seconds—it is not actually divided into three one-second parts, but it has the possibility of being so divided or measured, and the second is a standard unit of measurement. Then again, interval might be defined as a ratio —of string lengths, volumes, or cycles per second. But measurement of proportion is not a measurement of *interval* proper or the "distance" between points; it is the determination of a relationship of two simultaneous, co-present, or coextensive quantities (or rather, of two quantities regarded as co-present).

More generally, interval, however measured, implies co-presence, even if the pitches forming the interval are successive. The distinction between simultaneous and successive does not affect interval measurement (though we can, if we wish, make a distinction between "harmonic" and "melodic"). This is an obvious contrast to durational measurement—time points and time spans can be distinguished only by succession. (In the case of meter, for example, since all bars in a piece written in 3/4 are identical *as measures*, the ninth bar is a distinct unit only by being the ninth, or perhaps the first bar of a second eight-bar unit.) The difference is not that measured durations are temporal and pitch relations are atemporal. Intervals also necessarily have duration; but in the concept of interval, succession and duration are not opposed to one another. The pitches that "compose" an interval may be successive and, *as pitches*, may be conceived as mutually external, juxtaposed terms; but in their relationship as interval they endure whole and undivided. For example, a pitch is not a minor third higher than a succeeding pitch until there is that succeeding pitch, and there was never a time for this interval when the preceding pitch was not heard in relation to a succeeding pitch.

The duration of an interval in this way becomes utterly continuous. There is no durationless instant between two pitches that is interval, nor is each pitch "half an interval." Although there is an interval between two time points that is a duration, there is nothing "between" two pitches that is an interval—"betweenness" in this sense is not a tonal category. Both the pitches and the interval have duration, and the interval's duration continuously overlaps the durations of the pitches. This overlapping means that the first pitch endures throughout the entire interval in

that it is present together with the second pitch. Granted, the two pitches may still be regarded as distinct parts of the interval, but interval as the relation of these parts creates something new and undivided. Likewise, two time-points create something new and undivided (a time span or duration); but whereas part of a duration is a duration, and not a time point, part of an interval is a pitch (or, rather, a *tone*—a pitch that has entered into a tonal-intervallic relationship).

Schenker's theory, more than any other theory of interval, treats tonal relations as simultaneities. A *tone* is where it acts. By entering into a consonant intervallic relationship with a succeeding tone, an initial tone endures or is prolonged since the succeeding tone is, in fact, where the first tone acts. The two tones touch one another or become contiguous even if other tones intervene. The first tone is not actually prolonged *until* it is joined with the second—that is, until the second tone provides a determinate meaning for the first. In this union, the passage from the first to the second tone is reduced out, and the two tones are treated as a simultaneity. The temporal order of the two tones has no effect on their intervallic meaning or on their involvement in prolongations at higher durational levels.

In Schenker's theory, priority is given to simultaneity over succession. Thus, the given interval is "composed out" (*auskomponiert*) through temporal passage. In general, succession emerges from duration as the simultaneous becomes gradually transformed into the successive.[2] Transformation for Schenker means, primarily, a transformation of pure, undivided duration into suc-

---

2. "Within the poles of the fundamental line and foreground . . . the spatial depth of a musical work is expressed—its distant origin in the simplest element, its transformation through subsequent stages, and, finally, the diversity of its foreground" (Schenker 1979, p. 6). In the next paragraph (found in appendix 4 in ibid.), Schenker's comparison of the creativity of the fundamental structure to God's creativity points to the temporal character of the fundamental structure: "Between fundamental structure and foreground there is manifested a rapport much like that ever-present, interactional rapport which connects God to creation and creation to God. Fundamental structure and foreground represent, in terms of this rapport, the celestial and the terrestrial in music" (p. 160). From this comparison with God as Pancreator, the fundamental structure may be regarded as eternal or everlasting but not atemporal or "timeless" (for otherwise there could be no interaction or rapport). Schenker could mean by this that the fundamental structure exists independently from any manifestation as a universal, in which case it would have no concrete duration. But since it is the *rapport* that is manifested and not the foreground, the fundamental structure could be regarded as a concrete duration, everlasting and unchangeable through the entire content of the artwork.

cession. Pure duration is represented by the "chord of nature." Thus, "the overtone series, this vertical sound of nature, this chord in which all the tones sound at once, is transformed into a succession, a horizontal arpeggiation" (Schenker 1979, p. 10). It is with the arpeggiation of vertical sound that succession first emerges to create a "tone space" or "the horizontal fulfillment of the fundamental line" (that is, the consonant, arpeggiated members of the fundamental line, excluding the passing tones of the fundamental-line progression). And this underlying tone space precedes any particular shape that it may take. As Schenker writes:

> *Tone-space is anterior to form*
>
> Since the fundamental line is identical with the concept of tone-space, this in itself provides a fountainhead for all form. Be they two-, three-, four-, or five-part forms, all receive their coherence only from the fundamental structure, from the fundamental line in tone-space. Thus is the anterior nature of tone-space explained. (Schenker 1979, p. 16)

These remarks may suggest that Schenker regarded the "vertical sound of nature" as atemporal and ideal, or the fundamental structure (or structure at any level in relation to a "lower" level) as ideal in the sense of lacking any particularity. However, I believe this interpretation would not be entirely accurate. In a piece of music, neither the "chord of nature" nor the fundamental structure has any existence apart from its composing out. What these concepts seem to represent is the wholeness of a tonal composition as a single, undivided duration (a continuity made possible by tones).

> *The indivisibility of the fundamental line*
>
> No matter what upper voices, structural divisions, form, and the like the middleground may bring, nothing can contradict the basic indivisibility of the fundamental line. [Again, the same might be said of prolongational lines in the middleground.] This is the greatest possible triumph of coherence in music. (Schenker 1979, p. 12)

The priority of duration over succession is the priority of whole over part. The multiple collapsings of successions into simultaneities culminate in a single "vertical sound" that has duration—the duration of the entire piece. And although Schenker calls the fundamental structure 'arrhythmic,' he does not call it atemporal. (That Schenker calls the fundamental structure arrhythmic is the result of his practice of treating rhythm more narrowly as measured duration.) Nor does Schenker denigrate the actual temporal passage through which tones are prolonged:

> As a motion through several levels, as a connection between two mentally and spatially separated points, every relationship represents a path which is as real as any we "traverse" with our feet. Therefore, a relationship actually is to be "traversed" in thought—but this must involve actual time. Even the remarkable improvisatory long-range vision of our great composers, which I once referred to as 'aural flight", presupposes, indeed, includes time. . . . Today one flies over the work of art in the same manner as one flies over villages, cities, palaces, castles, fields, woods, rivers, and lakes. This contradicts not only the historical bases of the work of art but also—more significantly—its coherence, its inner relationships, which demand to be "traversed". (Schenker 1979, p. 6)

And this "traversal" is made possible by tonal relationship or tonal "motion."

Although Schenkerian theory is exceptional in the degree to which it gives priority to whole over part and simultaneity over succession, this priority and the continuity it establishes appear in most approaches to the analysis of tonal relationships. Certainly, tonal relationships (for Schenker, too) can arise only from a succession of events—harmonic and "linear" progressions, the introduction and resolution of dissonances, modulations, and so forth. And certainly, too, the order of events is essential to their meaning—a motion from tonic to dominant cannot be equated with a motion from dominant to tonic. But in our conception of tonal motion the boundaries of successive events often become blurred, with the result that succession, rather than articulating individual, externally related durations or time spans, can create a single, indivisible duration. In the case of a movement or modulation from tonic to dominant, for example, there is succession, but the tonic from which the departure was made and the dominant arrival become contiguous. The intervening span becomes a continuous passage from one tonal state to another. The two states are conceptually adjacent, and although there is passage, it would be difficult to say precisely *when* the change occurs, for in a sense it occurs throughout the entire duration as a single, undivided tonal motion. This "motion" from a tonally stable state to a relatively unstable state can be represented symbolically by two chords. In this representation the chords have duration, but the durations they represent are necessarily indeterminate.[3] The durations are not indeterminate simply because meter is no longer capable of measuring them— even if meter per se is no longer operative, we could, nevertheless, turn to a count of seconds, beats, bars, or "morphological lengths" for the purpose of measurement. The durations are indeterminate because there is no clear point of articulation. And it is because of this continuous passage that we find the word "motion" singularly appropriate for describing tonal connections. The duration or "time span" of the entire motion is not indeterminate—here we could easily measure the duration in seconds, beats, or bars. However, this would tell us nothing about the continuity of this duration other than that it is a certain number of (arbitrary) units long. Duration would then be a container for the tonal motion. Suppose, however, that we allow duration to partake in the continuity of tonal motion: then beginning and ending, rather than being quantified and represented by time points, would be regarded as inseparable phases of the duration of an event. (This, as we have seen, is Cone's position.) If beginning and ending are not points and yet are not separated at some point in the middle of the duration (as "halves"

of the duration), there will be no way of measuring the length of either beginning or ending— beginning and ending will be durationally indeterminate in the same way that the durations of the harmonic representations of tonal "states" are indeterminate. And if beginning and ending do not succeed one another as distinct parts, they are in this sense co-present or simultaneous in that both occur at "one time," the time of the whole event. This formulation seems paradoxical only if we posit "times" or time points that exist independently from the event and from the process through which its duration comes to be determined.

The idea of continuous tonal motion, based on the notions of co-presence and the priority of whole over part, points to a way of detaching duration from numerical measurement (though not from quantity or determinacy). That tonal relationships can be detached from durational quantity protects them from our customary ideas of time as number and allows these relationships to be viewed as more rhythmic than the mechanical counting of meter (much as "rhythmic accent" seems freer, more spontaneous—indeed, more *musical*—than "metric accent"). However, as rhythmic as tonal relationships may appear to be, they do not in themselves satisfy our intuitions of what rhythm is, particularly if they are regarded as durationally indeterminate. That tonal durations are continuous offends against our understanding of rhythm as something that involves regularity, repetition, and pattern formed by clearly articulated durational quantities. Schenker did not call his theory a theory of rhythm and explicitly renounced the claim that rhythm might exist at the durational level of the fundamental structure. Even at middleground levels there is a general lack of conformity between

---

3. For example, in their time-span reductions of groups at and above the level of phrase, Lerdahl and Jackendoff represent tonal events by stemless note heads to indicate that these events have no determinate duration: "Events at global levels are notated in black note-heads because at these levels there are no longer any dots in the metrical analysis with which durational values could be associated. This is our equivalent to Schenker's dictum (1935, paragraph 21) that rhythm does not exist at background levels. The crucial factor here is the fading of the perception

of meter over longer time-spans" (Lerdahl and Jackendoff 1983, p. 142). Lerdahl and Jackendoff define time-span structure as "the segmentation of a piece into rhythmic units within which relative structural importance of pitch-events can be determined" (p. 146). The reduction is similar to Schenker's: intervening events are reduced out in order to bring otherwise separated tonal "events" into a relationship of contiguity or to make, in Schenker's words, "a connection between two mentally and spatially separated points."

tonal motions and the articulations of meter and grouping. All attempts to reconcile tonal reduction and meter encounter the difficulty of bringing tones and metrical beats into correspondence. But this lack of correspondence is real and cannot be overcome by regularizing the placement of tones to conform to the "periodicities" of meter. Attempts to create conformity or to hypothesize an underlying corresponding are, above all, attempts to reconcile two apparently incompatible *theoretical* components—the tonal and the metrical. I have suggested that the incompatibility arises, at least in part, from differences in the way we conceive duration for the two components.

Furthermore, to the extent theories of tonal structure collapse successive events into copresent components of a structural whole, analysis will be removed from questions of temporality (or "real-time processes"). Although the concept of tonal relation I have sketched avoids problems of homogeneity and psychological atomism, it can easily lead to the conception of a timeless present where there is neither indeterminacy nor genuine novelty, but rather an essentially "preformed" whole that is fated to unfold through the medium of time.

In part II of this study I will attempt to develop an approach to meter that departs from counting and from the timeless "presence" of structures in an effort to minimize the conflict between meter and tone no less than that between meter and rhythm. In introducing this approach, I shall have to begin with a discussion of

several fundamental concepts that must precede a definition of meter as rhythm: temporal relations, duration as process, beginning and end, "now," durational quantity, and the determinacy of quantity. Two caveats may be in order before we enter part II. First, although I have raised the issue of tonal relations in this epilogue to part I, we will not return to this question until much later in this study, and even then the "rhythmic" nature of tonal relation will be considered only very cursorily. Since the focus of this study is on the question of meter, we will consider tonal relations only as they impinge on metrical determinations and then only in a relatively ad hoc manner. A systematic study of tone from a fully temporal, processive standpoint would require a separate study. I must also warn that some patience will be required in reading the following material. Only after a detailed and lengthy theoretical exposition will it be possible to turn to analyses of musical excerpts, and these excerpts will be very brief until some groundwork has been laid for considering the operation of meter on a scale larger than a few bars. If the pace of this presentation seems uncomfortably slow, remember that our goal is not simply a new technique of metrical analysis but a redefinition of meter. The path to this goal will lead us to consider a variety of traditional and not-so-traditional questions that concern musical meter. To the extent these questions can be systematically related, the goal, the path, and its "traversal" will be inseparable.

A Theory of Meter as Process

Tear 'repetition' out of 'experience' and there is
nothing left. On the other hand, 'immediacy,' or
'firsthandedness,' is another element of experience. Feeling overwhelms repetition; and there
remains the immediate, first-hand fact, which is
the actual world in an immediate complex
unity of feeling.

There is another contrasted pair of elements
in experience, clustering around the notion of
time, namely, 'endurance' and 'change.' . . . We
have certainly to make room in our philosophy
for the two contrasted notions, one that every
actual entity endures, and the other that every
morning is a new fact with its measure of
change.

These various aspects can be summed up in
the statement that every *experience* involves a
becoming, that *becoming* means that *something*
becomes, and that *what becomes* involves *repetition*
transformed into *novel immediacy.*

—Alfred North Whitehead, *Process and Reality*
(pp. 136–137)

SIX

Preliminary Definitions

All the things we call rhythmic are articulated; what is, in fact, utterly homogeneous or lacking internal distinctions cannot be rhythmic. And yet, the articulated parts or phases must be continuously connected—they must flow together as a whole, diversified but unbroken. Conceived as process, rhythm confronts us with the intellectual difficulties of reconciling from a genuinely temporal perspective notions of whole and part, unity and multiplicity, continuity and discontinuity. It might be said that we already have a satisfactory way of reconciling these terms, and that is through the concept of structure. Thus, we may say simply that the articulated parts are continuously connected through their mutual relationships in the context of the whole. Such a whole can be understood in this way as a totality of discrete elements joined through a system of relations or transformations. But in conceiving such wholeness, it is difficult to avoid positing a completed whole—something that exists all at once and in which all the parts and relationships are simultaneously, and thus instantly, present. "Present" in this sense means

timelessly present. In order to be presented to us for our inspection, the temporal whole must be completed, fully formed as an object awaiting our inspection. What is present as ongoing and in itself in the process of becoming formed in this view is merely our inspection or analysis of the whole.

As something fully determined, structure (no less than mathematical quantity) is removed from temporal process.[1] For this reason, the concept of a fixed network of parts and relations is incompatible with the notion of rhythmic continuity. Rhythmic continuity is a "holding together" of parts in transition or in a gradually, temporally unfolding process of becoming parts. In this transitory, fluid process, while it is going on (and unless it is presently going on it is not a process), nothing is ever fixed. In much the same way that we cannot arrest motion, which as a primary symbol of temporal continuity is often conflated with rhythm, we cannot arrest rhythm in an attempt to isolate distinct parts without annihilating rhythm. However, the temptation to do so is irresistible, for rhythm is not simply flux;

---

1. For a very sympathetic account of structuralist thought that nevertheless raises serious questions concerning problems of temporality, see Jean Piaget's *Structuralism* (1971). Throughout his study Piaget considers issues of the origin and genesis of structures and the question of formation versus preformation in a frank acknowledgment of the difficulty of interpreting structures in temporal terms.

it is an articulated flow that is in all cases comprehensible, ordered, and thus, in principle, analyzable. What is arrhythmic is disorganized and incomprehensible; and, in many cases, such formlessness is identified with stasis. For example, someone who finds a Jackson Pollock painting entirely disorganized, and consequently uninteresting, may well regard the painting as static and see no rhythm in it. An auditor for whom Stockhausen's *Kontra-Punkte* is incomprehensible could well consider the music static and lacking in rhythm.[2]

But if music presents us with some sort of comprehensible order, can we not hope to find some way of subjecting this order to intellectual analysis? The difficulty lies in standing outside process to distinguish parts, take measurements, and draw comparisons. Since we must freeze the flow of rhythm to treat it as an object for analysis, we may be inclined to conceive of time itself as something arrestable. Or, if time cannot be stopped, might there not be a standpoint outside time from which we can analyze temporal phenomena and make atemporal models of things caught up in time? From this standpoint, things might be removed from time and process. As I have already indicated, absolute time is useful for this purpose since it exists independently from the events that occur in it. Thus, a system of time points can be abstracted from events and used to measure their durations by marking discrete points of beginning and end laid out on an ever-present time line. Once this operation is completed, once events are fixed and assigned to a sequential order, time becomes a formality. The ordering of events, their durations, and their relations having been determined, process and becoming are exorcised—all events are equally available as parts of a completed whole. The future is a formal future; that is, rather than an undetermined realm of possibility, the future is a relation of "later than" applied to already existing entities. Likewise, the past is a formal past—a relation of "earlier than" rather than that which, having really perished (and thus being, in itself, irretrievable), exists in its potentialities for creative use in a newly emerging situation. The notions of permanence, temporal articulation as instantaneous succession, and the visual imagery of point and line—all of which Henri Bergson criticized as a "spatialization of time"—are useful intellectual tools for bringing flux under our control, but they do not seem adequate for understanding the diversified continuity of temporal experience.

The general dilemma of reconciling temporal continuity and discontinuity becomes especially acute for a discussion of rhythm because uses of the term point in the direction both of precisely measurable regularity and of fluid, articulated, but unbroken, change. The conceptual problems that emerge from this split are implicit in any analysis of musical rhythm and are, I think, responsible for much of the confusion that surrounds the topic. Like Saint Augustine in his quest for a definition of time, we know what rhythm is, but if we are asked to put this knowledge into words, we do not know what to say. We know what rhythm is because we experience it and can refer to a great variety of phenomena as rhythmic. As something experienced or observed, rhythm provides a special sort of link between the observer and a relentlessly changing environment. This connection might be described as a coordination of our attention with what is active and changing. We follow the activity and change with interest as our attention is drawn to it (and, of course, this following is it-

---

2. Alban Berg makes a similar connection between rhythm and comprehensibility. In his essay "Why Is Schoenberg's Music So Difficult?" Berg (1965) suggests that the reason for this difficulty is Schoenberg's extraordinarily rich and complex rhythmic practice: "[This is] the *only* reason, I maintain. For neither the other properties of his thematic writing (motivic development of multi-note phrases) nor his harmony—quite apart from his contrapuntal technique [which Berg views as an essentially rhythmic aspect of music]—are calculated to make his music difficult to understand" (p. 192). "[To] feel the beauty of such themes (and of this music in general) with the heart . . . requires the hearing faculty of an ear that is set to the most difficult task with regard to rhythm, which—here and everywhere in Schoenberg's music—rises to a hitherto unheard-of pitch of variety and differentiation. . . . One would either have to be very deaf or very malicious to describe a music that manifests such richness of rhythms (and in such a concentrated form both successively and simultaneously) as 'arrhythmic'" (p. 195).

self active). Thus, to experience rhythm is to participate or to become involved in an event as it is going on, and it might be said that the intensity of our experience of rhythm is determined by the intensity of our involvement.

If we are to follow the event, our attention must be relatively continuous—if our attention is broken, we stop following and are no longer with the event. But to "follow" is not to trail along behind the event or even to keep up with it "at every instant." It requires above all that we keep moving ahead, that we anticipate what is about to happen in order to follow what is happening. Since we do not, in fact, know the future, our anticipation is necessarily provisional and must not be too narrowly circumscribed. Anticipation in this sense is not the projection of a definite outcome but a readiness to interpret emerging novelty in the light of what has gone before. If what does happen cannot have been anticipated in this sense—if it cannot be felt to conform sufficiently to what has gone before—we may suffer a lapse of attention. Where rhythm is so broken, either we can refocus our attention, picking up whatever we can to return to the event, or, if we are unwilling to make this effort, we may lose interest and turn our attention elsewhere.

Following the rhythmic event involves both what is possible in light of what has happened and what has happened in light of what will or might be made of it. If there is to be anything approaching an analysis of rhythmic process, there must be found some way of speaking of future and past as they contribute to a presently evolving situation—a future that is potential rather than actual, undetermined rather than already determined (and thus, in effect, past); a past that, *in its effects*, is not fixed and immutable but that, in itself, is dead and gone and cannot be returned to (as if present). For this understanding of temporal relations I am indebted, above all, to the work of Alfred North Whitehead. And in the following account of musical meter I will employ several of Whitehead's distinctions. Most relevant for my account of meter is Whitehead's concept of repetition and his analysis of becoming. I will not, however, attempt to summarize Whitehead's views or to relate my peculiar uses of these ideas to a Whiteheadian metaphysics. An

EXAMPLE 6.1 Isolated sound
preceded and followed by silence

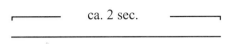

adequate discussion of Whitehead's system would demand far more space than can be afforded here, and in any case, I am hardly qualified to undertake such a task.

Beginning, End, and Duration

If meter is to be regarded as itself rhythmic, then the duration that is measured and the measuring itself must be related to present experience and to a becoming that is not given and not fully determined. Thus, I shall not begin with a given unit such as Mattheson's, which is divided, or with a given unit such as Koch's, which is multiplied, or, as Yeston does, with the givenness of pulse "strata" that interact to create meter. Whatever is given is already determined—it is something viewed as product rather than as process. How duration comes to be determined is the question that emerges when we inquire of process. To propose an answer to this question, I would like to start at the beginning, with a sound that has just begun.

In example 6.1 I have represented this continuous sound by a line segment and have indicated the approximate duration this length represents. The line shown here is given all at once. To imagine that this line represents passage, we shall have to imagine traversing the line without seeing any more of the line than has already appeared in the process of traversal, as by covering the line with our hand and moving our hand to the right to gradually reveal an increasing length. Let us say that the beginning of the sound represented here is sharply distinguished from a preceding silence. If there *is* sound, it has always (even from its beginning) had duration. Nothing that is actual—that is, nothing becoming or having become—is without duration. The sound could not be perceived as present if it were not going on, acquiring ever greater duration. Likewise, if we move our hand to the right across example 6.1, the very first thing we will see is a very short line (even if we are accustomed to calling a very short line a point). Nevertheless, we are inclined to regard the beginning of the sound as durationless (and the beginning of the line as extensionless). It is a durationless instant from which we can measure duration. We speak of the beginning *of* the sound, but here the beginning of the sound as a durationless instant is not a part of the sound, for there is no part of the sound that is without duration. This absolute beginning has zero quantity—zero duration. Without this point that is not durational, that is not already "in" duration or already a part of duration, we could not measure duration numerically.

But even apart from purposes of measurement, the postulation of a durationless now of beginning seems to be required in order to mark the instantaneous transition from not-being to being present. The fact that there *is* sound, that sound is present, means that sound is "going on" and that there is already duration. That sound is present means that the sound *has begun*. And as far back as we go in the history of the sound, there is no durational part of the sound that has not already begun. To break out of this infinite regress that seems to promise (retrospectively!) nothing belonging to sound and to the presence of sound that does not already have a past, we must posit an infinitesimal, purely present instant when there is as yet no sound but which, nevertheless, marks the sound as present.

Such a durationless instant is precisely this nothing that does not already have a past and that does not belong to sound. And yet, this instant, although it is durationless, is not nothing. As a time point it is a definite location "in time" or on a time line, and as such it exists independently from its functioning as a beginning. Its being this definite location logically and temporally precedes its being the beginning of an event. It is temporally earlier because this point precedes any point of sound that would define a duration. And its being a point logically precedes its being a beginning because it exists as a point regardless of whether it is a point of beginning. Being a beginning is merely a qualification of a location that already exists as one member of an infinite set of locations that constitute the time line. As classical "absolute" time flows independently from and logically precedes events that occur *in* time, the succession of durationless instants that compose temporal passage are independent from and logically precede events with which they might be coordinated.

Since there can be no sound without some actual duration, this durationless instant of beginning, since it is prior to duration, must precede sound. That is, there must exist an instant of beginning before the sound itself is present and in the process of becoming. If this prior and independent instant—let us call it "tn"—is itself regarded as present and durationless, an actual sound is future. But until there is an actual sound (or some point tn + x) that follows tn, this point cannot, in fact, be a beginning. At most, we could say that tn is a potential beginning, for when tn is present there is as yet nothing for tn to be a beginning of. To actually be a beginning, this point that is before sound and before duration will have to have become past. Thus, it is only by *becoming* past that tn *becomes* a beginning. Although there is a point tn before there is duration, there is no tn as a point of beginning before there is duration. We might say that tn has become t0—a point of beginning from which duration can be measured now that there is duration to be measured. But in this case, even if tn and t0 are in some sense the same, it will have taken time for t0 to be a beginning. Only with some nonzero durational interval after tn is there a beginning, t0; and to equate tn and t0—to say they are one and the same—is to suppress any temporal distinction involved with becoming and to maintain that tn was always a beginning, timelessly or eternally present as a beginning before anything was begun. In this case, there is no potentiality, no future that is not already present.

However, if to be a beginning requires becoming, then beginning cannot be said to be instantaneous, and beginning cannot be said to precede duration. Only when there *is* duration, and not before there is duration, is there a beginning *of* duration. But if this is granted, we will have lost the concept of a durationless instant of beginning.

In my criticism of the durationless instant I have, perhaps illegitimately, invoked categories that do not properly pertain to the concept—namely, process or becoming and real distinctions of present, future, and past. To retain the concept, we must deny becoming and we must regard present, past, and future merely as formal relations that apply to events or points that are already in existence and are never in the process of becoming. In this case, the point tn does not become past when there is sound—it simply *is* past for any succeeding point (or future for any preceding point). Here past simply means earlier than some point tn + x that is regarded as present. The point tn is always earlier than tn + x and does not become earlier than tn + x because tn + x is already and timelessly there, ready to be related to tn, as later to earlier. That a duration of sound is future for point tn does not mean that the duration is nonexistent at point tn. It means that there is a later point tn + x already given on the time line whose difference from tn is a duration.

From this perspective, events are tenselessly present, or present in the temporally indifferent sense of standing before us in a changeless relationship of succession, patiently awaiting our inspection. What is absolutely fixed are these relations of succession or the relations of before and after. However, we are free to assign the tense relations past, present, and future to the terms of succession as it suits our purposes. We need only fix a time point as present, and whatever lies before this point is past and whatever is after is future. Or, equivalently, this point is future for every point before it and past for every succeeding point. Our freedom to assign relationships in whatever manner we choose is won by treating a sequence of events as a stable collection of given objects, each of which is always available. Since the time line is already there, we can freely move backward and forward in time. The past event has not perished, for it can be retrieved as present by a move to the left. The future is not nonexistent, for it is already there, awaiting a move to the right. However, our experience of events bears no relation to such mastery of temporal passage. We can never return to an event that is past and experience that same event as present, and the future as something determinate that will become is forever unknowable.

The durationless instant or time point is a useful abstraction for the purposes of taking a measurement where it functions as an Archi-

medean point outside becoming and thus outside time. An ongoing event can be coordinated with the regulated motions of a clock, permitting us to count (starting from zero) the quantity of periods that elapse. Measurement in this sense is the coordination of two events. If our measurement is to be accurate, the two events must begin simultaneously, and if the events are simultaneous there is, ideally, no lapse of duration between beginnings—that is, their durational difference is zero. I say "ideally" because in comparing actual, physical events simultaneity can never be absolutely assured. To say that two events begin at the same time means that we have reached the limit of our ability to detect difference. This ideal lack of difference is regarded as an instant or a time point when, for the purpose of measurement, it is assimilated to the mathematical continuum, which demands the infinite divisibility of quantity.

But aside from taking a measurement, there is another use for the concepts of time point and time line. We can create a model of a temporal process by transposing the temporal to the spatial. In this case, succession becomes juxtaposition, and becoming is replaced by the timeless presence of a fixed and unchanging spatial configuration. The events represented by a spatial model are displayed along a line that represents temporal passage, and, as in example 6.1, any articulation represented in this model can be coordinated with a spatial location. But in order for this to be a model of temporal continuity, these locations must be without extension. Without infinite divisibility we would be left with indivisible, atomic units of time within which there is no passage and, hence (by definition), no time.

However, if we consider the sonic event represented in example 6.1 as something that is actually performed and actually perceived or experienced, there will be no reason to coordinate this event with a clock or with a spatial representation. If this is an actual event that we are attending to, the only coordination we could speak of would be the coordination of our attention with the event that we are attending to, and such an act of attention cannot itself be durationless.

When we first hear sound, sound will already be present and in the process of growing in duration. Here, being present will not mean already existing as an object. Instead, by saying that an event is present, I shall mean that the event is incomplete, that it is in the process of becoming complete or fully determined in all its particulars, and thus in the process of becoming the particular event it will eventually *be*. This process involves both the determinacy of having begun and the indeterminacy of being as yet incomplete. If beginning is durationless, it does not itself become and so cannot be present in this sense. However, I shall argue that although beginning is itself durationless, it is not something apart from duration or something that can be separated from duration. If beginning is involved and continues to be involved in the becoming of the event, there is, I believe, a sense in which beginning can be conceived as present with and for the present event and its duration.

As it is going on, the sound of example 6.1 has duration and is in the process of growing in duration. Since it is present and incomplete, its duration is not fixed. Only when the sound has ended and is past will it have a fully determinate duration. Nevertheless, while the sound is present there is always some duration already attained, and the "now" of our present awareness of the sound involves a feeling of attained duration—actual duration that is the realization (thus far) of the sound's potential for becoming. However, if the sound has not ended, if it is perceived as present, this potential for becoming is not exhausted. Thus, "now" is also a feeling of growth, a feeling of continually new and expanding duration, and a feeling of potential for becoming.

"Now" is not a point that is compared to a beginning point. If it were, we should have to imagine an infinite number of comparisons, and the continuous becoming of the sound would involve an infinite number of decisions not to end—that is to say, an infinite number of decisions not to make a now point an end point. I will postpone a closer analysis of the "now" of an event until we are in a position to consider the present in a broader perspective that includes the efficacy of past events for the becoming of a present event. At this stage in my argument, it will suffice to define the now of an event as a present awareness of the event in its process of becoming—an awareness of what the event has

thus far become, an awareness of its continual becoming, and, when it has ended, an awareness of what it has at last become.

Duration is not the difference between beginning and now, for in present becoming what an emerging duration *now is*, is just the duration that has been *and* continues to be attained—a duration that is wholly present and in the process of expanding. If duration were not now expanding, the event would not be present but past. Beginning is not something separate from this emerging duration, simply because there can be no beginning without duration. Nor can there be duration without beginning. There is not first a beginning and then duration. Beginning and duration happen at the same time, the time in which there is the becoming of the event.

However, even if we say that sound and duration are present and that beginning cannot be detached from the presence of sound and duration, is there not also some sense in which beginning is past, and could we not also say that the continual growth of duration that makes the sound present is, equally, the growing pastness of beginning? Certainly, beginning is in some sense always past for the sound begun. If there is a sound, the sound *has begun*. And yet, if beginning is to be past it must first be present. And if it is to be present it must have some independent existence or some thing-like or event-like character.

If beginning is regarded as a phase or a part of sound, then it is past in relation to any later part that is viewed as present. Thus we could say that the beginning of sound is the acoustically differentiated attack phase of the sound or an initial phase in our awareness of the contrast of sound and silence. In either case, beginning will itself be viewed as a sort of event. But may we not then ask when these events begin? And if they are past for some later phase or part, must not this later phase or part begin and the beginning phase end? As I have been using the term, "past" means completed, fully determined, and no longer in the process of becoming. Past in this sense refers only to events, to what can begin and end. But beginning cannot be an event. If beginning ends, it cannot continue to function as beginning. If there is a beginning phase, its beginning must continue to function as a beginning for the emerging event. Moreover, if beginning were an event, it would itself have to begin and end, its beginning would have to begin and end, and so forth, ad infinitum, until we finally arrive at a durationless instant—an event of no extension that is the ideal limit of this infinite division. The arrival at the durationless instant is the end of a search for a smallest part—a "part" with the durational value of zero. This is, of course, not a part of the event; however, it is a part of "time" or a part of the time line which is composed of such point parts. My objection to the concept of the durationless instant is not to its claim that beginning itself has no duration. Beginning must not have duration if it is not to be itself an event. Rather, my objection is that beginning is granted the status of a thing, or instant, that can have an independent existence and that can be conceived apart from event and duration and, thus, apart from being a beginning.

If beginning is not an event and does not end, in what sense is it past, and in what sense does it become increasingly past with the growth of duration? I shall argue that as long as the event is present, beginning is not, in fact, past. Rather, as long as the event is present, beginning functions to make the growth of duration possible, and the realization or actualization of this possibility is the pastness of the event's duration.

I said before that being present involves both the determinacy of having begun and the indeterminacy of becoming. These are inseparable aspects of being present. The past-like or event-like character we tend to ascribe to beginning arises from the determinacy or definiteness of anything that has begun. But as long as the event is incomplete and not itself ended, beginning must also participate in the indeterminacy of becoming and must in a sense be present with and for the event. Beginning might be thought to be itself determinate to the extent that it is thought of as a definite and irrevocable act. Once there *is* a beginning, nothing can alter the fact that an event is begun and is in the process of becoming. This act could be described as the bringing into presence of an event. Or the act of beginning might be called a decision—a decision for a new becoming. This decision involves, at the same time, a decision for ending—a decision to end the immediately preceding event and to

make this event past and no longer present, become and no longer becoming. In example 6.1, the contrast of silence and sound that marks beginning is thus the contrast of past and present—past silence and present sound. However, beginning is not itself this contrast and is not equivalent to the ending of silence. The act of beginning is directed solely toward the future becoming of sound. What is determined by beginning is the presence and thus the becoming of a novel event. Beginning is not itself this presence and this becoming. If it were, it would itself be an event—it would, in fact, be the event.

I maintain that the notion of "beginning" will be most productively understood as the potential of a present event for becoming. This is a definite potential because a definite decision has been made by beginning—a decision for the becoming of a novel event and thus a decision that is directed toward the future. If beginning is potentiality, it is not a being that precedes becoming, and there is no question of its having a duration. Beginning is a potential for, among other things, duration, and the actual duration of the event is the continuous realization of this potential. Since the only sort of becoming I wish to consider now is the becoming of duration, I will define beginning as a (more or less) definite potential for the becoming of duration. And since duration is already present with beginning, beginning is a potential for more or greater duration—always more or greater than zero.

In saying that beginning is a potential *for* duration, I mean that it is a potential that belongs to duration or a potential on behalf of duration—it is duration's potential for becoming. It is not a state of nonduration that precedes the presence of duration as a possibility that there will later be duration. A duration having begun has from *its* beginning potential for becoming, a potential that is being realized from the very beginning. And as long as the event is present and becoming, the potential for becoming is being realized.

What is realized is actual, not potential—it *is* or has become, and nothing that will happen can alter the fact of its having become. What is and has become is irrevocable and *in itself* determined and past. Thus, whatever is realized (or *actualized*) of the potential of beginning is past in this sense, and since potential was being realized from the beginning, actual sound, actual duration, is always past. Thus, what I earlier called the growing pastness of beginning is the progressive realization of a definite potential for duration. The present "now" of the sound involves a feeling of what the sound has thus far become and thus a feeling of past sound or duration thus far realized. However, if the sound is present, duration is incomplete, and "now" is equally a feeling of the incompleteness or becoming of the sound's duration.

I said that the duration thus far realized is in itself determined and past, but the "now" of a present, ongoing event is not realized duration in itself. The duration that is realized is also the duration that is being realized, and if there were a realized duration in itself, cut off from becoming, the event would be completed and past. That the sound is going on, that it is acquiring and can continue to acquire greater duration, means that there is still potential for duration, which is to say that beginning is still active, still functioning as a real potential for the event's becoming. This potentiality that has been and continues to be realized is the incompleteness of the event as a whole. And it is because of this incompleteness that the event is present. For this reason, I said that beginning is the making present of an event. This making present does not happen at an instant but continues to happen as long as the event remains present. It was perhaps inappropriate, however, to have called beginning an act. "Act" implies completeness, but beginning as potential or promise is not (like an event or a duration) something that can be completed—a promise can be met, a potential can be realized, but then it is no longer promise or potential. As a decision that there will be a new becoming or a decision that makes a new becoming possible, beginning is act-like, but it is not itself the duration that it makes possible, and thus, the notion of completion or end does not apply to beginning. Beginning does not begin and end—the event begins and ends.

When the event ends, beginning will have ceased to be active. Now that there is a determinate duration, there is no longer potentiality for duration. There is now a definite and past duration that had a beginning. This does not mean

that beginning is now actual. Potentiality cannot be actual—it is only duration that is actual. To say that beginning is now past is to say that the entire process through which duration was created is past and that the potential of beginning is exhausted. Beginning is thus past in the sense that it has ceased to function for becoming now that there is no becoming. Similarly, we could say that becoming is past or that the presence of the event is past now that there is no presence and no becoming. However, if past means determinate and complete, then becoming, presence, and potentiality cannot be past. These categories refer only to what is as yet indeterminate and incomplete. What can be completed and determined, and in this sense past, is an event and a duration.

The end of the event is both a completion or fulfillment of the event's potential for becoming and an annihilation of potential for becoming. The notions of completion and annihilation are complementary and are distinguished by a difference of perspective. This difference is expressed in our use of the word "end," a word that can mean, on the one hand, aim or goal and, on the other hand, cessation, limit, or stop. In conceiving of end as aim, our perspective is on the event for itself in its process of becoming. Here, end is the realization of a becoming made possible by beginning or, perhaps more accurately, the completeness toward which realization is directed—in this sense end is always future, never past. On the other hand, to view end as termination or a cutting off of becoming, and thus as a decision in which the event becomes fully determined, is to view the event from the perspective of a successor and a new beginning. Later, I shall consider the event from this first perspective and attempt to describe end as aim. For now, I would like to treat end as termination. However, even from this perspective, end cannot be detached from the becoming of the event. End "belongs to" the present event even as a denial of the activity of beginning and a denial of the continuation of the event's process of becoming.

When the event ends, it is past—no longer becoming, but become. To be past is being past in the presence of a new becoming, and in this sense it is a new beginning that ends the event and makes it past. However, the new beginning does not belong to the old event. Rather, the end belongs to that event as an annihilation of its potential for becoming. The decision of the prior beginning is for future becoming, a future that promises the progressive realization of a potential for duration. The end of the event as decision is not the realization of this potential. This potential is a potential for becoming and for duration. End is not becoming and is not a duration. The end is, rather, a renunciation of this potential—a decision that there be no more becoming and that beginning cease to function as a potential for the continuing presence of an event and the continuing growth of duration.

There is, however, a potential that end does realize. This is the potential—always "present" while the event is present—that this event will be succeeded by another, whereby the present event will be past. But this potential is realized only when there is a new event and a new beginning. I indicated this possibility earlier when I said that end and beginning are simultaneous decisions. However, to say that beginning and end are simultaneous might again open the possibility that beginning and end coincide in a durationless instant, a "purely" present point of zero difference.

In example 6.1, silence and sound are immediately successive. This means that there is no becoming of silence when there is sound and that there is nothing immediately before sound that is not silence and nothing after silence that is not sound. However, if silence and sound are immediately successive, the beginning of sound and the end of silence happen simultaneously. There is no interval or lapse of time that separates end and beginning, and we could not be aware of a beginning of sound if we were not at the same time aware of the end of silence. If end and beginning are simultaneous and silence and sound are successive, it would appear that beginning and end must be distinct from sound and silence. Such a conclusion would contradict my assertion that beginning and end belong to and are inseparable from what is begun and ended. And if to be simultaneous means to be present at the same time, the simultaneity or co-presence of end and beginning must be conceived as a durationless instant or time point, an instant of

no duration when there is neither silence nor sound.

Certainly there is no time at which silence and sound in themselves are both present, but this does not mean that there is a time—a point of time—at which there is no longer silence and not yet sound. Such a conclusion is reached by treating succession as a relationship that pertains to tenselessly present objects—in the case of immediate succession, objects that do not overlap in a duration, but that share a single, durationless point. Here silence and sound are both regarded as present and are only regarded as present. What makes them successive is solely the fact that they are not present at the same time. However, while it is true that silence and sound, considered individually, cannot be present at the same time, we could have no awareness of succession were we aware only of presence. Silence must be past for there to be temporal succession. And yet, silence *as past* does not precede present sound, for it is only when sound is present that the silence is past. Although present silence precedes present sound, there could be no succession were not past silence and present sound, in fact, simultaneous. Past silence and present sound happen at the same time—this time being the by no means instantaneous now when we feel the silence to be ended and past. Silence as ended and past does not precede the beginning of sound, and the beginning of sound does not follow the silence having become past.

The notion of simultaneity I have used to describe the coincidence of beginning and end does not mean co-presence. It does, however, imply a sort of "overlapping" and thus a reconciliation of continuity and discontinuity that I wish to propose as an alternative to the mathematical continuity of discontinuous, durationless time points. In example 6.1, present silence and present sound are absolutely discontinuous—there is no overlap in the presence of these two events. However, once there is a sound that succeeds silence there was never a time for this sound when silence was not past, or when this present sound was not a successor to silence, or when this sound was not being conditioned by the preceding silence as a contrast to sound. That is to say, there is no gap between past silence and present sound. The ending of silence, although functionally distinct from the beginning of sound, *was* never (was never past) before there *is* sound. And again, there can be no sound apart from a sound having begun—a sound that is not without duration. Nor is there a gap between silence as present and silence as past if we can imagine that the silence was experienced as an event—a silence that in the process of becoming acquired some felt duration (perhaps as a definite waiting for an event of sound). In this case, the presence or becoming of silence precedes its being past, but the end or completion of silence is not external to silence or something apart from its becoming. The end of silence is what silence has become, and it is only by having become that it is this particular silence—a silence of this duration and preceding this sound. This end is not instantaneous. It took time for the silence to become complete (this "time" being the entire felt duration of silence), and it will take some nonzero duration of sound for silence to be past. And this being complete is inseparable from having become past.

"Now"

In this account of beginning, end, and duration I have used the word "present" to refer to the incompleteness of an event as it is in the process of becoming. However, there is another meaning of the word that must be taken into account if we acknowledge that the becoming of an event involves anticipation and memory. If "present" is opposed to "absent," then any feeling of the potential for a future event or any past event that conditions a present becoming is in this sense "present." To make a distinction I shall use double quotes to refer to the "present" involvement of past and future in a present event.

There is also a sense in which the present becoming of an event itself involves past and future, apart from any other event. As I have pointed out, beginning as a definite, irrevocable decision is, in this sense, always past—if an event is present, it *has begun* and has duration, and whatever duration has been attained is past and irrevocable. At the same time, beginning is also a potential for duration, and as long as beginning is active, this is a potential for future becoming.

To be purely or absolutely present, beginning must be conceived as an instant or a now point in itself cut off from becoming. However, if a durationally extended event can be regarded as present, then past and future or the determinacy of what has become and the potential for what may become must be "present." To account for this "presence" of past and future I earlier spoke of the "now" of the event as a present awareness of the event's becoming.

This is an awareness of the novelty of the event as it is in the process of becoming. But this novelty is not something that, like an event, can be completed and past. Throughout its entire becoming the event is continually new, continually "now." But even when the event ends, novelty does not end, nor does now become past. When the event is past, its being past is a condition for there now being a new event that is its successor. If an event is past, it must be now past, and if the past event has any effect on a succeeding event, this effect happens now—not as a recollection of the past event as present, but as a condition for the particularity of what is presently becoming. If now is never past and never future, it cannot itself be an event and cannot in this sense be present. And yet, if now is continually new, it can only be an awareness of becoming, and if it is to be conceived as awareness, it cannot be a durationless instant. And because this is an awareness of and for (present) becoming, I shall continue to call now a "present awareness."

To avoid equating now with the event itself and to avoid calling now a time point, I suggest that now might be regarded as a continually changing perspective on becoming. Now is continually changing and ever new, because becoming is ever new and never fixed or arrested. What has become is fixed and past, but what is past becomes past only with a new becoming and is past only for what is becoming or will become. By calling now a perspective I mean that it is a "view" taken on present becoming from the standpoint of the particular opportunities offered by what has become and what might become. In this way, "now" might be considered most generally as a condition for freedom of action and more specifically as a condition for feeling rhythm.

The word "now" is extraordinarily rich in meaning. It can be used as a noun, an adverb, a conjunction ("now *that*"), and even an interjection ("now!"). As a noun, what I shall call "now" is a readiness to take a decision or to act. As an adverb, now is when action can be taken. Now might be called an "opportunity" for making and doing. Now is when something can be done with or made of what is past and when potentiality can be realized. Like beginning and end, now is not itself an event and does not have a duration. But unlike beginning and end, now cannot be regarded as a decision or act. Now is when a decision is being made, has been made, or can be made. What is present, past, or future is now present, past, or future. And yet, now is always a perspective for present becoming because it is only in the course of present becoming that action, making, and doing can take place. I suggest that now is not this making or doing, but rather a definite taking into account of what is available for the purpose of becoming. What is available for becoming is what is relevant to becoming, and this includes all that is past *for* present becoming and all that is potential for this particular becoming. Thus, now might be conceived as a definite perspective on the past and future, and a perspective without which there is no past and no future. It is a *definite* perspective because what is becoming has the definiteness of being this particular becoming with this particular past and this more or less definite potential for its immediate future. But since the past that is relevant to a present event also includes past, completed events that condition or qualify the present event and thus contribute to its definiteness or particularity, the perspective of now is not restricted to the immediate past of the present event. Likewise, now can also be a perspective on the potential for future events and can thus involve anticipation and a feeling of what the present might afford for future action.

By saying that now is a present perspective on the past and the future or that past and future meet in this now, and by saying also that now is not an event and does not have a duration, may we conclude that this present now, flanked by past and future, is a purely present, durationless instant? We may not if it can be understood that there is no perspective apart from whatever actual past and whatever definite potential are being taken into account. If what is now is "present," then past and future can in this sense be conceived as "present." The past, from this perspective, is not completed and fixed, because its relevance to or efficacy for becoming is continually changing. And the future *for now* is not indeterminate if there are definite and actual anticipations of what might come to pass. In calling now a readiness for action, I mean that the creative activity of becoming is readied or prepared by what is and readied in preparation for what will be. And this present readiness of what is and will be done, made, or created could conceivably involve the most distant past and the most distant future—a past and a future that are not, however, timelessly present but which are only "present" in a now that is continually new.

But, clearly, not all that has become or all that might become is available in perception. If all were available, there would be no change in perspective and, ultimately, no passage and no time. Now is selective. And to the degree it is a focused awareness, it is an awareness of particularity and an exclusion or limitation of relevancy. What is excluded is what is irrelevant and what does not contribute to the definiteness or particularity of what is now being created.

This understanding of "now presence" will, I hope, help to overcome the limitation of applying the notion of being present only to individual and relatively autonomous events. And even under this limitation, in my discussion of beginning and end I could not avoid invoking "now." When we considered the sound represented in example 6.1, the perspective of now was limited to this sound. But if events are in some sense "nested" within other events and can in this way be simultaneously present, now is always a multiple perspective. Thus, the last sound of a piece of music is present at the same time the last phrase, the last section, and the piece are present; and this "now" involves also the relevancies of many pasts, including, among others, many past experiences of listening to music. In saying in connection with example 6.1 that with the beginning of sound, silence is now past, I might have said that the (present) perspective of now involves both sound and silence and that silence is "present" for sound as a past event that continues to be a relevant factor in the becoming of sound (much like James's "thunder-breaking-upon-silence-and-contrasting-with-it"). This is, of course, not to say that silence and sound are simultaneously present or that the next to the last sound of a piece of music is itself present when the last sound has begun. Even if there are multiple perspectives of now and these perspectives are equally present or unified in the presence of now, they could not be multiple if they were not temporally distinct.

Although now involves the relevancies of past events, if it is a perspective on present becoming, now is always a readiness in regard to a present event. It is not a readiness in regard to a past event because a past event has become; and although something can be done with a past event, nothing can be done for an event that has ended and is completed. Thus, *the multiplicity of now is not the multiplicity of relevant pasts, but the multiplicity of present events.* And there is no now apart from one or more present events that are in the process of becoming. Also, if now is a focusing of awareness directed toward the definiteness or particularity of the event in its becoming, this focus can be relatively sharp or diffuse, and the several events that are now present need not be equally present or present in the same degree. And, too, since now is continually new, it is conceivable that what is felt as an event might emerge only after the event has begun, as it were, retrospectively, in the light of a new perspective. If this were the case, now could be regarded as creative for events and not merely as something dependent on the givenness of events. In this way, events would be neither temporally nor logically prior to now.

Durational Determinacy

By defining beginning as a potential for duration rather than as a point that together with an end point delimits a duration, I hope to open the possibility for viewing duration as process rather than solely as product. Of course, when an event is completed, its duration is a product—duration will then be determined and past. By saying that it is past, I mean that nothing can be done to alter this duration, and by determinacy I

mean this fixity or unalterability. But by saying that it is past I shall also mean that this duration is available as past for a present event—that it is or can be involved in the becoming of another event, for example, by being compared with another duration. Durational determinacy is achieved only when the event is past, but if this past event had no effect on a succeeding event or were not involved in the becoming of some larger event that included it, we could have no present awareness of durational determinacy.

If durational determinacy is linked to the effect a duration has or can have on the formation of other events, we may speak of degrees or types of determinacy. And later I will argue that a specific sort of determinacy characterizes the durations we call metrical. But before turning to this topic, I would like to qualify some of the remarks I made concerning the role of beginning and end in determining durational quantity.

I said earlier that beginning and end are definite decisions, and I implied that for there to be duration there must be a definite beginning and end. However, there are many events that do not have a definite beginning or end. For instance, the silence that precedes the sound in example 6.1 could be regarded as an event if we have some awareness of silence as such and thus feel a duration of silence. This silence might have a definite beginning if it ended a preceding sound and if we were to focus our attention on this beginning. But even without a definite beginning, we might become aware of silence as an event if we are awaiting an event that will break the silence. Since we live in a relentlessly echoic environment, what I have called silence here is simply a lack of interest in this sonic environment relative to our interest in the sound represented by the line in example 6.1. The silence I wish to represent by the empty space to the left of the line is the relatively amorphous silence that might be described as a relaxation of attentiveness to sound and a waiting for a sonic event that will catch our attention. If there is no definite decision to begin this waiting or this relaxation of an attentiveness to sonic events, beginning is indefinite. In this case, the now of silence will not be the feeling of a definite duration thus far realized. Instead, the now of silence is a relatively

EXAMPLE 6.2 Beethoven, Piano Sonata op. 2/1 in F Minor, first movement (conclusion) bs. 146–152

unfocused awareness of the sonic environment and a readiness for the coming of an event that could more sharply focus our attention. Since this readiness has a history, the silence can grow old, and we can feel some duration of silence. If we are aware of waiting and the absence of an event that would break silence, we can feel some length of silence. In other words, we can be aware of having deferred focus and having awaited a return to focus (in expectation that there will be an end to silence) for some time and feel this to be a relatively long or short time.

Nor does the end of an event that has a definite beginning necessarily create a definite duration. If there is not a definite beginning for a new event that would make the present event past, the end of the present event will be indeterminate and the duration of the event will be indeterminate. Thus, in example 6.2, it will be impossible to say precisely when this piece of music ends. Here, at the conclusion of the first movement of Beethoven's Piano Sonata op. 2/1 in F Minor, the last sound definitely ends with the immediately succeeding silence, but the movement does not end here. If applause begins when the last sound ends (questions of concert etiquette aside), the applause will have interrupted this movement, this coda, and the duration promised with the beginning of the last sound. It will take some indefinite amount of time for this movement to end and for the otherness of the sonic environment to gradually assert itself. The silence that ends this event (or, rather, this multiplicity of events) will gradually become a silence of waiting for a new beginning.

I have introduced these examples to show that definite decisions for beginning and ending are not necessary for a feeling of duration, and in

such cases we may say that duration is indeterminate. Presumably then, any event with a definite beginning and end will have a determinate duration. If beginning and end are simply points that delimit a duration, this distinction would suffice. However, even in events that are clearly delimited there is considerable variation in the definiteness of our feeling of duration. For example, a single sound lasting two seconds presents a duration that is in a certain sense more determinate than the duration of a sound lasting ten seconds.

In example 6.3a the duration of the first sound when it is completed is still "available" as a feeling of just this definite quantity—we can judge a second sound to be equal to this duration, or we can produce a second sound of equal duration (i.e., "reproduce" the duration of the first sound). However, in the case of example 6.3b we will find it very difficult to produce a second sound of precisely the same duration or to judge that a second sound is precisely equal in duration to the first. The duration of our ten-second sound is also still available as a feeling of a relatively long sound and can be compared to a noticeably longer or shorter sound, but it is available only as a relatively indeterminate duration and not as a precisely felt quantity.

We might say that the beginning has faded from memory and with it a potential for a determinate duration. As we are listening to the first sound, after, say, seven seconds, the sound's beginning is still active for the present event because *this* sound is still going on and still growing in duration—a duration that could now be felt as relatively long. But we can no longer feel the duration thus far realized as now entirely or vividly "present." After some time a feeling of the determinacy of past, realized duration will

EXAMPLE 6.3 Distinctions of mensural determinacy

abate, and the past act of beginning will cease to be available as a potential for a definite feeling of this sound's duration. Beginning is still active, and what is past of this sound must be relevant to its present becoming if we can now be aware of a single sound that has been going on for some time. What is now irrelevant and excluded is not past sound, but what had been a potential for a determinate feeling of duration. This was a potential of beginning, and this potential has now been denied. And whatever definite feeling of duration there was in the past will have become in itself irrelevant for what the sound has now become and for what is now its potential.

The potential that remains is the potential for more sound, or the possibility that the sound will continue, and the potential for a new beginning. And this latter possibility can manifest itself in an expectation of or expectancy for a new beginning and an opportunity to regain a feeling of durational determinacy—eventually, perhaps, in a feeling of impatience or boredom or in an inattentiveness resembling the feeling of silence I described earlier. In the course of its becoming, the duration of the sound will become increasingly indeterminate. Certainly, the sound has duration, but the now indeterminate duration of the sound—a duration that is gradually losing its memorability or potential for reproduction—is increasingly being measured by waiting and by a prolonged expectancy for a novel event. After ten seconds, when the sound has ended, the entire sound will be past, but the immediate past of the sound will be more vividly felt than its more distant past. And in a succession of very long,

unmodulated sounds, we will not hear from sound to sound, beginning to beginning, but rather from "ending phase" to "beginning phase." In such cases, I maintain that there is a gradual change of focus whereby our attention gradually shifts from duration realized to future becoming.

Since the sounds in examples 6.3a and 6.3b have definite beginnings and ends, their durations are, strictly speaking, determinate, but there is a clear difference in our feeling of durational determinacy. To make a distinction, I will call the durations in example 6.3a "mensurally determinate" and those in example 6.3b "mensurally indeterminate," or simply "determinate" and "indeterminate." I will say that a duration is mensurally determinate if the duration has the potential for being accurately or precisely reproduced. In this case, the duration can provide a definite measure of duration for comparison with another (latter or earlier) event. A feeling of determinacy together with the definiteness of this feeling is a condition for there being a precise reproduction or comparison. "Precise" here does not mean "objectively" precise, measured by the clock. Rather, it refers to a subjective judgment—a feeling of confidence that our reproduction is precise or that our comparison is an accurate comparison. Such judgments may depart from the measure of a clock. Thus, the second sound in example 6.3a might have a duration of slightly longer or shorter than that of the first sound, and we might, nevertheless, feel that the two sounds are equal in duration. Or our reproduction in example 6.3b might be proportionately as accurate as our reproduction in

example 6.3a, but even if this were the case, I believe that our uncertainty would be greater in
6.3b than in 6.3a. Since this feeling of precision
admits of degrees, the distinction between determinacy and indeterminacy often cannot be
sharply drawn. However, in examples 6.3a and
6.3b this distinction seems clear enough.

Since determinacy has been defined as a potential for comparison or reproduction, an actual
comparison or reproduction is not necessary for
a duration to be regarded as mensurally determinate—its "measure" belongs to it alone as a definite and past feeling of duration that may or
may not be used as a measure *for* a new event.
For a duration to be determinate in this sense,
the event must be completed—it must have a
definite beginning and end. And yet, while the
event is going on, there is, nevertheless, some
definiteness in the duration thus far realized, and
the active potential for its continued increase in
duration is also a potential for the becoming of
a mensurably determinate duration or for the
continuing "memorability" of its duration. If the
event goes on too long, it will have lost this potential, though not, of course, the potential for
growing in a duration that has become, increasingly, mensurally indeterminate. In this case, I
will say that the beginning has lost its potentiality for the becoming of a (mensurally) determinate duration.

In example 6.3a the two sounds are separated
by a brief pause of relatively indeterminate duration. By saying that this duration is relatively indeterminate I mean that if our attention is focused on the two sounds and on two beginnings, we may not be especially interested in the
silence as an event that begins and ends and that
attains a definite duration. If we actually produce
a second sound as a reproduction of the first
sound's duration, the silence could be regarded
simply as a gap between stimulus and response. If
we compare two sounds that are played for us,
the silence will be a waiting for a second sound.
Here the precise duration of silence will have little bearing on the act of reproduction or comparison. Of course, if the silence is too long, the
"memorability" or what I have called the relevancy of the first sound's duration will be lost,
and we will lose confidence in the accuracy of
our judgment. Since this memorability seems to

fade gradually and since our feeling of accuracy
admits of degrees, it is difficult to say precisely
when the silence might become too long or
when the mensural determinacy of the first
sound might be lost. But if the silence is not
too long—that is, if we can more or less confidently judge equality—this gap or nonevent has
little effect on the mensural determinacy of the
first sound. Certainly, the silence does function
to make the sound past and to end the potential
of the sound's beginning. But if we are not attending to the silence as an event, our attention
can be directed to the possibility of a second for
which the now fixed duration of the first sound
has become potentially relevant. The determinacy of the first sound's duration is also relevant
for a "larger" event that includes both sounds.
And this event will be past only when the first
sound has become the first of two sounds of
equal duration.

In example 6.3c I have indicated three
sounds. In this case, it will be possible to judge
that the first and third sounds are of equal duration or, if we are given only the first two sounds,
to produce a third sound equal in duration to
the first. And again, if the silences are not too
long, I believe we could be relatively confident
in the accuracy of our judgment or reproduction. If this succession of sounds is played for us,
the special relevancy of the first duration for the
third will emerge only when the third sound is
completed. Now we could hear in this sequence
the contrast of two durations—long and short—
and a "return" to the first duration. Thus, the
durational determinacy of the first sound is still
available after a comparison with the second
sound is made; and although the first sound has
now become something more particular—now
the longer of two sounds—neither its mensural
determinacy nor the determinacy of the second
sound's duration is affected by the act of comparing. I should add here that such judgment or
comparison is not limited to the simple distinctions of equal, longer, and shorter. By judgment I
mean a feeling of the particular similarity or difference of the two quantities, a feeling of just
these durations and their relative lengths.

In light of the preceding discussion, mensural
determinacy might be defined as the "presence"
of a past and determined duration as a definite

potential that can function as a "measure" for a later, but not necessarily immediately successive, event. I have focused primarily on equal measure because the mensural determinacy of the past duration can be most easily tested by attempting to reproduce the past duration (not the past event) as present. If we have decided to repeat the first duration, the beginning of the second sound is a definite potential or a potential for a definite duration—the beginning of the second sound is the beginning of a duration equal to the first. On the other hand, if the sounds are played for us, the possibility that the second sound might become equal in duration to the first is not especially privileged.

Assuming now that we are not producing these sounds and attempting to reproduce the duration of the first sound, the beginning of the second sound is not the definite potential for a reproduction of the duration of the first sound. If, in fact, the second duration upon completion is equal to the first duration and we judge the two durations to be equal, we must say that there was a potential for this judgment and that the determinacy of the first duration was a condition for this judgment. But there was, equally, a potential for the second to be longer or shorter than the first and a potential for judging the difference between the two durations. Here there is no "weighting" of potential in favor of equality.

The beginning of the second sound, like the beginning of the first sound, is a potential for a definite duration, but I will say that in neither case is this a definite potential or the promise of a particular durational quantity. Like the duration of the first sound, the duration of the second will be determined when it is past. But since the second sound does not begin as a duration equal (or unequal) to the first, the durational potential of its beginning is indeterminate and this potential is unaffected by the now determinate duration of the first sound. This is not to say that the second sound and its duration are unaffected by the first. If there is a comparison, then clearly what the second sound becomes is determined in part by what the first sound became. Although upon its completion the first sound will have a fixed duration, the determinacy of this duration is not past if it is a potential that is presently involved in the becoming of the second sound.

EXAMPLE 6.4 Reproduction of durational quantity

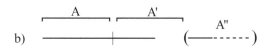

Although the two sounds shown in example 6.3a are mensurally determinate and can be judged equal in duration, this succession is not, as I shall say, "metrical." To be felt as metrical, the two events must be immediately successive—the beginning of the second event must make the first event past. In example 6.4a I have eliminated the pause between the two sounds. Here the beginning of the second sound functions to end the first sound and thus to determine its duration. As a result, the second beginning has a definite potential.

That this is a definite potential is demonstrated in example 6.4b. Here the second sound is shorter than the first, but if we can also feel the duration labeled "A'," the potential for duration beginning the second sound is not exhausted or realized when the sound ends. If the duration A' is realized—that is, if we come to feel a duration A'—the end of this duration is not determined by a new beginning. Rather, the end is determined by the durational quantity promised by the beginning of the second sound. When this promise is met, the second event, composed of sound and silence, will be past. If end and beginning are inseparable as a realization of durational potential and a simultaneous making present and making past, we could say that the promise of a second beginning is also a promise for a third event and that the potential of the second beginning for a definite end is also felt as the expectation of an immediately successive event.

In example 6.4b a third sound, A", is represented as a potential event. On the basis of the durational potential of the second beginning we can predict the beginning of A". If there is an actual third beginning, the realization of the duration promised with the second beginning will also be a realization of the potential for a new

EXAMPLE 6.5 Reproduction and mensural determinacy

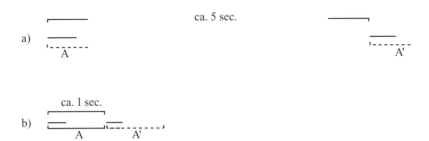

beginning. If there is no actual third beginning, the durational potential of the second beginning will still be realized, but the end of the second event will be somewhat indistinct. Since mensural determinacy is relative and thus somewhat flexible, the decision for a new beginning could be made a bit early or late by the clock and still be heard as the realization of the mensurally determinate duration promised by the second beginning. Thus, there is no precise "point" at which the possibility for a third beginning is denied, and the silence that belongs to the second event as a continued realization of its promised duration will not be very sharply distinguished from the silence in which this event is past.

The emergence of a definite durational potential for beginning is perhaps more clearly demonstrated in example 6.5. In example 6.5a two very brief sounds are separated by a relatively long duration. Here, the beginning of the second sound is simply the beginning of a very short sound, and I think that we will perceive two brief events of sound isolated from one another by a silence of waiting. In this case, the first event is the first sound, made past by the beginning of silence. By contrast, in example 6.5b the duration initiated with the beginning of the second sound can be heard to extend beyond this sound, and two immediately successive events can be perceived. Now, with the beginning of the first sound, there is also the beginning of an event that is not made past with silence.

To account for this difference, I suggest that in example 6.5b a potential for the creation of a reproducible duration is not exhausted when the first sound ends, and that this potential is realized

with the beginning of the second sound. In the case of example 6.5a, the beginning of the first sound, although it is the beginning of a determinate duration for sound, is not the beginning of a determinate duration for an event whose duration is determined by the beginning of a succeeding event—the second sound. Being the beginning of such an event was a possibility that is forfeited as the duration realized from the beginning becomes mensurally indeterminate. And as this duration becomes indeterminate, its potential for reproduction is lost. What potential for reproduction does remain is the realized and highly determinate duration of the first sound itself, and this sound and the second sound as the realization of a potential for reproduction whereby a comparison is made become the two events upon which our attention can now be focused.

Incidentally, it seems to me that Koch's argument for the proper barring of example 2.2b quoted previously from the *Versuch* (Koch 1787/ 1969, p. 303) shows an acknowledgment of definite durational potential. Thus, Koch argues that this example comprises not seven but four measures, even though the fourth measure is not notated as complete, and he justifies his barring on the basis of a cognizance and feeling of "the disposition of the extent and ending of the parts of the melody." Similarly, in the ending of the first movement of Beethoven's F-Minor Sonata shown in example 6.2 the final sound can be heard to open a mensural duration of two "bars." (But again, it is not clear precisely when this duration ends or when the movement as a whole is made past.)

SEVEN

Meter as Projection

"Projection" Defined

To make less cumbersome the discussion of the process in which a mensurally determinate duration provides a definite durational potential for the beginning of an immediately successive event, I would like to introduce the term "projection" (as a "throwing forth"). Example 7.1 provides a schematic representation of this process.

I will say that a potential duration for the second event (C') is *projected*, and I will represent the projected duration by a dotted line to indicate that this duration is potential rather than actual. When there is an actual duration C' that emerges as a reproduction of the first event's duration, I will say that the projected potential has been realized. The actual duration (C) of the first event, functioning for the potential duration of the second event, I will call "projective," and I will represent this function by an arrow aimed at the beginning of the second event. "Projection" as the act of projecting will refer to the entire process.

To forestall a possible misunderstanding, I should explain that the arrow shown in example 7.1 does not symbolize a first event (C) "leading to" a second event (C') or a first event implying a second event. Projective potential is the potential for a present event's duration to be reproduced for a successor. This potential is realized if and when there is a new beginning whose durational potential is determined by the now past first event. Projective potential is not the potential that there will be a successor, but rather the potential of a past and completed durational quantity being taken as especially relevant for the becoming of a present event. The arrow, in this sense, points to the possibility for a future relevancy.

My proposal of the terms "projective" and "projected" also demands a caveat. Lest it be thought that the opposition projective/projected implies an opposition of active versus passive or agent versus patient, I should point out that such an understanding would invert the relationship

EXAMPLE 7.1 Projection from the standpoint of durational products C and C'

EXAMPLE 7.2 Processive representation of projection in the actualization of potentials Q and Q'

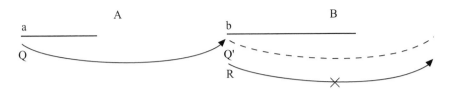

of the two durations: C is not itself active—it is past and has become a definite duration; C', on the other hand, *is* active—it is in the process of realizing a duration that begins as a reproduction of the duration of C. Thus, the duration C is projective as reproduced for C', and the duration C' is projected as a reproduction of C's duration. Although I have assigned two names and two symbols, it should be kept in mind that projective and projected are aspects of a single process—projection. However, because of the limitations of graphic representation and linguistic convention I shall often, for convenience and as an abbreviation, speak as if these were separate "things." In the preceding account I have, in fact, implied a separation of the two phases by identifying the process of projection with the two products C and C'. In order to make a clearer distinction between process and product, example 7.2 shows a more detailed representation.

Here, A and B may be understood to refer to two events or two durations as products abstracted or detached from process. (To avoid multiplying labels, I will avoid making a distinction now between an event and its duration.) "A" and "B" label two durations "given" for our inspection apart from any questions concerning their emergence. The designation "B," for example, means that we are "presented" with the second of two durations—in this case, the second of two equal durations. The lowercase letters refer to the beginnings of these durations. Each of these beginnings is a potential for duration—a, an indefinite potential; b, a definite potential (definite because of the projection Q–Q'). "Q" labels a projective potential realized with the new beginning b. This potential is not a's potential for a mensurally determinate duration—it is the potential for a mensurally determinate duration A to provide a definite potential for the

new beginning b. The realization of Q is the creation of a definite potential Q', which is shown here as realized in the duration B. Q' represents b's potential for duration. But with b there is also the emergence of a new projective potential R.

If, as in example 7.2, there is no new beginning c, Q' will be realized, but the projective potential R will not be realized in a projection. As Q' is in the process of realization, an R is emerging as potentially projective. I have drawn an "X" over the arrow of R to show that R does not in this case come to function in a projection. R is a definite potential for a projection, and here no projection actually occurs. It is a *definite* potential because Q' is a definite potential shown here realized in an actual duration B. Thus, if b promises a duration B, there is also the possibility of a projection when the duration B is realized and can be past *for* a new event C.

The difference between Q' and R is this: Q' is a potential for the becoming of B; R is a potential for B as past to affect the becoming of a new event, C. However, neither Q' nor R is itself a potential for a new event C. Since Q', as b's potential for duration, is a definite potential, Q' or b might be called the predictability of an end of B or the predictability of a new beginning that will make B past. Q' "predicts" how long B is likely to last or when a new beginning, c, is likely to occur. But Q' or b is not itself a potential for a new beginning, c; b is a potential only for the present becoming of an event B. If there is a potential for a C, this potential emerges from a now for which a potential C is relevant—for example, a now in which B is felt to be incomplete (the now of an event that B does not end) or a now in which we for any reason expect an immediately successive event. Nor is R a potential for a new beginning in the sense of being the promise of a new beginning. Rather, R is a potential for the duration of B as completed and past to determine how long the new event is likely to last or when this new event is likely to be succeeded by another. And until there is a new beginning, R shares whatever potentiality there is for a C. However, if we do not expect a projection there seems little reason to say that a projection is denied or that the projective potential R is denied, and I shall seldom represent nonprojection as a denial of projective potential. Nevertheless, it must be admitted that the promise of Q' for a definite duration opens the possibility for a definite end and that the potential for an end is inseparable from the potential for a new beginning. If we can predict an end for B or a beginning, c, our prediction is made on the basis of b's potential. Because of Q' we know how much time we have before B might end and, if we expect a C, how much time we have to prepare for the new event. And if Q' is not itself the potential for a new event, its realization in B requires a new beginning—either an actual beginning (of sound or silence) or the denial of a beginning.

In example 7.2 I have indicated that the projected potential Q' is realized in the actual duration B. However, since there is no new beginning c, the duration of B is somewhat indefinite. B is not completed until there is no possibility for a new beginning that would realize R. If we are expecting a new event, I will say that R is denied. However, if we are not expecting a new event, I would prefer to say that R is simply unrealized—nothing becomes of R, and its potential becomes gradually attenuated. In example 7.3a, since there is a new beginning, c, both Q' and R are realized and the duration of B is definite. In this case, c functions for the realization of Q' and R. But it is also possible that the beginning of a new event might not function in this way—C might begin too early or too late. In example 7.3 we will consider some situations in which c is early and in example 7.4 some situations in which c is late. Although it would be premature to embark on a systematic analysis of such "inequalities," a consideration of these examples will provide us with an opportunity to inquire more deeply into the relation of projective and projected potential and may serve also

to illustrate the flexibility of projective engagements. Since these situations involve fairly subtle perceptual distinctions, I should preface this discussion with some remarks concerning my graphic representations.

In the following examples (as in examples 7.1 and 7.2) generalized "events" composed of sound and silence are represented by line segments and spaces. In view of the variability of mensural determinacy and its dependence on many factors excluded from these simplified representations, there seems little point in attempting to assign specific clock-time durational values to these events. If we assume that the lines here represent single, relatively unmodulated sounds, the events labeled "A" in the following examples might be given a duration of between one and two seconds. Beyond two seconds, mensural determinacy rapidly deteriorates in such simple environments. Although these examples are offered as generalizations, the reader is invited to produce or to imagine concrete situations that might correspond to the various interpretations I will offer. This experimentation will likely involve adjusting durational quantity to the situation. From the reader's perspective, the point here is not to test which interpretation might be spontaneously chosen "all things being equal," but to test the variety of interpretations that might be chosen. (And later we will consider contexts that might favor one choice or another.) This said, let us turn to several situations in which a third sound begins early or too early.

It is difficult to say how early is "too" early. Since mensural determinacy is flexible, B can be felt as a reproduction of A's duration without being "precisely" equal, measured by the clock. However, this flexibility should not be taken to indicate an inability to feel differences among completed durations. It is, rather, a flexibility that accommodates the indeterminacy of present becoming to a definite potential for this becoming. (And I should add here that if in example 7.3 we expect a new event C, this expectation is a present potential.)

In example 7.3b let us say that B is noticeably shorter than A but at least three-quarters the length of A. (If A lasts 2 seconds, let us say B lasts between 1.5 seconds and 1.8 seconds.) If in this example we can feel an acceleration, we will

EXAMPLE 7.3 "Early" entries of a third event

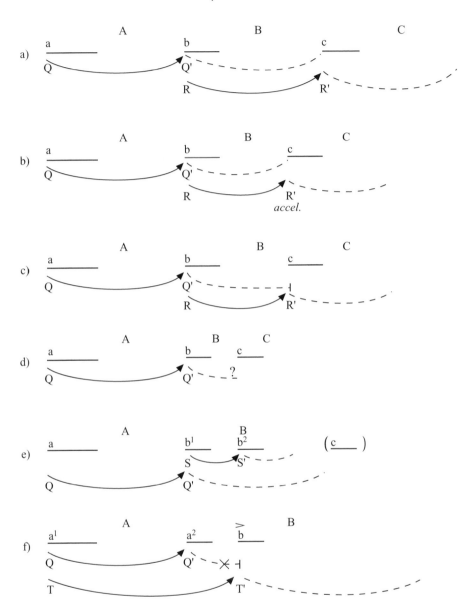

have felt the difference between the two durations *and* the realization of the projected potential Q'. Here we can make a useful distinction between "length" and "speed." B is shorter than A, but if we feel acceleration we will not feel that B is "too short" or that its promised duration is denied. If Q' is realized, B will repeat A's duration, but B will be faster than A—its duration will, in a sense, be realized more quickly. On the other hand, it is also possible to hear a shorter B not as an acceleration, but as "too short," interrupted by a C that begins too soon, as in example 7.3c. In this case, Q' will be denied complete realization. But this does not mean that Q' is denied as a potential. Q' is a definite potential for a duration B. Since B has begun and since there is no beginning apart from a duration that is in the process of becoming, there is from the beginning a realization of durational potential. C is too soon in relation to a projected duration that is being realized, and the beginning of C by interrupting this realization does not necessarily cancel the fact of realization. Nor does this interruption deny the potentiality of Q'. Q''s potential is preserved in the incompleteness of B's realized duration. If there is a feeling that C begins too soon, this feeling can arise only if Q' is presently functioning as a real potential. Q' is real in that it is efficacious in producing a feeling of "too soon" or a feeling that the completed duration of B is not the completion of a duration that b promised.

The decision to hear acceleration or interruption depends, in part, on our interest or purposes. If we expect a third sound, C, or if our interest is directed toward continuation, a feeling of acceleration will serve for prediction. In this case, the abbreviation of B will present for C the likelihood of being still "faster" and a definite possibility that a fourth event, D, will begin even sooner with the result that the projected R' will be shorter than the projective R. That is to say, the present projection R–R' can inherit a characteristic that the completed projection Q–Q' attained (again, *attained* as past and inherited as past for the present projection R–R'). If, on the other hand, our interest is directed toward the present becoming of B or toward B's completion, an "early" c can appear to cut short the projection Q–Q'. And yet, if there does emerge a "still sooner" d, a potential for acceleration may nevertheless be realized. For this "larger" becoming, the abbreviation of B is now relevant for a process of acceleration. But if we have, in fact, felt an "earlier" interruption, this feeling cannot be unfelt; and if an acceleration emerges, we will have felt an interruption that has become a factor in the acceleration.

In example 7.3d the third sound enters very early in the projected opening of a second duration. Since there is too great a disparity in the durations A and B for B to be felt as an accelerated replica of A, two metrically comprehensible alternatives emerge. In example 7.3e the projected Q' is realized in an event B. Here a projection S–S' can be completed within the duration promised by Q' and may function to enhance the mensural determinacy of the duration B. (In chapter 9 we will consider in more detail the question of such "division" within a projec-

tion). Although Q' can be realized without a new beginning, the emergence of c, shown in parentheses in example 7.3e, would enhance the definiteness of B and thus help clarify the relation of S–S' to the potential Q'. Moreover, any expectation of a new beginning c that might determine B's duration would be clear evidence of the continued "presence" of the projected potential Q'. In example 7.3f, projective potential is shown to be extended as the second event (beginning with a2) is assimilated to the duration of a first event. The accent shown above b in example 7.3f symbolizes an unequivocal second beginning that denies the projection Q–Q' in order to realize a larger projective potential T. Again, in cases such as example 7.3d, the variables of length and attentiveness and the countless qualifications and relevancies that are excluded from these general, schematic figures will all work together in an actual musical event to provoke a decision.

Now let us consider some situations in which c is late. If, as in example 7.4a, B is slightly longer than A as a result of a delayed c, we may hear deceleration—the "same" but slower. If the delay is much longer, as in example 7.4b, we may come to feel *hiatus* (symbolized | |)—a break between the realization of projected potential and a new beginning. Here the duration B loses its projective potential, and a new and relatively unconditioned projective potential S emerges from the beginning of event C.

Example 7.4c shows the possibility that a delayed c might come to function for a new projection R–R', which would break off from the emerging Q–Q'. In the projection R–R', Q' is denied both in realization and as the promise of a future projective potential. The projection R–R' will thus involve complex feelings occasioned by a rejection of the relevance of Q–Q' for the mensural determinacy of B. Indeed, this very denial of Q' will be inseparable from the particular duration B has now become.

In example 7.4d, a delay is created not by a third sound but by the second sound, which exceeds the duration promised with b. Here Q' is contradicted, or at least obscured, by an actual sounding duration B. In the case of example 7.4c, Q' can be realized (in the projection Q–Q') and subsequently denied by a new beginning c

EXAMPLE 7.4 "Late" entries of a third event

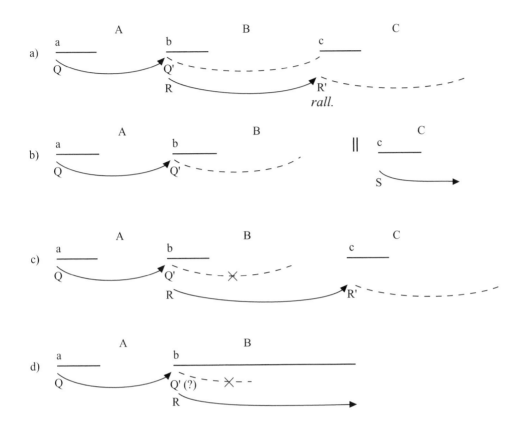

and the emergence of a projection R–R'. In example 7.4d, a realization of Q' is not subsequently denied by a new beginning (as in 7.4c)—Q' is simply never clearly realized. When B becomes too long to be a realization of Q', B's beginning is no longer the beginning of a projected duration, and the projection will have been denied. But since the duration of B will itself be relatively indeterminate (in the absence of a new beginning c) and since it is not at all clear "when" the projected potential Q' becomes exhausted, we may have little or no feeling of a potential denied.

If the foregoing analyses have helped clarify certain aspects of the projective process, they have also left a great many aspects of projection out of account. When we take up the topics of metrical accent, metrical type, and metrical levels in chapter 9, we will be in a position to consider a greater variety of interpretations than have been made in connection with examples 7.3 and 7.4. (For instance, we will encounter situations resembling example 7.4d in which Q–Q' can be realized by what will be termed a "virtual articulation" of a mensurally determinate duration A-B.) However, even in chapter 9 our examples will remain, for the most part, relatively general or abstract. A closer examination of factors that might contribute to particular projective decisions will be undertaken in subsequent chapters when we turn to specific musical contexts involving distinctions of tone and contour.

To conclude this preliminary discussion of projected duration, I would like to clarify several features of the graphic representation of projection introduced in examples 7.1–7.4. Although all of these examples incorporate both sound and silence, it should be understood that projection does not require an absence of stimulus during the projective or the projected phase. Thus, example 7.5a might have been substituted for example 7.2. But in the case of example 7.5a, although there is no less a projection, it may be

EXAMPLE 7.5 Distinctions between duration of sonic stimulus and projective duration

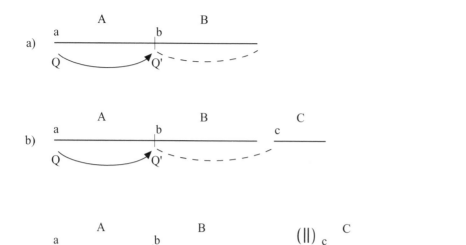

more difficult to feel projective potential per se or to isolate the process of projection from its durational products. Since in example 7.5a the second event is and actual stimulus of determinate duration, this sound will have this duration whether or not there is a projection. In the earlier examples, if we can feel a more or less determinate duration for the second event indicated in the diagrams, such a feeling can occur only if there is a projection. And in the following pages, I shall continue to use silence as a heuristic devise for testing projection, for it is in the absence of stimulus that the effect of projective duration can be most clearly isolated and tested.

In fact, example 7.5a does not entirely eliminate the problem of ascertaining the realization of projected potential. There is a definite b that terminates a's (indefinite) potential for duration. With b, A is fully determined and past for an emerging B. But, although there is an actual sounding event that corresponds to the realization of Q', there is no new beginning that definitely terminates b's durational potential. If, as in example 7.5b, a new event C begins after a brief silence, Q''s realization and the duration B might include this duration of silence. If, as in example 7.5c, this silence is lengthened, there may be ei-

ther hiatus (as in example 7.4b) or a new projection R–R' (as in example 7.4c). In the latter case, B will have become longer than A. And if this is a possibility, the duration B in example 7.4a cannot have been fully determined when the sound ceases, and a projective potential (R) will not have been forfeited with the beginning of silence.

Notice also that example 7.1 (which shows durational products) is more complicated than example 7.5a and differs from example 7.5a in two respects. The two events C and C' shown in example 7.1 are composite events or events composed of (in this case) sound and silence and, therefore, comprise more than one beginning and end. Although I have concentrated on beginning as the beginning of sound, there is also the beginning of silence. Also, in example 7.1 the two sound (and the silences) are of unequal duration. This sort of inequality has relatively little bearing on the projection. The duration of A' can vary from being very short to occupying the entire duration of C' without, I believe, greatly altering the projection. That is, the durations A and A' seem relatively independent from the projective C and the projected C'. A and A' begin and end: they have fully determinate durations that can be compared and judged equal or unequal. Their beginnings coincide with the beginnings of C and C' but, unlike the latter, do not function projectively.

If beginning is regarded as a time point—a self-sufficient entity—we could say that A and C (or A' and C') have the same beginning. However, if beginning is a potential for duration, these beginnings are not the same. The beginning of A becomes inactive and "past" while the beginning of C is still active and "present." Thus, in example 7.1, I count six beginnings (and six ends, for A, B, C, A', B', and C'), two of which—the beginnings of C and C'—function for projection. The postulation of a multiplicity of beginnings and ends within a single event will play an important role in the analysis of more complex metrical events I shall propose later in this study and will be invoked when we turn to a discussion of the problem of metrical accent.

Finally, it must be admitted that the above diagrams do not adequately represent projected potential as present activity. Thus, in examples 7.4c and 7.4d where the dotted line Q' with a "X" through it represents a denial of projected potential, I should perhaps have included another symbol for what is realized or actualized of Q' in the course of B's becoming. I have refrained form attempting this in order to simplify the analytic notation. But aside from the demand for economy, it seems impossible to adequately represent B's becoming—Q' is being realized from the start, and the dotted line will always have some actuality. It should be noted here that projective *denial* is always marked by a more or less clear feeling of incompatible potentials. Thus, in saying that a potentiality is denied, I mean that we can point to some more or less definite feeling of nonconformity or breach of promise—in the examples we have considered thus far, some feeling of "*too* short" or "*too* long." (Needless to say, there is great variety in the clarity and intensity of such feelings.) If, in example 7.4d, there is some feeling of denial— that is, if the second event in 7.4d is felt not simply as long but as "too long" in relation to the "expected" projected duration—then the projection is actual as the cause of this feeling of denial. However, it might be argued that even if there is little or no evidence of such a feeling, there must have been, in the early stage of this event's becoming, some feeling of a realization of projective potential, in which case the projection would have been actual even in the absence of a "subsequent" and definite feeling of denial. The only situation in which projection is clearly potential and not actual is where there is no beginning of a projected duration. Thus, "pure" or unequivocal potentiality belongs only to the projective phase. And projection is potential from the very beginning of the first event. From its beginning, the duration of the first event is potentially projective, and this potential is forfeited only if and to the degree that this event becomes mensurally indeterminate and, hence, unreproducible as a more or less precisely determinate duration.

My arguments thus far have been intended to support a claim that, given a relatively modest degree of attentiveness and in the absence of any competing durational relevancies, two immediately successive events begun with sound will necessarily result in projection if the first event is mensurally determinate and the duration of the second sound is not greater than that of the first event. If the duration of the second sound is greater than that of the first event, projection may nevertheless occur, but I will not claim that this is a necessary outcome. More broadly and, at this stage in my argument, more questionably, I will claim that projection is nothing other than meter—that projection and meter are one. But before I attempt to relate projection specifically to musical meter and to many of the problems posed by musical meter, I would like to consider the more basic question of why there should be such a phenomenon—why a second event should inherit the duration of a first event as a potential for its future becoming.

Projection and "Prediction"

Although our interest may be directed either toward the completion of the present event or toward the emergence of a new event, the opening of a durational span in which we can accurately predict end or beginning is created by a beginning that has acquired a definite potential. I have speculated that a beginning acquires such a potential by making past and determining the duration of an immediately preceding event and that the durational potential of this beginning is determined by the now actual duration of the past event. However, it must be said that prediction is also possible in the case of "nonadjacent" reproduction. Thus, in example 6.3a (where there is no projection) we can, if we choose, predict the end of the second sound and so predict a beginning for a third event based on an estimation of the duration that the second sound must have in order to reproduce the duration of the first. But it seems clear that in the case of example 6.3a this choice must be a conscious decision to regard the second duration from its beginning as a reproduction—there is no larger context shown here that would make such a potential reproduction especially relevant for the beginning of the second sound. In the cases of examples 6.4a, 6.4b, and 6.5b, I believe that the feeling of a determinate potential for reproduction with the beginning of the second event is involuntary, that we will feel the becoming of this more or less determinate duration whether we choose to or not (assuming, of course, a minimum level of attentiveness and the absence of any strongly conflicting relevancies).

Here it seems that the intense relevancy of the first duration for the second is created simply by the fact of immediate succession. This immediate feeling of promised duration has been the object of considerable study among psychologists. In the psychological literature emphasis has been placed on prediction of a new beginning, and the phenomenon is generally known as "synchronization," or the coordination of an action such as clapping with a series of periodic stimuli—coordination that is accomplished from the third stimulus on. Paul Fraisse comments on some of the special characteristics of this behavior:

> People fairly easily accompany with a motor act a regular succession of sounds. This phenomenon spontaneously appears in certain children toward one year of age, sometimes even earlier. . . . This accompaniment tends to be a synchronization between sound and tap—that is to say, that the stimulus and the response occur simultaneously.
>
> This behavior is all the more remarkable, as it constitutes an exception in the field of our behaviors. As a rule, our reactions succeed the stimulus. A similar behavior is possible only if the motor

command is anticipated in regard to the moment when the stimulus is produced. More precisely, the signal for the response is not the sound stimulus but the temporal interval between successive sounds. Synchronization is only possible when there is anticipation—that is, when the succession of signals is periodic. Thus the most simple rhythm is evidently the isochronal production of identical stimuli. However, synchronization is also possible in cases of more complex rhythms. What is important is not the regularity but the anticipation. The subjects can, for example, synchronize their tapping with some series of accelerated or decelerated sounds . . . The spontaneity of this behavior is attested to by its appearance early in life and also by the fact that the so-called evolved adult has to learn how to inhibit his involuntary movements of accompaniment to music. (Fraisse 1982, pp. 154–155)

The question remains why there should be an immediate, spontaneous, and apparently "involuntary" disposition for the reproduction of duration. I will address this question first by placing it within the framework of the notions of beginning/end, determinacy, and potentiality I have been developing. I will then depart from this framework to consider the utility such reproduction might have for our active engagement with events in the world.

Since the reproduction I have described occurs with the end of a durationally determinate event and the beginning of an immediately successive event, I would like to once again consider this crucial juncture of a simultaneous yet functionally distinct beginning and end. If two events are immediately successive and there is a clear articulation that marks a definite end and beginning, the beginning can, I think, properly be said to cause the first event to end (but only in the sense of being stopped, terminated, or made past—later we will consider end as goal or aim). Without a new beginning there could be no definite end for the first event and, assuming that the first event has a definite beginning, there could be no definite duration of this event. This assertion does not reverse the order of cause (beginning) and effect (end) or collapse cause and effect in a single durationless instant. The first event as present certainly precedes the second event. But the first event as past, ended, and completed does not precede the beginning

of the second event; and although end and beginning happen at the same time, this time involves duration—the (indefinite) duration in
which beginning, as I have argued, creates an
overlap in the making past of the first event and
the making present of the second.

If the new beginning is a cause of there being
a determinate end for the earlier event, and if
this end is a condition for the durational determinacy of this event, then the new beginning
can be said to participate in the creation of the
first event's determinate duration. But the new
beginning does more than end the presence or
becoming of the first event. It also makes this
event presently past and, in so doing, *necessarily*
(simply for there to be an awareness of succession) involves this past event in the now of the
present event. I will speculate that by functioning to determine the duration of the now past
event, the durational potential of the new beginning is determined by the actual duration of this
now completed event. However, the question
remains why the durational potential of the new
beginning should be conditioned by the duration of the preceding event, or why this past duration is especially relevant for the now of the
new event's becoming. Some light may be shed
on this question by considering what is unique
about duration among the many properties of an
event.

The now of the beginning of the present
event contains many givens. Assuming that the
event is a sound, there are, from the earliest
stages of our awareness of the sound, a variety of
definite qualities of sound—a particular timbre
and (possibly) pitch, a certain degree of loudness, a particular density or "texture," or a special
resonance. (In the attack phase of the sound
these qualities are unstable, but they quickly sta-
bilize and the attack itself has a definite quality.)
All these qualities from the beginning involve a
host of "associations" or past experiences. The
sound is the sound of a clarinet, or it is a rasping
or a velvety sound, or a B♭, or scale degree 1.
This sound is made particular, too, by its contrast
to the immediately preceding sound—it is a
higher sound, a softer sound, a sound with a particular intervallic quality. Any quality that has
been perceived is past and cannot be unperceived, and any "association" that is made is fixed

and cannot be unmade. Certainly, while the
sound is present it is possible for any or all of these
qualities of the sound to change in the course of
the sound's becoming (except, of course, for the
attack, which will become a completed event).
But these qualities do not have to change. From
the beginning, once the timbre, pitch, and volume of the sound are given, it is possible for
these qualities to remain relatively fixed. And if
they do remain fixed there can be no change in
their definiteness. If a sound begins with a particular timbre and does not noticeably change in
timbre, there is no becoming for timbre and no
becoming of timbre's definiteness. If it is the
sound of a clarinet, it can remain the sound of a
clarinet.

By contrast, *what cannot remain fixed and what
cannot be determinate while the sound is going on is
its duration.* Thus, while the qualities of sound
can be fully determined from the beginning, the
quantity of the sound's duration cannot be fully
determined. This quantity, by its nature, is always, until the sound is past, a potential for definiteness. This potential for the now present
sound can, however, be conditioned, just as the
qualities of the sound can be conditioned, by
pasts and futures that are brought into relevancy
for the becoming of the event. And just as these
relevancies contribute to the definiteness of the
sound's qualities, the relevancies of past durations
(and the anticipation of a new beginning) can
contribute to the definiteness of durational potential. But in the case of duration, since there is
only a potential for determinateness, these relevancies are not for what is, but for what will or
can become.

This necessarily uncertain or indeterminate
future of a duration's becoming definite can be
limited or to some extent "predetermined" only
if the beginning itself is given a definite potential. If, in the case of immediately successive
events, the beginning of the second event plays
an essential role in the determination of the first
event's duration as a making past of the first
event, what is immediately given for the durational potential of the nascent event and what is,
in part, created by the beginning as a making
past of the first event is the now determined duration of the first event. And it is because of this
now definite potential that a definite future be-

comes available as the predictability of a third event. For there to be a definite potential there must be a definite duration that is made past. The duration of the first event must itself be sufficiently definite to provide the second event with the definite potential of realizing "just this duration." It is doubtless misleading to call this process "reproduction" if "reproduction" is taken to mean making a copy of an event.[1] The beginning of the second event does not copy or reproduce the beginning of the first event—the beginning of the first event did not have a definite potential for duration. Rather, the new beginning uses the determinateness of the immediately past event *for its own end*; and if the potential it takes from that event is realized, the duration of the second of the two events will be emerging as equal quite apart from any comparison or any judgment of equality. From its beginning the second event is producing equality.

The duration of the first event, even in its process of becoming, is a potential for determining the duration of an immediately succeeding event or, as I shall continue to say, being "reproduced" by or for a successor. Thus, what I have called mensural determinacy is a narrowing or focusing of potentiality or a limitation of what is possible. And it seems that in acts of perception we actively and involuntarily seek opportunities for such limitation.

Thus far, I have approached the question of reproduction from what might be called an "ontological" perspective. However, since we are considering perceptual acts and the limitations imposed by perception, we must also view this question from an "ecological" or "environmental" perspective. From this perspective, prediction plays a primary role. Here I suggest that the "reason" we can feel a determinate potential for reproduction is that we *must* in order to act and survive in a world that involves so much periodicity. If we are to coordinate our actions with periodic phenomena, we must have time to prepare our actions, as in the case of clapping with a third beat. This involves anticipation or feeling in advance when the next event is likely to occur or when the present event is likely to end.

The periodic events we encounter in the world are produced primarily (but not exclusively) by organisms—other organisms and our own. And such periodicities are often not very precise. Very precise periodicity in our world of "middle-sized" durations is encountered primarily in the workings of machines. But we have not evolved to respond to machines. We have evolved to respond to, among other things, creatures that we must capture and creatures that we must evade. Since our locomotion and the locomotion of many other creatures involve various periodicities, much of the information we need for our interactions with the environment comes from aural, visual, and kinesthetic perceptions of more or less equal durations. "More or less" is an important qualification. Focusing now on chase (which, of course, is not the only of our activities that involves a sensitivity to periodicity), it would be as dangerous for the prey to behave with a high degree of regularity as it would be for the predator to assume a high degree of regularity. By altering speed, direction, and various bodily movements, creatures can avoid too obvious a regularity of motion. In sports, too, it is important to be unpredictable and to avoid telegraphing one's movements. But even though irregularities can camouflage periodicity, for many creatures (ourselves included) they cannot entirely obscure it, particularly because only two "points" of beginning are needed. In fact, just two beginnings may be especially relevant to action, since to act effectively in many cases we

---

1. Along the lines of the perceptual theories of J. J. Gibson, Ulrich Neisser also argues against the notions of copy or representation in his account of the role of memory in the formation and activity of "anticipatory schemata"—that is, "more or less specific readinesses (anticipations) for what will come up next, based on information [the listener] has already picked up" (1976, p. 27). As Neisser writes: "It may be wise to avoid the connotation that there is a final, constructed product in the perceiver's mind; that we see internal representations rather than real objects. This, I think, is not true. By constructing an anticipatory schema, the perceiver engages in an act that involves information from the environment as well as his own cognitive mechanisms. He is changed by the information he picks up. The change is not a matter of making an inner replica where none existed before, but of altering the perceptual schema so that the next act will run a different course" (p. 57).

may need to be highly attuned to last-minute information and flexible enough to make last-minute adjustments. Certainly, vision provides much of the information we need for action, but we would be at a great disadvantage without the contributions of the ear (and without an intimate coordination of ear, eye, and muscle groups —large and small).

I shall return to this "worldly" aspect of felt duration in connection with various questions concerning musical meter. My immediate purpose in introducing this perspective is to account for an aspect of reproduction that the "ontological" perspective did not touch upon, and that is the imprecision—measured by the clock—of our feeling of duration. If there is a reproduction of mensurally determinate duration, why should we be confident and yet wrong by the clock? This disparity would seem to indicate a perceptual defect. However, I would suggest that for the purposes of acting in a world of imprecision (and, possibly, deception), such perceptual precision would be dangerous and would thus be a greater defect. This perspective also might account for the durational constraints for mensural determinacy. In this view, such limitations would roughly correspond to the durations of events that for our purposes must be immediately comprehended or "grasped."

EIGHT

Precedents for a Theory of Projection

Before I turn to an analysis of various problems of musical meter viewed from a projective standpoint, I would like to acknowledge and evaluate the work of two theorists who have discussed in detail the phenomenon I call "projection." The account of projection I gave in connection with example 7.1 is similar in many respects to Hauptmann's definition of duple meter and to Neumann's description of the "rhythmic pair," a concept that for Neumann points to an *Urphänomen* of the rhythmic and a scheme that is manifested in the largest and most complex of rhythmic formations.

Neumann's concept of the rhythmic pair differs from my account of projection most obviously in its isolation of the pair as an autonomous "whole," its separation of rhythm and meter (as "inner" versus "outer" time, *Zeitgestalt* versus *Zeitmaß*), and its invocation of time point for the determination of an event's boundaries. Neumann's initial discussion of the rhythmic pair is very condensed, and his thought will be better related by quotation than by paraphrase. Since Neumann's examples 1–4 (shown in our example 8.1) closely parallel several of the examples of projection I discussed earlier, I will include his entire commentary.

Having defined discrimination (*Aufmerkung*) as the determination of an event's beginning and

end points, Neumann proceeds to a discussion of the intervals spanned by these points:

> We turn now to the inclusiveness [*Enthaltensein*] of discriminations and begin with the simplest case in which two discriminations are contained in a discrimination of higher order. To this end we place two real or imagined, temporally adjacent events delimited by points at a certain easily comprehensible distance from one another (ex. 1). This interval might amount to about one second, but within certain limits a larger or smaller interval could be chosen, depending on the rhythmic capability of the reader.
>
> Given the two events A and B, *two* discriminations are defined, one from A to B and one from B to a concomitant, unknown potential limit (S), such that the intervals A–B and B–(S) are, in fact, equal (ex. 2). The existence of this potential limit is immediately known to us when a third event C enters. We are then easily, and with great accuracy, able to say whether C coincides with (S) (ex. 3a), or if it enters earlier (ex. 3b) or later (ex. 3c). Upon the fact of the potential limit, just explained, and its coming to consciousness is based the ability for time-comparison and consequently all beating of measures, counting of measures—in short, the temporal theory of measurement or *Metrik*.
>
> How then is event C related to the unity and wholeness of the higher-order discrimination? Most neutrally, certainly, in the case of ex. 3c. Pro-

EXAMPLE 8.1 Friedrich Neumann, *Die Zeitgestalt,* examples 1–4, p. 3, Beispielband

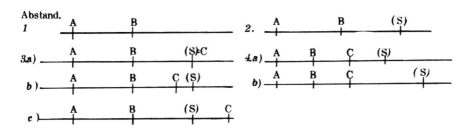

vided, that we enter the process A–B–(S) with a clear conception of its two-part structure, a C that comes too late can no longer interfere with the rounded-off completion of the duration, particularly if C does not enter too quickly afterwards. It is obvious that, in the opposite case, with a C that comes too early, as in ex. 3b, the wholeness of A–B–(S) will be entirely abolished. In the case of ex. 3a this wholeness is affected in a different way. It can no longer be at once destroyed since, indeed, C=(S) corresponds to the appropriate place in the completion. And yet, with the event C the threshold to a greater discrimination is crossed, robbing the process A–B–(S)=C of its closure to make it a part of a larger process. The discrimination that has attached C to itself brings along with it a new potential limit (S'), and indeed C–(S') can be either equal to A–B (ex. 4a) or equal to A–C (ex. 4b).

If, therefore, the wholeness of A–B–(S) is not to be broken, the potential limit (S) must not be realized, either in actuality or in the imagination. . . .

An uninterrupted whole made up of two discriminations of equal duration and determined by two events and a potential limit we shall call a "*rhythmic pair*" or also, simply, a "pair". (Neumann 1959, pp. 18–19)

Again, in Neumann's separation of rhythm and meter the given equality of the two durations is itself a purely rhythmic phenomenon (*innere Zeit*) upon which the possibility for a quantitative comparison or measure (*äußere Zeit*) is based. In this way, the givenness of equality logically (if not temporally) precedes measurement. And although Neumann does not offer any suggestions as to why there should be a promise of equality in the emergence of a potential boundary (S), he does offer a psychological and temporal account of the process that unites the pair—a

process that generates a temporal and rhythmic *content*. The extensive, point-delimited container is filled with expectation and recollection, future and past. If it is also filled with "time," this time is merely time as quantity—extrinsic or outer time, the time that is measured. In Neumann's conception (and Hauptmann's as well) there can perhaps be found traces of Goethe's anti-Newtonian sentiments; however, Neumann, in granting the reality of absolute "outer" time, recognizes two opposed principles with no possibility for sublimation.

Neumann's illustration of the process through which the content of the "rhythmic pair" is formed can be seen in a comparison of example 8.1 with example 8.2 (Neumann's example 5 in which the three vertical lines correspond to A, B, and (S) in his example 2):

Now further, in order to experience the temporal *content* of the rhythmic pair it is necessary that we set out and traverse the pair as a closed event that is surveyed in advance. Here two opposed qualities are revealed to us with some clarity. Namely, on the way from A to B temporal consciousness is directed predominantly toward the future, toward the arrival of B. This state we will label as *expectation* [*Erwartung*]. From B to (S), however, the direction of our attention is reversed; consciousness glances back toward the past stretch A–B and avoids any thoughts of the coming potential limit (S) in order that the wholeness of the pair not be disturbed. This state we will label *recollection* [*Erinnerung*], and expectation and recollection form complementary qualities whose order may not be reversed without destroying wholeness. It lies in the nature of expectation that it *intensifies* with the growth of duration, and in the nature of recollection that it *dies away*.

EXAMPLE 8.2 Friedrich Neumann, *Die Zeitgestalt,* example 5, p. 3, Beispielband

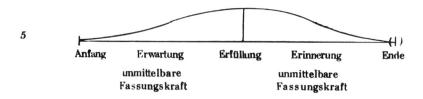

Besides expectation and recollection, the power of direct comprehension [*unmittelbare Fassungskraft*] is also still active, and upon this rests, above all, the ability for time-comparison. The first discrimination, filled with expectation, will be taken up by direct comprehension. At the beginning of the second discrimination a new act of direct comprehension enters; simultaneously, attentiveness springs back recollecting the beginning of the first discrimination and leaves this discrimination once more to elapse as a temporal *measure for comparison.* . . .

With regard to expectation and recollection, the time-points which delimit and articulate the rhythmic pair further obtain a special meaning. The first discrimination becomes *beginning* from which there follows a mounting *expectation* as the content of the first discrimination; expectation *endures,* indeed, *over-endures* with all its might until its goal, *fulfillment* [*Erfüllung*], takes place; and this in turn forms a transition, as a boundary between both discriminations, to *recollection;* recollection, however, *crumbles away,* as it were, before its *end* [*Ende*], in the form of the potential limit, is reached (ex. 5). Already here we point toward the difference between the unconscious end and the conscious conclusion. (Neumann 1959, pp. 19–20)

I should explain here that *conclusion (Schluß)* is a perceptible part of an event—a discrimination that comprises the last part, or the beginning of the end. Discrimination (*Aufmerkung*) is directed solely toward beginning, which is identified with *being.* The beginning of discrimination is active and clear and corresponds to wakefulness and consciousness. End is *nonbeing*—passive and diffuse, it corresponds to sleep (or timelessness) and to the loss of consciousness. For this reason, in his example 5 Neumann encloses end in parentheses, for it is nothing to be experienced. Similarly, he writes in connection with the temporal whole A–B–(S) shown in his

example 2 (see our example 8.1) that the potential limit (S) "must to some extent remain unconscious; indeed, consciousness itself must actually be for a moment extinguished and be submerged in the subconscious in order for the rounding-off of the duration to be completed."

Neumann's conception of "content" is in certain respects reminiscent of Riemann's, though it is more clearly and systematically formulated. Neumann's time-span (*Zeitintervall*), delimited by time-points, is itself empty—it is a container. But Neumann does not say that its content is one of duration, of objects (tones for example), or of sensible qualities. Contrasts of sensible quality provide points of beginning and end for *Aufmerkung,* but such discontinuities cannot account for our spanning of time. For Neumann, the time-span is filled with the activity of recollection and expectation. The particular course of recollection and expectation is the time-span's content; and since recollection and expectation are active and dynamic, content is active and dynamic and, thus, intrinsically rhythmic. The time-span also contains *time,* "absolute" time that can be measured. But this, again, is "outer," "external," extensive, or spatialized time—the time of meter (*Zeitmaß*), which is opposed to an "inner" and purely temporal, rhythmic time of *Zeitgestalt.*

The rhythmic pair is not a metric pair; it is not derived from nor does it know of quantitative measure (though through the agency of properly rhythmic qualities a comparison of quantity can be made). This freedom from quantitative determination allows the pair to be interpreted as a scheme for a great variety of rhythmic formations and, as we saw in chapter 3, permits Neumann to detach "rhythmic weight," as a property derived from temporal phases of attention, from metrical accent as a graduated

EXAMPLE 8.3 Friedrich Neumann, *Die Zeitgestalt*, examples 29–32, p. 7, Beispielband

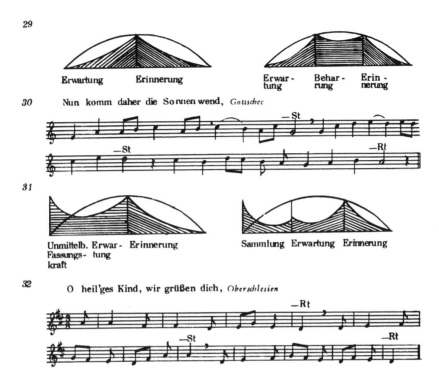

ordering of stresses. And although the pair functions as the elementary *Urphänomen* that first reveals the basic rhythmic qualities of expectation and recollection, Neumann does not find it necessary to reduce other formations to an underlying *Paarigkeit*. Rather, by expanding the catalog of rhythmic qualities Neumann is able to describe three- or five-part schemes and variations within the two-part scheme as fully particular *Zeitgestalten*. Neumann's rhythmic distinctions are manifold and intricate, and there is no need to pursue them here. However, I would like to reproduce his diagrams contrasting duple and triple forms, in part to show the considerable difference between this interpretation of triple "rhythm" and Hauptmann's triple meter. Although the distinctions shown in his examples 29 and 31 (see our example 8.3) could presumably be applied to beats of a barred measure, Neumann, here and throughout this study, is concerned with "time shapes" that encompass many bars. The rhythmic shapes of duple and triple are not limited to a single form, nor is any

single representation capable of describing the complex interaction of rhythmic qualities. In his illustrations of the contents of triple *rhythm* (examples 30 and 32) Neumann takes "harmonic" or tonal organization as the primary determinant of shape. He begins by contrasting triple with duple (the "rhythmic pair") represented by an arc constituted of rising expectation [*Erwartung*] and waning remembrance [*Erinnerung*]:

In the triple-time scheme this arc is divided into three equal parts and yields three contents, namely: *expectation* in the first part; an expectation that is in part realized and consequently diminished, joined with a beginning recollection in the second part—this state we will call *persistence* [*Beharrung*]; finally, in the third part after all expectation is realized there is exclusively *recollection*.

Here the concluding notes take the form of tension-tones [*Spannungstöne*, -St] at the end of the first and second segments, and resting tone [*Ruheton*, -Rt] at the end. Example 30 serves as an illustration.

We should however also call attention to the

fact that every expectation arises from direct comprehension. Thus, the first part of the rhythmic pair comprises, intersecting with one another, a direct comprehension that dies away and a growing expectation. Represented graphically, the rhythmic pair appears as is shown in example 31. The three-part form then yields the following contents:

In the first part, the waning direct comprehension crosses over into a slowly rising expectation—this state we will call *accumulation* [or concentration, *Sammlung*]; in the second part *expectation*; in the third part *recollection*.

In respect to harmony the resting tone corresponds to the state of accumulation; thus the cadential tones of this type of three-part scheme are -Rt, -St, -Rt (ex. 32). (Neumann 1959, p. 33)

Although Neumann describes the process through which a rhythmic pair (or a rhythmic "triple") might become unified as a "higher order" discrimination, he does not consider the process through which equality is produced and removes the phenomenon that I have called projection from meter in order to characterize an exclusively rhythmic order that in many respects resembles Riemann's dynamic, "organic" model.

By contrast, Hauptmann is concerned with the process whereby determinate duration and equality are created and proposes a theory in which meter, quite apart from rhythm, is regarded as a dynamic, organic phenomenon arising from an innate human disposition for equal measure. Our measuring is not an act applied to given units of duration as a counting or a comparison. It is, rather, a feeling of measure in the creation of equality. Here equality emerges or becomes. Metrical formation is, Hauptmann says, the "product that originates from an evolution of a first beat [*Zeit*] established as a beginning." The elementary unity is again the pair, but a pair that is conceived as a unity of measuring and measured beats. And yet, although there is process in the formation of the pair, this process does not extend beyond the pair. Pairs as elementary unities and as products become for Hauptmann givens for combination in the construction of metrical types that order a properly rhythmic content. For this reason, Riemann could with some justice criticize Hauptmann's theory as an abstract and schematic reduction in which the particularity and dynamism of *Takt* are suppressed.

EXAMPLE 8.4 Moritz Hauptmann, *Die Natur der Harmonik und der Metrik,* p. 212

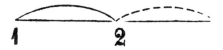

In many respects, my account of projection at the beginning of the previous chapter resembles Hauptmann's analysis of the formation of duple meter. Hauptmann starts from the same observation: that with the beginning of a second sound and from this beginning, there can be heard a reproduction (*Abbild*) of the duration spanning the two beginnings (*Bild*). The result of this process is not simply an addition of two durations, but rather a complex and irreducible unity, *die metrische Einheit*:

If *one* impulse cannot determine a space of time or a definite length of time, but rather only a beginning without end, we do obtain a temporally determinate *whole* with two immediately successive impulses, in which the interval enclosed by the two impulses is the *half*. The first metrical determination is not simple but duple, a repeated time-interval. [See example 8.4.]

These two impulses comprise only *one* extent of time. But with these two impulses we obtain not one but two determinate beats. With the second impulse, with the end of the enclosed space of time, there is given at the same time the beginning of a second which is equal in duration to the first. At the end of this beat we can expect a new impulse which, if it is not to give rise to an interruption, a cutting short of the time that is determined by the two impulses, may not follow earlier than this end-point.

A simple duration is not a metrical unity and cannot emerge as a metrical whole. A simple has meaning for a metrical determination only as a part of the whole, as a *first* for a *second*; for the metrical whole is from its first determination an inseparable double, a unity of two [*eine Zwei-Einheit*]. (Hauptmann 1873, pp. 211–212)

The two phases I have called projective and projected Hauptmann calls *Bestimmende* (determinative) and *Bestimmte* (determined): "A first time-phase, since it is metrically always a first for a second which can be equal to it, is for its second the *determinative*. This second is the *determined*. The first compared with the second has the energy of beginning and therefore the metrical *accent*" (Hauptmann 1873, p. 228).

Because Hauptmann analyzes the phenomenon of meter as a process, he is able to avoid a reification of metrical units as objects that are given for the operations of multiplication and division. In this respect, Hauptmann's theory of meter is radically different from traditional theories:

> It is clear from the preceding remarks that metrical organization does not consist in the division of a given whole, even less should we imagine the whole to be a joining together of units as a multiplicity: metrical formation is always only the product that arises from the evolution of a first beat established as a beginning, and all manifold formation can here issue first of all only from this simple antithesis of that which is established as a unity, i.e., from its duplication. (Hauptmann 1873, p. 225)

What Hauptmann does, nevertheless, reify is the pair first/second (*Vorbild/Abbild, Klang/Nachklang*) or the single *metrische (Zwei-) Einheit* as a product—a closed unit in which the first is necessarily accented in relation to the second. While there is process in the formation of this unity, the unit, once formed, is a given into which all metrical formations or measures are resolved, and meter is viewed as a series of measures that mete out time and thus provide measure for the freedom of rhythm:

> We shall call the constant measure according to which the measurement of time is carried out, *meter*; the kind of motion in this measure, *rhythm*.
>   This measure, according to its external character, results in *two-*, *three-*, or *four-*part unities; motion in the measure, which itself can be of endless multiplicity, will, as measured, find its intelligibility only in regulation, an intelligibility that results from the metrical conception. (Hauptmann 1873, p. 211)

For Hauptmann, meter is prior to rhythm as an order that limits an otherwise anarchic freedom. And this law is expressed in the recursive

EXAMPLE 8.5 Moritz Hauptmann, *Die Natur der Harmonik und der Metrik*, p. 228

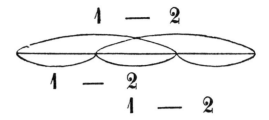

application of the process of unification that results in two-, three-, and four-beat units—measures that, prior to the complications of rhythm, are always composed of a real succession of equal units produced by successive metrical accents. Thus, all instances of triple meter, for example, derive from the underlying superimposition of pairs, as can be seen from Hauptmann's diagramatic representation shown in our example 8.5. Here, the third beat can only be a copy (*Abbild*) of the second beat as model (*Vorbild*). And because the primitive metrical unity, as product, is hypostatized as a *Zwei- Einheit*, triplicity must be viewed as an overlapping of two unities (as a "higher order" of metrical formation), each of which retains its accentual form. As a result, the first two beats are accented and the third is unaccented. To distinguish between the accents of the first two beats, Hauptmann suggests that since the second beat is accented as a member of the second (and, hence, unaccented) unity of a higher order, the second beat suffers a degradation in accent:

> Accordingly, the second third in triple meter receives the accent that belongs to it as the first beat in a metrical pair of a lower order. This accent it has in equal strength to the first third. However, the first third carries an accent of higher order: that of the first of the *pair*; and it is this accent which allows the first beat of the triple measure to stand out as the primary stress. (Hauptmann 1873, p. 230)

Likewise, larger, more complex formations arise as the pairs themselves are accented as a single "determinative" duration:

> Together with this determination of accent [that of the simple metrical pair], which concerns the

parts only in regard to the pairs they form, there enters another, higher order in the joining of pairs, namely a determination of accent for the pair itself. Just as everything that would be brought together in the conception of a unitary succession can have only *one* beginning, *one* first rather than a repeated, reiterated beginning or first; thus, for every order of metrical formation, one part will be the first and what follows will be the equal other part. And if the formation should be carried farther, these two parts can again be joined to form a first part for an equal second part. (Hauptmann 1873, pp. 229–230)

In Hauptmann's view, priority is given to the simple pairs. Although the lower and higher orders might be understood as arising in some sense simultaneously, the determination of accent for the lower order constituents precedes the formation of higher order unities and the determination of their accentual structure. Hauptmann proposes this priority in order to establish a hierarchy of accent, for it is a determination of accent and not a determination of duration that is the goal of Hauptmann's process of metrical formation. And it is the scheme of accents, what Hauptmann calls meter's "form," that provides order for the fluid and intrinsically formless rhythmic content:

> Metrical form is a rigid skeleton, the bones upon which the body, wherein life resides, is shaped in rounded and, in themselves, unbroken forms which cannot do without this solid support— forms which themselves however do not reveal, or reveal only in veiled, softened semblances, definite outlines. (Hauptmann 1873, p. 343)

But by assimilating meter to a fixed scheme of accent, Hauptmann relinquishes the dynamic and more clearly temporal interpretation he accorded the original pair. Furthermore, this turn can easily lead to an understanding of meter that closely resembles the theories that he sets out to circumvent. Theodor Wiehmayer, Hauptmann's successor and apologist, follows this path, finally to reaffirm the operations of multiplication and division. Commenting on Hauptmann's theory of metrical formation and metrical form, Wiehmayer writes:

> The study of meter is now placed on solid footing. We know that the scheme of metrical stress represents a *fixed framework*, an *invariant artistic measure* arising from a feeling for order and symmetry which, *without regard to musical content*, produces for all sequences of equal durations the same determination of accent. Upon this fixed order the musical content can unfold in full freedom . . .
>
> Since the metrical division always begins with a stressed value, all metrical groups are *falling*. The metrical measuring thus knows no development. It permits only the *unification* of two or three groups in a single group of a higher order and, correspondingly, the *resolution* of the measuring unit, or the single beat, into metrical time-divisions. (Wiehmayer 1926, pp. 451–452)

In attempting to develop a theory of meter as projection, I shall have to address many of the issues that Hauptmann raises in the exposition of his theory. My solutions vis-à-vis Hauptmann involve, among others, the following assumptions: that there is no separation of rhythm and meter—there is simply metrical rhythm (and also nonmetrical rhythm)—that reproduction does not necessarily involve accent as a distinction between strong and weak beats, and that meter need not be reduced to a uniform succession of equal pulses or beats.

NINE

Some Traditional Questions of Meter Approached from the Perspective of Projective Process

Accent

Since projection has been described without invoking the distinction between strong and weak beats, the equation of projection and meter carries the implication that the existence of meter precedes or is not necessarily dependent upon this distinction—that there could be meter without there being a distinction between strong and weak. Although such a conception departs from most recent definitions of meter, I will argue that meter can profitably be regarded as something that is, in a sense, prior to the metrical distinction between strong and weak (a sense of "prior" I will clarify).

Later I will specifically engage the problems posed by projections that involve a triple or unequal grouping of equal durations. But for now I would like to consider only duple or equal metrical groupings. The difficulties presented by triple meter arise from a privileging of *Paarigkeit*. Such a privileging is, I think, justified, but not on the grounds of a metrical unity composed of weak and strong beats. From the standpoint of projection, there is a privileging of immediate succession, and immediate succession can involve only two terms. But projection does not require that the projective and the projected durations stand in the relation of strong and weak.

In example 9.1 I have indicated two projec-tions—the potential for a third projection is not realized because there is no beginning of a fourth sound. If the tempo is slow and we attend to three beginnings, it should be possible to hear three "beats" without feeling the distinction strong/weak. The tempo here must be slow, but not so slow that the three durations become mensurally indeterminate.

To hear three "ungrouped" beats here may require some effort, but I think this can be accomplished by focusing our attention on three beginnings or by attempting to hear the beginning of B, for example, as a starting over again rather than as the beginning of a duration that continues a duration begun with A. The question here is not whether this is a common or easily accomplished perception—clearly, it is neither. Instead, the question is whether such a perception is at all possible; and I think that patient introspection will show that it is. If we are successful in this exercise we will have heard three "strong" or accented beats. But if the word "accent" refers to a distinction or difference among beats, as a contrast to "unaccent," there can be no accents here—all three beats are equally accented.

To make a distinction between accent and "unaccent," we could say that the beginning of each sound is accented and the rest of the sound is unaccented. Clearly, if beginning is regarded as a durationless instant, this statement will make

EXAMPLE 9.1 Successive projective beginnings

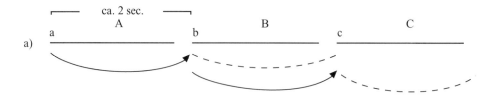

little sense—if beginning is something that can be distinguished from the sound and separated from the sound's duration, accent in this case could not be perceived and regarded as a psycho-acoustic attribute. A solution is to regard accent as beginning, but not to detach beginning from the event begun. We could then concur with Hauptmann that metrical accent is the accent of beginning—*die Energie des Anfanges*, that "energy" being an active, creative potential for duration.

What, then, would constitute a weak beat or "unaccent"? It could, I think, be said that any articulation or any possibility for articulation within the promised duration of the event begun would be "unaccent," or not the beginning of the event. If there is a new beginning and this beginning does not end the prior beginning's potential for the creation of a mensurally determinate duration—if the earlier beginning is still "present" and active—this new event will be unaccented or "not-beginning" in relation to the larger event that has already begun and continues to be in the process of becoming. Thus, the new beginning functions as continuation, much like the unarticulated continuation that precedes and follows it, except that this continuation is a definite decision—a decision for a new becoming that will participate in the becoming of an event previously begun. Such a possibility is represented in example 9.2.

EXAMPLE 9.2 Beginning
and continuation of a
duration

In this example I have introduced two new symbols: | and \. The vertical line labels beginning. Three beginnings are identified here: the beginnings of two quarter-note durations and the beginning of a duration that is two quarter notes long. The slanted line labels continuation of a special sort. During the progress of this measure there is always continuation, but with the beginning of the second beat there is a definite *decision* to continue—that is, a decision not to end or a decision against making a new beginning that would make the first beginning past or inactive. There is, nevertheless, a new beginning—one that creates a first beat and a second. Now that there are two beats, each beat necessarily has a beginning. And now that there *is* a first beat, *it* is past. This first beat, since it has become, always had this beginning in the sense that only when there is an actual first beat is there this particular beginning of this beat and this (now completed) realization of a beginning's potential for duration. However, there is also a beginning whose potential for duration has not been realized and which will be the beginning of a definite, completed duration only when silence begins. The second beat begins as a projection of the duration of the first beat, and while it is present there is a potential for the projected duration to be realized. When this potential becomes actual the second beat will be past, and the half-note duration of the measure will be past. The particularly felt durational equality of the two actual beats is a product of projection, and the felt duration of the half-note measure is conditioned by the entire process of projection. To make a distinction among these various beginnings, I will sometimes call the beginning of the larger measure, as distinct from the beginning of the first beat, the "dominant" beginning—a beginning that remains active when the beginning of the first beat is past and inactive.

The symbols | and \ might be taken to stand for strong and weak, in which case we could just as well use the traditional symbols ¯ and ˘. However, there is a distinction here that justifies the introduction of new symbols. The vertical line in conjunction with a slanted line does not refer to the first (accented or strong) beat. Instead, it refers to the entire duration, or rather to the entire becoming of a duration that in this case includes two beats. If there were only two "things"—a first and a second beat—we might adequately describe the situation simply as a binary opposition of strong and weak beats, the first beat being strong or accented in relation to the second weak or unaccented beat.

As properties possessed by the beats, "strong" and "weak" are traditionally viewed as external relations. However, I argue that our feeling of strong and weak arises from internal relationships. There is no first beat (strong or otherwise) until the new beginning with a second beat makes a first *now* or "presently" past, and there is no metrically weak beat apart from its function of continuing a duration already begun. The decision to label the second beat \ rather than | is not made by comparing two given beats; it is made in response to a feeling that this articulation continues a process initiated with the beginning of the first sound, and that with the second sound the duration previously begun is still present, active, and expanding. Two equal beats are not given at the outset; they are formed through a process that itself generates the metrical qualities we call strong and weak (or beginning and continuation), and these qualities cannot be added to the products or detached from the process. When the event is completed there are, in fact, two equal durations in the relation strong/weak, but for there to be such a relationship the two durations must be united under the perspective of a single beginning, a process Koch called *Vereinigung unter einem Gesichtspunkt.*

The tradition that regards the qualities "strong" and "weak" as external relations is that of accentual theories, and I think it is fair to say that these theories have not produced very satisfying accounts of musical meter. The tradition that these theories gradually succeeded in replacing regarded metrical quality as *quantitas intrinsica.* In this view, meter is not caused by accent; rather,

meter is a condition for a distinction in feeling. This distinction has been called the difference between accented and unaccented, strong and weak, heavy and light, good and bad, or even long and short. Wolfgang Caspar Printz, for example, refers to the difference between long and short:

> Further, the position in the measure has a particular power and virtue which cause notes equal to one another, according to the time signature, to seem [somewhat] longer or [somewhat] shorter. . . .
>
> The apparent different length of notes that are equal according to their time or value is called *Quantitas Temporalis Intrinsica,* or the inner duration. . . .
>
> To know these quantities correctly, one must know that every note is divided into either two or three like parts.
>
> If the subdivisions of notes are duple, all odd numbered notes 1, 3, 5, 7, etc. are considered long and all even numbered notes 2, 4, 6, 8, etc. are considered short. . . .
>
> I explain here that every semibrevis or entire *Tactus,* according to the inner quantity, is also long because it is figured with an odd number, one, since this number always begins on the downbeat of a measure.
>
> Also each and every syncopated note is long because the odd and even numbers are mingled together and mixed in it.
>
> If the subdivisions (of a note) are three in number, the first is long and the second and third are short.
>
> When the first part is silent, the second is long and the third is short. (Printz 1696, p. 18, as translated by Houle 1987, p. 80)

We will return to several of Printz's observations later. Here I would note that although the ascription of *length* to an accented or "stressed" beat derives from the terminology of classical prosody, this ascription of greater length to the first of two notes acknowledged to be equal in length may be more than purely metaphorical—it may, in fact, be supported by a real distinction in feeling. Thus, for example, in a duple measure consisting of two equal beats, the reader should find it possible to imagine a "longer" first beat because the beginning of the whole duration (which Printz views as itself intrinsically long) coincides with the beginning of the first beat.

EXAMPLE 9.3 Complex projection
R (Q–Q')–R'

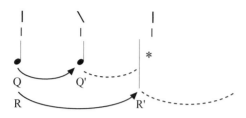

Similarly, the second beat may seem shorter be-cause continuation is necessarily shorter than what is continued.

The potential for a half-note projection in example 9.2 is not realized. In example 9.3 it is. The asterisk in example 9.3 represents the be-ginning of a projected duration. The duration of the sound here begun is unspecified except to say that it is very short. The reason I use an as-terisk is to avoid having to choose a specific note value. To the degree the two beats of the first measure are unified as a single determinate dura-tion, the projected duration begun with * can be spontaneously realized in the absence of a con-tinuous sound. And by making this new sound-ing duration very short, we can test the determi-nacy or strength of the projection. It should be noted here that continuation, or, in this case, the formation of two beats, enhances or keeps alive the larger projective potential. Thus, in example 9.3 if the tempo is relatively slow (say, quarter note at M.M.60), the projected potential R' would be less determinate if this first measure contained only a single sound rather than two equal beats.

If, as Yeston (1976) suggests, meter is the in-teraction of at least two pulse "strata" whereby the slower pulses group the faster pulses, exam-ples 9.1 and 9.2 are nonmetrical. If meter is the alternation of weak and strong beats, example 9.1 is nonmetrical. However, examples 9.1 and 9.2 both involve projection, and by equating meter and projection I mean to call both metri-cal. Here I follow Matteson and also William Benjamin (1984), who grants metrical status to a series of equal but "ungrouped" pulses (but not Neumann, for whom an "irregular" succession is also metrical). Certainly, in most musical con-texts we will not encounter anything resembling

example 9.1. And even in situations where pulses are relatively homogeneous, we will spontane-ously group them by hearing distinctions of strong and weak (if the tempo is not too slow). Certainly, too, without feeling the distinction strong/weak we will not feel "duple meter."

Such "marked" beats are the products of meter and, as products, can be effectively used to describe metrical phenomena. However, meter, temporally conceived, is also process—a process in which potentiality and becoming are constitu-tive of events. The language and logic of products will tend toward a "substantialist" view of meter in which beats are regarded as fixed *things* (Koch's *Gegenstände* and Sulzer's *Sachen*, for example) that possess properties—among others, the property of accent. The properties do not constitute the things, but are attached to them—that is, the re-lations of things are the relations of their proper-ties and do not alter the things themselves.

From a perspective of process, however, *events* are intrinsically relational and are constituted by relationship. From this perspective, we can still speak of products—the realization of potential, the determinacy of the past—but such products cannot be understood as independent entities or things that can exist apart from an evolution that continually creates new relevancies. And it is in order to approach meter as process that I have proposed the notion of projection—a concept that requires creativity and that encompasses fu-ture, past, and present, potentiality and actuality.

Thus, in example 9.2 there are not two beats with the qualities accented and unaccented apart from a projection that involves the creative po-tential of beginning. From this perspective, the question of whether meter arises from the divi-sion of a given unit or the multiplication of a given unit (or the coordination of discrete strata) does not arise. From this perspective, units are not given—they are created under the pressure of antecedent events and are creative for present and future events.

If metrical accent is the distinction of begin-ning, in example 9.4 B is weak or unaccented as a continuation of the duration C. If we view A and B as objects, we could say that A is ac-cented and B is unaccented. But from this per-spective, how does the relation accent-unaccent arise? B is a cause of there *being* an A—because B begins, A is past and its duration is deter-

EXAMPLE 9.4 Metrical accent represented as process

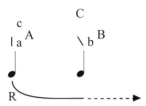

mined. However, B does not cause A to begin. What becomes A was accented from the beginning; if B were not continuation (as in example 9.1), A would still be accented. Nor is A a cause of B's being unaccented—B is unaccented because its beginning is denied as a beginning that would end the duration begun with c. There is a distinction between strong and weak because the simultaneous decision to end A and begin B does not deny a projective potential R and because this decision does not end the potential for duration promised with c. It is because of this "priority" of c and R that I said projection can be understood to precede, both temporally and logically, the distinction strong/weak.

Division

Now let us consider several instances of projection within one of the phases of a greater projection. Of the many issues that arise from such projective complexity, only three will concern us in this section: (1) the subordination of smaller projective potentials to the larger (or dominant) potential they help constitute; (2) the distinction between "open" and "closed" projective types; and (3) the possibility of interpreting division as acceleration. We will return to the first of these topics in the following chapter when we consider the reproduction of projective complexity. The remaining two topics will be discussed in greater detail when we turn to the question of projective types in chapter 13. A discussion of acceleration at the end of this section will also

serve to introduce a pattern that will be the focus of our investigation of types in chapter 13.

But before we consider these topics, it may be helpful to discuss the notation of our examples. Since note values are now being used to represent durations, I should explain how these representations are to be interpreted. I have not employed meter signatures, since these symbols refer to possible events and possible durations rather than to the actual durations that compose a measure. Thus, 4/4 may contain four quarter notes or two half notes, and it is not, in all cases, necessary to imagine that the half notes represent or "stand for" two quarters or that two quarters are actually felt. For now, I will use bar lines to mark beginnings that do not also function as continuations (or, more accurately, beginnings that are not regarded as continuations from the perspective of the event whose becoming we are interested in). In order to feel these as "dominant" beginnings or beginnings that do not also function as projective continuations, the reader may wish to supply a dynamic accent. But a dynamic accent is not necessary for feeling a beginning—we can simply choose to hear a new event and a new beginning. Thus, if we choose to do so we can hear a second half note as continuation even if it is considerably louder than the first. And although the bar lines in these examples indicate measures, I ask the reader to understand "measure" in a more general sense than is customary—as a word that can refer to a variety of metrical or projective durations. A measure that corresponds to the notated bar I shall call a "bar measure." But since "measure" here means "a measure *for*," or a more or less determinate projective potential, I shall use the term also to refer to durational determinacies that do not correspond to the notated bar. Thus, we will often have occasion to speak of larger and smaller measures (e.g., a "two-bar measure" or a "half-note measure"); and when we turn to more properly "musical" examples we will frequently encounter situations in which bar lines do not indicate measures.[1]

The decision to group beats metrically is a

---

1. The confusion of projective or measured duration with the objects of conventional notation has been a powerful factor in obscuring the creativity, spontaneity, and complexity of meter. Fortunately, the terms "bar" and "measure" present us with a helpful distinction. Since "bar" clearly refers to a notational device (which

decision to regard new beginnings as continuations and expansions of a presently emerging (and "reproducible") durational quantity. Crucial for such a decision is the length of the beats involved. No metrical grouping will occur if the total duration becomes mensurally indeterminate. However, since this determinacy admits of degrees and is tied to context, and because each of the examples that will be presented here is contextually unique, the relation of "objective" duration (i.e., duration measured by the clock or metronome) to determinacy and to the coherence of the group will vary from case to case and from listener to listener. For this reason I will leave it to the reader to choose an appropriate tempo. However, I suggest that in most of these examples the quarter note be taken at a metronome marking of about 76. This duration seems to function as a comfortable span for purposes of grouping and lies toward the shorter, more easily graspable end of the scale of durations for pulses or simple (noncomposite, unmodulated) events that can function projectively—a scale that seems to run from about 0.2 second to about 2 seconds.[2]

In example 9.5 several projections are indicated. In example 9.5a the second half-note duration in the projection Q–Q' is interpreted as continuation, and within this continuation there is a projection R–R'. The question I would now like to consider is whether the projective potentials T and U shown in example 9.5b are realized. Or to put the question more generally, can continuations engender projective potentials that are independent of the dominant projective potential? Strictly speaking, the answer is no. To support this judgment I will approach the question first from a systematic and then from an empirical perspective.

I have defined projection as a process that involves two beginnings. It follows, then, that a continuation cannot be projective for a beginning and that a beginning cannot be projective for a continuation. This latter formulation will seem puzzling only if it is thought that the labels "beginning" and "continuation" (| and \ ) refer to two *parts* of a measure—an accented and an unaccented part. But it should be remembered that the theory of projection is not an accentual-extensive theory. Thus, in example 9.5a the beginning of the first *bar measure* is not the beginning of the first *half-note measure*, and it is the first half-note duration (Q) that is projective for the second half-note duration. For the realized first half note, the beginning of a second half note is a second beginning, a beginning again. For the beginning of the bar measure—the beginning regarded as "dominant" here—the second half note functions as continuation. Likewise, the second quarter note functions as a continuation of the duration begun with (and now promised by) the second sound. The second quarter note is also a continuation of the duration of the bar measure, which now has a very definite durational potential.

Note, however, that the projection U–U' in example 9.5b can be realized only if the beginning of the second half-note duration (b) is regarded not as continuation, but solely as beginning, thus denying the relevance of the dominant beginning (a); and in this case, the beginning * will not be a second beginning but, rather, a third beginning. Such a denial is not, I think, entirely out of the question—U is a real potential, and its

---

may or may not mark a projective duration), the term "measure" may be reserved to refer to any duration that can function projectively (whether or not this duration corresponds to a notated bar). It will often be convenient to refer to notated objects when identifying measures—for example, a bar measure, a two-bar measure, a dotted half-note measure—but, as we shall see in the following chapter, such labels should be used in full awareness of their abstraction from durational complexity and particularity.

2. Given the variety and particularity of experience, such limits are, of course, quite arbitrary. An upper limit of about two seconds has been found in our ability to in-

tegrate successive pulses whereby the intervening silence is in a sense "filled" with a palpable durational quantity (see Fraisse 1956, p. 41). The lower limit for projective activity is much more difficult to gauge. Certainly, projective distinctions can be felt in durations shorter than two-tenths of a second, but we will not have occasion to consider such fine-grained perceptions in the present study. Incidentally, my suggestion for a metronome marking of 76 for a pulse corresponds roughly to the range of the "indifference point"—an interval of about three-quarters of a second postulated as a sort of optimal span for reaction to a stimulus. For a thoughtful and historically astute summary of pertinent psychological research, see Fraisse 1963, pp. 116–135.

EXAMPLE 9.5 Projective boundaries

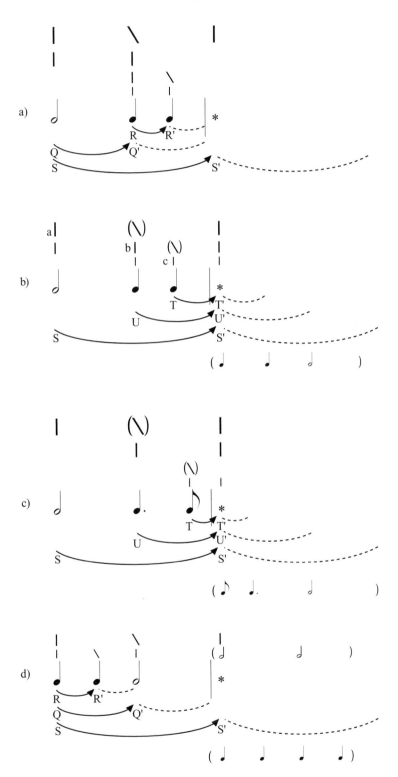

realization will depend on how we attend to these events. If our interest lies with the projective potential S, we will not be inclined to focus on a projective potential U, but rather to focus on a projected potential Q' (in example 9.5a) as a continuation of the potential S. If, however, we are especially interested in what might happen early on in the new event begun with * we might be more inclined to focus on what a U could offer for the becoming of the new event and to withdraw our attention from the relevance of a projective potential S. But we cannot have it fully both ways—one perspective will detract in some measure from the other. The projection U–U' in example 9.5b gives us a higher degree of determinacy—U is mensurally more highly determinate than is S. But this determinacy is purchased at some cost to a feeling of the larger potential, S (and the larger potential for realization, S'). To realize the projective potential T is to suppress to some extent both S–S' and U–U' and to gain information about the immediate future of the duration begun with *.

I have argued that the three projections shown in example 9.5b are incompatible. However, it might be argued that they are fully compatible—that we can have it both, or all three, ways. Thus, if we can hear in the projected S' "virtual divisions" of half-note or quarter-note durations, the projections U–U' and T–T' will have functioned to measure the becoming of S' and will have enhanced the determinacy of the larger projection. (We will not now inquire whether or how vividly such virtual articulations might be felt in a particular case; it matters here only that the possibility for such perceptions be accounted for in a projective interpretation.) If we can feel such virtual divisions in the second measure, it may be argued that such a feeling could arise only because the beginning of a second half-note duration (b) and the beginning of a second quarter-note duration (c) in the first bar created these durations (U and T) for a subsequent reproduction (U' and T'). But if projection were responsible for these virtual articulations, we should expect to find the palindromic division quarter-quarter-half shown in parentheses in example 9.5b, rather than a division of four quarters. And in example 9.5c an eighth-note division (the realization of T') should be

felt. Moreover, projection does not seem to account for the possibility of feeling the quarter-note divisions shown in example 9.5d. Instead of attempting to account for these (possible) feelings of division as products of projection, we might say that they are the products of the relevancy of what has occurred in the first completed bar measure for the becoming of a second measure. If the first measure presented half and quarter as continuations and the second measure promises a reproduction of the first measure's duration, there is now a definite possibility for the realization of S' to involve half and quarter continuations. These smaller durations are our only clues for action that might be taken in the process of S's realization, and if we have difficulty "holding onto" a projected potential S', we can use the smaller, more highly determinate durations to enhance our feeling of continuation as a realization of projected potential.

In the case of example 9.5c it may even be possible to feel eighth-note continuations beginning with * if we are for any reason especially interested in the possibility for such continuations. But without this expectation there seems little reason to focus our attention on such small durations. And in any case, the duration of an eighth note at moderate or fast tempi gives us little time to act and too little time if large motor groups are to be involved. On the other hand, the duration of a half note does give us ample time to act. In general, larger durations are potentials for action and smaller durations are opportunities for gaining accuracy in prediction. And what counts as large or small depends on our aims or the action we intend. Thus, the virtual half note shown in the second bar measure of example 9.5d may be interpreted either as a potential for action or as an enhancement of projective potential that strengthens our feeling of how long the second bar measure is likely to last, or when we could expect a third bar—how much time we have to complete an action or when we might act and how much time we have to prepare.

In example 9.5a the projection Q–Q' creates a definite first half-note duration and a definite potential for a second half note. With the beginning of the second sound as continuation, the completion of a measure is promised and a beginning of a second measure can be predicted. For this completion or for the potential projection S–S', the quarter-note durations are in a sense superfluous. Although R–R' does enhance the determinacy of Q' and S, the projections Q–Q' and S–S' can be realized without the division of Q'. However, if the quarter notes are not needed to realize the projected potential Q', they do, nevertheless, function to point toward a new beginning, *, and are thus clearly effective in directing our attention toward the second bar measure. If there is no beginning of a second bar measure, we may feel the denial of such a beginning or some incompleteness in the end of the first measure, a denial or incompleteness that we would not feel so strongly if the measure were composed of two half notes. Again, this denial might be identified with the denial of U and T in example 9.5b. But if this were the case, we should, presumably, be able to intensify a feeling of denial by slowing the tempo. Thus, at a tempo of quarter note = M.M.40 it should be easier to hear the beginnings of the second half-note duration (b) and the second quarter-note duration (c) as beginnings detached from their function as continuations—that is, as beginnings detached from the dominance of a beginning a. In fact, the result is quite the opposite: the faster the tempo, the greater will be our expectancy for a second bar measure. It seems that to the degree Q' is mensurally determinate and does not need a definite continuation to be vividly felt, the quarter notes are free to direct our attention toward a new event. If the shorter durations do not leave us time for action within the promised span of a present becoming, they can, nevertheless, help us prepare for future action and enhance the accuracy of our prediction. (We will consider such distinctions in greater detail in the section of this chapter devoted to the topic of anacrusis.)

In example 9.5d the quarter notes also point toward a new event, but here the goal of this pointing is a continuation. In distinction from the quarter notes in example 9.5a, the two quarters in example 9.5d are hardly "superfluous." Here there is no definite projective potential Q' apart from the projection R–R'; nor does the beginning of what will become this event or this complex of events have any definite potential for

duration until there is the beginning of a second sound (the second quarter note). In example 9.5a there is a definite potential Q' and the promise of a definite potential for S before and apart from R–R'. (To say this is not to deny the importance of R–R' in the creation of the projection Q–Q' and the projective potential S.) The first bar measure in example 9.5a might be called "open" since it points toward a new measure; and the first bar measure in example 9.5d might be called "closed" since the pointing is toward continuation or completion. These metrical/rhythmic functions are analogous to the tonal/harmonic functions of opening and closing. A virtually identical distinction is made by Narmour (1990) in his definition of "cumulative" and "countercumulative" durations.

If we are to regard meter as genuinely processive, we must acknowledge in the preceding examples not only heterogeneity, but also real change. In examples 9.5a and 9.5d the functions of opening and closing also involve speeding up and slowing down—in the first measure of 9.5a the attacks get faster, and in 9.5d they get slower. In mechanical terms, in acceleration there is increase of kinetic energy and in deceleration loss. From the standpoint of everyday observation, speeding up is generally a sign that motion is likely to be continued; slowing down generally precedes stopping. We might say that there is an acceleration in example 9.5a simply because quarter notes are faster than half notes. However, I would like to make a distinction between the *increased activity* of division and *acceleration* as a feeling of "the same" but faster. If in example 9.5a we focus our attention on the half-note division, it will, I think, be possible to hear the quarters simply as subdivisions of the half-note pulse. There is more activity in the second half-note duration: attacks are faster. But if our attention is directed toward the slower equality we need not feel an increase of activity as acceleration: the pulse we are attending to does not change speed. Nor, from a mechanical perspective, does the multiplication of standing waves in a system (for example, a string vibrating in one, or two, or four parts) require that energy be added to the system—thus, there will be no increase in kinetic energy.

If acceleration can be viewed as a transforma-

EXAMPLE 9.6 "Nested" repetitions interpreted as acceleration and deceleration

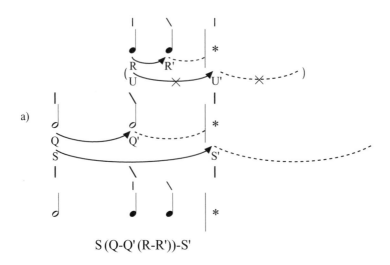

a)

$$S\,(Q\text{-}Q'\,(R\text{-}R'))\text{-}S'$$

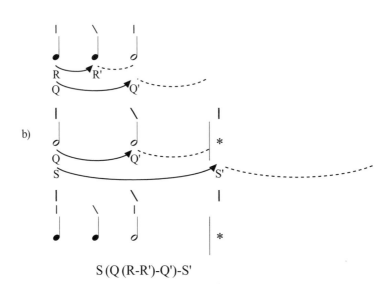

b)

$$S\,(Q\,(R\text{-}R')\text{-}Q')\text{-}S'$$

tion or a change in events that are in some sense regarded as "the same" or of the same kind (and thus invariant as instances of the same kind), we could say that there is acceleration if "the beat" gets faster, or if, in the case of example 9.5a, what counts as a beat changes from half to quarter. For this to happen, we shall have to shift our attention in some degree from the invariance of pulse (two half-note durations) to the invariance of beat (three articulated or "struck" sounds). In terms of projection, this would also imply a shift

from Q–Q' to R–R'. But conceived projectively, such a perception involves two *events* that happen at the same time—the projection R–R' is realized while Q–Q' is being realized. I would now like to ask if it is possible that a feeling of acceleration might be enhanced if we can come to feel not only a faster beat, but also a faster or condensed projection. In the case of example 9.5a, could we interpret R–R' as an accelerated "repetition" of Q–Q'?

Example 9.6a reproduces the pattern shown

in example 9.5a, but here I have separated the two projections graphically, placing the faster one above the slower one. A projection S–S' is indicated, but not a projection U–U' as in example 9.5b. U–U' is excluded because R–R' is here interpreted as continuation—a replication of Q–Q' that takes place in the duration made possible by the "dominant" beginning of the bar measure.

To feel this replication, we shall have to direct our attention simultaneously to both (or all three) projections. This will require some effort. I encourage the reader to attempt this by first performing the two projections separately, hearing one as faster than the other, and then performing the whole as a composite of the two projections. The special effort required to carry this out argues strongly against the likelihood of this interpretation being spontaneously chosen, and even with this effort a feeling of repetition may be elusive.

In example 9.6b a similar interpretation is made of example 9.5d. There is an interesting disparity between examples 9.6a and 9.6b. Again, note that in example 9.6a the projective potential of the two quarter notes is unrealized—the beginning, *, is not a new beginning that would realize a projective potential (U) engendered with the completed quarter-note projection R–R'; indeed, I have argued in connection with example 9.5 that to the degree there is an active potential S in example 9.6a there is no projective potential U. In example 9.6b the projective potential (Q) of the half-note duration comprised of the two quarter notes is realized (in Q'). In this sense there is a clearer match between the faster and the slower components than in example 9.6a. However, I do not suggest that this correspondence makes it easier to hear a replication; in fact, a feeling of replication seems to me more elusive in example 9.6b. Perhaps the reason for this is that in example 9.6b there is no correspondence until the first projection (R–R' or Q–Q') is itself past—become and no longer becoming. Thus, the two events shown in example 9.6b are not simultaneously present or co-present in that the initial, smaller projection is completed before the larger projection. In the case of example 9.6a, the two projections are completed simultaneously.

Although the replications shown in example 9.6 are perceptually quite dubious, it is possible to devise a situation in which two projections are both co-present and more fully congruent. Example 9.7 presents a projective scheme commonly used to create closed units that nevertheless involve a feeling of acceleration. (In chapter 13 an investigation of projective schemata or types will return us to the schema shown in example 9.7 for a more detailed discussion.)

If the beginning of the second bar measure can be felt also as continuation (thus forming a two-bar measure), the two projective complexes S(Q–Q')–S' and T(R–R')–T' will match quite closely. Here the projection R–R' is projective for a continuation T', and the projection T–T' is simultaneously embedded within the continuation S'. Of course, we may hear the quarter notes simply as divisions of a half-note pulse; but I suggest that an attempt to hear acceleration and an attempt also to hear replication are rewarded with some novel intensity of feeling—perhaps a feeling of, among other things, a special directedness toward the last half-note duration, which, as continuation of a continuation, completes the whole.

The scheme represented in example 9.7 is especially useful where a closed unit with some impetus for continuation is called for. Because of its directedness toward the final and relatively late phase of a projection, the figure acquires some "kinetic energy" at its end and for this reason is more suitable for opening rather than closing a composition. And because it is itself closed, the figure usually comprises more than a single bar. In its larger incarnations this scheme can be found, for example, in the units Schoenberg called *Sätze* or "sentences."

A customary example of the sentence, the opening of Beethoven's Piano Sonata in F Minor, op. 2, no. 1 is shown in example 9.8. This is a good example because of the explicit repetitions in bars 5 and 6 of the opening two-bar units. As a result, it is difficult to avoid a feeling of acceleration and to hear bars 5 and 6 simply as another two-bar measure. As continuation, the concluding two-bar unit (bars 7–8) is complicated. The large-scale acceleration has as its aim the beginning of a final two-bar measure as continuation of a second four-bar measure. The two

EXAMPLE 9.7 "Nested" repetition interpreted as acceleration

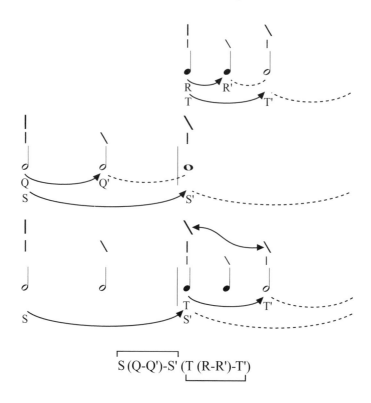

$$S\,(Q\text{-}Q')\text{-}S'\,(T\,(R\text{-}R')\text{-}T')$$

EXAMPLE 9.8 Beethoven, Piano Sonata op. 2/1 in F Minor, first movement, bs. 1–9

offbeats and the change of harmony in bar 7 contribute to a continued acceleration—a replication of the eight-bar pattern, long – long – short – short – long, on the four-bar level. Note also the correspondence of the two melodic ascents: Ab–Bb–C as short-short-long in bars 5–8 replicated in the bass in bars 7–8. The tonal end or goal (dominant harmony, scale degree 7) is greatly delayed. Nevertheless, a tonal goal (or end) is reached with the beginning of measure 7–8—c3 (scale degree 5). This tone, consonant with the final, offbeat E♮, remains a goal throughout the realization of the two-bar measure. And compared to the similar tonal gestures, Ab–F and Bb–G in bars 5 and 6 (and 2 and 4), the completion C–E♮ is slow—comparable, perhaps, to a dissipation of kinetic energy and coupled with a real dissipation of energy in the diminuendo from fortissimo to piano.

Hierarchy

In discussing examples 9.5 and 9.6 I might have simplified matters by invoking the notion of hierarchy and by speaking of quarter-note, half-note, and whole-note "levels." Indeed, my diagrams show levels. In example 9.5a, for instance, symbols for the beginnings of the two quarter-note durations are placed below the symbols for the beginning and continuation of a second half-note duration. And in example 9.7 the "embedded" replications are aligned above the larger projections in which they occur. Such graphic devices are useful representations of simultaneity—thus, in example 9.5a the beginning of the second quarter note is "at the same time" a beginning, a continuation, and a continuation of a continuation. However, the notion of simultaneity or "the same time" is problematic, for there would seem to be different "times" represented by the repetitions of the symbols | and \ if it is remembered that these symbols do not refer to instants.

The hierarchy represented in example 9.5a is a hierarchy of beginnings as potentials for duration. The beginning of the third sound produces a first quarter note as past but does not terminate the potential that was created with the beginning of a second half-note duration. For both quarter notes this is a dominant beginning, just as this beginning is a continuation of a dominant beginning of the bar measure. And since the third sound continues the duration of the bar measure, the beginning of this greater duration is a dominant beginning for the duration of the third sound. The notion of "dominance" comports well with the connotations of the term "hierarchy." But it must also be remembered that the "power" of dominance is derived from dominating and that continuations as denials of beginnings that would end dominance also function to realize the potential (*potentia*) or "power" of the dominant beginning, to keep this becoming alive, and to enhance its mensural determinacy or its projective potential.

From a different perspective, the durations shown in example 9.5a, if they are understood as *products*, can be viewed as components of what might be called an "extensive" hierarchy or a hierarchy of containment. The second half-note duration contains two quarters, and the bar measure contains two half-note durations. But if a half note is the equivalent of two quarters, and if we supply a signature of 4/4, the bar measure must be regarded as containing four quarter-note pulses. Certainly, the first half note could have been subdivided without altering the metrical type, 4/4; but certainly, too, examples 9.9a and 9.9b differ in rhythm.

For one thing, there is no acceleration in example 9.9a; for another, there is actually a quarter-note pulse in 9.9a before there is the beginning of a projected half-note duration, and, thus, in 9.9a we can predict the beginning of a second half-note duration—in 9.9b we cannot. From the standpoint of projection, these differences are rhythmic *and* metrical. From the standpoint of an extensive hierarchy, the difference is one of content (in example 9.9a the first half-note division contains two quarters), and these contents are regarded as products or objects—fully "present" half notes and quarter notes presented in a hierarchical arrangement. Although the arrangement is not a process, the formation of the hierarchy or the formation of hierarchic relations among the objects (or elements) can be interpreted as a process or transformation—a process of analysis or division or a process of synthesis or multiplication.

EXAMPLE 9.9 Metrical difference in two bars of "4/4"

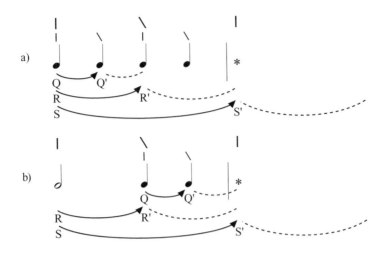

In the tree diagram of "pulse levels" shown in example 9.10a we will read a process of multiplication or synthesis if we proceed from top to bottom (pulse levels C to A—quarter to whole) and a process of division or analysis if we proceed from bottom to top (pulse levels A to C—whole to quarter). The "accent levels" shown in example 9.10 mirror the pulse levels and are produced by the periodic alternation of accent. Here I have indicated accents and "unaccents" using the symbols ´ and ˘. In the pulse levels, moving from top to bottom—or reading from accent to accent—will produce multiplication (in the case of duple meter, 2 × 1). Or, equivalently, multiplication will allow us to proceed to a graphically lower level. Here the accents are necessary agents of transformation since it is only by identifying recurrent accents that we can move to a slower or larger pulse level. That is to say, starting at level C, for example, we must find a next accent to proceed to pulse level B, composed of half notes (2 × 1 quarters). In this sense accents *produce* multiplication. Conversely, if we move from bottom to top, division will produce the accents (by the rule: first half accented—second half unaccented). But here accents are superfluous, in the sense that we do not need accents to divide and to proceed to a "higher" (faster, smaller) level.

These two interpretations of example 9.10a carry temporal implications in the transformations they assert, and by making some of these implications explicit we will better understand the differences between extensive and projective hierarchy. Moving upward presents formation from an atemporal perspective. Here we start from the givenness of the measure's duration—a whole note. For this duration to be given for division, the measure and its formation must be completed and (viewed temporally) past. It is only as completed that the duration is available for analysis or division. And if to be completed is to be past, this duration is past and must be represented for a present analysis or separation into parts. But the present representation can be regarded as identical to the past formation of the measure only if there is no temporal distinction present/past. This perspective is much like Mattheson's, only we are now free to extend the privilege of *Zeitmaß* to any durational level. Thus, the half notes in example 9.10a are also given and logically precede their division into quarters. If this is the case, there is no reason to postulate an underlying sequence of quarter notes in order to generate the arrangement (half-quarter-quarter) shown in example 9.9b. Nor did Mattheson find it necessary to postulate an underlying pulse stream within the measure. Koch, on the other hand, did find this pulse stream a necessity in his efforts to interpret meter as a process of synthesis. And although Koch recognized only one such stream—that of *Taktteile*—a consistently synthetic method will posit a pulse stream for every periodic durational quantity.

EXAMPLE 9.10 Extensive-hierarchic interpretations

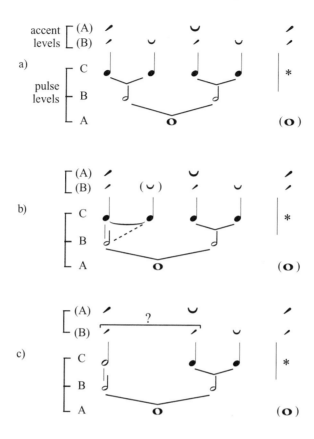

Moving downward introduces the distinction past/present as the distinction before/after. There are quarter notes before there are half notes—quarter notes grouped together by accent to form half notes. Similarly, there are half notes before there are whole notes. There is, however, no whole note and no level A until there are at least three half notes or a recurrence of accent at the whole-note level. Therefore, if we wish to continue the process of generation to the level of whole note, there must be a second whole note or a second whole-note accent that will unite the two half notes and move us down to the next level. It is perhaps for this reason that many accentual theories require at least two bar measures for there to be meter. In any case, what is *given* here is the homogeneous pulse stream C. Pulse levels B and A are not given but are produced or generated by the accents shown in example 9.10 as "accent levels" (A) and (B). There

is no accent level (C) because there is no accent apart from the distinction between accented and unaccented pulses, and it is this distinction or alternation that produces pulse level B. Therefore, C itself must be regarded as metrically "uninterpreted."

To continue reading downward we will need to find at each level a continuous alternation of accents and unaccents. Thus, for the pattern half-quarter-quarter, if we do not posit a second quarter note, shown in example 9.10b as tied to a first quarter note, we shall have to read up at the second half note in level B. Since accent is a signal to move down to a slower durational level and since there cannot be immediately successive accents, we must either posit a second unaccented (and unsounded) quarter note or say that there is no level C "before" there is a level B. This latter alternative, shown in example 9.10c, violates a "left–right" distinction of before and after and violates a consistent (downward) direction of generation. It is also similar in some respects to a projective reading. Certainly, there is a first notated quarter note (i.e., the second "sound" of example 9.10c) before there is a second half note as a container for the two quarters, but there is no accented quarter note before there is an unaccented half note, as there was in example 9.10a. The first sounding quarter note in example 9.10c is accented only as the first of two *divisions* of an unaccented second half note, and the second half note is unaccented only when there is a recurrence of accent in level (A) and a second bar. Thus, if we do not posit an underlying stream of quarter notes as in example 9.10b, we cannot from a purely accentual perspective maintain that the two quarter notes in example 9.10c precede the second half note. A similar conclusion is reached from a projective standpoint: in example 9.9b the projected potential R' precedes the projection Q–Q'.

In several other respects, the projective interpretation shown in example 9.9b combines both upward and downward readings. What is given is something resembling level A in example 9.10 —a beginning of what will become this whole-note duration. However, unlike A, this duration is not given and past, but present and becoming, and also future in the sense that it will be completed and past. With the beginning of the second sound (what will become the second of three sounds) we move to level B. There is now a completed first half-note duration (R) and the beginning of a potential half-note duration (R'). However, this projection returns us to level A in example 9.10 because now that there is a projection there is a definite potential—not only for the becoming of a second half note but also for the becoming of the duration begun at level A. If there is a projection, the initially indefinite durational potential of the beginning at level A is now and only now a definite potential for being the beginning of a whole-note duration. Again, this can happen only if the beginning of the second half note is felt as unaccented or as continuation.

Likewise, the second quarter note in example 9.9b as continuation of a second half-note duration (R') returns us to level B (example 9.10) to enhance the determinacy of the projected

potential R' and also the determinacy of the whole—a whole that is now directed toward a new beginning, *, as a projective potential S. If the second half note (level B) and the second quarter note (level C) are continuations, we must also return to level A for the emergence of a projective potential that has become progressively more definite as the potential for a completion of the duration begun at level A has become more definite. And if the second quarter note leads us to expect a new beginning, *, such an expectation will enhance the relevance of a projective potential S initiated with level A.

From a projective standpoint, there is no reason to posit a division of the first half note. In fact, if there were a division as in example 9.9a, the entire projective field would be altered. Transfering the labels of example 9.10a to the projective situation shown in example 9.9a, we would again begin with level A, but since the second sound is a quarter note we should have to jump to level C (for the projection Q–Q') before arriving at level B with the beginning of the third sound. From a projective standpoint there is a more radical metrical difference between examples 9.10a and 9.10b than that shown in the tree diagrams. In these diagrams, levels A and B are the same in each case (and if we posit a second quarter, levels C will be the same). But if we permit changes of "direction" in reading these diagrams, there can be no identity. Lower and higher levels will themselves be altered by the interaction of levels, which is to say that products as fixed and past nevertheless have histories, and how they become products is inseparable from the particular products they have become. From the standpoint of projection, nothing is *given* except for more or less definite potential. But here there is no uninterpreted level. Accents and unaccents—beginnings and continuations—are not applied to given objects (or pulses) that could exist independently from or prior to interpretation.

I draw attention to these issues in order to warn the reader of a deficiency in my analytic notation. To the extent my graphic representation implies an extensive hierarchy, it is a misrepresentation of projection. Since these are graphic representations, they cannot truly represent temporal progress or process. They will always give

EXAMPLE 9.11 Remaining possibilities for a measure (S) "four quarters long"

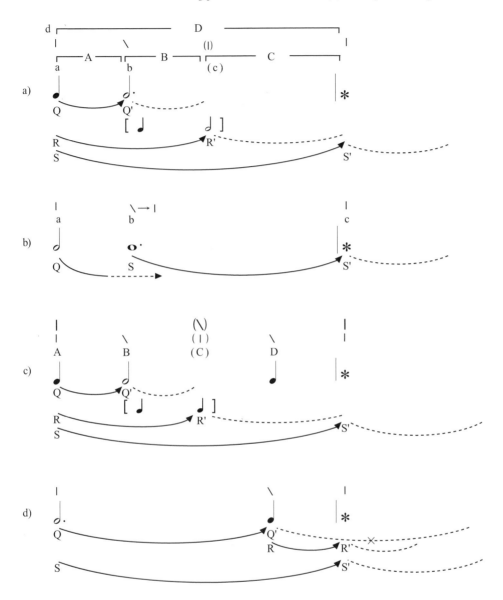

the impression of an extensive hierarchy because, as spatial representations, "time" or duration will be shown as extension. Linguistically, too, it will be difficult to avoid spatial or extensive expressions (e.g., "small/large," "short/long"). I will not attempt to avoid spatial terms altogether, but will ask the reader to understand such terms as substitutions for more cumbersome temporal descriptions. And even words

that seem fully temporal often carry problematic "extensive" connotations—for example, "before" (in front of) and "after" (behind) can easily be taken to mean "to the left of" or "to the right of" quite apart from the temporal categories past, present, and future. With this caveat in mind, let us consider the remaining possibilities for composing our bar measure of quarter notes and/or half notes as shown in example 9.11.

Because of the projection R–R' in example 9.11a, it may be possible to feel some trace of a projection Q–Q' in spite of the long, sustained second sound. The continuation B that might realize Q' fulfills the promise of a quarter–note duration. However, the realized duration of the second sound exceeds the projected potential Q'. The excess duration, C, was not promised. Nevertheless, to the degree Q' is realized (and the duration Q–Q' does not exhaust durational determinacy) a projective potential R will have been created. Since with the new beginning, *, a projection R–R' can now be realized, there may be some trace of a "virtual" articulation, (c). We might say that such a feeling is "retrospective," but this formulation is somewhat misleading. There is a projection R–R' (and a realization of S) only when the first bar measure is past or completed. But what this measure has become is inseparable from its becoming, and a virtual articulation could not be imagined if the projection R–R' had not become (in the course of the bar measure's becoming) a definite potential. Again, the strength or relevancy of this potential is dependent upon tempo and our interests. If we expect a new beginning, (c), we may be prepared to supply a virtual second half-note duration (or even a virtual quarter-note division of C) "before" *. If the tempo is quick and we do not need the projection R–R' to enhance the durational determinacy of S, we may have no feeling of virtual articulation. If the tempo is slow and/or if we have no interest in the emergence of a third sound, it may be that the potential projection R–R' becomes especially relevant only with the beginning of a second bar measure. Or, as in example 9.11b, if the durational determinacy of our dominant beginning, a, is exceeded we might reinterpret b as a second beginning. (Note here the use of the arrow as a symbol of projective reinterpretation: \ → |.)

If we do hear a virtual division in example 9.11a, this is not the same as hearing a real division or a sounding half note, C. One way of naming this difference is to say that example 9.11 is syncopated. Syncopation is something felt, and the feeling of syncopation could be called a feeling of the suspension or denial of a promised (and awaited) beginning and thus a prolongation or extension of continuation. Ex-

ample 9.11c is also syncopated, and here the effect of syncopation may be more intensely felt. Since the third sound (D) is continuation, the absence of a second half-note beginning is also the denial of a beginning for this continuation.

Example 9.11d is problematic. There is no trace of equality here. There is a potential projection Q–Q' denied, and in its stead is the projection S–S'. There is perhaps the possibility for a projection R–R', but, again, this projection can be realized only at the expense of S–S'. Although I have labeled the last beats of examples 9.11c and 9.11d as continuations, they might also be regarded as anacruses, and it is to the topic of anacrusis that I would now like to turn.

Anacrusis

In the theory of projection I have presented thus far, there are only two metrical possibilities: beginning and continuation. However, anacrusis is not beginning, and it seems, in some respects, to be functionally distinct from continuation. Beginning, or downbeat, sounds "grounded" and fixed. Continuation, or afterbeat, is not itself grounded but is, nevertheless, anchored in the duration begun with the downbeat. Anacrusis, or upbeat, seems rather like a continuation released from its dependency on a prior beginning, unanchored, and (in some cases) seeming to come, is it were, "from nowhere." Anacrusis points forward; it is anticipatory, directed toward a future event. Continuation in a sense points backward as a denial of ending for a prior beginning.

In example 9.12a I have designated the second sound as anacrusis with the symbol /. Without the new beginning * there will be no anacrusis, and, in this case, there will be little, if any, grounds for hearing a measure composed of "dotted half and quarter." In example 9.12b, without a new beginning * the bar measure can be realized, but the second quarter will not function as anacrusis. As we have noted, a realization of this measure and its projective potential does not require the second quarter note. However, this beat will greatly enhance our expectancy for a new beginning * and therefore for a realization of the measure's projective potential. If there is no new beginning, we may feel this possibility as denied (or we might, depending on the circum-

EXAMPLE 9.12 Anacrustic detachment

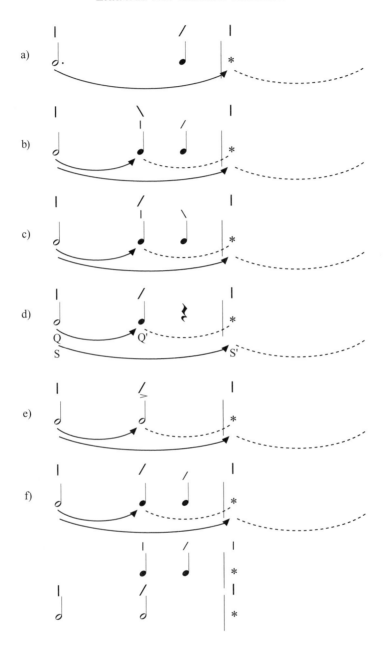

stances, reinterpret the entire projective situation). If there is a new beginning, our expectation will be fulfilled, and we might say that, as a cause of this expectation, the second quarter note has engendered a possibility that is realized with the new beginning. In this way, the last beat of the measure could be thought to function not only to continue the measure's duration but also,

and more especially (since it is not "needed" as continuation), to intensely direct our attention toward a new beginning.

In example 9.12c the second half-note duration is interpreted as anacrusis. In this case, however, the second half-note pulse *is* needed for there to be a bar measure, and it may require a special effort (or a larger context) for this second pulse to be heard as anacrusis. Nevertheless, I would suggest that to the extent we for any reason expect a new beginning and to the extent our attention is focused on the half-note "pulse level," we may be inclined to feel the second half as anacrusis. (And here tempo will play an important role.) Furthermore, I suggest that "given" only two equal beats, as in example 9.12d, shortening the second sounding duration might enhance its potential for becoming an anacrusis. I reason here that silence during the realization of a projected duration Q' will lead to some insecurity in the prospects for an emerging Q–Q' (and S), and that for this reason we may be more inclined to focus our attention on the emergence of a new event that would reduce this indeterminacy. (Here, if the tempo is very slow, expectation of an end may result in an underestimation of projected duration, and if the second sounding duration is not much shorter than the first, we may be satisfied with the realized continuation and less inclined to expect a new beginning.) A similar effect can result from providing the second sound with a dynamic accent (as in example 9.12e), which, it seems, can also enhance expectancy for a new beginning. And accenting and shortening combined should further intensify the potential for anacrusis.

In the case of example 9.12e, it would seem that the second half-note pulse can serve a double function—as if, having already (with its beginning) promised the completion of a bar measure, it can, as an actual, realized duration, in some sense break away from the bar measure as continuation and come to be, with the advent of a new beginning, a duration oriented toward this beginning. In example 9.12f, both half- and quarter-note pulses are interpreted as anacruses. With some effort it should be possible to hear acceleration and an intensification of the anacrustic character of the third beat (along the lines of example 9.7).

The difference between "anacrustic continuation" and "nonanacrustic continuation" (or "anacrusis" and "continuation," to abbreviate these terms) is a difference we have encountered before: the distinction between attentiveness to the emergence of the next event (how much time we have to prepare for such an eventuality) and attentiveness to the fullness of the present event (how much time we have for this event). Like all the other metrical distinctions I have drawn attention to, the distinction between continuation and anacrusis admits of degrees. The distinctions between continuation and anacrusis shown in example 9.12 depend on what we might call grouping or segmentation and require a decision that attention be directed either toward the completion of a present event or toward the prospect of a successor. Two points need to be made here. First, this decision is fully metrical and has an effect on projection. For instance, the interpretations shown in example 9.12 can, I think, result in a more highly determinate projected potential for the second bar measure than the interpretation shown in example 9.9b, in which the second half-note duration is oriented more toward the realization of a projected potential R'. Second, the factors that lead to such a decision are extremely complex. They can involve any of the qualitative distinctions sound is capable of sustaining (tonal function, contour, articulation, loudness, etc.) and any of the relevancies that can contribute to the particularity of the emerging event (i.e., any past experience or novel desire that can enter into the composition of present experience). Indeed, these are the same factors that lead to the distinctions between beginning and continuation in the multiplicity of present events or, as we might say, in the multiplicity of "projective levels." For this reason, in projective theory meter is not given the sort of independence or autonomy that would place it in opposition to or in conflict with grouping or the articulation of phrases and phrase constituents.

Although there is a definite distinction in feeling between continuation and anacrusis, it may or may not be sharply drawn. And their differences notwithstanding, continuation and anacrusis are similar at least in their clear distinction from beginning. Although I labeled anacruses in example 9.12, all of these beats or pulses function also as continuations. Thus, I have argued that anacrusis is a type of continuation—a continuation that becomes in some sense disengaged from beginning. And since there is anacrusis only in relation to a later event and continuation only in relation to an earlier event, we might posit a process whereby continuation is transformed into anacrusis. When in example 9.12

EXAMPLE 9.13 Anacrustic decisions for two successive sounds

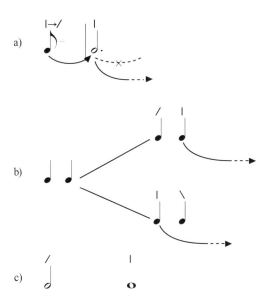

there is the beginning of a second measure, and to the degree this beginning is felt as a goal, the continuation in the first measure will have become anacrustic. Thus, it would seem that continuation in some sense precedes anacrusis, in that there must be a duration begun and continued "before" there can be an anacrustic disengagement.

My attempt to relate continuation and anacrusis is not motivated solely by systematic considerations, but by the thought that the distinction strong versus weak is the more general distinction and that continuation and anacrusis must be united as forms of the "weak." The connection of anacrusis and continuation, however, becomes problematic if we consider the eighth-note anacrusis to the first bar measure in example 9.13a.

Here there is no beginning for which this initial eighth note might be a continuation. The eighth-note upbeat is felt as weak, and I have defined "weakness" as an attribute of the function "continuation." But since there is actually no beginning preceding this eighth note that it might be a continuation of, how can it be continuation, or, equivalently, why is it not a beginning? It is, of course a beginning for itself and as such is potentially projective. However, even at much

slower speeds than that implied in this example we cannot avoid grouping. If the second sound is a beginning, the first cannot be a beginning, or, as we might say, the first will be denied as a beginning. Put in other terms: we cannot hear a quick succession of strong beats, and if the first beat is weak in relation to the second, it is not the beginning of a metrical unit. In the case of "afterbeat," weak beat is the continuation of a definite beginning and a *part* of the duration begun. Continuation is necessarily a part. Anacrusis or "forebeat," since it, too, is felt as weak, is also a part in the sense that it sounds incomplete or not anchored to a definite prior beginning. It was perhaps an overstatement to have said that it "comes out of nowhere," but I do believe that a feeling of anacrusis often involves a feeling of "coming from," the "whence" of this coming being relatively indistinct. In this interpretation, the anacrusis shown in example 9.13a could also be regarded as a continuation, the beginning of which is indistinct or undefined. The indefiniteness of beginning would then be taken as the reason for a putative feeling of incompleteness and for the dependency of this upbeat on the ensuing downbeat—perhaps, too, for the special focus that accrues to the downbeat. In such cases it appears that we are not willing, for one reason or another, to stake our prediction on an unpromising beginning or on what comes to be felt as an unpromising beginning.

In the case we are considering, without the succeeding downbeat there will be no anacrusis and no feeling of weakness or continuation. This first event is not weak in relation to a strong beginning that precedes it—silence precedes it. If this event is felt as anacrustic and continuative, it is only because the second event makes it so felt. Thus, the first is weak only in relation to the second. Furthermore, this relation is one of smaller to larger (realized) duration. Since the second sound is considerably longer than the first (and is not subsequently confirmed as continuation), it is not a realization of projected potential, and a possible projection is denied or unrealized. For this reason the second sound must be interpreted as beginning and not continuation. If the possibility for projection (or "periodicity") is relevant for us, the relation smaller to

EXAMPLE 9.14 Stephen Handel, *Listening—An Introduction to the Perception of Auditory Events,* figure 11.1, p. 387 (annotated). Copyright © 1989 MIT Press. Used by permission.

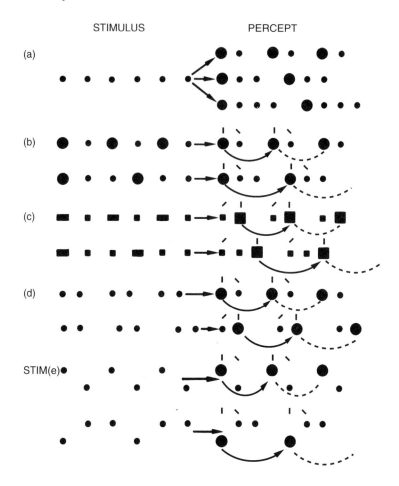

larger can be interpreted as the relation continuation to beginning. But in saying this, I do not mean to detract from the power of anacrusis; this short "first" sound can provide information that might become relevant for the projective future of the second beginning as an indication of possible continuations or "divisions." Indeed, such information may be crucial to our success in quickly grasping a newly emerging durational order. The choice of taking this "forebeat" from the start as the prelude to a dominant beginning or of making this decision only when a succeeding dominant beginning has manifested itself depends (as always) upon context and admits of limitless variation.

The decision for hearing anacrusis seems no less spontaneous than that for hearing beginning and continuation (as "afterbeat"). Stephen Handel has summarized some findings of research concerning "subjective rhythm" that are pertinent to the distinction between "afterbeat" and "forebeat." Example 9.14 reproduces Handel's figure 11.1, to which I have added a metrical analysis. The following is Handel's commentary:

A series of identical elements, as in (a), is perceived to form groups of 2, 3, or 4 elements. The initial element of each group is perceived to be accented (represented by the bigger filled circle), and the time intervals between elements do not appear equal. If every second or third element is more intense, as in (b), the elements are perceived to form groups so that the more intense elements begin each group and there appear to be longer intervals between groups. If every second or third element is longer, as in (c), the elements are perceived to form groups so that the longer duration elements are the last elements of each group, the longer duration elements appear accented, and there appear to be longer intervals between groups. If every second interval between two elements is increased so that the elements form groups temporally, as in (d), then the first elements of each group appear accented if the longer interval is slightly greater than the other intervals, but the last element of each group appears accented if the longer interval is much greater than the other interval. If the elements are different frequencies, as in (e), then the elements are perceived to form groups so that the higher-pitch element begins each group and appears accented, and the interval between groups appears longer. If one note occurs less often, it may appear to be accented and begin each group. (Handel 1989, p. 387)

I would call attention especially to two of Handel's observations: the judgments that afterbeats are "closer" to the prior beginning and forebeats are "closer" to the new beginning, and the effect of length in the anacrustic groupings. In my own very informal experiments, I have found a strong tendency to interpret the first of the two short sounds such as those shown in example 9.13b as an anacrusis. I imagine that this decision is made because without a third sound to terminate the second event, the second event is, in fact, longer than the first. And I believe that even at very slow speeds, where we might be able to hear separate beginnings, if the second sound is longer than the first (as in example 9.13c), we may nevertheless come to hear the first as weak. Thus, in example 9.11b the first beat might have been labeled / rather than |.[3]

If anacrusis preceded by silence is conceived

as continuation without a definite beginning, is it possible that a beginning might become definite—that "later," "retrospectively," a definite beginning could emerge? From the evidence of example 9.15a this does seem possible. Here tonal differentiation is employed to support distinctions between beginning and continuation.

If in example 9.15a the duration of a whole note is projected with the beginning of the second bar measure, projective potential will have been created from the beginning of the first measure and from the silence that will have begun the first measure. This beginning will be definite because it acts as the beginning of a definite potential and the beginning of a determinate duration that is reproducible. Such a "silent beginning" will emerge only as it comes to function as a beginning; that is, it must function for the creation of an actual, determinate duration. And the only basis for asserting the existence of an actual beginning and an actual duration here is evidence that this beginning and this duration have a real effect on a subsequent event. The silence of "silent beginning" is meant literally. As should become clear from the following analysis, a "silent beginning" is a *functional* beginning and will only in rare circumstances leave any trace in feeling as a "retrospective" virtual articulation.

In the case of example 9.15b, I think it would be difficult even in the most favorable of circumstances to identify a projection beginning with silence. Indeed, since there is so little context given here, it will be difficult to say anything very definite about feelings of durational potential. However, the projective issues that arise from this minimal situation may be instructive for our attempt to define the conditions under which a "silent beginning" can emerge.

If (as we are now assuming) the first eighth-

---

3. Although the question of "large-scale meter" will be taken up in chapter 12, it may be appropriate here to mention that anacrusis is not limited to brief durations. Consider, for example, the opening of Brahms's Third Symphony, in which a two-bar "introduction" may come to be felt as anacrusis to a four-bar measure (bars 3–6). Such a transformation can occur only when the beginning with bar 3 emerges as a dominant beginning for a four-bar duration—that is, the beginning of a larger duration for which bars 1–2 *cannot function as a projective potential*. In this connection, I will also take the opportunity to remind the reader that "anacrusis" in a projective sense does not refer to a vague sense of "leading to," but rather names a smaller durational "part" (or continuation) that precedes and directs attention to the dominant beginning of a larger duration.

EXAMPLE 9.15 Emergence of a "silent beginning" for projective potential

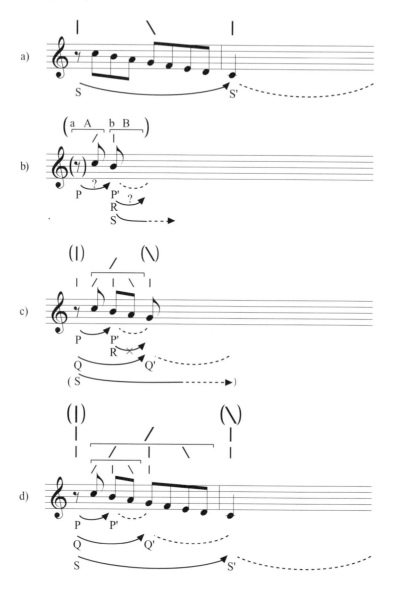

note beat can be heard as anacrusis, the duration of the second beat will be longer than the duration of an eighth. How much longer is not at all clear. I have indicated the possibility of a projection P–P′ and a hypothetical duration A begun in silence. However, such an interpretation does not accord with projective distinctions we have thus far developed. To argue for a projection P–P′ is to posit two beginnings, a and b. But since the durations of A and B do not exhaust mensural determinacy (here represented by the open or indeterminate potential S), a and b cannot both be dominant beginnings. If b is a dominant beginning, a must be continuation of some prior beginning, in which case a projection P–P′ would cross projective boundaries—a situation we disallowed in our earlier discussion of division. Moreover, there is no projective evidence of such a prior beginning. The alternative is to imagine that b is continuation for a prior beginning a. But there can be no evidence of a continuative b in the absence of a new beginning c. Note also that lengthening the durations of A and B so that they would approach the limits of durational determinacy would at the same time have the effect of detracting from the continuative or anacrustic character of the first beat.

The only evidence for something approaching projection here is the possibility for feeling some trace of eighth-note, or perhaps quarter-note, divisions beginning with the second beat. Thus, we may, depending upon our interests and attentiveness, hear virtual division in the continuation of the second duration. But even if there were such a perception, it is not likely to be very clear, nor can the realization of a second duration be very definite. In an attempt to make metrical or projective sense of this event, we simply have very little information on which to act—potential is relatively unfocused or indefinite. "Given" an initial continuative/anacrustic eighth note in example 9.15b, we can produce eighths and quarters for a new beginning on the chance that such division will become relevant for this present becoming; and if we are interested in the course this becoming is likely to take, eighths and quarters are all we have to go on.

In example 9.15c we do have more to go on, and here a realization of the projected potential P' should be more definite. Nevertheless, we must assume much of the interpretation shown here: namely, that the third sound is continuative for a quarter-note duration begun with the second sound, and that this quarter-note duration does not function as a projective potential R. If, in this case, the quarter-note duration (P') can function as continuation for a greater duration (Q) begun in the silence preceding the first sound, evidence of such a function will be the emergence of a projected potential Q'. These are perhaps strong possibilities, but they cannot be fully realized until there is a completed projection Q–Q'. And in the limited context of example 9.15c there is no reason to assume that this projection must be realized. (Dynamic accents in support of this interpretation would certainly strengthen these possibilities, but accents cannot eliminate indeterminacy or guarantee realization in the face of incompatible future developments.)

In example 9.15d, decisions have been made that will have reduced the indeterminacy or range of possibilities encountered in example

9.15c. Here the projected potential Q' is realized in a projection (assuming now that the pitch G is heard to begin a half-note beat). Now that there is a past and *effective* projective duration Q, there can be no durational indeterminacy, and the measured silence preceding the first sound will have come to function as a beginning. If conditions allow the second half-note duration (Q') to be perceived as continuation, there will also be a projection S–S' (provided that we hear the low C as goal and the beginning of a second measure). In this case, three projections will have begun with silence.

What is peculiar about such situations is the fact that there is no beginning until there are continuations. The creation of a "silent beginning," since it is dependent upon subsequent events, has, as I have said, a retrospective character (as has *anacrusis* in general). However, once there is a beginning and once these "subsequent" events are present or past, there will, in a sense, always have been such a beginning for these events. Thus, the beginning of the first bar measure in example 9.15a becomes a beginning because it comes to function as a beginning, and once we have reached the second bar measure—once there is, in fact, a first measure—there will never have been a time when *this* measure did not have a beginning. Again, in such situations there will rarely be any evidence of hearing such a beginning as a virtual articulation; but this is hardly an issue if it is remembered that beginning here is not regarded as a thing (a beat) that could be isolated from the becoming of the event.

In examples 9.15c and 9.15d the projective complex comprising the first three eighth notes is bracketed and labeled as an "anacrustic group." In example 9.15d a larger projective complex comprising seven notes is also identified as anacrustic. These labels assert the possibility of feeling no clear "resolution" of anacrustic suspense, no end to this pointing forward, until the projective goal is secured. Incidentally, in order to indicate this larger gesture I might have labeled the durations marked "P'" and "Q'" as anacrustic and shown a "hierarchical" accumulation of anacruses: in example 9.15d, an eighth-note anacrusis leading to a quarter-note anacrusis leading to a half-note anacrusis leading to the beginning of a second bar measure with the low

EXAMPLE 9.16 Haydn, Symphony no. 101 in D Major, first
movement, bs. 24–30

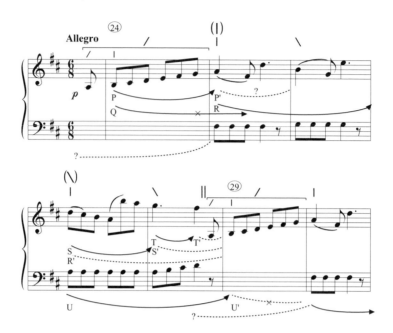

C. Such an interpretation is, in fact, implied by the notion of anacrustic group. But for greater clarity I have chosen instead to label "P''' and "Q'" as beginning in order to show the immediate resolutions of the anacruses that lead to these projected realizations. Nor have I attempted to label every eighth note in example 9.15d. An attempt in cases such as this to identify every constituent duration as either "pure" continuation or anacrusis is not likely to prove very satisfying and can easily lead to hairsplitting—an unreasonable attempt to make very fine distinctions in terms of only two categories. Since anacrusis is a sort of continuation, it is often difficult and unrewarding to make a very sharp distinction between the two. Where we can draw a distinction we might say again that anacrusis points forward toward a new beginning and that continuation remains in the thrall of a prior beginning, or that there is continuation only in relation to a prior beginning and anacrusis only in relation to a subsequent beginning. But anacrusis always bears some trace of incompleteness or of being detached from a prior beginning, whether definite, as in the case of examples 9.12 and 9.15, or indefinite, as in example 9.16.

As example 9.16 indicates, the opening phrase from the Allegro of Haydn's Symphony no. 101 begins with a long anacrustic group leading to a two-bar (and possibly a four-bar) measure. The anacrustic group is especially fluid as a scale pattern rising an octave from scale degree 5 and in contrast to the highly segmented and projectively closed figures of bars 25 and 26. Note that it will take some time for a feeling of anacrusis to emerge. The initial eighth note will quickly be heard as anacrusis. But bar 24 cannot be interpreted as anacrusis until there is some evidence of a larger two-bar measure begun with bar 25. Were we to stop with the beginning of bar 25, a two-bar projective potential Q could be formed (as a result of a projection P–P'), in which case bar 25 would be interpreted as continuation. However, Q is not realized. Instead, a projective potential R emerges leading to the projection R–R'. In fact, because of contrasts introduced in bar 25 there may be some feeling of a potential R (evidence, that is, of a new, dominant beginning) even before bar 26, in which case there will also be some feeling here of an anacrustic group.

Although bar 24 has a definite beginning, if it

is heard as anacrustic this duration will begin, as it were, in medias res. And the preceding eighth-note anacrusis will further vitiate the effect of a definite beginning. Note that all these factors also call into question the projection P–P' and therefore the projective connection of the anacrusis group as a whole to the remainder of the phrase. As evidence of the incompleteness of anacrusis arising from the loss of a prior beginning, the juncture of this first phrase and its repetition is especially revealing. The first phrase ends in bar 28 with three completed projections: R–R', S–S', and T–T'. The eighth-note anacrusis at the end of bar 28 in no way detracts from these completions. However, as the new anacrustic group emerges, the second phrase will become projectively detached from the first. As anacrusis, bar 29 will necessarily be continuation, but not the continuation of a prior beginning in the preceding phrase. The preceding phrase itself closed with the continuation S' (and if bars 25–28 form a measure, S' will be the continuation of a continuation, R'). Since there is no beginning from which the anacrusis might have emerged, the two phrases will be projectively disjunct. And as we enter into the second phrase it may seem that there was a projective break or hiatus (||) separating the two phrases.

If it is directed toward beginning, must anacrusis be regarded as in some sense "external" to measured duration? Certainly, Riemann did not regard anacrusis in this way, though his elevation of anacrusis did provide him with a means of breaking the bar and of conceiving of *Takt* as a rhythmic-metric phenomenon. For many other theorists, anacrusis (together with the "end accent" of tonal cadence) has pointed to a separation of meter and rhythm. Again, Lerdahl and Jackendoff make a sharp distinction between meter and grouping based, in part, on the overlapping of boundaries occasioned by anacrusis. However, if meter is not understood as an extensive (spatial) arrangement of "time spans" there will be no grounds for conflict. Anacrusis will, in a sense, "belong to" the measure it precedes, in a special focusing of attention on a new beginning in an overlapping of measures. And since anacrusis contributes to the determinacy and particularity of the new beginning, it cannot be detached from the new metrical/projective field.

Pulse and Beat

In the preceding discussion of meter I hesitated to speak of pulses or beats in reference to the examples, using instead expressions like the "second sound" or "event" or "quarter-note duration." Both "pulse" and "beat" imply a sequence of equal, ideal divisions that might underlie a heterogeneous sequence of actually sounded durations. Thus, in the case of example 9.10b or 9.10c, we could speak of a second quarter-note beat apart from the question of its being perceived. To avoid circumlocution I would like to use the word "beat" in a rather unconventional sense to refer only to perceived durations and without regard to periodicity. Thus, in reference to example 9.9b, by "first beat" I mean the sounding half note, by "third beat" or "second quarter-note beat" I mean the last notated quarter, and, since I maintain in this case that the realization of a projected potential is perceived as a real duration, I will call this realization a "second half-note beat." By "pulse" I will mean one of a series of equal divisions implied by metrical notation and considered apart from questions of perception.

Meter signatures indicate groupings of pulses. Modern signatures explicitly indicate one pulse level—the "conductor's beat." However, our notational system implies other pulse levels: thus, a half note is assumed to contain two quarters, each of these quarters is assumed to contain two eighths, et cetera. And, incidentally, the assumption is that division will be duple. If we wish to indicate other divisions, special notational devices are required—for example, the notation ♪♪♪. Compound signatures make some concession to triple division, but even here pulses must be indicated by dotted notes—one and one-half times the note value.

What I wish to call beats are real performed or perceived articulations of duration. In some cases there is no distinction between pulses prescribed by the signature and beats—for example, in a 4/4 measure containing four quarter notes. Where there is a distinction, the difference between pulse and what I am calling beat is often regarded as the difference between meter and rhythm, and it is only by finding a common denominator regarded as a pulse that beats which are not pulses can be regarded as metrical (measured by the smaller pulse). Since pulse levels other than the one indicated in the signature are implied and since we can, in any case, multiply by any factor we choose, any beat can be accommodated to the metrical structure. In this way, the rhythmic irregularity and heterogeneity of beats can be reduced to an underlying metrical regularity and homogeneity of pulses. In this reduction, meter may seem to be something of an abstraction. Thus, the "rhythms" shown in examples 9.5 and 9.11 are particularizations of a single, invariant meter—4/4 or 2/2. And for the purposes of analysis the distinction between 4/4 and 2/2 is largely irrelevant. There is, at least implicitly, a half-note pulse and a quarter-note pulse and, were it called for in the analysis, an eighth-note and a sixteenth-note pulse.

However, pulses are abstractions only if they are detached from beats. If we can perceive a pulse or feel an actual articulation or beginning, this pulse is a beat. Such a felt articulation need not be notated or produced by the performer. Thus, if we hear what I have called a "virtual articulation," this articulation will be no less real (though less vivid) than a sonic articulation. Of course, once there is a projection that involves two bar measures, the first of which expresses the notated pulse (or a division implied by the notation), there will be definite possibilities for feeling pulses that are not sounded. I will suggest, however, that not all such possibilities are equally relevant and that potential divisions implied by notation are often suppressed. Since relevance is a matter of degree and is determined in an actual experience, it will be precarious to assert that a potential division will not be heard. But in order to avoid treating meter as an extensive hierarchy of continuous pulse streams, I would prefer to err on the side of heterogeneity and to favor the relevancy of sounding articulations over virtual articulations.

The problem of virtual beats obviously leads to more general issues of interpretation and the question of whose experience is being described in analysis. Although we will be able to confront these issues more directly when we turn to extended analyses of musical compositions, I would like to at least broach the question here by drawing attention to a difference between the per-

ceptions of performer and listener. Consider, for instance, the opening *adagio molto* of Beethoven's First Symphony, shown as example 13.4b (chapter 13). A conductor whose duty it is to determine the durations of these initial half-note beats might rely upon a feeling of subdivision here. However, a listener need not have a clear perception of subdivision in order to feel the second half-bar durations as realizations of projected potential or to feel that these durations are "just right." I should add that an experienced conductor might well choose not to beat quarters in performance and might choose to suppress a feeling of subdivision in favor of feeling a unitary duration. In general, beginners or inexperienced performers have greater need for subdividing as a corrective for the inability to feel larger projections—to ensure against rushing or "cheating" rests and sustained notes. A listener, on the other hand, does not have the responsibility for actually producing the durations prescribed by the score and may often feel projective potential differently from the performer. This is not to deny that the performer's feeling is also communicated to the listener and that the possibility for projective *Fernhören* can be enhanced or blocked by a performer's realization.

I mention this difference between performer and listener because in testing projective potential and projective realization in examples for which there is no recorded performance, the reader is put in the position of performer and asked to make judgments that may not accurately reflect the perceptions of a listener. Clearly, this difference is most problematic in the judgments I offer. I can by no means guarantee that the judgments I propose will correspond to those of "the listener" or to those of the reader as performer. I can, however, hope that the questions raised by these interpretations are pertinent to the issue of projection and, moreover, that the concept of projection can account for differences of perception and offer us a way of understanding and valuing such differences.

Metrical Types—Equal/Unequal

If all potential divisions of a measure are not perceived, there is, nevertheless, incontrovertible evidence for the relevance of virtual articulations if we can feel "the" meter, or a definite metrical type, in the absence of sounding pulses. Thus, in example 9.11, if we can feel "duple meter" in the bar-measure projections, we must have felt the effect of articulations that are not actually sounded. Whether we interpret these bars as examples of 2/2 or 4/4 (whether our attention is focused on half-note or quarter-note pulses), we will in any case sense equality—duple, equal measures. If signatures are somewhat misleading if they are taken to promise homogeneous division, they do, nevertheless, indicate metrical, projective types that in limitless instantiations can usually be felt (though the degree of such feeling is, as I shall argue, highly variable).

I would now like to turn to the question of metrical types by considering the difference between two types—duple (or equal) and triple (or unequal). To avoid problems of virtual articulation, I will represent the pulses given in the time signatures as beats. Although in the following examples the measures we shall consider are notated as bar measures, the analysis should apply equally to smaller or larger measures—measures within the bar or measures comprising two or more bars.

As types, duple and triple are universals— every duple measure is an instance of duple meter, and, in this sense, every duple measure is the same. Thus, we might say that for a piece "in" 2/4, meter, at least at the level of the bar, is invariant. But again, if meter is regarded as repetition of the same, particularity and novelty will be ascribed to rhythm as something other than and therefore opposed to meter. Later I will argue that meter, even when viewed from the perspective of metrical type, is fully particular and never "the same." But to argue against a reduction of meter to type is not to dispute the reality of distinctions of metrical type as distinctions of feeling. And in the following discussion I will attempt to account for the emergence of such feelings from the standpoint of projection.

We have already considered many examples of duple meter. Duple meter is created when the projected duration functions as continuation for the beginning of the projection. Since projection is essentially binary and requires that the two terms be immediately successive, and since

EXAMPLE 9.17 Projected beats for (**a**) duple and (**b**) triple meter

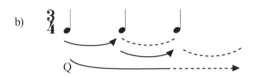

projection results in equality, a projective account of triple, unequal meter is problematic. Therefore, my discussion of metrical types will be focused primarily on the problems posed by triple meter. Instances of duple and triple meter are given in example 9.17.

In comparison to the projection shown in example 9.17a, projective potential Q is extended in example 9.17b. Here there are two weak beats or two distinct continuations that prolong the activity and presence of the beginning (and, consequently, the projective potential that emerges from this beginning). The beginning of the third beat, like the beginning of the second, is denied as a beginning that would make the beginning of the nascent measure past. The third beat does, nevertheless, make the second beat past, thereby confirming the projected duration of the second beat and the completion of a projection. This might suffice for a description of triple meter if we were to view projection as an abstract scheme. Since we have substituted a beginning that lasts throughout the group and continuations that "prolong" the beginning for Hauptmann's binary unity of an accented and an unaccented pulse, there is no systematic problem raised by a third pulse (or a fourth or fifth pulse). However, the problem that *is* raised is a perceptual one. If we allow a second continuation, why can we not allow a third or a fourth? That we cannot is given by the fact that we do not. Presented with a series of "objectively" homogeneous pulses (at a moderate tempo), we will spontaneously create groups of two or three (or multiples of two or three) and

EXAMPLE 9.18 Projective decisions for equal and unequal measure

a)

b)

c)

d)

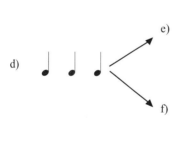

e)

f)

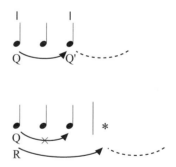

not groups of five or seven. And if we are given a group of five (at a moderate tempo) we will hear this as a composite of duple and triple groups. Moreover, the evidence of musical practice shows that duple and triple (or equal and unequal) measures constitute two basic forms of metrical organization. In the following section I shall attempt to account for this limitation of types through a systematic development of the notion of projection.

I said earlier that in example 9.17b the third beat, like the second beat, functions as a continuation. However, it must be noted that the initiation of the third beat functions as a more complex denial of ending than did the second beat.

The third beat cannot function exactly like the second beat simply to continue the duration begun "before" there were any beats, for now that there is a second beat there is also a real potential for projecting a half-note duration (the potential Q in example 9.17a). In order to function as a continuation, the beginning of the third beat must deny this potential. In contrast, the beginning of the second beat denied no potential—rather, it created one projection and the potential for another.

It may be helpful here to review this process in detail. (See example 9.18.) The beginning of sound is a potential for an as yet indefinite duration. As potentially reproducible, a presently emerging duration is also potentially projective, and (in the absence of a prior projection) this projective potential is also durationally indefinite. In example 9.18a an indefinite projective potential P is indicated in parentheses. With the beginning of a second sound (example 9.18b) there is a projection. Since the second sound presents a new beginning, a projective potential initiated with the first sound is realized, and this potentiality is realized before the projected duration is realized. If the second sound is also a continuation, the beginning it continues retains projective potential because this beginning is still "present." But now it is a definite potential (Q in example 9.18b) because the projected duration of the second sound is definite as a (more or less) definite potential. And yet, to the extent that the dominant beginning has the potential for remaining active beyond Q, there is also a greater and still indeterminate projective potential P. If, as in example 9.18b, nothing happens after the second sound, Q will not be realized, P will be denied, and the beginning will have become past and inactive. However, as example 9.18c shows, we may have to wait some time after the second sound has ended to be sure that the beginning is really past (and that the potential P is really dead). And, in general, it seems that we hold onto beginnings for as long as we can.

In example 9.18d, with the introduction of a third sound, two possibilities are presented. If, as in example 9.18e, the third beat emerges as a new beginning (rather than a continuation), the projective potential Q will be realized, and the beginning of the third beat will project the duration of a half note. If, as in example 9.18f, the beginning of the third beat is perceived as a continuation, the projective potential Q will be denied and will be replaced by the projective potential R. (The possibility for an R was shown in example 9.18b by P.) This is the denial of a definite potential and the affirmation of a potential beyond Q that becomes definite only with the new beginning *.

Since the denial of projective potential shown in example 9.18f is a special sort of denial—different from continuation as a denial of ending and different, too, from the denial of the projective potential Q shown in example 9.18b—it will simplify our discussion to give it a name.

"Deferral" seems an appropriate word since it implies postponement, delay, putting off to a future time, and also the renunciation or the yielding of a claim. Deferral involves the cancellation of a prior and definite projective potential (Q in example 9.18f). Since there is a postponement of a decision that would create a definite *projective* potential from Q to R (or a yielding of Q to R's projective claim), I will call this characteristic of triple meter "the deferral of *projective* potential." But this is only one aspect of deferral and cannot in itself account for the phenomenon of triple meter. The other aspect of deferral directly involves not the expansion of projective potential, but the expansion of a projection. Of these two aspects of deferral, the second—expansion of a projection (or what I shall call the deferral of *projected* potential)—is conceptually the more difficult to grasp and will therefore require closer analysis. Again, we must consider both what constitutes the event's self-fulfillment and what the event can offer beyond itself as datum for a successor.

In examples 9.18e and 9.18f it was assumed that the beginning of a third beat offered the possibility of beginning a new "half-note" measure. Now it may be fairly asked why we should imagine such a possibility for a third beat. Earlier, I suggested the following reason. Just as the second beat makes the first beat past, the third beat ends the second beat and makes the second beat past. However, since the second beat is a continuation that completes a projection, the third beat in making the second beat past also functions to make this prior and completed projection past.

But in triple (or unequal) meter the third beat does not function in this way—it is, in fact, a continuation of the nascent measure, and not a new beginning that promises to reproduce the duration of a completed two-beat measure. If, in a perception of triple meter, the third beat does not begin as a reproduction of a two-beat unit, what does it reproduce? Clearly, it reproduces the duration of the second beat. If, as in example 9.19a, the third beat, C, is not a new beginning or "accented" in relation to a continuative, "unaccented" second beat, we can regard each of the first two beats as projective. We will then recognize two projections: S−S' and T−T'.

EXAMPLE 9.19 Deferral

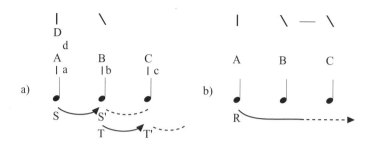

It will be remembered from the section of this chapter on division that an "overlapping" of this sort would be suppressed if a two-beat projective potential (Q in example 9.18e) were to be realized in a projection (Q–Q'). However, in this case, since no projection Q–Q', in fact, emerges, C can reproduce the duration B as B reproduced A. In view of this "transitive" relationship, it should be possible for C, in reproducing B, to reproduce something of B's special relationship to A—namely, the function of continuing a dominant beginning (d in example 9.19a). Thus, it would appear that what is given for a newly emerging C is not simply the projective potential (T) of B, but also a completed projection (S–S') in which B has functioned as continuation of a greater duration begun with d. If C is also continuation, it will therefore be the reproduction of a continuation (B in example 9.19b). Furthermore, by reproducing B as continuation, C will, presumably, reproduce something of the specific form of this continuation—a continuation that completes a projection. As in example 9.19b, I will use the symbol \ — \ to indicate this reproduction of function. To summarize: in functioning as continuation (rather than as a new beginning) C *defers* the *completion* of a projection S–S' to open the new projective potential R shown in example 9.19b.

As a result of deferral, the projective situation is complicated. A duration A–B has been created—there is now a unit A–B (| \), which is completed when C appears, and since A–B is past it is irrevocable and necessarily given for C (just as the duration A is past and given for B as B's projected potential). C reproduces B *and* continues the beginning of the nascent measure. But what does C's inheritance mean for the larger measure's projective potential? I have speculated that by reproducing B, C can also reproduce B's function of completing a projection. In this case, C is nothing apart from this projection and will, in this sense, belong to a single projection A–B–C as an extension of continuation through a reproduction of the projected duration already realized by B. If C reproduces the projected duration of B, C is not merely added or tacked onto the completed A–B. Its novel contribution is to alter the entire projective situation. C results in an enlargement of the projection and a deferral of its completion. Finally, if the ending of B is now no longer the ending of a projection and C is not a beginning that will make the projection past, then C will have reproduced a result of B's adjacency to A—that is, the duration of B *as* projected duration (something that B inherited from A as a result of projection). In this case, deferral means deferral of the realization of a projection or, to abbreviate this formulation, a deferral of *projected* potential—a denial that the projection is completed with the ending of B.

That there should be two aspects to deferral—the deferral of *projective* potential and the deferral of *projected* potential—follows from the dual nature of projection, which necessarily involves both a projective and a projected component. These two aspects of deferral are fully complementary. By reproducing B's realization of a potential for duration that would complete the projection (B's promise for an end of the projection) and thus deferring the completion of the projection, C also defers the projective potential of A–B as a unit (Q in example 9.18e). By deferring the projective potential of A–B, C also becomes a continuation (and not a beginning) that can reproduce the continuation B and, hence, B's function of completing a projection. These aspects of deferral are inextricable. Their difference emerges as a difference of perspective—the difference between whether we regard the event for itself (the creation of a unified duration) or beyond itself (its potential for reproduction).

Since I have characterized deferral negatively, as denial, I wish to remind the reader that the reinterpretation effected by deferral involves more than denial or negation (as the delay or postponement of projective completion). Deferral also involves the creation of a novel projection and a novel projective potential (through the renunciation of a more limited, "duple" claim). Likewise, the continuations created by the second and third beats are denials in that they deny the possibility of making the beginning past or inactive for the creation of duration. But continuation (as denial of negation) is obviously creative—as continuations, the second and third beats keep the beginning present and active. Like continuation, deferral is a definite decision, a decision against realizing a definite potential, and, at the same time, a decision for the creation of new potential. Thus, I suggest that the third beat has two functions—it functions, like the second beat, as a continuation, but in order to do so it must also function as a deferral. And continuation, like deferral, must be understood in terms of both what the event is for itself and what the event is beyond itself.

The reader may have had the suspicion that the preceding account of deferral is an attempt, like Hauptmann's, to fit the round peg of triple meter into the square hole of *Paarigkeit*, or an attempt to reduce triplicity to an underlying duplicity. In defense of this account (or at least to keep the question open), I assure the reader that I would not present the hypothesis of deferral if I did not think it justified primarily on experiential grounds. However, I must concede that such a suspicion is not entirely unjustified; for, although I do not claim (as Hauptmann did) that a triple is created from the superimposition of two discrete duples, I cannot deny that the governing hypothesis of projection is grounded in the twoness of immediate succession. If the notion of deferral is not to be regarded merely as a

methodological convenience, it must be asked if there is any evidence for the claims made by the hypothesis of deferral.

In the succession of three quarter notes in example 9.18d, if we hear triple meter, we do not first hear duple meter (example 9.18e) and then a change from duple to triple (example 9.18f). In fact, the reader should find it virtually impossible in this example to hear both triple meter and the projection of a half-note duration initiated by the third beat, simply because once deferral has happened there is no possibility for such a projection. Since the potential for projecting a half-note duration is not realized, there is now no feeling of duple meter; and now that there *is* a completed projection involving three beats, this projection was incomplete "before" there were three beats. Evidence for deferral cannot be adduced by treating a denied possibility as if it were a realized actuality. But this does not mean that the denied possibilities involved in deferral are unreal. Moreover, the possibilities denied by deferral are definite possibilities that must make a difference in, or contribute to, the particularity of what is realized. If there is evidence of deferral, it will come not from a direct perception of what is denied, but indirectly from a perception of the particularity of what is actually created.

In the case of continuation versus beginning, there is a feeling of weak versus strong: for duple meter, a succession strong-weak; for triple meter, a succession strong-weak-weak. However, I do not think that the third beat in triple meter is necessarily felt as "weaker" than the second. In certain contexts such a feeling may arise. For example, as Printz (quoted earlier) observes, if a triple measure lacks a first beat, the third beat can sound weak in relation to the second (as the first *sound* of the measure). However, there are also contexts in which such a distinction is far from clear. Thus, it is possible to perform example 9.19b without feeling that the third beat is definitely weaker (or "more continuative") than the second. And for this reason I maintain that categories of accent cannot account for the particularity of triple measure.

My introduction of the notion of deferral is an attempt to account for the special feeling of triple meter or the difference in character be-

EXAMPLE 9.20 Contrasted characters of unequal and equal measure

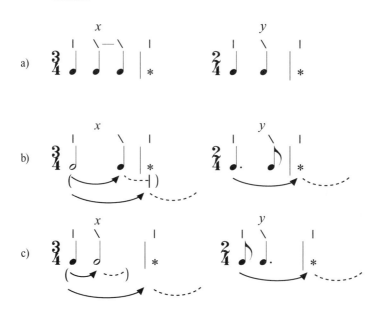

tween duple and triple. Traditionally, this has been called the difference between equal and unequal measures (*temps egaux/inegaux, gerade/ungerade Taktarten, battuta eguale/ineguale, tactus inaequalis*). Although this difference could be conceived simply as the difference between even and odd numbers, "equal" and "unequal" have referred to an essentially qualitative distinction. To use other words, we might say that duple sounds balanced, even, or "square"; triple, by contrast, sounds off-balance, uneven (rather than odd), lilting, or, perhaps, "sprung."

Again, if deferral is the denial of a possibility, it will be impossible under normal circumstances to feel a projective potential that is not realized or the completion of a projection that is denied as a completion. Nevertheless, some indirect evidence of deferral might be adduced from the contrasting characters of equal and unequal measures. In example 9.20a, a feeling of the inequality of X compared to the equality of Y might be understood to arise simply because X contains two adjacent continuations or, in comparison to Y, an "extra" continuation. However, if this felt difference between equal and unequal involves the distinction between balanced and unbalanced—if X sounds somewhat off-kilter compared to Y—the fact of having an extra

continuation does not in itself account for this feeling. We could propose a rule that adjacent pulse continuations will result in a feeling of inequality, but we should still have to ask why this should be the case (and later I will suggest that this is not always the case). Example 9.20b, I think, intensifies the feeling of inequality and presents clearer evidence of deferral as the denial of projective potential (as example 9.20c presents clearer evidence of the denial of projected potential).

To hear the distinctions I wish to draw attention to, it will be helpful not to reduce the rhythms shown in examples 9.20b and 9.20c to the form of example 9.20a—that is, not to divide the dotted half note by counting "one-two-three." If such subdivision is not performed, I think that the beginning of the second measure (*) in example 9.20b, X, can be felt to happen "too soon," as if interrupting the duration initiated with the second sound. A comparison with an analogous situation in duple meter may help sharpen this feeling. In example 9.20c, I would ask the reader to notice a feeling that the beginning of the second measure is in some sense delayed, as if the half-note duration begun with the second sound were suspended. In the case of the comparable duple figure, the second sound could

EXAMPLE 9.21 Projective consequences of immediate succession

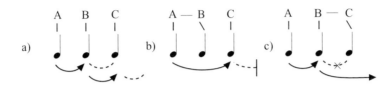

also be called "suspended," but it lacks, I think, the "sprung" character or the "suspense" of the triple figure.

The purpose of example 9.20 is to draw attention to the particular feelings that seem characteristic of unequal measures—what I have called feelings of "interruption," "too early," "delay," and "suspension." To intensify these feelings, I have departed from representing triple measure as a succession of equal durations. But although examples 9.20b and 9.20c introduce factors not encountered in example 9.20a, they are no less instances of triple meter, and I believe that some traces of "too early" and "delay" can also be discerned in feeling the inequality of triple meter in 9.20a. In discussing examples 9.20b and 9.20c, I called attention to an apparent divergence of the two aspects of deferral that, as I have argued, are inseparable. We will consider this divergence in more detail later. Here I would note that although one or another aspect may gain perceptual prominence, both are necessary for a feeling of triple measure. Either can be made to account for a feeling of inequality, but without both I cannot account for the particular sort of inequality that characterizes triple meter.

In attempting to draw attention to the feeling characteristic of unequal measure, I found it necessary to contrast this feeling with that of equal measure. I did not find it necessary to refer to inequality when discussing duple measure. This in itself is a sort of privileging of duple. This sort of privileging is common in discussions of meter and is even expressed linguistically in the "marked" form, "*un*equal" (or, as I have suggested, "*off*-balance"). Thus, "unequal" implies a departure from equality, or *not* being composed of two equal parts. Why should there be such a privileging of equal division and such

a strongly felt difference between duple and triple? The notion of deferral is intended to provide a response to this question which does not suggest that duple is in any sense more "natural" than triple (although it may be in some sense simpler).

Although deferral is by no means unnatural, it is, nevertheless, linked to the incontrovertibly binary nature of projection. Since projection occurs only where there is immediate succession, it always involves two "adjacent" events. Given three equal durations (or, rather, three durations that are not "given" but which are created equal by successive reproduction), A, B, and C, no projection above the level of single durations can be realized. Thus, in example 9.21, A is adjacent to B and B is adjacent to C, and the projected durations of B and C are realized (example 9.21a). On the other hand, A – B is adjacent to C, but C does not realize the projection (example 9.21b); and A is adjacent to B – C, but B – C does not realize the projection (example 9.21c). However, if B and C are continuations, then by renouncing its claim to beginning, C has no choice but to become incorporated into a projection that entered into realization with the beginning of B. I do not suggest that we have a predilection for duple grouping. I do suggest, however, that the feeling of inequality results from a complication of projective/projected potential, a potential that is disposed toward equality. By this account, a disposition toward twoness or *Paarigkeit* would not result from the regulation of attention by heart or lungs (the two phases of which are, in any case, unequal), or from our experience as bipeds (for if we had three or five legs we would still move by "adjacent," immediately successive steps).

In connection with example 9.20, I attempted to provide clearer evidence of deferral

EXAMPLE 9.22 Unequal measure,
deferral intensified

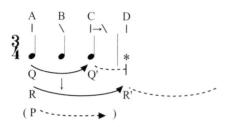

sible to notice a change from duple to triple taking place with the new beginning * , after C is begun (or perhaps even after D has begun—here "before" and "after" are not entirely clear). The projection A–B can be heard as actually completed and only afterward augmented with the incorporation of C into a triple measure. In this case, the reinterpretation appears to be retrospective. What, then, is the proper interpretation? It is exactly what was experienced—a feeling of triple meter having "replaced" a feeling of duple meter. There is now no duple meter per se—that feeling is past (and also past *as denied*), and a feeling of triple meter is present. However, that feeling is relevant for triple measure in a feeling of the interruptive character of the now present second measure and in an intense feeling of inequality for the first measure now past.

To push this situation to the extreme, we might consider the case shown in example 9.23. Here, as I suggest with the unusual time signature, there is no reinterpretation. C begins as, and remains, a beginning. The projective potential Q is realized, and a projection Q' is begun. D interrupts this realization but does not create a reinterpretation of C. As a beginning, C projects the duration Q'. However, to remain a beginning (and not to be reinterpreted as continuation), C must create a new projective potential S, a quarter-note duration. Since C is not reinterpreted, neither is Q. The entrance of D is again interruptive of the projection Q', but since C is not a continuation, there is no projective potential R (as there was in example 9.22). R is not denied, for there is, in fact, no R distinct from the initial indefinite projective potential P. We

by devising situations that I hoped would intensify the feeling of inequality. If there are degrees of intensity in the feeling of inequality, then inequality and, consequently, deferral are relative. Since deferral as a feeling of denied potential is dependent upon some feeling of that potential, projective and projected potential must also be relative. If this is the case, we should attempt to locate the extremes or limits of deferral. Let us first consider the case in which deferral of projective potential and the immediate completion of projection is strongly asserted.

In example 9.22 the projective potential, Q, actually results in a projection, Q'. Initially, the third beat, C, begins with a potential for reproducing the half-note duration A–B. This potential is denied by the beginning of a second measure, D. As a result, C is reinterpreted as a continuation. (This reinterpretation is symbolized by | → \ .) However, since the projection Q' has, in fact, begun to be realized, D is also an interruption of projected potential (represented by the symbol - - - - ⊣). For C as a beginning, D arrives too soon. And yet, D as a second beginning now makes the first measure past and realizes the projective potential R. As a result, the projective potential P of the beginning of the first measure (or, rather, the beginning of what would become the first measure) is reinterpreted. The projective potential of the beginning (P) is not denied—it is reinterpreted and enlarged. This double reinterpretation—C changing from | to \ and the projective potential changing from Q to R—can be felt here as an actual succession. To test this, the reader should perform the first two quarters in 2/4, begin a second bar of 2/4, and, interrupting this duple measure, begin another measure with D. If this is done, it should be pos-

EXAMPLE 9.23 Equal measure, contraction of projective potential

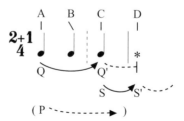

have, in effect, created three measures: one of 2/4 followed by one of 1/4 followed by one (potentially) of 1/4. As bizarre as example 9.23 appears, it is not, I believe, entirely out of the question. At a very slow tempo, it is, I think, possible (although very difficult) to hear something resembling this interpretation. The tempo must be slow enough for individual pulses such as C and D to be immune from involuntary or "spontaneous" metrical grouping, and we must struggle against an inclination to hear D as continuation and thus to reproduce a measure of 2/4 — that is, we must by an act of will attempt to block the relevancy of Q. To the degree we are successful in doing this we will have succeeded in hearing three measures and not the two bar measures indicated in the example. In this case there will have been no deferral. (In effect, this would a be a "contraction" of meter or a reduction in the scope of mensural determinacy — a phenomenon that does occur in more complex projective situations, as we shall see in later chapters.) Example 9.22 represents a limit of deferral and example 9.23 a situation in which this limit is exceeded.

Let us now consider the limit to deferral in the opposite direction — toward the weakening of projective and projected potential. Here, since these potentials become increasingly attenuated, we cannot look for so precise a limit. The question we must ask is, rather, what the result of an utter absence of deferral would be. If, as in example 9.24, there were no deferral of projective potential, we would be left only with the deferral of beginning, i.e., pure continuation (| \ \).

And if there were no deferral of projected potential, we would also be left only with pure continuation — two completed projections within the measure and a realization of the projection R–R' (or a definite but unrealized projective potential R if there is no beginning of a second measure).

In example 9.24 we can perhaps still speak of 3/4 time, a real measure composed of three equal beats, the second and third of which are continuations of a single beginning. But unless we take inequality to be simply an arithmetic distinction between even and odd, or ground the distinction between equal and unequal in physiology (and both assumptions are highly problematic

EXAMPLE 9.24 Pure continuation, no trace of inequality

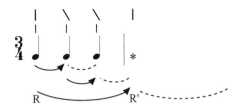

lematic from a perceptual or psychological point of view), we must ask what it is about example 9.24 that is unequal. I suggest that to the degree deferral is attenuated, what we call triple measure loses its distinctive character of being unequal (unbalanced, lilting, etc.) and becomes less distinct in feeling from duple measure or a feeling of equality. In this case, the difference will tend to become one of quantity or the difference between 2 and 3 as "lengths." If there is no felt projective/projected potential that is denied — if, as in example 9.24, the indefinite projective potential P is simply realized as R — there is nothing but equality: three equal beats and the (potentially) equal reproduction of the duration of a dotted half note with the beginning of a second measure (*). In the extreme case, the characteristic difference between equal and unequal would be lost, and to determine the metrical type we should have to resort to counting beats. This may, in fact, happen more frequently than is generally acknowledged. Certainly, students often have difficulty identifying metrical type, but even well-trained, mature musicians may not always be fully cognizant of metrical type and may have to count to identify the type. However, even in cases in which it is found difficult to explicitly identify triple measure, it cannot be assumed that there is absolutely no feeling of inequality. I do not suggest that the absence of a feeling of inequality is necessarily a defect in hearing — in fact, it has the considerable advantage of strengthening the greater projection of a "three-beat" duration. But I do suggest that a distinctive property of what we call triple meter will have been lost.

Having identified extreme situations, I should reiterate my point that virtually all experiences of triple measure fall somewhere between these

EXAMPLE 9.25 Projective possibilities for a group of
five pulses

a)
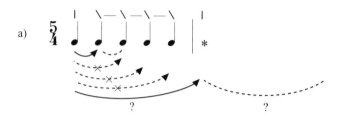

b)

c)

d)

extremes. (Indeed, there is enormous variety in the particularity of deferral or metrical inequality.) Obviously, situations resembling that shown in example 9.22 are rarely encountered, particularly once a triple meter has been established (that is, if the measure begins as the realization of a projected duration "three beats long"). And although the extreme case of feeling absolutely no trace of inequality in the perception of triple measure may perhaps not be so rare, I would question the decision to call such a case a perception of triple (unequal) measure. Nevertheless, the feeling of deferral is often attenuated, in

which case the feeling of simple continuation (deferral of new or dominant beginning) seems paramount. Again, the result of a weaker feeling of deferral is that more attention can be given to the greater projective potential. If this is the case, can we not gain an even greater projection by extending this process, further suppressing projective potentials and completions, and "adding" continuations? In the following I will argue against this possibility and against the extension of deferral to inequalities of more than three beats.

In example 9.25a, four continuations and

EXAMPLE 9.26 Projective possibilities for a
group of four pulses

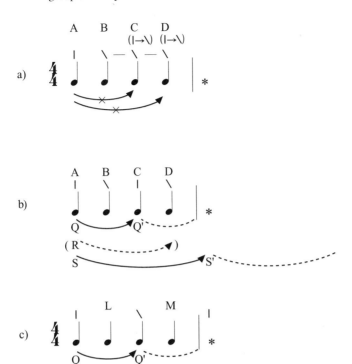

three deferrals are indicated. However, as experiments concerning "subjective" or "spontaneous" grouping show, it will be very difficult (and at moderate tempi perhaps impossible) to suppress a feeling of duple or triple measure (examples 9.25b and 9.25c) to hear the continuation of a single beginning and the projection of a duration equivalent to five quarter notes. It seems that we are not willing to defer making a projective decision for such a long time given the opportunities available in example 9.25a. These projective potentials (shown as denied in example 9.25a) are opportunities to strengthen or enhance the durational determinacy of the group. If we fail to take advantage of them (or realize them), we run the risk of losing a feeling of durational determinacy and, consequently, risk losing our abilities to predict and to act upon the basis of the durational information offered to us by the stimuli.

If this series is performed much faster—say, as five 16th notes or five 32nd notes (example 9.25d) —we may, indeed (depending on our attention and the context), hear no internal group-

ing. If grouping has as an aim the enhancement of durational determinacy or the enhancement of our ability to hold onto a beginning, there would appear to be little need for grouping within a relatively short durational unit. Or from the standpoint of prediction, if potential projections are too brief to be acted upon, it will do us no good to realize them, and we will be better off choosing a projection that better suits our purposes and motor abilities. If, at fast speeds, there is no grouping but, rather, a series of continuations, this situation resembles that of "triple measure" in which a feeling of inequality is suppressed with the suppression of deferral. However, in the case of example 9.25, I will argue that interpretation a should be rejected in favor of b, c, or d, or, more generally, that deferral be limited to the inequality of triple measure.

If we extend our measure to include four beats (example 9.26) and allow that there are definite projective potentials greater than the potentials for reproducing individual beats and smaller than the potential for reproducing the bar measure (i.e., the potentials that were disallowed in example 9.25a), there will be no reason to speak of deferral.

Although, as in example 9.26a, it is conceivable that there might be two deferrals before there is a beginning of a second measure (if for any reason there should be a reinterpretation | → \ of C and D), these deferrals cannot be maintained once there is a bar measure. As example 9.26b shows, with the advent of a new beginning *, Q is, in fact, realized in the projection Q–Q', and so there can be no definite potential, R. Now if there is a measure of four beats, it must have a single beginning. Since the projection Q–Q' creates two durations, L and M in example 9.26c, the second of these, M, must function as continuation. In this case, all projective potentials are realized, as are all projections.

Let us now consider a measure composed of five beats. Example 9.27a duplicates example 9.25a, an interpretation I rejected on empirical grounds. Now I would like to consider other reasons for excluding deferral in this case (and, thus, reasons for our choosing duple and triple rather than purely quintuple grouping, or example 9.27b or 9.27c rather than 9.27d or 9.27e). Again, we ask what are the projective consequences of creating a measure. In the case of 5/4 there are several possibilities. In example 9.27b projective potential Q is realized, but the projected duration Q' is not. Instead, the third beat, C, initiates a triple group and, consequently, an embedded deferral. Since C is a beginning and not a continuation, there are two measures: one of 2/4 and one of 3/4. To form a single measure, there must be, with the beginning of C, a beginning of M that functions as continuation. In this case, there is no deferral in the sense I have used the term—no projective potential has been denied (Q is realized), and no completion is deferred (there is no second continuation succeeding M). In fact, the measure L–M is a duple measure, albeit an unequal duple measure. Certainly there is a feeling of lengthening with M or a feeling that N is delayed, but M is not involved in a deferral—no projective potential is denied by the beginning of M.

In example 9.27c, projective potential R is realized at the expense of Q to result in a triple group, A–B–C, and a projected duration R', which is not realized. Again, there is a deferral in

the triple group, but there is no deferral that would distinguish a measure of 5/4 from a sequence of two measures—one triple, the other duple. Here the inequality results in a feeling that M is too short or interrupted by the beginning of a second bar measure (*).

In example 9.27c a projective potential (Q) is denied by M, but M does not complete a projection R–R'. There could be a deferral only if M were to reproduce the continuation C as a reproduction of a reproduction of B. However, M does not reproduce C; M is two beats long. Similarly, in example 9.27b, M is three beats long and so does not reproduce B. (The possibility of a denial of projective completion is represented by a dotted line connecting continuations in examples 9.27b and 9.27c.) In the case of example 9.27c, could M, in principle, reproduce the continuation B–C? It could not, because to be reproducible, B–C would have to be a unit—a relatively self-sufficient entity with a single beginning. Certainly B and C are each units, but there is no deferral of projective completion, B–C, apart from A. That is to say, B can be reproduced and C can be reproduced, but if B–C as deferral is to be reproduced, it can be reproduced only with a reproduction of A–B–C (| \ — \). I raise this question only to clarify the systematic relation of deferral to reproduction. In examples 9.27b and 9.27c such questions need not arise because deferral is excluded for a more obvious reason, as is shown beneath the examples. In example 9.27c, for M to complete the projective potential begun with A–B–C, it would have to be continuation. However, in order for there to be an M, there must be an L made past by the beginning of a third sound— that is, a beginning in relation to the continuative C or B–C. M can be a continuation for the duration realized in L, but not for the duration realized in C—to be a continuation for C (or even for B–C, if this were possible) would mean no L and thus no M. As a result of there being an L and M there are two groups and a deferral limited to the triple group—which is to say, there is no "quintuple deferral."

In example 9.27d an attempt has been made to escape groupings of two and three beats. The potentials Q and R, shown in parentheses, are denied in order to assert a real projective poten-

EXAMPLE 9.27 Projective possibilities for "quintuple deferral"

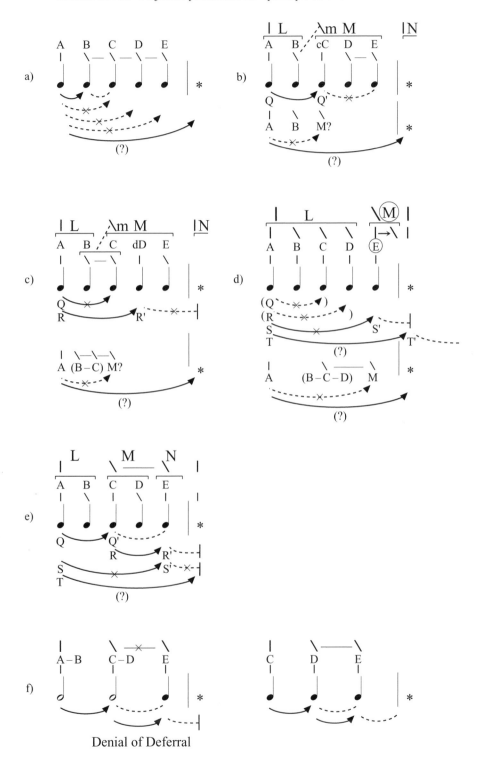

Denial of Deferral

143

tial S, "subsequently" denied with *. This extremely unlikely interpretation may be tested by attempting to hear four ungrouped beats, followed by a beat E that would initiate a second duration of four quarters, followed by the beginning of a second measure (*). If this can be accomplished, E will be reinterpreted as continuation. It must be said, however, that to the extent we are successful in carrying out this performance, E will sound much more like a break in continuity than a continuation, and as a result of this reinterpretation, the projective, T, shown in example 9.27d will not, I think, emerge. The problem here, or rather one of the problems, is that the projective potential S must be realized in order to be denied. For there to be an M as a continuation in relation to an L (and, consequently, for there to be an L), M must be distinct from B, C, and D as a beginning distinct from continuations. Thus, in example 9.27b there is a continuation M distinct from the beginning C because there is a C that functions as a beginning phase of M. However, in example 9.27d, M and E are identical—they are the same duration. Without the realization of L and S (like the realization of L and Q in ex. 9.27b), there would be no M. And yet, without the denial of S there would be no final beat of 5/4, E, and no projective, T. Example 9.27d in many respects resembles example 9.22. However, in example 9.22, through the agency of deferral, a third beat could be assimilated to the measure and a projection could be realized. In example 9.27d, there is no deferral, and the fifth beat is not incorporated into the unity of a nascent measure. I maintain that a measure—that is to say, a unitary duration with a definite projective potential—cannot be formed in this way.

As outlandish as example 9.27d certainly is, it may point toward a more plausible possibility for a genuinely quintuple deferral. Assuming that we were not successful in entirely eliminating a feeling of grouping in the first four beats of example 9.27d, we will have heard the segmentation 9.27e (for reasons discussed in connection with example 9.26). Now there is a triple division and, conceivably, the initiation of a deferral with the beginning of beat E. Example 9.27e can be performed by producing a measure of 4/4 (or 2/2), beginning a second measure with

E, and then interrupting this beginning with a "downbeat" at *. In this case, the beginning of E coincides with the beginning of a projected half-note duration, R'. However, if there is deferral here, it is a deferral denied. N does not, in fact, reproduce M. Certainly, a projective potential S is denied, but the projective potential, T, that replaces S is smaller than that promised by deferral R–R'. Had deferral been realized, the measure (and its projective potential) would have been six beats long and not five beats long.

The question I would like to ask concerns the "status" of S—how definite is this denied possibility, and how is it denied? S must be denied for there to be a T. Thus, S in a sense precedes T—we can (if we try) hear a third half-note duration begun "before" we hear T, as in example 9.22 we can hear the beginning of a second measure of 2/4 "before" we hear the beginning of a second measure of 3/4. (I place "before" in double quotes because in another sense both these feelings occur at the same time—the time of the created measure.) But in example 9.27e, it is deferral and not, as in example 9.22, simply projective/projected potential that is denied with *. These two situations are contrasted in example 9.27f. In example 9.27e a rejection of S is also a rejection of a potential deferral that would enlarge projective potential by reproducing the continuation M. For this reason I suggest that, to the extent we attend to this S as a possibility that is unrealized, we lose a feeling for the reproductive potential, T, that is realized.

Now there seems little point in choosing the denied deferral shown in example 9.27e when we can more economically choose the realized deferral shown in example 9.27b, in which E functions as a deferral in the context of the triple group, $C - D - E$. But I would argue that the choice is not driven exclusively by economy—that our interests are not served entirely by the conservation of energy, but by an optimally productive use of energy. Presented with a measure of five beats, a denial of deferral as a process of integration will leave us with a poorly integrated duration. By contrast, if we realize a deferral in beats C, D, and E, we can better grasp the duration and better predict a future. This choice for greater determinacy can, I think, be observed in the performance of example 9.27e, where, even while trying to realize the deferred S and trying to hear the beginning, *, as interruptive, it will be difficult to avoid feeling the "retrospective" formation of a triple, C – D – E, with the beginning, *. It may be possible to suppress to some extent this triple and its realized deferral by concentrating our attention on the denied deferral L – M – N; however, to the extent we are able to do this, we will have had to suppress T and, consequently, T'.

It must be said that the preceding demonstrations concerning example 9.27 are circular, since deferral has been defined precisely to account for the feeling of triple unequal measure. Indeed, it is my hope that they are circular, because if this circle is truly closed, deferral will distinguish triple measure from all other varieties of unequal measure, and the distinction will be one of kind and not merely one of degree. Certainly, there is a clear difference in feeling—quintuple sounds more unequal than triple. If triple sounds lilting, quintuple sounds limping. Thus, I would like to suggest a division of metrical types into three categories: equal, mediated unequal (3/4, for example), and nonmediated or "pure" unequal (5/4, for example). By the term "mediated unequal" I mean to suggest an accommodation of inequality to a demand of equality or reproduction. Through deferral, a third beat extends a unitary duration by becoming assimilated to a projective potential created by an initial two beats. The third beat, although it does not immediately succeed the first beat, nevertheless draws on the projective potential of the first beat (or, more accurately, the projective potential of what becomes the first beat) by reproducing the first beat's immediate successor, a reproduction in which the dual function of the second beat for the first is repeated: the function of continuation (whereby a first beat was created) and the function of realizing a projection (whereby the projective potential of the first beat became actual). Or, from a different perspective, it might be said that in reproducing the second beat, the third beat inherits the particular relevance the first has for the second.

Although, for convenience, I have used (and, for convenience, will continue to use) the terms "duple," "triple," and "quintuple," such terms are not appropriate for the distinctions I have made.

As was noted in connection with example 9.27b, a measure of 5/4 can take the form of duple unequal. Likewise, a nonmediated triple might be represented by 8/8 as 3+3+2, for example. "Oneness," "twoness," "threeness," "fourness," "fiveness," et cetera, are real properties that cannot be detached from metrical formation, but I do not believe that the feeling of meter is the feeling of these numerical quantities per se, but rather the projective possibilities that such quantities offer. Indeed, these projective possibilities, special for each cardinality, may be involved in feeling the distinctiveness of various numerical quantities.

Before leaving the topic of inequality, I would like to consider briefly the projective shortcoming of "pure" unequal measure compared to the other two types. In example 9.27 I placed question marks beneath the projective potentials indicated for 5/4 measures to suggest projective indeterminacy in these cases—that with the beginning of a second bar measure (at *) the projective potential for a definite duration is not very clearly felt. Obviously, nonmediated inequality detracts from projective potential. In examples 9.27b and 9.27c the continuations M do not realize the projected potentials Q' and R', respectively, and thus do not complete a projection. The new beginnings with N complete a previous measure, but this measure itself is not composed of a completed projection above the level of individual beats. In the case of 3/4, I have argued that although the measure is unequal, it is nevertheless composed of a completed projection. One of my reasons for introducing the notion of deferral is to offer an account of why metrical types such as 2/4, 3/4, 4/4, 6/8, and 9/8 seem (at appropriate tempi) to have similarly strong projective potential, whereas metrical types such as 5/4, 7/8, and 3+3+2/8 are projectively much less determinate. Example 9.28 points to a further complication that can arise in "pure unequal" projective types.

From a reproductive standpoint, a second measure of 5/4 demands considerable reinterpretation, especially if, as in examples 9.28c and 9.28d, the tempo is slow enough to open the possibility for the emergence of a smaller projective potential, R. If there is any ambiguity in the projective "hierarchy" (S versus R), realized pro-

EXAMPLE 9.28 Contrasting projective potentials for "mediated unequal," "equal," and "pure unequal" measure

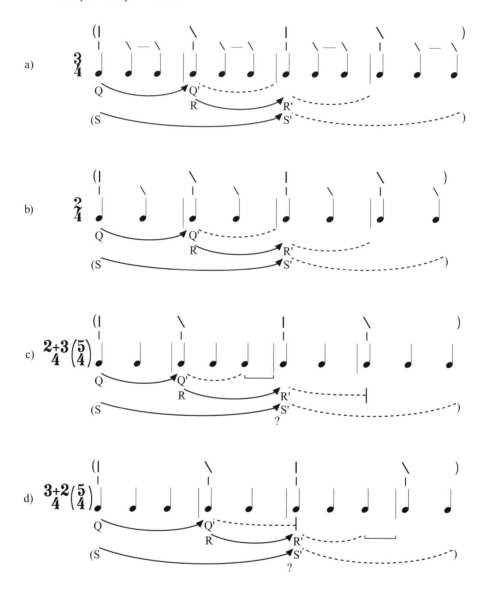

jective potentials (Q and R) will issue in failed projections (Q–Q' and R–R'). In the case of 3/4 or 2/4, et cetera, no such reinterpretation need arise—all realized projective potentials result in completed projections. This is not to say that 5/4, 7/8, and so on are unnatural or confused. It is to say that such measures are complex. They are in a sense underdetermined and in a sense overdetermined—underdetermined in that the smaller projections involved in the two-measure projection are unrealized or denied and so do

not enhance the determinacy of the larger projection, and overdetermined in that within each measure decisions among equally possible alternatives (in the case of 5/4, 2+3, or 3+2) must be made. For this reason, 5/4 is not as flexible as 3/4 or 4/4. If we are to feel quintuple measures, we will not be able to depart very far from an explicit presentation of five appropriately grouped beats. Due to their greater determinacy, measures of 3/4, 4/4, and so on can support a greater variety of patterns and can withstand greater departures from an explicit presentation of composite beats once there is a definite projection (i.e., a second measure).

In the case of "subjective" or "spontaneous" grouping (groupings within a continuous pulse train in which none of the pulses is "objectively" accented), quintuple groupings are not chosen. Duple, triple, or quadruple groupings will be chosen, and this choice is doubtless based upon the interaction of many factors—tempo, attention, and interest. However, I believe that, in general, there will be an inclination to choose equal over unequal measures with triple grouping, in a sense "mediating" between duple and quadruple. At slow tempi (say, one or two seconds per pulse), as it becomes possible to hear continuation rather than individual beginnings only, duple grouping will be heard. Continuations will function to keep dominant beginnings projectively active and will thus function to expand the range of prediction. At somewhat faster tempi we might be prepared to sacrifice some degree of determinacy for a greater projection. But doubling the duration—as in the case of moving from duple to quadruple grouping—although it would

increase predictive range, might result in too great a sacrifice of determinacy; and it will do us little good to predict if our predictions miss the mark. However, the choice of triple grouping would offer an increase of projected potential (predictive range) with a more modest loss of determinacy (predictive accuracy). If triple grouping is more complex owing to the operation of deferral, this loss of economy might be compensated for by an increase in the range of duration in which a relatively accurate prediction can be made, the advantage being that we will have won more time in which to act effectively. Again, the question arises, why there should be such durational limits for attention, why this trade-off between durational quantity and determinacy, or why the added complexities shown in examples 9.28c and 9.28d do not seem for us worth the effort. And again, I suggest that such limitations or conditions for the grasp of duration arise from our adaptation to a particular environment, an environment and an adaptation that constitute our world. For without some sort of limitation there would be no determinacy *and no world.*

TEN

Metrical Particularity

Now it must be admitted that in the "natural" world, no less than in the "artistic," musical world, simple series of isochronous pulses are rarely encountered. The operation of meter is far more flexible and complex than has been suggested by our preliminary investigations concerning the metrical grouping of pulses. By concentrating on the question of metrical types, we run the risk of losing sight of what is rhythmic about meter. If any measure is reducible to an instance of a type and thus to a typical organization of equal beats and if meter is equated with this "underlying" organization, the uniqueness or particularity of any actual measure will be viewed as a product of rhythm and not meter.

The problem here is not the identification of type but the reification of the type or an identification of the type with a particular instance. Thus, unequal or triple meter, for example, is often identified with a succession of three equal beats (even in cases where these beats are not actually sounded). The three beats together with their accentual distinctions are then said to constitute "the" meter, and it is against this underlying regularity that a less regular and more rhythmic "surface" is heard. The hypostatization of three beats gives the measure a considerable degree of autonomy. Once "*the* meter is established" it can be thought to perpetuate itself, reproducing again and again groupings of equal beats.

The measure and each of its reproductions are relatively immune from context. The only contextual pressures that affect the measure *as* measure are those that would alter the metrical type and thus subvert its perpetuation. If "the" meter is sustained, individual measures may differ considerably, and some of these differences may be called metrical differences; but the ruling meter as a grouping of pulses remains unchanged, and each measure, as measure, is identical to all the others. Certainly, as representatives of a single metrical type, such measures are identical, but to identify meter with type robs meter of the particularity that will tend to be assumed by its opposite—rhythm.

Just now, I have used the word "meter" conventionally to mean notated meter and "measure" to mean notated bar (or felt "bar" if there is a discrepancy between notation and feeling). There is much to recommend this understanding of meter. The meter signature indicates a grouping of equal beats that (in some styles) is often repeated in the course of the piece; and there may be situations in which such beats can be felt even when they are not explicitly articulated. In many cases, we can, and often do, count pulses or beat time without consulting the notation—certainly, dancing to music clearly shows the relevancy of the articulations indicated in the signature (though it should be pointed out that expressive dancing shows many other relevancies as well). The notated or felt bar thus seems to be a privileged measure. Typically, the duration of the bar accommodates a comfortable projective potential—one that is long enough to permit us to act (with hands and feet, arms and legs) on the basis of a projection, but not so long that the projected duration would lose a determinacy that will permit accuracy in execution. Often, a feeling of the notated pulse or the "conductor's beat" can enhance the determinacy of both projective and projected potential. If we are in danger of losing a desired degree of determinacy we may, in fact, imagine and feel an expected beat when none is actually sounded. However, bars can also be composed of a complex of projections and can compose projections involving more than two bars. And in order to feel the determinacy of a projection it is not always necessary to feel beats that are not actually articulated. Although the bar is often a favorable environment for projection, projection itself is not limited to the bar and does not require a homogeneous train of pulses.

If meter is identified with projection, there will be no reason to identify meter with bar or to presuppose an invariant procession of equal beats. In this case, the rhythmic particularity of a bar will be inseparable from its metrical particularity. And each measure or each metrical unit could be viewed as a unique projective situation in which uniqueness or particularity arises both from the measure's internal constitution and from its assimilation of prior events (and its potential for being assimilated to future events). Although I will continue to focus attention on the bar measure as a primary metrical unit, I will use the term "measure" indifferently to refer to any mensurally determinate or reproducible duration. Likewise, "meter" will not be taken to mean "the" meter or the information supplied by the time signature, but will refer instead to the operation of projection at all "levels."

It is the continuous repetition of metrical type that seems most lawlike and deterministic and most opposed to the spontaneity and creativity of rhythm. If meter is regarded only as a grouping of equal beats and is reproduced only as a grouping of equal beats, the only *metrical* particularity that can be ascribed to a measure is

the particularity of a metrical type (or a composite of types such as duple, triple, and quadruple—subdivisions of the measure's beats). While I reject the notion that meter is reducible to a fixed organization of equal durations representing a metrical type, I cannot deny the fact that metrical type can be replicated in successive measures. However, I maintain that reproduction always involves more than a reproduction of type and that this latter reproduction is an outcome of the potential for reproducing a measure in all its durational particularity.

Particularity and Reproduction

In discussing meter as projection, I claimed that the projected duration is a potential for a reproduction of the projective duration, but I did not claim that in projection the "contents" or the particular metrical decisions that constitute the projective duration are reproducible in the projected duration. There are, however, grounds for making such a claim. In example 10.1a the constitution of the second bar measure is very different from that of the first. The second may be regarded as a duple equal measure, but it will not be heard as simply duple; in fact, it may not be felt as a duple equal measure at all, but rather as a syncopated figure in which the second sound can be heard to enter too late. Here the beginning of the second measure projects something more than the potential for a dotted half-note duration. In example 10.1a a possible feeling of "too late" is accounted for by regarding the third beat of the first measure as projective for the following beginning (in violation of the rule we established in the last chapter). The projection Q–Q' is not realized, and on the basis of this real potential the second sound or beat of the second measure is felt to be too late. If we also feel that the second sound is syncopated—that it begins as a weak or continuative phase of an expected second beat (and does not end with an expected beginning of a third beat)—it might be argued that we will have felt a realization of projected potential (Q') and a definite but acoustically suppressed beginning (| \) indicated in parentheses in example 10.1a. However, to regard the third beat as projective, we must detach it from

EXAMPLE 10.1 Inheritance of
projective complexity

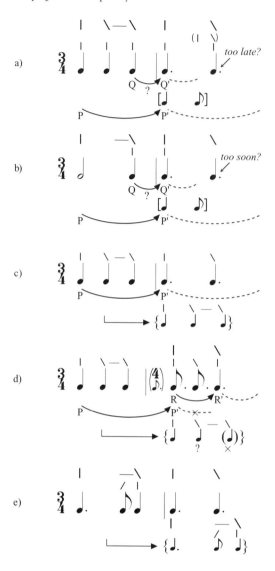

content of the first measure provides a potential for reproduction. By "durational content" or simply "content" (an unfortunate word perhaps) I will mean the particular ensemble of projective potentials and realizations that constitute the measure. This potential is represented by the copy of the first measure, enclosed in braces, that appears below the second measure. This device of copying the first measure may be misleading. I do not mean that the first measure is re-presented or re-called while we are attending to the second measure. I mean, rather, that there is a potential for reproduction, or, more precisely, that the range of possibilities available for the becoming of the second measure is narrowed by the definiteness of the now completed first measure (and thus the copying of the first measure is a very crude representation of this complex durational *relevance*).

This potential is, in fact, inseparable from projective potential. The projective potential of the first measure cannot be abstracted from the actual first measure and from everything that is involved in its becoming just this measure with just this projective potential. As I indicated earlier, the events that constitute the measure (in this case, a first, second, and third beat) can enhance or (as in the case of 5/4, for example) detract from its projective potential. *The projective potential or the duration of the measure is nothing apart from its constitution.* It is also for this reason that the term "content" is misleading. What I have been calling projective potential is not an abstract quantity or a "span of time" in which the event is contained. Nor is a measure or a duration simply a span of time reducible to the descriptions "three beats long" or "two seconds long." I did perhaps imply the contrary in using expressions such as "a dotted half-note duration." But a feeling of duration is always a feeling of particularity. Thus, even performing our poor example 10.1a again and again, the feeling of duration will not be precisely repeated. "Content" here refers to the *particularity* of a projective potential. Again, this particularity may be more or less relevant for the realization of projected potential, depending on our attentiveness and interest. Indeed, to the degree such particularity or complexity is *not* relevant, the projected duration will more resemble a "span of time" (but a felt rather than a counted span).

its context in the first measure and hear it simply as a beginning. Certainly, the third beat does have a beginning and can, presumably, function projectively for the following sound. But I do not believe that this interpretation can entirely account for our feeling of the second measure. And in the case of example 10.1b a similar interpretation will not account for the possibility of feeling that the second sound of the second measure enters too soon.

Example 10.1c presents an alternative interpretation of example 10.1a. Here the durational

Earlier, I said that projective reproduction is not here conceived as a reproduction of beginning by beginning. (As a *potential* for duration, beginning is not, strictly speaking, reproducible.) Instead, I argued that projective reproduction arises from a simultaneous making present and making past effected by the beginning of a new event. However, once a projection is effected— once there *is* a new beginning and the emergence of a more or less definite projected potential—the second beginning can, in fact, reproduce in its durational potential something of the realized duration of the first beginning; and if this potential is realized, the second event will have repeated (*in its own particular way*) the actual duration of the first event. Thus, in the course of its becoming, the second event has the potential for reproducing what became of a prior beginning; and if this potential is realized, there will in effect be a reproduction of beginning by beginning.

Directed by this (durational) potentiality, the now of the second event specifically involves (durational) relevancies of the now past first event. And the repetition of the first measure below the second in example 10.1c is a crude device for indicating such relevance. The realization of projective potential in a projection may be considered the relevancy of the first measure for the becoming of the second measure's duration. And since the actual duration of the first measure is the particular product of all that has transpired in the course of its becoming, its projective potential is also that particular product. The durational content of the second measure may depart from a repetition of the content of the first. But to the degree we hear departure as contrast (e.g., too late, too soon) or as a repetition denied, the particularity of the first measure is to this degree relevant for the second.

Contrast arises from departure, but there is no departure apart from reproduction. If there is divergence, it is divergence only *with respect to* reproduction or correspondence. If the second measure comes to differ greatly from the first and does not develop projective correspondences with the first, the first measure, as measure, can lose relevance for what the second is now becoming. Since the two measures (and, more generally, the two events) are immediately successive, the first will necessarily have some rele-

vance for the second, but if the divergence of projections is too great, as in example 10.1d, the metrical or projective organization of the first measure will not be corroborated and the projection will be denied. In example 10.1d, although the second measure is "objectively" equal in duration to the first, it will not, I think, be easily heard as equal or as a realization of the first measure's projective potential. Instead, the relevance of the first measure is expressed in a feeling of faster tempo and the contrast between unequal and equal measure. The projective function of the third beat of the second measure (the dotted quarter) now excludes the projective relevance of the first measure.

To put the matter in more "environmental" terms, initial correspondences in a projection enhance projected potential and thus predictability. It may happen that the present event ceases to corroborate predictions made on the basis of the projection, in which case we may be inclined to eschew the projection as irrelevant and turn our attention to more immediate projections that offer better predictive results (as in the second bar measure of example 10.1d) or turn to the relevancy of other durational levels. But even if an immediately preceding event ceases to serve predictive aims, it must retain some relevance, if only as a contrast that sharpens the particularity of the newly emerging event. More generally, in the formation of a new event all the relevancies in the horizon of "now" can come into play, but the immediately preceding event is especially privileged. And according to the intensity of our involvement with this process, the particularity or definiteness of the previous event will be especially relevant. Moreover, if (as I suggested in chapter 6) there are in the horizon of "now" manifold presents, there are also manifold pasts or immediately preceding events whose definiteness can be taken into account. Or, to put this in other words, if there are several metrical or projective levels, each level's projected duration will draw upon the definiteness of a completed projective phase. The projective "hierarchy" or the coordination of or movement within these levels will therefore produce a wide range of relevancies that are (variously) brought into play according to the demands of the newly emerging situation.

In view of this complexity, it is clear that issues of metrical particularity and reproduction cannot be adequately addressed in the very limited contexts of the preceding examples. If we are to inquire into more complex and subtle projective relevancies, we will need to consider musical examples in which projective potentials are much more sharply and richly defined. In particular, we will need the differentiation provided by tonal quality and contour. Such differentiation can create abundant opportunities for durational correspondence (whether in conformance or contrast) and can play a primary role in the distinction of end, beginning, and continuation (or anacrusis). Indeed, larger projections or projective complexes cannot arise in the absence of tonal differentiation. In each of the subsequent chapters of this book, analyses of excerpts from a variety of musical compositions will provide us with opportunities to explore questions of metrical particularity and reproduction in more detail. And in the next section of this chapter we will begin this exploration with an analysis of excerpts from two Bach Courantes for solo cello. Our analysis of the Bach will continue the argument presented here to assert that metrical type is an abstraction that, if reified and given priority over all other metrical characteristics, will result in the reduction of meter to a deterministic repetition of pulse. But before we begin this analysis I would like to return to example 10.1 to consider the role of "virtual" beats in the creation and reproduction of metrical type.

In the syncopated second bars of examples 10.1a, 10.1b, and 10.1e an actual feeling of an acoustically absent second and third beat may occur and may be more or less vivid, especially if we are performing rather than listening to a performance. If the tempo is slow, we may be inclined to subdivide the second bar measure. If the tempo is faster, the projected duration of the second measure will be more highly determinate and we may simply fit a duple division into this "container" without imagining a triple subdivision (in which case a feeling of syncopation will be diminished). Certainly, experienced performers do not have to rely on subdivision in such situations. To perform a quintuplet, for example, it is possible to feel the projected duration more

generally as a "span of time" in which to play five notes without relating this division to a previous duple or triple division. Likewise, at the other extreme, in cases where projected potential is most highly conditioned by the durational determinacies of a preceding event, we should not assume that it is the pulses of an imaginary metric grid that direct the performer's (or the listener's) perceptions. Having developed both a capacity for comprehending relatively long projections and a keen sensitivity to durational relevancies, an experienced performer does not have to imagine the pulses that are often indicated in metrical analyses. And I believe that this capacity and this sensitivity can be communicated in performance and valued as especially "rhythmic." Of course, there are situations in which subdivision becomes necessary, but only as a feeling of durational determinacy fails us or when, as beginners, we are learning to read from metrical notation.

In examples 10.1b and 10.1e I have not indicated quarter-note subdivisions, and although I did copy the three quarter notes of the first measure beneath the second in example 10.1c, I do not mean to imply that these three beats are repeated; in fact, they are not. It may, however, be objected that there is one very good reason for postulating a succession of three beats—or, rather, pulses—in every bar. How else could we account for the first measure of example 10.1b or 10.1e, for instance, being felt as a triple unequal measure? To feel inequality we do not need to feel three beats; we need only feel a deferral of projective potential, as is indicated in examples 10.2a and 10.2b.

Without a deferral of projective potential, however, there will be nothing to distinguish what I have called "mediated inequality" from "pure" inequality. (Conversely, in example 10.2c without a third beat there will be deferral of projected potential but no fully explicit deferral of projective potential.) Certainly there is a clear distinction in feeling. Examples 10.2d and 10.2e can also be heard to present a deferral of projective potential, but they clearly sound more unequal than examples 10.2a and 10.2b (unless, of course, through the vagaries of mensural determinacy we can hear in example 10.2d and example 10.2e *rallentandi*). The first duration in

EXAMPLE 10.2 "Retrospective" emergence of metrical type

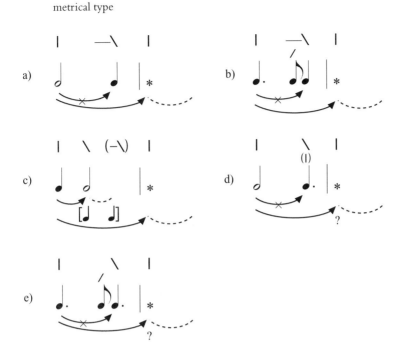

example 10.2d is not, as in example 10.2a, exactly "twice as long" as the second. It might be said that simplicity of proportion results in a greater feeling of "equality." But unless we assume that there are specific feelings of numerical proportion—"twice/half as long" or "two-thirds/one-third as long" (or, in the case of the eighth note in example 10.2b, a feeling of "a quarter as long as the half-note duration" or "a third as long as the dotted quarter")—it seems we must grant some sort of perceptual reality to the acoustically suppressed "second pulse."

Let us assume that we hear something resembling example 10.2a without having heard a preceding measure of 3/4 or without a prior decision to hear this as a measure of 3/4. In this case, we will first hear a measure of 3/4 only with the beginning of a second measure (*). To say that the second sound of the first measure is now heard as, in some sense, a "third" beat would seem to imply that we have retrospectively divided the first half note. I think that this could be taken as an adequate account, provided that the notion of "retrospective division" is clarified.

The first measure is now past for the second measure. The second measure, or what is becoming a second measure, is present and is being constituted, in part, by the "presence" of the first measure as projected potential. Thus, it is this definite potential that is "retrospective." And the "division" is therefore a potential division. Now that there is the possibility of reproducing the particular projective potential of the first measure, there is a great variety of metrical arrangements that could conform in one way or another to this potential. If there is an actual second beat articulated in the second measure, it will be a division of the half note as reproduced for the second measure and a confirmation of the relevancy of the first measure as a mediated unequal measure. What was "given" to the second measure by way of potentiality includes a potential for subdivision, and what is "taken" by the second measure by way of realization is an actual division. If there is no actual second beat in the second measure, the potential for division is nonetheless real, and the first measure will be, "retrospectively," no less a mediated unequal measure. (And, of course, in the becoming of the two-bar measure decisions pertaining to "type" are in flux until the end of this larger present.) Although I have used unequal measure as an example since it is more problematic, a similar analysis applies to equal measure in situations where what we might regard as beats are suppressed (as in syncopations, dotted figures, and ties).

Having acknowledged a real potential for division, I will not argue that the practice of including indications of all "virtual" beats in a metrical analysis is entirely inadequate as a representation of metrical organization. But I do argue that this practice oversimplifies the issue of meter in two ways: first, by implying a reduction of meter to a coordination of more or less autonomous (and essentially atemporal) pulse "strata," and, second, by eliminating a distinction between "virtual beats" that are clearly felt and those that are not. Among those that are felt there is a great range in the vividness of feeling, and this variation contributes to the rhythmic/metrical particularity of musical experience. Both of these reasons have, I think, far-reaching implications for our study of meter and rhythm.

Two Examples

I opened the preceding discussion of metrical reproduction with the assertion that meter, or the feeling of what we call "meter," is always particular, and then I proceeded to consider the particularities involved in immediate reproduction. The examples we have considered certainly raise many more questions than I have attempted to answer. And the limitations of these few, contextually impoverished examples invite us to think of other examples that would raise new questions or put the questions I have addressed in a different light. A comparison of the opening measures of two Courantes from Bach's *Suites for Unaccompanied Cello* (examples 10.3a and 10.3b) will allow us to consider the metrical particularity afforded by broader musical contexts and to contrast two measures that, from the standpoint of pulse division, appear identical. But before presenting this analysis I would like to review some of the points made above and consider briefly some of the problems raised by presenting an analysis.

As a temporal phenomenon, a measure is constituted gradually. At every stage of its evolution

what will eventually become its parts are adjusting to an as yet undetermined composition. The quantitative or qualitative determination we ascribe to the completed measure may be described abstractly as something shared by all like measures; but an experience of a measure (which is, of course, always more than the experience of *a* measure pure and simple) is eminently particular, both in the sense that it is an experience of just this measure of just this piece and in the sense that it is the unique act of attention performed at this moment by this human being. Regarded as components of an act, the various determinations we would attempt to describe analytically may eventually become more or less fixed as the act is completed, but as components they must also bear traces of the process that led to an unpredetermined completion. Those determinations we might call metrical arise from the process whereby a more or less comprehensible durational unit is formed, and they characterize the particular feelings an experience of the unit calls into play according to whatever categories we choose to ascribe to the metrical —the categories, for example, of duration, number, proportion, gesture, accent, grouping, and "phase" (arsic, thetic, anacrustic). In no two experiences will these feelings be precisely replicated. Thus, any description or analysis that would attempt to characterize *the* experience of meter will necessarily be abstract. And, of course, the descriptive categories are by nature abstract. Apart from these problems of abstraction, but at least as problematic for analysis, is the fact that the description of an act of hearing is not that act. At best, analysis can be only a speculation on certain possibilities of experience. And yet, this speculation is another and different experience. Even an analysis that would take process into account can do so only by another process—one of reconstruction.

These limitations might lead the reader to ask whose experience is being described. I have often used and will continue to use the plural "we" in describing hypothetical experiences. The reader may, justifiably, find this a somewhat irritating convention. However, the use of "I" is at least as problematic. The fact of the matter is that no description replicates the thing described. If to write "I hear" is to claim to report on an actual experience (or on many actual experiences), it must, nevertheless, be understood that this report is something other than that experience (or those experiences) and is guided by many things other than hearing. Although I have also used and will continue to use the first person singular, it should be noted that writing "I hear" can be misleading to the extent that it implies a seamless continuity of report and experience. Belief in the unity and autonomy of the ego lends to introspective reports an authority that, though limited, appears inviolable and that can seem to cover the gap between experience and report. Writing "we" is not much better, but at least it implicitly opens this gap. It is also an invitation to the reader to test a written hypothesis against an aural experience. However, this testing is just as problematic as is the framing of the hypothesis, because the sort of aural experience I wish to consider is not a test of anything; it is just the enjoyment of music. The testing of a particular hypothesis is an experience in its own right. Also, the experiences I attempt to describe do not consist of an aggregate of the individual features that I shall have to draw attention to separately. Whatever feature I might describe is intended to represent one aspect of the particularity of an experience from which nothing can be truly isolated. If there is a sense in which an analysis of component features might correspond to a musical experience, it is certainly not that some isolated feature can, in and for itself, be extracted from that experience. However, it is conceivable that a component isolated by analysis could be taken as a sensible distinction that contributes to the definiteness of an aural experience. That is to say, testing is not a matter of finding a correspondence between an analytic object and that selfsame object in an experience, but of asking if there is some effect or feeling that could be imagined to result from the distinctions an analytic object hypothesizes.

With these caveats in mind, let us consider the beginning of the C Major Courante (example 10.3a). Example 10.3b shows the beginning of the Eb Courante, which we shall turn to after a close analysis of example 10.3a.

Although the two Courantes differ in tempo (the C major having more the character of a Corrente movement), both are in 3/4 time and begin

EXAMPLE 10.3 J. S. Bach, openings of the Courantes from the Suites for Unaccompanied Cello in C Major and Eb Major

with the same pattern of durations: an eighth-note anacrusis preceding a bar of six eighth notes. The two opening measures are nevertheless rhythmically and, I will argue, metrically very different. Whereas the first measure of the Eb Courante comprises a complex pattern of changes in harmony and contour, the Courante in C opens with a fluid, unbroken gesture. Our impression of fluidity and speed is enhanced if we hear the beginning of the Courante in the context of the ending of the Allemande (example 10.4, bars 23–24) in which the downward arpeggiation of the tonic triad took place more erratically and slowly. Moreover, a connection of Allemande and Courante could be expected in this style.

Metrically, the beginning of the Courante is most clearly related to the figure in bar 23 of the Allemande in that the distinctions between strong and weak (or beginning and continuation) that mark the tones of the first measure of the Courante closely correspond to the metrical distinctions between these "same" tones in bar 23. Notice also that the anacrusis (c') beginning the Courante is picked up from bar 24 and that the strong eighth notes in the beginning of the Courante (c'–e–G–C) repeat the pitches of the final chord of the Allemande, thus supporting a connection of the two movements.

There may even be a sense in which the opening of the Allemande is indirectly involved in the formation of the Courante's first bar measure (see example 10.4). The figure appearing in the second half of bar 23 of the Allemande begins as a repetition of the first bar (or a transposed repetition of bar 13—the beginning of the second section). By comparison, it fails to present a complete arpeggiation, lacking a low

EXAMPLE 10.4 J. S. Bach, Suite for Unaccompanied Cello in C Major,
bs. 1 and 23–24 from the Allemande and b. 1 from the Courante

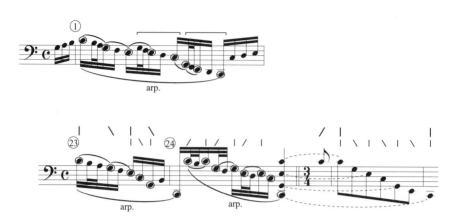

E, which, were it presented in place of the B, would result in a more complete closure, making the remainder of bar 24, I think, somewhat redundant. Also in relation to the opening of the Allemande (and bar 13), the arpeggiations in bars 23 and 24 happen more quickly. In the beginning of the Courante the arpeggiation is complete and happens even more quickly in a single, relatively undivided gesture. When it ends, the Allemande is fully closed—it certainly does not need a low E or a complete arpeggiation from c′ to C in bar 24 to effect a satisfactory conclusion. However, to the extent we can sense the correspondences I have described (among others), we may hear in the complete arpeggiation that begins the Courante a closure that can bring to light some latent openness in the Allemande (and thus a connection or "overlapping" of Courante and Allemande). If this is too grandiose a claim for "our" hearing, I will suggest that we can at least hear in the beginning of the Courante a gathering and acceleration of previous events or a quick, fluid, unimpeded running of tones in contrast to the slower pace and the more constrained and complicated patterns of the Allemande—as if solid has suddenly thawed to liquid. Although the tempo of the Courante is faster (comparing eighth notes, which in the Allemande often provide a focal pulse), there is a sense in which the Courante feels more relaxed or expansive than the Allemande, owing to the deferrals of unequal measure and the dominance of a pulse formed by

bars that contain relatively simple and not highly differentiated articulations. If I am correct in this observation, the Courante would not sound quite so relaxed and fluid without the preceding Allemande.

When the first measure of the Courante returns in the repetition of the first section, its rhythmic/metrical character is in part colored by the measures that immediately precede it (example 10.5). It still sounds very fluid and quick, but if we can sense a complex acceleration and condensation in bars 37–40, bar 1 will now come to sound newly broad and expansive—almost leisurely in this new context. The acceleration and compression in bars 37–40 is perhaps most easily represented by harmonic analysis, as in example 10.5. In bars 39–40 there is an acceleration of harmonic change that compresses the harmonic activity (tonic-dominant-tonic) in which this closing gesture is itself embedded. Of course, the harmonic articulations shown in example 10.5 represent only one aspect of the metrical particularity of this passage, and only in abstraction can they be isolated from the many other factors that contribute to cadential intensification at the end of the first section.

The possibilities for interpretation here are limitless, and the particularity of any interpretation will be no less dependent upon events preceding this phrase than will the repetition of the opening be dependent in its particularity upon this phrase when it is completely determined or *performed*. Nevertheless, I will take

EXAMPLE 10.5 J. S. Bach, Suite for Unaccompanied Cello in C
Major, Courante bs. 36–40 and 1–2 (in repetition)

the liberty of extracting this phrase from its context and isolate several factors that might contribute to a feeling of acceleration. As I have indicated in the staff above the example, bar 37 and bar 38 each offer the opportunity for a continuative "arrest" or suspension in the ascent to a second (quarter-note) beat followed by an anacrustic group directed toward the following bar measure. Beneath the example I show an alternative interpretation in which emphasis given to the fourth (continuative) eighth note in each bar will result in the suspended "arrest" of syncopation at the expense of anacrusis. In either case, the opportunity for a comparatively sharp delineation of successive quarter-note beats in bar 39 can lead to an intensely focused closing gesture. In example 10.5 I have also indicated a correspondence of melodic figure with the labels "a," "a'," and "a''." The repetition of these figures need not be emphasized in performance, but if there is any hint of these correspondences, the displacement—"too soon"—in bar 39 will contribute to a feeling of acceleration and condensation.

In contrast to this phrase, and particularly in contrast to the erratic contour of the last two bars, the repeated opening of the Courante now has a new feeling of breadth and spaciousness. Even the break in contour and register in bar 2, which might initially have sounded abrupt, could now sound like an expanded and quite leisurely anacrusis in comparison to the anacrusis figures in bars 37–39—the turns leading to the beginning of bar 38 (A–B–G–A) and bar 39 (G–A–F♯–G). (And compared to a possible "expanded" anacrusis figure shown in parentheses above bar 39 the anacrusis in bar 2 can be heard as especially smooth or fluid.) Although the repeated beginning of the Courante takes something by way of contrast from the last phrase of the section, it does not continue the process begun there. This lack of connection is a necessary component of binary forms in which the repetition of the first part interrupts the progress toward the second part, leaving the potential of dominant harmony unfulfilled and bringing to light the openness of what had seemed a close. In fact, the first measure is in many ways less connected to the last phrase of the first section than it was to the ending of the Allemande.

EXAMPLE 10.6   J. S. Bach, Suite for Unaccompanied Cello in C Major, Courante bs. 1–2

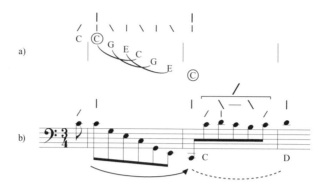

My primary purpose in dwelling on all these qualifications of the beginning of the Courante has been to demonstrate some senses in which the interpretation of a "given" metrical unit is dependent upon previous experiences and thus to show that such a unit cannot be taken as self-sufficient or autonomous. And here it should be added that "previous experience" can include all sorts of things—for example, our familiarity with tonic triads or with dance movements of the Corrente variety.

My discussion of the beginning of the Courante has thus far focused on the past. I would now like to consider present and future. If the first bar measure of the Courante is not autonomous, it is nevertheless separable as an event among other events—a unit differentiated from other units. As it is presently coming into being, this event uses aspects of previous events in its self-formation. However, in order to become a contrast to earlier events, the fluidity or unbrokenness of this event must also be a product of the unit's "internal" organization. If this contrast is taken to be a salient feature of the opening of the Courante, we might describe the metrical organization of the initial measure in terms of its unbrokenness. (This is, of course, not the only "salient" feature or the only approach we might take.)

In the first measure a feeling of triple (unequal) as opposed to duple (equal) involves the grouping of eighth notes in pairs. But since there are no changes in harmony or contour, eighth-note pairs are not very sharply articulated (as they are, for example, in bar 39), and no other

groups emerge to break the continuity of the gesture. There is, however, another possible grouping that serves continuity by inhibiting clear articulations within the measure (see example 10.6a). The repetition here of the succession of scale degrees, 1–5–3 (C–G–E), does not result in a syncopated arrest, but it does result in giving identical scale degrees different metrical functions or qualities—assuming, of course, a realization of the notated meter and a performance that does not emphasize the fourth eighth note of the bar, c (assuming, that is, the relevance of the signature for the performer). The only coincidence of "metrical accent" with a repetition of scale degree occurs between the c' that begins bar 1 and the C that begins bar 2. In this way, the C at the beginning of bar 2 functions to complete a "cycle" as a single, relatively unbroken unit.

The completion of this cycle in bar 2 raises questions of what constitutes a metrical unit and when it is completed. We have already considered the first question in some detail but have given less attention to the second question. There is no first measure in 3/4 time until the low C initiates a second measure. This new beginning simultaneously creates a unit of the preceding three pairs of eighth notes and opens a span equal in duration to the span it closed. Even if nothing were played after the first note of bar 2, we could feel the full duration of the measure (example 10.6b). The five eighth notes that do follow fill the remainder of this duration and thus realize the projected potential created by the beginning of a second measure. At the same time, these notes point toward the initiation of the next measure. As I have indicated in examples 10.5 and 10.6b, the five-note group, by directing our attention toward a third bar measure, can function as an extended, syncopated anacrustic figure. In this interpretation, the five-note group as a whole could be thought to prolong the anacrustic, offbeat quality of the c' that initiates the group. Although this c' as a weak or continuative eighth immediately "resolves" (metrically) to the following d', the figure this c' initiates resolves as a syncopation only with the d' beginning bar 3. In a sense (a sense I shall later qualify), the five-note figure is not needed for the completion of the second measure—the duration of this measure has already been created with the appearance of the low C as a downbeat. That the low C here succeeds in establishing two unequal measures seems clear enough. But it is not so clear when this C actually becomes a downbeat and, consequently, when the first notated bar becomes articulated as a measure. When the low C is sounded, it has the potential for being a downbeat. Whether or not this potential is realized depends on the course of future events (in the context of a larger becoming). If this potential is not realized, the projective potential of the first (notated) measure will not be realized. Thus, the formation of a first measure is affected by "later" events that follow the low C. That a failure to realize a projected potential can result in the denial of a projective potential is a possibility that arises from the inseparability of projective and projected in a projection.

In examples 10.7b–f I have altered the course of future events in several recomposition of example 10.7a, each of which (regardless of its flaws) results in a feeling of duple equal measure. The potential inequality of the opening arpeggiation survives in all but the first of the recompositions (example 10.7b). Thus, in the third recomposition (example 10.7d) it is possible to feel triple meter until somewhere in the neighborhood of the third bar. (The possibility of salvaging triple meter even here is shown in parentheses.) However, once we are in the third bar, the high d' in bar 2 will have become the initiation of a measure. If we resolutely attempt to hear triple meter, we will find jarring the

reinterpretation that takes place in the second bar. However, if we relax this resolve somewhat or hear a relatively unprejudiced performance, the potential inequality of the opening may manifest itself, less disruptively, in a sense of urgency associated with the beginning of the second measure—as if this articulation, on the heels of the abrupt leap preceding it, happened in some sense too soon. The second recomposition (example 10.7c) presents a similar situation with regard to metrical alteration, except that here pattern repetitions emerge much sooner to reinforce duple meter (and here the urgency of the second bar is intensified in the third bar). In the first recomposition (example 10.7b), the potential for inequality is withdrawn through a reinterpretation of the initial arpeggiation. Instead of being construed as a cyclic return to C, the gesture is broken by the arrest of the low G—an articulation that arises largely through the agency of the G that begins bar 2. (Notice also that this opening sounds particularly plodding in relation to the ending of the Allemande.)

Examples 10.7c–e take advantage of the potentiality of d' in Bach's bar 2 for being interpreted as initiating a change of harmony (the beginning of a new event) and thus the potentiality of the first c' to function solely as an anacrusis to this d'. The considerable mobility of interpretation is further illustrated in the recomposition shown in example 10.7f. Here I have combined both interpretations of d'. Although metrical irregularity can certainly be heard here, I believe that if we are able to withdraw some attention from the beginning of a second measure (initiated with the low C) and attend more to a broad gesture leading to the high f' (say by imagining a crescendo from d' to f') we may be less aware of the irregularity and hear unequal measure rather than a change from unequal to equal.

I stated earlier that the first measure of the Courante is not fully formed until the low C initiates a second measure. But, as example 10.7 shows, it is not clear precisely *when* this happens (and if "when" refers to a "point of time" the question will have little meaning from our perspective). The recompositions indicate that this is a progressive development in which successive *events* confirm or deny metrical implications of prior *events*. Recompositions 10.7c–e

EXAMPLE 10.7 Recompositions of the opening of the C Major Courante

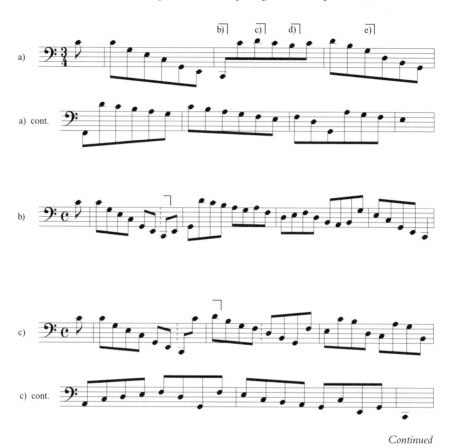

Continued

also show the sense in which the five-note figure leading to d' in bar 3 is necessary for the projection. It confirms the thetic quality initially presented by the low C—a quality variously denied in the recompositions. I do not maintain, however, that as we listen to the opening of the Courante we ever experience any uncertainty concerning "the" meter. In this passage nothing occurs that would deny the potential for unequal measure. By the third bar the meter will, from the beginning, have been triple. But much more than triple meter will have been decided. Among other things, a two-bar metrical unit (i.e., a single "6/4" measure) will have been created. The particular metrical properties of this unit come into focus as the various components both adjust and contribute to a gradually evolving whole. Upon its completion, this unit will have achieved its particularity or definiteness by having realized certain possibilities at the expense of

others. And once formed, the metrical properties of this unit will, in part, determine potentialities for ensuing events. If we can speak of potentiality in the formation of metrical units and thus speak of the future and indeterminacy, we can regard meter as an aspect of emerging novelty rather than as reproduction of the same. Of course, in the Courante there is reproduction— 168 bars of 3/4—but there are no metrical identities. The "threeness" of quarter-note division is but one aspect of meter and is interpreted differently and to different ends in each bar. The reproduction is, rather, of fully particular events, or rather aspects of these events, variously used in the creation of new events.

In order to make a case for the particularity of meter in a bar of the C Major Courante, it seems hardly necessary to contrast this bar with one taken from another piece. Nevertheless, I would like to consider the opening of the E♭

EXAMPLE 10.7 (*continued*)

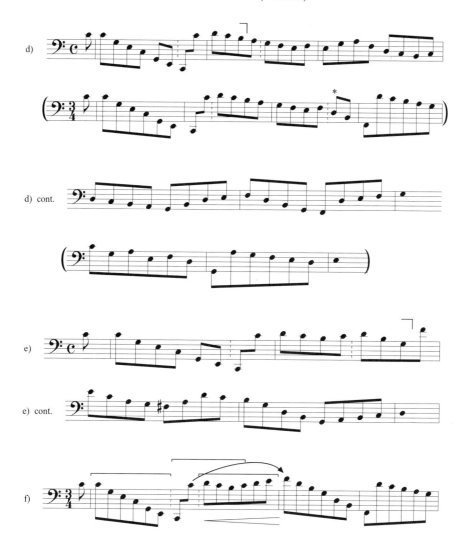

Major Courante (example 10.8), not just because of its metrical difference but because an account of its particularity will involve a closer examination of tonal relations. Compared to the first bar of the C Major Courante, the opening of the E♭ major is quite complex, broken by articulations of harmony and contour. Coincidentally, its first bar very closely resembles bar 39 of the Courante in C (example 10.5). However, a comparison of these two measures reveals considerable metrical-tonal-"formal" or, more generally, *rhythmic* difference.

In bar 1 we can identify changes of harmony that correspond to the three quarter-note beats

of the measure. These harmonic units are again indicated in example 10.8a with the functional labels "T." (tonic), "D.P." (dominant preparation), and "D." (dominant). I would like to consider briefly the grounds for such segmentation. In the tonal context provided by the Allemande (and particularly by the final "chord" of the Allemande shown in example 10.8c), the E♭ in bar 1 and the following B♭ are *con-sonant*—E♭ and B♭ "sound together" as an expression of tonic harmony. Since the two tones are consonant, E♭ is still "harmonically active" when B♭ is sounding and E♭ is no longer sounding (see example 10.8b). In this way B♭ can be said to "pro-

EXAMPLE 10.8 J. S. Bach, Suite for Unaccompanied Cello in E♭ Major, opening of the Courante, conclusion of the Allemande

long" the activity of E♭. The next tone, C, is not consonant with B♭ and ends the harmonic activity of B♭. C is consonant with E♭ and can prolong E♭, but only by altering the immediate harmonic/intervallic qualities given to E♭ by B♭. The following tones, A♭ and F, are consonant with C (and with E♭, granted the consonant status of the "essential dissonance"). The final tone of the measure, D, is consonant with F but not with the preceding C—A♭ (and E♭). As a result, the F would seem to be removed from its affiliation with the unit C—A♭. However, since this alteration occurs only with the leading tone D and is not supported by a change in contour, the segmentation shown in example 10.8a seems to overstate the metrical "regularity" of the passage. The D, rather than being simply present with F to articulate a third beat, could also function as a resolution of a suspended E♭ made dissonant by the F, and as an anacrusis that brings to mind the anacrusis that introduces the first bar (example 10.8b).

The point I wish to make is that, although there are three (quarter-note) beats in this mea-

sure, the articulation of the second beat by means of harmony and contour is made clearer than that of the third. Certainly, to stress three equal beats in performance would rob the passage of its potential liveliness. I will not attempt to say how this measure ought to be played, but I would like to consider some of the options afforded by context.

The initial context is provided by the close of the Allemande (example 10.8c). Here the correspondence of the bracketed figures suggests a performance that might more strongly articulate a third beat in bar 1. If we consider only the portion of the Courante shown in example 10.8c, this beginning sounds like a *close*—particularly if it is heard as a repetition of the final cadence of the Allemande. It is also conceivable that the correspondence of the ascents, C—D—E♭ (the pitches circled in example 10.8c), might favor the articulation of the second beat in bar 1. However, this correspondence seems less striking, in part, because the C in the Allemande resolves to B♭ and is thus not very strongly connected to the following D.

EXAMPLE 10.9 J. S. Bach, Suite for Unaccompanied Cello in E♭
Major, Courante bs. 1–2

Interpretation 1

Although the Allemande may influence a metrical interpretation of bar 1, it is the particular closure effected in bar 2 that provides an occasion for this correspondence. By completing a "clausula vera" cadence, the low E♭ in bar 2 heightens the metrical articulation of the third beat of bar 1 as anacrusis. As is suggested by the interpretation shown in example 10.9, it may be possible to feel something resembling a succession "long–short/short–long" in these two measures (with the sixteenths in bar 2 functioning as a complex anacrusis figure). This sort of metrical gesture is often encountered in triple meter, where it functions to create a relatively closed two-bar unit—closed in the sense that a mobile, anacrustic deferral in the first measure leads to a second measure that inverts the "directionality" of this gesture through a realization of projected potential that is not directed toward a third measure. (We might conceive of a harmonic analogy to this metrical gesture by a comparison with the harmonic progression T.–D.P.–D.–T.) Although the closure involved in this interpretation accords with a (possible) feeling that the beginning of the Courante repeats to some extent the final gesture of the Allemande, such closure does not entirely accord with a feeling of continuity in the opening bars of the Courante. If this interpretation is taken too literally, the sixteenth-note figure may seem relatively detached from the opening gesture as a rather superfluous bit of passage work that fills out the projected measure and leads to a second two-bar phrase. And if this figure is thrown away as passage work, the two phrases themselves will seem relatively disconnected. There is, however, another interpretation of the first bar, which would enhance the continuity of the two phrases

and enhance the role the sixteenth-note figure plays in their connection.

In the context of the final cadence of the Allemande, the third beat of bar 1 emerges as a more or less clearly defined metrical unit where both D and F function as anacruses. Example 10.9 (interpretation 1) is intended to show that this articulation of a third beat in bar 1 becomes especially relevant in the early stage of the emergence of bar 2 as a measure. However, as I mentioned previously in connection with example 10.8, in the limited context of bar 1 alone, contour and harmonic affiliation seem to favor the articulation of a second "half-note" beat. Example 10.10 (interpretation 2) shows a sense in which this construal of bar 1, latent for the early stage of bar 2, becomes more relevant with the sixteenth-note figure that connects the two-bar phrases. Here I have traced an ascending line from B♭ in bar 1 to B♭ in bar 3 (the tones circled in example 10.10b). The B♭ in bar 1, which, as it happens, is the only pitch common to bar 1 and the close of the Allemande, is shown here as an anacrusis to C. C is regarded as consonant and prolonged as harmonically active until D makes it past. Although D makes C past, it does not make the "half-note" duration initiated by C past. For this duration, D is continuative and functions as anacrusis for the beginning of a second bar measure. Of course, D is also continuative for the duration initiated by the low F. As a tone that is consonant with F, that prolongs F, and that together with F articulates a new harmonic unit, D prolongs the duration begun with F as a continuation. On the other hand, if D can be heard as a continuation of the ascending line shown in example 10.10b, and, thus, if D can be heard in some sense as "coming from" C, then D is con-

EXAMPLE 10.10 J. S. Bach, Suite for Unaccompanied Cello in E♭ Major, Courante bs. 1–3

Interpretation 2

tinuative for the entire continuative phase (begun with C) of the measure. The choice between these two alternatives depends on what is taken as a beginning. If we select interpretation 2, the "arrest" with the low E♭ in bar 2 will be mollified, and we will hear a continuous gesture leading to the second two-bar phrase (and perhaps more strongly feel a two-bar measure).

The metrical structure of bar 2 is very complex, and I will not attempt a detailed analysis. It is tempting to reduce this complexity as in example 10.10c to show a durational parallel between the two ascending tetrachords, B♭–C–D–E♭ and F–G–A–B♭. However, these two gestures are far from identical metrically, and to reduce the second gesture to four notes is to lose much of its particularity and the particular relevancies it accepts and offers. Nevertheless, example 10.10c does point to the question of acceleration or change of "speed." Sixteenth notes are, of course, twice as fast as eighth notes, and we cannot but feel an increase of speed in bar 2. However, as I indicated earlier, there are situations in which a change to faster note values is heard less as an acceleration than as division of a slower pulse. In the present case, for example, if a performance strongly favors interpretation 1 and suppresses interpretation 2, and if the sixteenth

notes are, as I said, "thrown away" or treated simply as filler for the projected duration and as a filling out of tonic harmony (E♭–G–B♭, circled in example 10.9), bar 2 could sound "slower" or less animated than bar 1, which is constituted of comparatively rapid harmonic change. On the other hand, interpretation 2 favors a detailed hearing of the sixteenth-note figure, which features numerous replications. To the extent replications or correspondences are brought to light, feelings of acceleration and deceleration will involve more than a general sense of increased or decreased animation. Rather, acceleration and deceleration will also, and more specifically, involve feelings of "the same but faster" or "the same but slower." I would argue that this sort of acceleration or deceleration is, properly speaking, a metrical category, if only in that meter can play a significant role in producing the correspondences that lead to perceptions of "the same" and that feelings of acceleration and/or deceleration can strongly affect protective potential.

Above example 10.10a I have indicated in parentheses a correspondence that may contribute to a feeling of acceleration: eight notes in each of the two gestures. Earlier I argued that counting need not play a role in the feeling of meter, particularly the counting of more or less

EXAMPLE 10.11 J. S. Bach, Suite for Unaccompanied Cello in E♭ Major, Courante bs. 22–26 and 1–4 (in repetition)

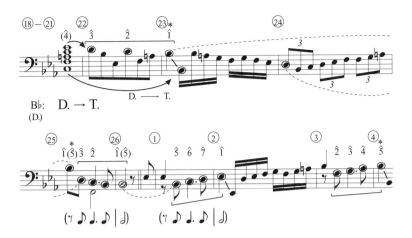

abstract pulses. However, I will suggest that within certain limitations ("seven, plus or minus two," perhaps) it is possible to feel the quantity of events, though not necessarily in cognizance of the "number" we might attach to this quantity. This is not itself a feeling of meter—in example 10.10a the two groups of eight are not metrically congruent—for example, the first group creates an unequal measure. However, there are various correspondences between the two groups that do arise from metrical distinctions, and if we can feel (however vaguely) a repetition of quantity, meter will have played a role in this feeling.

The two tonal/metrical interpretations discussed here are not entirely incompatible. In a performance that is not "overinterpreted," aspects of both could be heard, just as the polyphonic complexities upon which these interpretations are in part based can be heard. (Nor, I should add, do these two interpretations exhaust the complexity of this passage.) However, it is possible to give prominence to one or the other. And I would suggest that interpretation 1 might be more appropriately favored at the beginning of the movement and interpretation 2 favored in the repetition of the first section. As I argued above, interpretation 1 is most congruent with the ending of the Allemande and seems to me a more obvious interpretation. On the other hand, the ending of the first section presents a very favorable environment for the more fluid interpretation 2, as is shown in example 10.11.

The close of the first section, D–C–B♭ (scale degrees 3-2-1 in the dominant) in bars 25–26, clearly focuses our attention on B♭ and invites us to follow the retrograde of this line in the repetition of bar 1 (B♭–C–D). Moreover, this closure was anticipated in the upper register in bars 22–23, and the last phrase of the first section plays within the limits of this B♭ octave. That the high B♭ is regained in bar 3 and more conclusively in bar 4 presents an opportunity for hearing the first few bars in repetition as a relatively continuous gesture and the beginning of bar 4 as a moment of arrival that could supersede the return of the first bar. In contrast to a beginning of the movement that favored the closure of interpretation 1, the repeat seems designed to delay closure and to focus our attention on the active scale degree 5 rather than on the tonic in bar 2. Among the lures for hearing interpretation 2 shown in example 10.11 note the repetition of durational pattern in bars 25–26 and bars 1–2 and the numerous correspondences between bars 22–23 and bars 1–2. (The sixteenth-note anacrustic figure in bar 2, for instance, is an inversion of the corresponding figure in bar 23.) There is some similarity between the two Courantes in respect to the repeats. In both I feel that the first bars are more fluid in repetition. However, the fluidity of the C Major Courante is achieved by a contrast that creates a sharp break, whereas, in the E♭ Major, fluidity results from a continuity that

EXAMPLE 10.12 (**a**) J. S. Bach, C Major Courante bs. 1–2 (transposed to
E♭); (**b**) synthetic recomposition; (**c**) J. S. Bach, E♭ Major Courante, bs. 1–2.

more radically reinterprets the opening bars and blurs division.

The first bars of the two Courantes are similar in very many respects. Metrically, each contains three subdivided beats. And yet they are also, as I have argued, metrically dissimilar. Certainly, their similarity is a basis upon which to judge their dissimilarity, but such a judgment involves much more than a reference to three beats. As an experiment, I have composed in example 10.12b what might be called a "duple version" of the first Courante (transposed to E♭).

Is example 10.12a more similar metrically to example 10.12b or to example 10.12c? If "metrical" is reduced to the distinction duple versus triple, the answer is clear. If not, the answer is not so clear. Of course, example 10.12b replicates a variety of features found in example 10.12a and so makes it difficult to disentangle metrical similarity from these "other" similarities. But this is the point I attempted to make earlier—that the metrical cannot be detached from the whole of musical experience as process, which whole and which process we have no better word for than "rhythm." This is not to deny, however, that there is a definite similarity of metrical type between examples 10.12a and 10.12c. (Nor, by the way, is this to deny the fact that there are also striking *metrical* similarities between example 10.12a and example 10.12c, which are not solely the prod-

ucts of "triple meter.") Since both can be felt as triple or "mediated unequal" and since this feeling must involve some perception of three equal durations (*and*, as I have suggested, a feeling of deferral), should we say that three beats form the basis upon which finer metrical distinctions are apprehended? Or to put the question more pointedly: For these measures, does their being in 3/4 logically, temporally, or perceptually precede their being these particular instances of 3/4? In fact, by reducing these examples to a pattern of three beats that constitute "3/4 time," we are no longer simply comparing these two individuals, but relating each to a third, ideal or prototypical, entity—a universal form that enters the phenomenal world by being "expressed" in a limited (and thus "impure") individual. And from such a perspective, generality can be said to precede particularity. I will not attempt to pursue the issue of universals here. But I would point out that if there are universals, then any of the metrical features I indicated in the preceding analyses could also be regarded as a universal or something that can be repeated in various individuals, in which case there would seem to be no reason for privileging "three beats" over any other repeatable.

Certainly, our past experiences of hearing music in 3/4 precede our present experience of hearing one of these measures, but all of these past experiences were fully particular, and their relevancy to a present experience cannot be divorced from the uniqueness or novelty of this present experience. It must be acknowledged that abstractions, too, are experienced and are not without relevance. Our experiences of the abstraction "3/4 time" arise in the course of our practical and theoretical training—experiences of learning to read music or of considering various theories of meter. Although the latter experiences tend to have relatively little relevance for acts of listening, the former experiences are doubtless relevant, particularly if we have developed habits of counting or beating time as we play or listen. However, as I remarked earlier, the practice of counting and subdividing can inhibit rhythmic fluency and seems to be abandoned with experience. For example, a cellist who gives too much attention to the articulation of three beats in these Courantes will likely produce a rhythmically and metrically dead performance.

It is true that the description of these measures as three-beat units is in some sense more general than many of the other descriptions I proposed. Thus, for example, the two metrical interpretations I offered for the first bar of the E♭ Courante could be regarded as qualifications of an "underlying," simpler metrical structure. Although the order of my presentation may have implied the "givenness" of the three-beat unit, my intent was to show that all these metrical distinctions arise together. If descriptive generality were grounds for "priority," then we might say that just as being a measure of 3/4 precedes being this particular measure, being a measure

precedes being a measure of 3/4. But I argue that this measure, this measure of 3/4, and this 3/4 measure constituted in just this way, although separable in analytic description, are inseparable in experience and that none of these categories logically or temporally precedes the others. From this point of view, the first bar of the E♭ Courante is no more three subdivided beats than it is a long thetic beat followed by a short anacrustic beat (interpretation 1) or anacrusis to a long, suspended arsic beat followed by anacrusis to a second measure (interpretation 2). The three beats will seem logically prior to any other interpretation if it is assumed that we must know the 3/4 structure in order to make distinctions of strong and weak (beginning and continuation) or thesis, arsis, and anacrusis. But in an experience of the Courante all these distinctions come into being simultaneously, with the emerging perception of a particular measure in which "threeness" or "inequality" is only one of its properties. From a temporal point of view, there is no more reason to say that the feeling of 3/4 is the simple foundation upon which the other, more complex interpretations are constructed than to say that the feeling of 3/4 is constructed out of these complexities. Finally, it must be said that once there is the beginning of a second measure and a projection, "threeness" will, in a sense, be "given." But as I argued in the previous section, it is not simply any "threeness" that is given—rather, it is a particular "threeness" that is given or, more accurately, *taken* as a datum relevant for the becoming of the new measure.

ELEVEN

Obstacles to a View of Meter as Process

In my analyses of the two Courantes I have argued for the particularity of meter and the relevancy of context in the creation of particularity. In this discussion I have attempted to treat meter as a process in which the determinacy of the past is molded to the demands of the emerging novelty of the present. "Novelty" here implies freedom—the freedom to make decisions and to create experiences that are not mere repetitions and that are not, therefore, predetermined. Viewed in this way, meter is not distinct from rhythm as "general" is from "particular" or as "law" is from "freedom." There are, however, two customary interpretations of meter that do support such a distinction and therefore demand refutation: the reduction of meter to the mechanical repetition of equal durations conceived as habit, and the identification of meter with measures conceived as time spans that contain rhythmic events and which can be joined as contents of yet larger containers. I have argued against the first of these views in the preceding chapter, noting that a present measure inherits much more than the possibility of instantiating a metrical type. But before undertaking a critique of the second view, I would like to consider the notion that a pulse stream once secured by repetition will be sustained by a sort of mental inertia and will in this way resist forces that would threaten its continuation.

Meter as Habit

The presumably deterministic character of meter is thus often regarded in (nontechnical) psychological terms as habit, and it is often said that the repetition of pulse, once established, will persist or perpetuate itself in spite of rhythmic irregularities. An analytic representation of continuous strings of pulses can in this way be justified by an appeal to habit or inertia. The irregularities that appear where underlying pulses are not actually sounded could then be regarded as rhythmic differentiation of a metric grid formed by a persisting pulse train.

I would argue, however, that the "persistence" of a past metrical determination is limited to the immediate past of the projective phase of a projection or a more distant past that is taken as relevant, and that, in either case, the persistence is not achieved passively as habit but actively in the self-creation of the new event. From an "environmental" perspective it would be dangerous to be easily lulled by habit and inattentive to novelty. Certainly, given a high degree of regularity or conformity in reproduction, we may withdraw our attention and focus it elsewhere. Or, at the opposite extreme, if there is a high degree of irregularity and little evidence of projection, we will be unlikely to attend to projective potential. But in either case

EXAMPLE 11.1 Stefan Wolpe, *Piece in Two Parts for Violin Alone,*
second movement, bs. 121–124. Copyright © 1966 by The Joseph
Marx Music Company. Used by permission of the publisher.

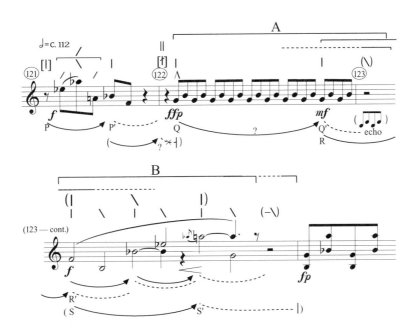

we should be prepared to refocus our attention when the need arises. And although we may equate habit with inattentiveness, I see no reason to equate meter with inattentiveness or with constant regularity or homogeneity.

In many eighteenth- and nineteenth-century compositions there is, in fact, a high degree of repetition—of measure, pulse, and subdivision of pulse. "Given" such repetition, it is tempting to view the repetition as more or less automatic. However, such repetition is not given—it is continually being created anew, and if we attend carefully we will be prepared to feel distinctions or differences that are no less metrical than they are rhythmic and to break with regularity when repetition is no longer relevant for the becoming of a present event. Certainly, many musicians are able to maintain a relatively fixed tempo throughout a piece in spite of considerable local deviation and can often very accurately reproduce that same tempo on different occasions. Such facts of musical life do not, however, require us to imagine that our actions are coordinated by an independent mechanism conceived as an internal clock (or a set of clocks). The complexity

and subtlety of these acts of memory attest, rather, to massive relevancies in the now of a spontaneous performance heavy with the past. To posit a central (cortical) "pacemaker" as a device that might account for our "time sense" is to ignore the fact that all processes take time and that their durations—their particular ways of "taking time"—are inseparable from what these processes become.

There do seem to be cases in which pulses may persist when not actually sounded, but these situations are, I think, better explained as products of active reproduction than as products of habit. In the second movement of Stefan Wolpe's *Piece in Two Parts for Violin Alone* (excerpts shown in example 11.1 and example 11.2), projective complexity requires, for an active engagement with this music, attentiveness to detail and a readiness to adjust to novel projective situations. To follow this music we cannot allow our attention to lapse; indeed, to "follow" is to be attuned to real projective possibilities.

Here silences are charged with uncertainty. In example 11.1 we may, I think, spontaneously hear eighth notes, indicated in parentheses below bar 123, as a sort of echo continuing the group marked mezzo forte in bar 122. I reason that this perception arises because the change of dynamics before bar 123 creates a new beginning, and in the silence that continues the projected duration we may actually reproduce the projective event in the absence of an acoustic stimulus. Although the projection here is not likely to be highly determinate, the new beginning at the end of bar 122 does seem to call for continuation; and we may hear not only continuing eighths but also a "phantom" continuation of the alternating pitches G and B. Here the possibility for a persisting pulse is enhanced by an ensuing silence—in the absence of an acoustic stimulus, all that we have to go on is the continuation of actual stimuli. In bars 115–116 (example 11.2) I also find evidence of an echo, though less, perhaps, than in bar 123. Here we might account for such a continuation by claiming the relevance of the figure in bar 113—the eighth-note figure in bar 115 being regarded as a replication of the earlier figure a step lower. (Note also that the repeated pitches G and F have similar tonal or intervallic qualities acquired from the preceding pitches C♯ and B, respectively.)

These distinctions, although they are subtle and perhaps not entirely conclusive, illustrate the two limitations for persistence I listed earlier: the immediate reproduction effected by projection and more "distant" reproduction effected by the relevance of a past event. A closer projective reading of the excerpts shown in examples 11.1 and 11.2 may allow us to better understand the complex interaction of these two sorts of relevancy.

Throughout this movement, the eighth is the smallest notated durational value (apart from grace notes). With few exceptions, eighths form duple equal projections, as do quarters. Half-note durations are more variable, composing both equal and (mediated) unequal projections, and it is these values that most clearly correspond to Koch's *Taktteile*, giving this movement a very quick tempo. However, to imagine that these various beats are discrete, homogeneous pulse levels constantly ticking away beneath a rhythmic grouping and to imagine that it is this

grouping that provides diversity for an otherwise mechanical coordination would be to ignore what is so fascinating about this movement: the exhilarating play of durational determinacies that engages our attention and gives us in return such a richly imagined world of kinesthetic experience. From moment to moment—phrase to phrase, section to section—the projective field is formed through kaleidoscopic activity. What was just felt as pulse or beat can now change in size, character, or determinacy. Complexity or ambiguity can intensify or relax, suddenly or gradually. Variable, too, are speed, acceleration, and the distinction between these categories.

It is with such factors in mind that I did not identify continuative beats in bar 122 of example 11.1 and did not wish to assert a clear projective potential Q. In bar 121 there is reason to believe that our attention will be focused on small divisions or beats (especially if we take into account the previous bars). Assuming that a projection P–P' is created, the silence beginning bar 122 should function as a new beginning that would promise at least a half-note duration. Since this possibility is not realized, the silence may be felt as hiatus (‖) or a gap in the projective field. Or, if the possibility is sufficiently strong that we can feel a silent beginning with bar 122 as Wolpe has suggested by his barring, this will be a possibility *denied* and the violin's fortissimo-piano attack will feel interruptive. In any case, there will be no clear projective potential given to the new beginning in bar 122, and to represent half-note and whole-note beats here would, I think, be to misrepresent the character of this passage. With its startling, explosive beginning and its lack of internal articulation, the figure begun in bar 122 seems much closer to a measured tremolo than an instance of 4/2 meter. Without clear internal projections this duration will not be highly determinate, and the projective potential Q' may therefore have relatively little relevance for the new mezzo-forte beginning. Consequently, there should be little, if any, feeling of interruption with the new beginning in bar 123. If there does, however, emerge a projection R–R', one result will be that the mezzo-forte figure in bar 122 will have broken to some extent from the

EXAMPLE 11.2 Stefan Wolpe, *Piece in Two Parts for Violin Alone*, second movement, bs. 109–118. Copyright © 1966 by The Joseph Marx Music Company. Used by permission of the publisher.

"tremolo" it continues. And because this mezzo-forte beat will be projectively connected to the forte half-note figure of bar 123, the two parts shown in example 11.1 as A and B are joined across the highly charged silence in which we can hear the echo. Note, too, that events A, and B are of similar length (at least as measured on the page). But in contrast to A in which the projective and projected potentials Q and Q' are relatively indefinite, the articulation of two parts in B may give rise to a larger projection S–S',

shown in parentheses. In any case, distinctions between beginning and continuation at the half-note level (and therefore mensural determinacy) are much clearer in B than in A. And yet, while the potential Q in A may not be very definite, we may, nevertheless, come to have some feeling of the adequacy or correspondence of the two durational products A and B. If we do, this would suggest that for a "larger" becoming the durational determinacy Q–Q' indeed retains some relevancy.

Before leaving the Wolpe, I would like to consider projective engagements in bars 111–117 (example 11.2), again drawing attention to the interaction of relevancies within a projection and relevancies among or across projections. In example 11.2 I have broken this passage into three segments (A, B, and C) and have aligned these on separate staves. Although this segmentation is a considerable oversimplification of the larger event, it will be useful for indicating several projective correspondences that serve as important ingredients in the formation of this larger event. The immediate context for bar 111 is the projective potential O initiated in bar 110. (Part of the context for O is shown in the immediately preceeding projection N–N'.) The projection O–O' is realized in bar 111, but compared to the potential O, the projected realization O' is more relaxed—no silent beginning, no syncopation, and perhaps less anacrustic detachment in the deferral. The new projection P–P' is not fully realized. However, since P (in bar 111) is a product of deferral, there may be little feeling of interruption when P' is cut short with the new beginning in bar 113 and in its stead a projective Q is realized. At this tempo or, as we might say, in this projective environment, deferral at the half-note level does not produce a highly determinate duration. The feeling of a denial of P' here, though difficult to describe, might be said to resemble acceleration as a feeling of earliness—a closeness or immediacy that brings the beginning of the eighth-note figure of bar 113 into especially sharp focus. In this sense, the potential Q acts as a sort of contraction of P. The new projection Q–Q' is realized with the beginning of the mezzo-forte figure in bar 113. And yet, when there is an unambiguously new beginning with bar 114, clearly comparable to the beginning of bar 111 (and to the syncopated first sound of bar 110), the final half-note duration of bar 113 must be reinterpreted as continuation, or, more specifically, as anacrustic deferral $| \rightarrow - /)$. To the extent there is a projection Q–Q' there will emerge a projected potential R', the denial of which will cause the new beginning with bar 114 to be interruptive, intensifying the anacrustic character of the preceding mezzo-forte beat. As a result of these reinterpretations there will now arise a projection S–S'.

Like P, S is not highly determinate (and perhaps less determinate than P as a result of the reinterpretations). For this reason, the new projective T can be felt as urgent but not interruptive. On the other hand, the projective U at the start of bar 115 is interruptive—in part, because the projective history of a new beginning with the repeated notes in bar 115 involves no quarter-note deferrals such as might incline us to interpret the half note and quarter rest at the start of bar 115 as a triple unequal measure; and in part, because of the relevancy of the preceding phrase constituent A. In comparison with constituent A (in bar 113) the pianissimo eighths of constituent B (bar 115) enter too soon. As we have seen, the vividness of an echo in bars 115 and 116 may depend on just this relevancy. And yet, this very relevancy must cause the echo itself to be interrupted as the (silent) beginning of bar 116 comes to function not as a continuation of the projective U but as a beginning comparable to that of T in bar 114 (and perhaps to P in bar 111 and/or O in bar 110).

If these relevancies are operative, a phrase constituent B will have emerged as a reproduction of constituent A and as a potential for the emerging C to reproduce. Notice that the opening of constituent C reflects both the syncopated beginning of constituent B and the forte arpeggiation at the end of constituent A (bar 114) through its lower grace note. This latter relevance involves also the arpeggiated figures of bars 110 and 111 and has consequences for the segmentation of a larger event that we will not consider here. More pressing is the emergence of a constituent C "modeled on" the preceding B, much as B was on A. Here, however, there seems little reason to feel a half-note deferral. A projection V–V' is realized in bar 116. Again, an interruptive eighth-note figure follows; but now this figure is briefer and promises a duple equal projective potential W (in part, because of V–V'). Moreover, this potential is realized in a projection W–W'. Let us now compare this projective complex with that of constituent A and with that of constituent B.

In A there is clear deferral in the projective potentials P and S, relatively little sense of interruption with the start of eighth notes in bar 113, and a fair degree of closure in the formation of two small events: P–P' in bars 111 and 112 and S–S' in bars 113 and 114. Constituent B is considerably shorter; its eighth-note figure (bar 115) is quite interruptive, beginning too soon in comparison to A; and the eighth notes do not lead to a projective completion—instead, they lead to a silence interrupted with the beginning of constituent C. C is smaller still, but although the eighth-note figure is again interruptive and even shorter, there is no projective break with the following half-note passage in bar 118—a passage that will emerge as the beginning of a new phrase.

In this larger process of abbreviation and intensification of durations is there also a transition from unequal (longer, less sharply determinate) measures to equal measures? If it can be said that the unequal measures shown in constituent A (P and S) are relatively clear, as are the equal measures (V and V', W and W') in constituent C, we might inquire more closely into the projective relevance of A for B and B for C and the possibility that constituent B might serve as a transition from unequal to equal measure. The deferral I have shown in constituent B as projective potential T is far from unambiguous. This interpretation takes into account the relevance of constituent A and the relevance of Wolpe's bar line at 115. In regard to the later, it should be observed that Wolpe is, in general, very careful in his metrical notations; for example, the crescendo-decrescendo beneath C♯ in bar 114 will help to alert the violinist to a feeling of syncopation. There are also other factors that could enter into a decision for deferral. Most immediately, the last two quarter notes in bar 114 (D♯ and G) present an opportunity for anacrusis (similar

perhaps to the anacrustic detachment of the mezzo-forte "half note" at the end of bar 113). Furthermore, the first of these quarters, D♯, as the beginning of a half-note duration can be heard in context to resemble the half note E at the end of bar 111: as E "moves" to C♯, a third below (and thence to G), D♯ now "moves" down a third to B (and on to F). These decisions will also have consequences for bar 116: a hearing of the pitch B in bar 115 as a new, dominant beginning (T', interrupted by U) will enhance the determinacy of a duple equal projection V–V' in bar 116 where the pitch B is also a dominant beginning (preceded again by a continuative and anacrustic A♯ and G).

Do all of these "reasons" mean that this segment at the beginning of our constituent B must be heard as an unequal measure (or an instance of 3/2)? Not at all. An alternative interpretation shown in parentheses in example 11.2 is, I think, entirely plausible. There is no change of bow with the pitch B at the start of bar 115, and, all things being equal, higher pitches will be chosen as beginnings over lower pitches (cf. Handel, cited in chapter 9). Although I invoked the relevance of bars 111–112 for an interpretation of this segment as an unequal measure, there is no prior projective potential that would generate a three-beat projected potential here. Moreover, a duple equal measure will be mensurally more highly determinate than an unequal measure. In this interpretation there will be no deferral, and the projection Y–Y' in constituent B will closely correspond to the projection V–V' in constituent C.[1] If both interpretations are possible, must we then decide between them?

By claiming that both interpretations are possible, I mean that the passage is projectively am-

1. But, then, what should we make of the crescendo to E that Wolpe asks for in bar 116? To say that a dynamic intensification opens the possibility for beginning a new measure with E (and deferral for the preceding B) is, I believe, an oversimplification; but so perhaps is our projective analysis of this moment. In contrast to the earlier "half-note" figures in bars 111–112 and bars 114–115, the concluding beat in bar 116 is now of the same pitch (E) as the succeeding eighth-note figure. This early arrival, together with the early arrival on the pitch B in bar 116 compared to bar 115, is the culmination of a process

of abbreviation and compression that characterizes bars 111–117. A crescendo to E and the repetition of pitch (forte-pianissimo) can have the effect of breaking this beat from the projection V–V' to momentarily focus our attention on a much smaller projective world in which the two beginnings with E in bars 116 and 117 are successive beginnings. I maintain that such a change of focus will not interfere with the projections V–V' and W–W' or with the relevance of these projections for the events begun with bar 118.

EXAMPLE 11.3 Stefan Wolpe, *Piece in Two Parts for Violin Alone*, second movement, bs. 114–117. Copyright © 1966 by The Joseph Marx Music Company. Used by permission of the publisher.

biguous. Certainly, a performance might favor one or another interpretation, but I believe the continuity of the phrase will best be served by respecting, insofar as possible, the projective ambiguity of the passage. "Ambiguity" here should be taken in its positive meaning—the presence of two or more possible meanings. It is true that the two interpretations cannot be heard "at the same time"—a beat cannot be heard simultaneously as continuation and beginning. The first beat of bar 115 is not at the same instant (metrically) strong and weak. But we should not imagine that there must be so simple a choice. If measures are not reducible to metric types (e.g., 3/2 or 2/2) we may acknowledge a great variety in the degree of definiteness a measure may present. In the case of constituent B, some indeterminacy could serve the particularity and coherence of the larger gesture. That is, ambiguity in such cases should not be confused with vagueness—there will be nothing vague about keenly felt possibilities adjusting to novel experience. And it can be argued that coming to "know" a piece involves a heightened sensitivity to complexity and ambiguity and, thus, particularity. Should it be doubted that such subtleties can be heard or such fine distinctions felt? With attentiveness and musical involvement, far more can be felt than we could possibly touch on in description. And unless we are dulled by the *an*aesthetic effect of habit, each hearing (even if it be the repeated hearing of a recorded performance) will be an opportunity for novel, vivid experience.

Example 11.3 displays an interpretation of bars 114–115 that I did not consider. From bar 111 to bar 117 a half-note pulse can be maintained. Indeed, the projective interpretation in example 11.2 shows most of these pulses as beats up until bar 115. Example 11.3 shows the persistence of this pulse through bar 116. If we are habituated for so long a time to a half-note pulse, we should, presumably, be able to maintain this pulse through the relatively small deformation of bar 115 and renounce it only in bar 117. Of course, if we wish to do so, we can maintain such a beat (say, by tapping and attending to the tapping), but I do not think this will be a spontaneous response if we are listening attentively and with the pleasure of some kinesthetic involvement. On the other hand, if we can feel the interruptive character of the eighth-note figure in bar 115 (and possibly a slight hiatus) we will have adjusted to a novel projective situation without being for an instant lulled by habit. And to make this adjustment we shall have to attend to immediate projective potentials and to the relevancies of past events while at the same time remaining open to the adventure of a present becoming that has yet to be fully determined.

"Large-Scale" Meter as Container (Hypermeter)

If repetition is not automatic but involves an essentially creative realization of projective potential and the selection of past and future relevancy, one obstacle to the assimilation of meter to rhythm will be removed. Another obstacle arises from the discrepancy, in certain styles of music, between the apparent homogeneity of meter and the irregularity of larger units such as phrase and section. If the repetition of bar measures is not regarded as automatic, it can nevertheless be seen to create a fixed unit for the measurement of larger events. But unless phrases and sections are interpreted as measures, the measurement by bars will be very different in character from the measurement that creates the bars themselves. Instead of functioning metrically or projectively, bars will measure larger units by numerical quantity or count. Such a count could, presumably, provide an index of relative length and lead to an analysis of proportion or an analysis of varying degrees of regularity and irregularity; but in this case, measures will be deprived of their particularity, and the function of meter will be reduced to that of providing a numerical count. If bar measures are simply replications of a given unit, they are all equivalent and are differentiated only by position in a given count.

Such an interpretation arises from a reification of meter. Rather than being viewed as a process, meter is identified with products conceived as spans of time. Regarded as products, bar measures can be treated as containers that in turn form the content of larger containers. In this way, bars function to segment the musical fabric into a succession of relatively small units. These unit products are then combined to form larger unit products in a hierarchy of segmentations that leads from measure to subphrase to phrase to phrase group to section and finally to the unity of the entire composition. Thus, meter can be assimilated to "form" considered as a segmental hierarchy of products. However, the transition from bar measure to phrase presents a break in the composition of the hierarchy. While bar measures in many compositions are all of the same length, units above the level of bar are generally far less regular. The constancy of the bar measure can thus seem to provide a homogeneous medium for the rhythmic diversity of larger units and their nonmetrical contents. If there is activity, "motion," or rhythm that would animate the hierarchic arrangement, it would seem to be provided not by the homogeneous metrical content but by contents that provide goals for boundary points and correspondences among units. As we saw in chapter 5, it is, above all, tonal relations that seem to make a segmental whole a rhythmic whole. Although tonal events

can also function to create metrical boundaries, they are free to transgress these boundaries and thus to diversify and enliven the underlying homogeneity and regularity provided by the relentless succession of measures.

Like the notion of "automatic repetition," the notion of metrical homogeneity rests on the observation of an apparently "given" regularity. And while it might be granted that each bar measure is rhythmically (and, as I have argued, metrically) unique, the particularity and diversity of measures would seem to play no role in the creation of large-scale events. The problem here is that of connecting meter, which seems to operate only "locally" for relatively brief time spans (Lorenz's "rationale Rhythmik"), with form viewed as large-scale rhythm (the "more organic principle" Cone opposed to the metrical). One solution—though, as I shall argue, a partial and ultimately misleading solution—is to expand the scale of meter and regard constituents larger than the bar as genuinely metrical units. It is to this solution or the analysis of "hypermeasure" that I would now like to turn.

There is considerable disagreement among musicians as to where the transition from metrical to "formal" unit (Cooper and Meyer's "morphological length") occurs. Many musicians insist that a true feeling of meter rarely exceeds two-bar measures; others find evidence of meter in larger spans, particularly in phrases as measures. A choice between these alternatives obviously depends upon what is to be meant by "meter" or "measure." If meter simply means equal division and thus "regularity," there is no limit to the duration of a measure, provided that we are given equal durations. If meter refers to a feeling of the distinction strong/weak, there would appear to be rather narrow durational limits to the operation of meter. However, the feeling of strong and weak is not always sharply drawn, especially in larger projections, and as metrical determinacy becomes attenuated it becomes difficult to clearly distinguish "metrical accent" from other types of accent. If there were, in fact, a sharp distinction in feeling, there would be no controversy.

Perhaps because it provides a less ambiguous

criterion for meter, regularity or equal division is often taken as the primary factor in ascertaining the limits of meter. Cone, who links regularity and homogeneity, identifies the bar as the largest metrical unit in most music of the Classical period. This limit is chosen in light of the irregularity and rhythmic diversity of the phrase:

> One sometimes hears remarks about the tyranny of the four-measure phrase during this period. It is true that the four-measure phrase—or rather some sort of parallel balance—can usually be felt as a norm; but it is never, in the music of the masters, a tyrant. This is because it is for them a rhythmic, not a metric entity. Conceived metrically it would tend to become as fixed and invariable as the measure; conceived rhythmically, it is as flexible as the musical surface itself.

> In the Classical period, as we have seen, the measure was usually the largest metrical unit. Its steadiness served as a constant support for—or counterpoint to—the variety of motif- and phrase-construction. When measures combined to form phrases, they did so not in any regular metrical way but as components of freely articulated rhythmic groups whose structure depended on their specific musical content. (Cone 1968, pp. 74–75, 79)

Since the criterion for meter here is regularity, Cone is willing to grant metrical status to phrases if they approach the regularity and homogeneity of bars:

> In Romantic music, on the other hand, one can find long stretches in which the measures combine into phrases that are themselves metrically conceived—into what I call hypermeasures. This is especially likely to occur whenever several measures in succession exhibit similarity of motivic, harmonic, and rhythmic construction. . . . It is here, and not in the preceding style, that we can justly speak of the tyranny of the four-measure phrase! (Cone 1968, p. 79)

Although meter as pure quantity may be distinguished from rhythm by its regularity and homogeneity, the qualitative category of accent can be applied to virtually any constituent. Thus, it is possible to import metrical terms for the description of larger, "formal" events—for example, "large-scale anacrusis" or "structural downbeat." In this way the qualitative or "functional" attributes of meter can be detached from mensural or durational attributes. Lerdahl and Jackendoff, who recognize metrical units of up to eight bars (even in music from the Classical period), make an explicit distinction between two forms of accent: "By *structural accent* we mean an accent caused by the melodic/harmonic points of gravity in a phrase or section—especially by the cadence, the goal of tonal motion. By *metrical accent* we mean any beat that is relatively strong in its metrical context" (1983, p. 17). Since the same term, "accent," is applied in both cases, this separation seems to widen the gulf between meter and rhythm or form. "Structural" upbeat or downbeat and metrical upbeat or downbeat are related by analogy but are unrelated in their process of formation—the structural arising from tonal "motion" and the metrical from equal division. And this disparity can lead to numerous problems of reconciling tonal and metrical accent—for example, the problem of tonal "end accent" or the appearance of an accented tonal arrival in an unaccented metrical position, or, more generally, the difficulties of coordinating the placement of "structural" tones with metrical articulations. Because of these problems it is difficult to avoid concluding that meter, even if extended to the level of phrase, functions as a scaffolding for the play of rhythm.

A solution to the problem of reconciling meter with the irregularities encountered in many phrases is offered by Schenker's concept of expansion (*Dehnung*) or, more generally, by positing an underlying regularity that is capable of retaining some sort of identity under transformations that result in "surface" irregularity. Such an approach has many antecedents (in the theories of Koch and Riemann, among others) and has recently been developed systematically in the work of Carl Schachter and William Rothstein. For Schachter, repetition is again the primary cause of large measures, though repeated spans need not necessarily be immediately successive or "adjacent":

> Within long time spans . . . meter may very well recede in importance compared to tonal motion

and the tonal rhythm associated with it. Yet if the long span is a durational unit that recurs, and if it is articulated by a network of regularly recurring smaller spans, it has a metrical organization which is in principle no different from that of a bar. (Schachter 1987, p. 7)

Accent limits the extent of large measures—only if some distinction of strong and weak beginnings can be sensed can a measure be identified. Depending on the context, Schachter identifies in his examples "regular" measures consisting of two, three, four, eight, and sixteen bars. However, irregular lengths—that is, measures that are neither three nor powers of two bars long—are not nonmetrical if they can be heard as transformations of an underlying regular count. The underlying form is called the *prototype*, after Schenker's *metrisches Vorbild* (Schenker 1935, pp. 192–193).

As an example of a relatively simple expansion, I quote in example 11.4 Schachter's analytic representation of the Trio from Mozart's *Haffner* Symphony, K. 385. (A score is provided in example 12.1.) Here bars 16–20 are interpreted as an extension of the fourth bar of a four-bar metrical unit beginning in bar 13 (see levels e and d). The prototype for this transformation is the four-bar unit, bars 9–12, which presents a similar middle-ground structure (prolongation of scale degree 2 by the upper auxiliary C♯). Schachter also recognizes a large measure of eight bars formed by the first part of the Trio—a complete phrase, bars 1–8. And, thus, the twelve bars of the second section (bars 9–20) are also regarded as an expanded eight-bar phrase measure based on the prototype of the first section. The entire twenty-bar (or expanded sixteen-bar) formation is not in this case regarded as a metrical unit because it is not repeated:

> . . . might we infer a metrical relation of strong-weak between the downbeats of bars 1 and 9? The answer must be no. Time spans of twenty bars (the sum of the first two phrases) or of sixteen (the first phrase plus the eight bars that underlie the second) do not function as durational elements in this piece; there are no recurrent sixteen- or twenty-bar spans. (Schachter 1987, pp. 7–8)

Schachter does acknowledge an "accented" first phrase, but in the absence of recurrence this accent cannot function as a metrical accent:

> Of course a special emphasis accrues to the downbeat of bar 1, partly because it is the first downbeat and partly because it carries the opening tonic. In this sense, therefore, the downbeat of bar 1 may indeed be "stronger" than that of bar 9. But its priority is not metrical; it results from what Lerdahl and Jackendoff call a "structural accent." (Schachter 1987, p. 8)

Incidentally, treating the second eight-bar phrase as unaccented in relation to the first might imply that the second phrase is "continuation" in relation to the first and that the (accented) reprise in bar 21 is a second beginning. Although this interpretation would seem to accord with the Schenkerian notion of interruption, Schachter does not pursue such a parallelism.

In the case of the Trio, the four-bar prototype (bars 9–12) and the eight-bar prototype (bars 1–8) are "literal"—they occur before the transformations as explicit models to which the expansions can be compared. However, the presence of a literal prototype is not necessary for there to be a transformation. Later events and more "abstract" middleground structures can also provide models. And, following Rothstein (1981), Schachter notes that the difference between literal and nonliteral prototype is not as great as it might appear since the prototype, even if literal, is not, in fact, *present* in itself for the transformed replica:

> If the expansion has no actual model in an earlier passage, its underlying metrical structure exists "only at some higher level that is not literally expressed [Rothstein 1981, p. 170]." A literal prototype, of course, announces its metrical structure more directly, but in the expanded variant, the meter of the prototype no longer occurs in the immediate foreground. It, too, withdraws to a higher level, though the listener's memory of the earlier passage helps him draw the necessary inferences. (Schachter 1987, p. 44)

Although Schachter does not bring up the question, it might be argued that certain metrical prototypes (for example, the four-bar phrase) are

EXAMPLE 11.4 Carl Schachter, "Rhythm and Linear Analysis: Durational Reduction," *Music Forum*, vol. 5, edited by Felix Salzer, example 8. Copyright © 1980 by Columbia University Press. Reprinted with permission of the publisher.

given as stylistic norms "prior" to the composition (as residues of past experiences). In any case, the opening of meter to the apparent irregularities and heterogeneity of the musical "surface" through the prolongation (by expansion) of a "hypermetric beat" suggests a novel construal of metrical hierarchy:

> By connecting the idea of expansion to his theory of levels, Schenker made it a far more powerful analytic tool than the old and familiar notion of "phrase extension," which it obviously resembles and from which it almost certainly derives. The superiority of Schenker's approach lies first of all in his taking into account the levels of tonal structure and diminutional content that are associated with the prototype and the expansion; it is never simply a matter of counting extra bars. In addition Schenker brings a new perspective to the study of purely metric phenomena. An expansion—especially a large-scale one—can establish its own metric structure. As Rothstein acutely observes, "in such cases we must distinguish two levels of hypermeter: a higher level, which is the level of the metric prototype; and a lower level, the level of the hypermeasures within the expansion. . . . Accordingly, we may speak of hypermeasures of higher or lower *structural order* [Rothstein 1981, p. 172]." (Schachter 1987, pp. 44–45)

Thus, the expanded fourth measure shown in level e of example 11.4 is, as it were, "composed out," forming a subsidiary four-bar metrical unit (or what is potentially a four-bar unit—the fourth bar being shown in parentheses).

Rothstein (1989) pursues this idea and develops a distinction between "surface hypermeter" and "underlying hypermeter." However, he also acknowledges that in very large expansions it may become difficult to retain a feeling of the underlying measure:

> Expansions of any length tend to fall into their own hypermetric patterns, resulting in a conflict between the *surface hypermeter* within the expansion and the *underlying hypermeter* of the basic phrase. Often it is possible for the listener to perceive both hypermeters simultaneously; at other times the underlying hypermeter may be pushed so far into the background that it virtually disappears. (Rothstein 1989, p. 97)

That the underlying hypermeter might become relatively obscure does not result so much from the length of the extension as from complications that arise in the structure of the extended phrase. To give some idea of factors that are involved in the formation of such a metrical hierarchy and factors that contribute to ambiguity, I would like to refer to Rothstein's analysis of a passage at the end of the exposition of the first movement of Mozart's Piano Concerto in C Major, K. 467 (bars 171–194). In example 11.5 I have represented Rothstein's analysis in schematic form. The prototype for the expansion in bars 180–194 is the preceding eight-bar phrase (bars 171–178), a hypermeasure composed of two four-bar hypermeasures. Bars 180–185 repeat bars 171–176 in many respects. And the cadence in bars 177–178 is clearly reiterated in bars 192–194. The "added" bars (186–191) delay the cadence of the second phrase and are read by Rothstein as an extension of the sixth "bar-beat." Of the two subsidiary or foreground hypermeasures (bars 184–187 and bars 188–191), the second is regarded as a *parenthetical insertion*. It contributes to the metrical expansion, but it is subsidiary to the first foreground hypermeasure in the sense that bar 187 could have proceeded directly to bar 192 (as a resolution of the C♯ diminished seventh):

> The metrically weak m.187 leads to the metrically strong m.192, *as well as* to the surface downbeat of m.188. The parenthetical passage, once perceived as such, recedes in the listener's mind to make way for the larger connection. Comparison with the preceding basic phrase facilitates this metrical hearing. (Rothstein 1989, p. 98)

Rothstein acknowledges two factors that in this case weaken a "feeling of long-range metrical continuation." One reason is that the surface hypermeter overlaps the underlying hypermeter in bars 184 and 185; that is, bars 184 and 185 are simultaneously the fifth and sixth measures of the underlying hypermeter and the first and second measures of the surface hypermeter. The other reason is that bar 185, the sixth bar of the "basic phrase," could not be directly followed in the solo part by the seventh bar, bar 192.

EXAMPLE 11.5 Mozart, Piano Concerto in C Major, K. 467, first movement, bs. 171–194, after William Rothstein's analysis (Rothstein 1989, example 3.16).

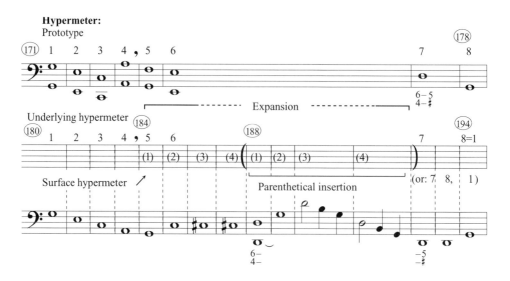

Although he is less explicit in his treatment of problems of meter than is Schachter, Rothstein more explicitly links large-scale meter to the phrase as an essentially rhythmic phenomenon. And while Rothstein makes a sharp distinction between hypermeter and *phrase structure* (similar to Lerdahl and Jackendoff's distinction of meter and grouping), he unites the two in the notion of *phrase rhythm*. While expansion is only one of several transformations of metrical regularity, it is the one that most clearly offers a metrical analogy to the tonal hierarchy of Schenkerian theory. Like the perception of middleground tonal structure, an appreciation of underlying hypermeter would (assuming there are such perceptions) require a good memory and an ability to make long-range connections—in short, a capacity for *Fernhören*:

> Phrase expansions often create complex, multilayered hypermetrical structures; these consist of a surface hypermeter plus one or more levels of underlying hypermeter. (More than one level may exist especially when a phrase, having once been established, is expanded still further.) Underlying hypermeter may be defined as the hypermeter of the basic phrase. The perceptibility of an underlying hypermeter may vary: in some cases it will be nearly self-evident . . . ; in others it may be vaguely intuited, perceived only with difficulty, or missed

altogether, depending in part on the listener's capabilities. (Rothstein 1989, p. 99)

Although I shall offer an account of larger metrical formations that differs considerably from that of Schachter and Rothstein, I should point out that their construal of "large-scale" meter succeeds to some extent in closing the gap between meter and rhythm by allowing inequality to be interpreted in purely metrical terms and by introducing process through the notion of transformation (though, as in all structuralist accounts, the temporal nature of such transformation is not at all clear). However, two difficulties attend this view of hypermeter. First, for very large measures projective/projected potential becomes, at best, highly attenuated, so that it becomes difficult to grasp meter in the same way or with the same confidence with which we grasp smaller measures. If measures are formed by repeated "lengths" (and these lengths can be expanded internally), it is conceivable that the duration of a measure could be very long indeed. If being a measure can be a property of being a phrase, and if, as Rothstein says, large phrases could be construed as "periods, sections, and ultimately as whole movements or pieces" (1989, p. 13), a large section could conceivably be a measure. Although such interpretations seem possible theoretically, Schachter and Rothstein are very careful to limit hypermeasures to more or less plausible lengths—the duration of a metrical unit never exceeds the level of a period. However, even this limitation may seem an excessively liberal construal of measure. Phrases or periods are by definition "units," and their formation is surely dependent upon meter, but this does not necessarily mean that they are "metrical units."

The other difficulty concerns the metrical transformations allowed in the formation of hypermeasures. Such transformations as expansion or parenthetical insertion (among others) are not permitted in the formation of smaller measures—for example, a bar of five or six eighth notes as a transformation by expansion of an underlying measure of 4/8. For this reason, what is more conventionally called meter still seems removed from the rhythmic freedom accorded to hypermeter.

Because of these difficulties, it is indeed appropriate to make the terminological distinction between "meter" and "hypermeter." Although Cone did not intend for hypermeter to be understood in this sense, the term might be used to refer to the "more organic rhythmic principle" Cone opposed to meter. In his attempt to connect meter and hypermeter, Rothstein suggests that the usual definition of meter (requiring that "strong and weak pulses must alternate in some specified and regular way") must be revised "to accommodate a new and more complex reality" (1989, p. 40). This revision draws on Zuckerkandl's view that "what is essential to a metrical pattern is not so much the maintenance of equally spaced pulses as the establishment of a kinetic cycle consisting of a moving away from and moving toward a series of goal points (that is, downbeats)" (quoted in Rothstein 1989, p. 43). To this conception Rothstein adds the requirement that "equally spaced beats of the conventional metrical model retain their relevance as a point of reference—a norm against which all deviations are to be measured . . ." (p. 43). However, these two views of meter are not clearly reconcilable—an understanding of meter as "motion" or dynamic quality and meter as equal division, measurement, and quantity. In the end, Rothstein leaves this question open:

It would exceed the boundaries of this study to address the psychological and epistemological questions raised by the existence of underlying hypermeter, but those questions surely need to be explored. In particular, the nature of meter itself needs to be reconceived if underlying hypermeter is to be accommodated within a general theory of musical meter. (Rothstein 1989, p. 99)

If there is some question whether hypermeasures are, in fact, felt as measures in the conventional sense, we might say that hypermeter, rather than being itself meter, is a feeling of metrical correspondence in the relevancy of a past "model" for the formation of a novel phrase or period. Thus, in example 11.5, for instance, without claiming a properly metrical connection of bar 185 (weak) to bar 192 (strong) it might be possible to claim, even without great connoisseurship, a feeling of two phrases in which the second phrase, which is easily felt to be longer than the first, could be heard to begin and end like the first. Without metrical correspondences (which are numerous and extend, I would argue, into the "added" measures) we could still feel a difference of length, but not the similarity of beginning and ending. Nor could we feel in bars 180–194 this particularly broadened and intensified response to (and, possibly, extension of) bars 171–180. This, I believe, is the essential contribution of meter to "form"—that whatever the piece becomes will be as much a product of metrical process as any other process: thematic, harmonic, contrapuntal, "textural," or process in any other domain in which we can locate distinctions in feeling. (In fact, to appreciate the contributions of meter to this passage we might need to consider a larger context and the interactions of several domains—for example, the failed cadence in bars 162–163 and the successful cadence in bars 168–169, the similarities of bars 180–183 and bars 154–157, and the possibility of a four-bar projected potential engendered with bar 192.)

However, to rob the hypermeasure of its status as a metrical unit is also problematic. In eighteenth- and nineteenth-century European music there are metrical or, at least, meter-like units composed of more than one bar, and there is often considerable repetition of two-bar, four-bar, and sometimes eight- and sixteen-bar units. (Nor is this the only musical culture that employs repetitions of this scale.) Also, I think it could be said that there is often a feeling of regularity or at least "rightness" in the duration of larger groupings. There are apparently measures that are longer than bars (and bars that are not measures). Again, if the durational limits of measures were clearly felt, Cone and Schachter would not disagree in their use of terms.

TWELVE

The Limits of Meter

The Durational "Extent" of Projection

I would now like to pursue the question of these durational limits by referring the question to projection. Since we have not bound the concept of projection to the notated bar, we have no need of the term "hypermeter" to refer to *metrical* formations larger than the bar. (And given Cone's aesthetic valuation of hypermeter, I suspect he may have had the derogatory connotation of the prefix in mind: "more than normal" or "excessive"—as in "hypertrophy.") If meter and projection are synonymous, the problem is simply that of determining the durational limits of projection. If, nonetheless, "hypermeter" is intended to name a measuring of duration that is distinct from meter and yet meterlike, we might also ask how this measuring is carried out and how it is related to meter proper.

To seek the maximum length of projection is to ask how far mensural determinacy can be stretched. Obviously, there can be neither a general nor a definitive answer to this question. Since mensural determinacy is gradually attenuated, evidence of projection or projective potential will, as a rule, become progressively weaker as duration increases. But since mensural determinacy can be enhanced or reduced by any fac-

tors that contribute to the particularity of the event (including the relevance of other events) there can be no general or context-free limit to determinacy. Furthermore, since we are concerned here exclusively with real events—individual acts of musical attention—the "same" bit of music can give rise to a multitude of occasions for feeling durational quantity. If we cannot hope to arrive at an exact numerical answer, we can, nevertheless, expect the question of limits to shed some light on the nature of projective phenomena.

Let us begin by asking how we might detect the failure of an event's duration to be taken as a potential for reproduction by an immediate successor. The simple test I proposed earlier is to stop with the beginning of the projected phase and ask if we can feel the opening of a duration more or less commensurate with that of the projective phase, or ask if we can confidently predict the end of the projected duration and a new beginning. This test often works quite well for relatively short durations—projected potentials of up to about two or three seconds. Should we conclude that if this test fails there is no projection? To answer this question we should ask what is being tested. I introduced the device of stopping with the beginning of the projected duration in an attempt to separate the two phases of projection and to demonstrate the operation of potentiality by focusing our attention on feelings of anticipation. However, I also said that the projective and projected phases cannot, in fact, be separated and that the process of realizing projected potential is part of the process of projection. The device of stopping and imagining a continuation in the ensuing silence is not a neutral or "objective" test—that is, it does not succeed in objectifying potentiality or revealing potentiality per se. Our imagined continuation is no less a definite realization of projective potential than is a "given" sonic continuation. It is important to recognize that our imagined continuation is an act that is fully particular. This act affirms that there was a potentiality offered by the projective phase by creating a particular realization of that potential, but it does not reveal that potential in itself—a potential that could be realized in countless ways. Thus, a failure of this test does not necessarily mean that some acoustic event could not function as a realization of projective and projected potential. And yet, if we renounce this test altogether how can we find evidence of projection?

We might point to a feeling of reproduction or the repetition of equal durations. However, we should have to distinguish projective repetition from a judgment of equality. I have claimed that in the case of projection, the second event is, from its beginning and throughout the entire process of its becoming, a reproduction of the duration of the first event. Here reproduction (or the potential for reproduction) is expressed primarily as a feeling for how much longer the present event will go on or when a new event might begin. Reproduction in this sense is a process and not a comparison of quantities as products. In the case of a judgment of equality, the evidence of repetition arises after the fact in completed events or products as a judgment of sameness or difference. But even here it must be admitted that there is a potential for reproduction —if there were no such potential, there could be no such judgment. To distinguish this from projective potential I have said that in the case of judgment there is no "weighting" in favor of reproduction—that as the second duration is being formed, it is in the process of becoming a duration that is neither equal to nor unequal to the first duration. In the case of projection, the

special relevance of the first duration for the second is felt from the beginning of the newly emerging projected duration as a spontaneous and apparently "involuntary" feeling of how long the new event will last.

If the weighting of durational potential in favor of reproduction is the defining characteristic of projection, and if this potential is subject to enhancement in the course of realization, it will be impossible in all cases to distinguish a feeling of projection from a judgment of equality. How strongly must we feel a potential for reproduction, and how can we gauge this strength? If projected potential can be enhanced in the course of its realization, how can we distinguish process from product to say whether or not the projected duration had from its beginning this potential? Indeed, it is the lack of a clear boundary that will prevent us from placing an exact limit on projection.

To refer these questions to a specific case, consider the Trio from Mozart's *Haffner* Symphony, no. 35, K. 385, shown in example 12.1. Since an eight-bar unit here seems to be the largest plausible candidate for measurehood, let me begin by asking if there are any grounds for regarding an eight-bar duration as potentially projective. For now we will consider questions of the projective potential given for a new beginning with bar 9 and not the potential for a beginning again with the repeat of the first phrase.

On the basis of repetition, Schachter has identified a hypermetric phrase beginning the second part of the Trio. To simplify matters I have included beneath bar 16 in example 12.1 an alteration of the passage that would produce a clear eight-bar phrase (bars 9–16). In this case, we can easily feel a correspondence between bars 1–8 and 9–16 and perceive the equality of the two durations—a unit of two four-bar phrases, itself repeated, followed by another unit of two four-bar phrases. Are these, then, two measures, the second a realization of the projective potential of the first? Certainly, if we stop with the downbeat of bar 9 we cannot feel the opening of a definite eight-bar duration. In the ensuing silence we can feel at most, I think, a projected duration of two bar measures. However, if we recognize bar 9 as the beginning of a

EXAMPLE 12.1 Mozart, Symphony no. 35, K. 385 (*Haffner*), Trio

Continued

EXAMPLE 12.1 (*continued*)

Continued

EXAMPLE 12.1 (*continued*)

187

new section, and thus in some sense as a second beginning, we may we feel the promise of more than two bar measures.[1] Yet, what might ensue is quite open. There is a possibility for two four-bar units, but there are many other possibilities as well, and if we wish to say that an eight-bar phrase is especially privileged, we would presumably have to show that a denial of this possibility would be felt as a denial. That is, if there is a projective potential of eight bars realized with the initiation of the second section in bar 9, a denial of this potential must have some effect: it must make some difference in our feeling of the passage—a feeling that the event is in some sense "too long" or "too short" or *not* what was promised.

In example 12.2a I have altered this passage to form a six-bar phrase. This unit, to my ear, does sound short, but it is not entirely clear that it must be heard as an abbreviation of what should have been an eight-bar phrase. There may be some feeling here that the third two-bar unit is in some sense too short or a somewhat abrupt ending of the phrase, but such a feeling could more immediately arise from the denial of a four-bar projective potential created by bars 9–12. In example 12.2b the second "section" has been reduced to four bars. Here I believe the phrase definitely sounds too short to fulfill the promise of a second section. It might be argued that a feeling of its being too short could arise not from a denial of projected potential, but rather from a denial of stylistic expectations. But this argument begs the question, for we should still have to ask whether projection plays a role in the creation of stylistic "norms." Also, as a result of the recomposition in example 12.2b, I hear two, not three, sections in which this third four-bar unit (bars 9–12) belongs to and concludes the first section (here bars 1–12) renouncing its claim to independence. If this is not an eccentric perception, it cannot be ac-

counted for simply on the basis of convention. In any case, examples 12.2a and 12.2b provide some evidence of a projected potential of greater than four bars at the beginning of the second section. Or, to put this in another way, we could say that if a second phrase is to develop, there is at least the promise that a new beginning in bar 13 will be a continuation. How much longer than four bars this phrase might last seems more open.

In Mozart's Trio the possibility for two four-bar units is enhanced in bars 13–14, but even as late as bar 16 it is possible, I think, to create a larger second phrase without feeling this to be a denial of an eight-bar unit. One such continuation is shown in example 12.2c—a ten-bar phrase (bars 9–18) overlapping with a new beginning in bar 19. Mozart's solution is to allow the potential eight-bar unit to be completed or realized but to immediately undercut this completion by reinterpreting bar 16 as the beginning of a two-bar unit. Nevertheless, if there is a realization of an eight-bar unit (whether somewhat ambiguous, as in Mozart's composition, or unambiguous, in the case of my "regularization" in example 12.1) and if this unit is felt to be equal in duration to the preceding unit (bars 1–8), there can be no doubt that there has been a potential for this correspondence. Furthermore, when there is a correspondence—when the second large phrase is a fait accompli—it becomes evident that this was a "strong" possibility. We could not feel such long durations as precisely equal and thus in some sense mensurally determinate were there not, all along, projections and relevancies that kept this possibility alive—were this "measuring" not also a fait accomplissant.

If we are to allow an eight-bar projective potential, it must be admitted that the potential for a realization of the projected duration is incomparably less definite than that of the bar measure. A duration of twelve seconds (in the case of the

---

1. I say "more than two bar measures" rather than "more than three seconds" because projective potential here is not simply a time span (measurable by the clock), but a measured duration—that is, a duration measured by the coordination of many projections. If there is a projective potential given to the new beginning with bar 9, it will

be a potential created out of a definite four- or eight- bar duration (bars 1–4 or 1–8), and part of the definiteness of that duration is its formation as a complex of projections involving one-bar measures and two-bar measures. As was claimed in chapter 10, projective potential is nothing apart from its constitution.

EXAMPLE 12.2 Recompositions of Mozart, Symphony no. 35, K. 385, Trio, bs. 9–20

Trio) is simply too great to be determined from the outset. It would seem that for relatively long durations we are not prepared to forego opportunities for revising our expectations. Were we to place too much trust in long-range predictions, we would not be prepared to adjust to novelty and to act on the basis of more immediate projective possibilities. Assuming for the moment that a larger projected potential emerges and becomes realized, as, for example, in bars 9–16, we will lose nothing by feeling this reproduction, and we can gain some information that may be useful in directing the course of our attention. Evidence of large-scale repetition may, in fact, allow us to relax our attentiveness to the potential for novelty. And in this case, we may experi-

ence boredom. Thus, my revision of the Trio in example 12.1 results in a quite tedious composition. The projective reinterpretations Mozart calls into play in bars 16–20 forestall a lapse into inattentiveness.

Shall we then call bars 1–8 a measure and speak of a projective potential of eight bars? If we do not, we must ignore the definite potential for a correspondence that if realized can share something of the spontaneous and "involuntary" character we attributed to projection. But, again, how can we precisely determine or measure projective potential? I said earlier that we might test the strength of a potential by denying it and asking if there is any feeling of denial. But this test has limitations similar to those of "silent continuation." To test potential in this way we must select a particular continuation—one that results in particular realizations and denials (e.g., example 12.2a, 12.2b, or 12.2c). But this does not exhaust potentiality per se, which would reveal itself differently in a different continuation.

Thus far we have focused our inquiry on the feeling of durational adequacy—specifically, the feeling that bars 9–16 are "just the right length" in conformation to bars 1–8. This sort of correspondence is the strongest argument for those who would regard phrases as large-scale metrical formations. However, the results of this inquiry have been far from conclusive. Our devices of "silent continuation" and recomposition, although suggestive, cannot satisfactorily resolve the question because these tests are "intrusive"; that is, they require an alteration of the object we wish to test. The perception of durational adequacy or correspondence, on the other hand, is a non-intrusive or observational test, but this test also is not entirely decisive. If we have felt a correspondence, this does not necessarily mean that meter or projection is the basis for this feeling.

It could, for instance, be argued that the correspondence is a result of reckoning or computation, that the perception arises from a sort of counting applied to "morphological lengths." Along these lines, it might be imagined that we perceive bars 1–8 as *two* four-bar lengths and each of these four-bar lengths as *two* two-bar lengths (or two-bar measures, perhaps) in order to judge the magnitude of this larger unit and to feel it equal to an immediately successive eight-bar unit similarly constituted. If interpreted literally, this sort of "counting" would seem to imply a measuring of duration radically different from that of projection. In this case we could imagine projection providing the durational units—one- or two-bar quantities of the "how much" sort—which are then measured by count, or quantity conceived as "how many." We would then have to assume that the durational extent or magnitude ("how much") of four- or eight-bar units is not experienced directly in the way that projective duration is felt. Instead, such durations could be experienced only indirectly, as it were, through a translation into number ("how many"). Such a *representation* of durational quantity would be very different from our categories

of duple and triple measure in which all the durations involved are mensurally determinate.

In support of some such discontinuity in measuring, two factors could be taken as decisive. The first of these concerns metrical accent. The strongest argument for denying that repetitions on the order of phrase are metrical has been the disappearance at these durational levels of any clear distinction between "strong" and "weak" beats. The second factor concerns "adjacency" or immediate succession—a category that formed the basis of our initial definition of projection, but one that seems dispensable in cases involving larger and more complex repetitions. I would like to consider each of these questions in detail and in each case ask whether it is possible to save the phenomenon of projection for "phrase-length" durations.

In the case of a small measure, if there is division, we can hear the distinction between beginning and continuation as a distinction between strong and weak. This distinction is remarkable in that beginning and continuation are felt as palpable qualities that are not acoustic properties. (Again, there is no contradiction in a weak beat being louder than a strong beat.) Is there then a similar distinction in the case of bars 9–16? Bars 13–16 are certainly a continuation of the beginning of the second part of the Trio, but to be a metrical continuation these bars must be the continuation of a mensurally determinate duration. Since, most immediately, bar 13 is the beginning of a four-bar unit, it may be heard simply as strong. Note in particular that bars 9–12 are harmonically closed (V–I) and that the new small phrase starts *subito piano* with a repetition of bar 9—clearly a "beginning again." On the other hand, it may be possible to hear some trace of a metrically weak continuation and to detect some feeling of duple equality if we very clearly feel this eight-bar unit as a repetition of the duration of bars 1–8 and attempt to suppress a feeling of "beginning again" with bar 13. Such a feeling is tenuous at best and cannot be easily tested. However, I think a palpable distinction may emerge in our attempt to hear the four-bar unit as continuation: if we succeed in hearing this unit as continuative or in some sense "weak," the entire passage will sound more fluid and less broken or "square" than if we hear bar 13 as a beginning comparable to the beginning in bar 9 (and less a contrast to the more continuous phrase in bars 1–8). But to convince ourselves that such a hearing is *possible* does not mean that it is necessary or even desirable (and later I will argue against this interpretation of bars 9–16).

If the distinction strong/weak does not seem very compelling here, should we for this reason deny to bars 13–16 the function of metrical continuation? If the perception of weakness is an indication that the potential of a prior beginning for the formation of a mensurally determinate (i.e., reproducible) duration is still in force, does not the complete absence of such a perception indicate that we have exceeded the limit of mensural determinacy and that the prior beginning is no longer dominant? Since ours is not an "accentual" theory, we need not draw this conclusion. Although metrical weakness seems to be a sufficient condition for metrical continuation, we are not obliged to regard it as a necessary condition. We are, however, obliged to find some sensible evidence for continuation if we are to speak of larger projections. Is there, then, any palpable qualitative distinction that might mark the difference between beginning and projective continuation for durations on the order of our eight-bar examples? I believe there is such a distinction, though it is subtler than the distinction strong/weak. Like strong and weak, it is a difference that involves equal durations (most often duple equal, for reasons we shall discuss later). The customary terms that perhaps come closest to naming this distinction are "antecedent" and "consequent." But since these terms are used in ways that are not always connected to metrical distinctions, we might more generally speak of the difference between "first" and "second." Like Riemann's *proposta/riposta*, this difference names our feeling that the second answers or is a response to a first and thus continues a single, "symmetrical" event composed of two commensurate or equal parts. Such a feeling of "secondness" would not, however, correspond to the notion of "counting" as representation I spoke of earlier. Note that "second" in this sense (from *sequi* "to follow") names a perception of continuation and is not, properly speaking, a quantitative-numerical category. If it can be granted that

there is such a feeling of continuation associated with commensurate durations, this does not necessarily mean that the measuring of duration in this case is the same as that we have described as projection. It would mean, however, that even if there were two distinct kinds of measuring, the difference between the two would not be so drastic as that between projection and "counting." Or, if we were to regard this as an extension of projection, we must acknowledge that there is a real change in our feeling of continuation. We shall return to this question after we have considered a second and perhaps less serious objection to speaking of projection here.

If we pause for two or three seconds between the two eight-bar units there will be relatively little impairment of our ability to feel the correspondence of durations. This appears to run counter to two observations I made earlier in this study concerning projection. In examples 6.4a and 6.3a I distinguished between a feeling of projective reproduction and a judgment of equality, a distinction made on the basis of the "adjacency" or immediate succession of mensurally determinate durations. And in my "ontological" account of projection I speculated that projection occurs, in part, because the new beginning ends or determines the duration of the prior event as it makes it "presently" past. Let us quickly review these conditions in connection with examples 12.3a and 12.3b, which return to representations of simple, abstract events such as those shown in examples 6.3 and 6.4.

In example 12.3a two sonic events are separated by an unmeasured silence of waiting or a hiatus (symbolized by | | in the example). To say that there is hiatus here is equivalent to saying that a projective potential Q is not realized and that the duration from M to N is mensurally indeterminate. Note that although M has a determinate duration (ended by silence), it is not clear when Q is forfeited. In this example, "(Aa)" labels the possibility for an event that might have realized Q. Such an event could arise only if there were a new beginning (b) that would end (A) before mensural determinacy runs out. In example 12.3b such a possibility is shown actualized. Here there is a completed projection Q–Q'. For this reason there is a more or less definite end to event B as Q' is realized and also a more or less

EXAMPLE 12.3 Relevance of complex
projective potential

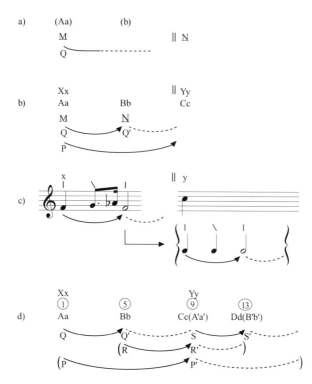

definite end to event X if B is continuation. That is, unless the durations involved are very brief, a new beginning c or y is not needed to end B or X. If X is very brief (say, one second) and there is no immediately successive Y, this situation may resemble that of example 12.3a thus: the possibility for a greater duration remains so strong that the completion of X (like the completion of M in ex. 12.3a) will leave a projective potential P open until, at some time during the ensuing silence, mensural determinacy runs out. If, however, X more nearly reaches the limits of mensural determinacy and ends more or less definitely as a result of the completed projection Q–Q', could we now speak of a realized projective potential P in the absence of a new beginning? From the standpoint of the present theory of projection we can. In example 12.3b, X is a measure if, as past, its duration has acquired sufficient determinacy to be reproduced. Whether it is, in fact, reproduced—whether there is, in fact, a projection P–P'—does not affect X's measurehood (though it does, of course, affect X's relevancy).

Our next question concerns the possibility of a projection P–P' if, as in example 12.3b, there is a hiatus separating X and Y. In example 12.3c I have provided an illustration that, I believe, indicates such a possibility. If, after a brief pause, we are inclined spontaneously to continue a duration in some way modeled on the preceding measure, I can see no reason why we should not speak of projection here.

In order to devise a more or less convincing illustration, I found it helpful to provide some tonal differentiation and to turn from abstract representation to a specifically musical example. If our complex duration X in example 12.3b is to be taken as a measure for Y, some special relevance may be not only helpful, but necessary. In such situations heightened relevance will be crucial for durations greater than a couple of seconds.

Since it appears that there can be "broken" projections involving durations on the order of the notated bar, we can scarcely object to regarding phrases as measures on the grounds that a relatively brief pause between phrases may have little effect on our sensing their adequacy. But beyond countering this objection to phrase-length measures, the observations we have made in connection with example 12.3 may clarify our more general problem if joined to the question of metrical accent.

In example 12.3d I have represented two hypothetical eight-bar phrases, X and Y, joined without hiatus. Each phrase will be imagined to have a duration on the order of twelve seconds. If, as in this example, we are to very clearly perceive the durational adequacy of Y to X, or, as we might say, the "symmetry" or "balance" of these two phrases, each phrase must be composed of two four-bar units and each of these must be composed of two-bar units. Although our representation here is highly schematic, it will be understood that for X and Y to be conceived as musical phrases they must be imagined to represent complex tonal events composed of many mutually reinforcing projections. Let us assume for the sake of argument that there is a projection Q–Q' involving the four-bar durations A and B. And let us assume, also for the sake of argument, that the new beginning b is not perceived as metrically weak. I say "for the sake of argument" because we could draw similar conclusions by altering the durations of these events—X might be four or sixteen bars long. However we construe these dimensions, A and B must be regarded as mensurally determinate and yet not give rise to clear feelings of strong and weak. I would now like to consider two interpretations: one in which the first eight-bar phrase is regarded as a measure that leads to a projection P–P', and a second interpretation that denies that there is a true projection P–P'.

If we do not make the feeling of metrical weakness a necessary condition for the formation of a duple equal measure, there is nothing to prevent us from considering a projection P–P'. With the beginning of Y (or what might become Y) there will be the promise of a duration more or less commensurate with X, or, judging from our experiments in example 12.2, a duration greater than four bars (i.e., greater than half of X). Because of the attenuation of mensural determinacy and the complexity of these events, there will be considerable flexibility in the realization of projected potential. For these

same reasons—the attenuation of mensural determinacy with greater length and the complexity that makes such lengths viable—the projective potential P will be relevant only to the degree that an event Y in fact emerges and develops sufficient correspondences with X. I have indicated this relevancy by including the alternative labels "A'" and "B'" for the two four-bar measures (C and D) of Y.

It is important to remember here that Y's beginning is not instantaneous (and neither is C's or A''s). It will take time for evidence of Y to emerge. In fact, it will also take time for the end of X or B to emerge—the projection Q–Q' will not actually be completed until a new beginning c or a' denies the possibility of a continuation of B beyond four bars. It is impossible to say precisely when there is enough evidence to justify the label "Y". This is a gradual process, and Y will not be absolutely definite until it is past. But judging from example 12.2b, where the third four-bar measure seems too short when followed by a new noncontinuative beginning in bar 13, I am inclined to say that a Y is more or less clearly emergent before the end of the third four-bar measure. Certainly, there must be some evidence of a projection if a beginning b' can be felt as continuation. Finally, it should be recalled that once there *is* evidence of an event Y, *this* event *from its beginning, y*, was always an immediate successor to X.

Now let us consider an alternative interpretation. Since the new beginning b is not perceived as metrically weak, we will take this as an indication that B is not a projective continuation and, therefore, that the greater projective potential P is not, in fact, being created. Event B is, nevertheless, the continuation of the *phrase* X. Now if (again, for the sake of argument) the four-bar measure is taken as the maximum durational quantity that can function as projective potential, we should expect a projection R–R'. However, a projection R–R' would contradict our perception of Y as a second phrase. That is to say, in a projection R–R' event C would reproduce the duration of event B; but if Y is to be taken in any sense as a reproduction of X, it will be event A, and not event B, that is especially relevant for the third four-bar unit. We ask again when and under what circumstances such a correspondence might arise.

The durations of A and B as constituents of a phrase X can only be relevant when there is a completed and past phrase X—a phrase made past by a successor Y. But this cannot happen immediately with a new projective beginning at bar 9. Even when the projection Q–Q' is completed and made past with a new beginning, the phrase is not necessarily over—bar 9 could begin a duration that would extend the phrase (not the projection) beyond eight bars. Thus, it will take some time for Y to emerge as a second phrase and, consequently, for X to be completed and past in the presence of Y. This having occurred, a choice will have been made for A' and B' over C and D (that is, for the relevance of the first four-bar phrase for the third).

If we choose to say that there is no projection P–P', we cannot, however, deny that the two phrases are in some sense mensurally determinate. To account for the reproduction of four-bar durations in example 12.3d, we do not need to take into account the correspondence or even the formation of the eight-bar phrases. For example, if we can predict the end of the last four-bar unit, we can attribute this prediction simply to the projection S–S'—a projection that would emerge regardless of whether there were any evidence of an eight-bar phrase. Obviously, what is lost in such an interpretation is our perception that this last four-bar unit is also the continuation and completion of a phrase, and that the third four-bar unit does not itself fulfill the promise of a second phrase commensurate with the first phrase. But if the last four-bar unit is thus heard as continuation and completion of a duration promised with the third four-bar unit does this not *in effect* make the eight-bar phrase a measure, and does not this effect duplicate or at least mimic the effect that would have arisen from the projection P–P' shown in example 12.3d?

If we answer these questions affirmatively, we are, I think, obliged to recognize the mensural determinacy of our hypothetical eight-bar phrase. And in so doing we will have accounted for the meter-like effect of our eight-bar phrases while maintaining that the means by which this sort of measuring is accomplished is different from that of bar measures. From this perspective, phrases can use the determinacy of lower order

projections to extend our grasp of durational quantity—but only by creating novel forms of continuation that have the effect of overriding the closure of projective potential. They may give the appearance of projective continuations because they, too, expand a duration by leaving open the potential of a prior beginning and because the entire duration is measured—measured, that is, by smaller, constituent projections. If this difference in kind is granted, should we say that our grasp of duration in such situations is illusory—a "trompe l'orielle"? Does musical art in this way offer us the illusion of extraordinary durational quantity? I see no reason to make such a distinction or to mistrust the particular sensitivity to durational quantity that music can offer us. Nor do I find this cause to begin erecting the oppositions of natural versus artistic or innate versus learned.

Our dilemma here is, I would suggest, largely terminological (but not "merely" terminological). From a projective perspective, I have attempted to make plausible arguments both for and against an extension of meter proper to durations on the order of the musical phrase, and I believe either position could be productively elaborated. How, then, shall we choose between these two interpretations? The question here is not whether there are differences of determinacy and relevancy among various "levels" of duration. Indeed, a positive outcome of this inquiry has been an analysis of some of these differences. The question is whether these are differences of degree or of kind. This sort of question is both difficult to avoid and frustrating, given the complexities and continuities of perception. Our logic demands sharp distinctions and clearly delineated categories—in a word, abstractions. However, our experiences are not so clear-cut.

We have made a distinction between more generalized feelings of beginning and continuation and the feeling of beginning and continuation as strong and weak. But where precisely do we draw the line? In the Trio, for example, there may be some question whether we can hear the distinction strong/weak in four-bar "subphrases." If there are honest disagreements concerning these subtle qualitative distinctions, a simple classification will be arbitrary. In such cases we

EXAMPLE 12.4 Mozart, Symphony no. 35, K. 385, Trio, bs. 1–8

might more profitably turn our attention to the particularity of the continuations in question. In bars 1–8, for instance, we can note a difference in continuation or weakness between the two small phrases.

As I have indicated in example 12.4b (an analytic reduction of example 12.4a), the second violins in bars 3 and 4 repeat the connection C♯–D made by the first violins in bars 1 and 2 and repeat also a very prominent scale degree 5—the pitch E, which, from a Schenkerian

perspective, could be regarded as *Deckton*, prolonged in the upper voice by a descent to B. This repetition in bars 3–4, if heard as a "beginning again," would have the effect of detracting from the continuative quality of this second two-bar measure, as would also the change of "texture" in bars 3 and 4 where the second violins' emphasis of E accents the continuative phase of each bar measure and thus checks the momentum leading from bar to bar. By contrast, the second small phrase (bars 5–9) is very fluid.

The cadential descent to A with bar 7, far from creating a conflict of "structural accent" and metrical "unaccent," considerably enhances the continuative character of the closing two-bar measure. (A tonic close with bar 7 can scarcely be heard as a new beginning!) Here I might also mention that a much better case could be made for hearing some trace of metrical weakness in this first eight-bar measure than in the eight-bar measure of the second section (bars 9–16). Although there is a clear beginning again with bar 5, the new beginning also resolves the prolonged dominant of the first small phrase and a prolonged seventh (D from bar 2 in violin I and bar 4 in violin II) in the C♯s beginning bar 5. (See also example 11.4, where Schachter shows a connection A–B–C♯ in bars 3–5.) By functioning to close the large phrase tonally, the second four-bar measure more clearly functions as continuation, thereby enhancing the mensural determinacy of the eight-bar product.

If the boundaries that would define feelings of weak and strong are not sharply drawn, neither are the boundaries that would define "adequacy." My definition of adequacy as a feeling of "just right" is perhaps an overstatement of the precision with which we feel such correspondence. Needless to say, there is a great range in our discrimination of equality or the reproduction of durational quantity, and with the waning of mensural determinacy an attempt to distinguish between "just right" and "about right" will hardly be very rewarding.

Although the question of adequacy is generally most problematic for large durations where mensural determinacy is highly attenuated, projective complexity and ambiguity can detract from a clear feeling of adequacy or reproduction in relatively small durations. In the analyses that conclude this chapter we will consider several examples in which we may question the mensural determinacy of two–, three–, and four-bar units.

According to the model I developed in connection with example 12.3d, a "hypermeasure" (i.e., the *simulation* of a measure, different in kind from measure proper) can be no more than twice the length of a "proper" measure—that is, a measure in which continuation is felt as metrically weak. Again, this will be a fairly loose limit, given the uncertainties of metrical accent. For

example, if it is claimed that there is no distinction or insufficient distinction between strong and weak among the two-bar measures of bars 1–8 of the Trio, we could speak at most only of four-bar measures (or "hypermeasures"). Or, if it is claimed that the second four-bar measure as continuation can here be felt as metrically weak, we must recognize the possibility of a sixteen-bar measure. Since the eight-bar phrase is repeated, the first section is, in fact, sixteen bars long. There is, to be sure, little evidence here of even the simulation of a sixteen-bar projective potential. Because the first eight-bar measure is tonally so strongly closed and because the repetition is exact, the (quite literal) sense of beginning again will greatly reduce a feeling of continuation and therefore reduce the mensural determinacy of the sixteen-bar duration. This repetition, nevertheless, does continue the first section, and were there a closely corresponding sixteen-bar consequent (perhaps composed also of a repeated eight-bar measure) I believe we could feel the adequacy of the two durations. If this possibility is granted, we must say that the first section of the piece is to some degree mensurally determinate, regardless of whether there is an actual correspondence in a second large phrase.

In the alternative interpretation of example 12.3d in which we recognize a difference of degree rather than a difference of kind for "phrase-length" measures, I suggested placing the same limitation on projective potential "proper" (i.e., one projection beyond the last trace of strong and weak). However, it must be admitted that here there seems to be no systematic or theoretical requirement for imposing such a limit. If a case can be made for distinguishing some form of continuation and for sensing the adequacy of the durations in question we could, presumably, speak of very large projections. Here the criterion of adequacy becomes extremely problematic. Our feelings (or judgments) of adequacy will now be very imprecise. And because the durations of such events will be highly complex, composed as they are of a great variety of mensural and tonal determinacies, we will risk considerable oversimplification in an attempt to reduce them to unitary durational quantities. However, it would be wrong for this reason to dismiss altogether the effects of such quantities. Although our feeling of quantity may be quite imprecise, owing to the attenuation of mensural determinacy, we should not discount real feelings of adequacy (of the "about right" sort) that clearly share the character of projections. If, after a large phrase (or section), a new phrase is begun, this can be from its very beginning a large phrase with the promise of attaining a duration more or less commensurate with its predecessor; and if the new duration falls short of this promise it may be felt as "too short." The spontaneous and processive character of this opening up of a large duration with a new beginning could be taken as a strong argument for the extension of projection to very large durations. On the other hand, since such feelings of commensurate duration are so imprecise, and because the durations involved need not be reducible to a compounding of duple measures, we might in such cases speak of yet another sort of measure—a second or third sort of measure, different in kind from "true" projection or, if we prefer, from the meter-like effects of "hypermeasure."

The difficulties we encounter in attempting to locate "essential" discontinuities in our sensitivities to durational quantity are reminiscent of the difficulties psychologists have encountered in trying to give precise limits to categories of memory ("immediate," "short-term," "working," "episodic," etc.) or to the dimensions of the "conscious present." These difficulties should remind us of the great variability of individual experiences and the oversimplification of the "law" of averages. (And it is for this reason that I have not attempted to correlate the extent of mensural determinacy with the various findings of psychological research.)

It has been a postulate of our theorizing that the category of mensural determinacy is both highly variable and contextually defined. Certainly, there are significant qualitative differences between our experience of bar-length and phrase-length duration. But there are differences also in our feeling of eight-bar phrases and their constituent four-bar "subphrases"; differences between the felt character of two-bar measures and one-bar measures; differences, too, among the "same" durational units in different parts of a piece or among durations of the same clock-time length in different pieces. To ask for the

sharp distinctions that a difference in kind would require is to underestimate the complexity and "mobility" of projection and to invite oversimplification.

For all these reasons, I think it would be ill-advised to place precise limits on projection or on measurehood (i.e., projective potential). This is not to say that we can afford to ignore the qualitative differences that characterize measures of various lengths. Indeed, nothing could be further from the spirit of projective theory than the homogeneity or leveling that Leonard Meyer has called the "fallacy of hierarchic uniformity." Our analyses should be as sensitive as possible to variations in determinacy and relevancy that characterize the rhythmic articulation of musical passage. If the richness of expression offered by metrical diversity is not regarded as simply decorative, as mere "surface" as opposed to depth, or, to use Hauptmann's metaphor, as a supple flesh that covers the structural skeleton of metric regularity, we will have no reason to seek limits to meter's effectiveness in organizing durations of any length.

The Efficacy of Meter

I began this discussion by asking how we might relate meter to large-scale rhythm or form. An attempt to ascertain the largest plausible measure as an attempt to secure for meter a role in the creation of phrase and period or large-scale rhythm will not answer this question and may lead us again to equate meter with regularity and homogeneity by simply transferring the determinacy and lawfulness of meter to "higher levels." But surely Cone is right in rejecting such a metrical understanding of phrase (though wrong, I think, in accepting such an understanding of the bar). However, if measure is not equated with time-span and if neither form nor meter is reduced to an extensive, segmental hierarchy, it will not be necessary to place limits on the efficacy of projection or to seek large measures in order to capture meter's contribution to form or rhythm on any "scale."

Again, the concept of *Dehnung* would seem to offer a promising solution in that meter is not reduced to the homogeneous return of the

EXAMPLE 12.5 Carl Schachter's analysis of Mozart, Symphony no. 35, K. 385, Trio, bs. 13–20 (cf. example 11.4)

same. Here repetition results in *in*equality. Furthermore, since expansion is a transformation, we are permitted to speak of process in the formation of relations between unequal measures—a process that involves both "prototype" and extended replica. Although the concept of expansion posits an "underlying" correspondence, it need not be understood as positing an underlying equality and thus need not be understood as reductive. On the other hand, by breaking with the metrical "rule" of equality, the notion of expansion cannot be reconciled with a theory of projection or with more conventional views of meter.

In Schachter's analysis of the second section of the Trio (example 11.4 and example 12.5) bars 17–20 are interpreted as a metrical expansion of bar 16. Certainly, these measures function to continue the phrase begun with bar 9. And, more specifically, they function to "extend" the arrival on the dominant in bar 16 in what Erwin Ratz has called "*Stillstand auf der Dominant.*" The tonal goal achieved in bar 16 promises a return to tonic that takes place in bar 21, and in bar 19 (or perhaps even in bar 20) we are in a sense in the same "place" we were in bar 16. From a projective standpoint, the potential for an eight-bar duration is realized with bar 16, which functions both as an end of the phrase and as a beginning for the extension of the phrase. Both of these observations are entirely compatible with what Schachter called "the familiar notion of 'phrase extension.'" What Schachter's interpretation adds to this notion is an acknowledgment of the relevancy of an experience of bars 1–8 for an experience of bars 9–20 (and bars 9–12 for bars 13–20).

Bar 16, by functioning as continuation and end (as a fourth or eighth bar) and as beginning,

belongs to both measures. These two functions can be ascribed to bar 16 whether or not we take into account the prototypes (bars 1–8 and 9–12), and we could presumably speak of "phrase extension" without invoking any context greater than bars 13–20. However, to function as the beginning of a hypermetrical extension, bar 16 will have to be interpreted in light of its correspondence to bar 8 and bar 12. Here the relevancy of the prototype is asserted in the subordination of bars 17–20 to the prototypically replicated bars 9–16 and 13–16. Thus, bars 17–20 function to extend not only the phrase but also a bar of that phrase. If this is the case (and I see no other way of interpreting Schachter's analysis metrically), a twelve-bar duration (bars 9–20) will have come to function as the realization of an eight-bar projected potential, and an eight-bar duration will realize a four-bar projected potential, and, more immediately and more problematically, a five-bar duration (bars 16–20) will realize a one-bar potential (bar 16). To conceive of such possibilities we should have to imagine a metrical *Stillstand*—an arrest in the becoming of duration. But "time" does not stand still, and, as I shall argue, the process of projection in bars 16–20 is not held in the thrall of the prototype.

My objection to *Dehnung* as the expansion of a measure could arise from taking the concept too literally. If hypermeter is something distinct from meter, we might interpret the expansion of bar 16 more loosely as the expansion of continuation—bar 16 is continuative as the end of an eight- and a four-bar measure, and the measure it begins is continuative for the large phrase or section. In this case, my comments should not be taken as criticism but as an attempt to distinguish such a hypermetrical account from an analysis of meter. But in this case we should

EXAMPLE 12.6 Mozart, Symphony no. 35, K. 385, Trio, bs. 15–21

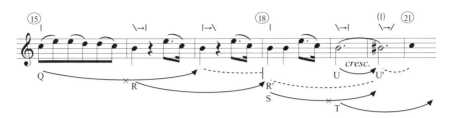

then ask how this extension functions metrically. If we do not ask this question, a hypermetrical interpretation will have obscured the contribution of meter to large-scale form or rhythm.

If bars 17–20 are an expansion of the phrase, they are also a contraction of projective activity (see example 12.6). If there is a four-bar projective potential realized with the beginning of bar 17, it is not affirmed. Indeed, because bar 17 repeats bar 16, reiterating the tonal goal B, there is little promise in this beginning for a larger projection, and so a projective potential of only two bars (Q in example 12.6) emerges as relevant. With bar 18 this measure is denied, and bars 16 and 17 will have become, respectively, beginning and continuation. The projective potential R is realized, as is the projected potential R'. Bar 20 does not, I think, function as deferral to create a three-bar measure. Instead, bars 19–20 break off from the emergent potential S to form a duple equal measure (U–U'). Although bar 20 is certainly felt as continuation, I would suggest that it could be heard to some extent also as beginning—a novel event that breaks off from the projective potential T. It is true that this B♯ "comes from" or is immediately connected to the B of bar 19. But it might be argued that this B♯ also "comes from" the goal of bars 9–16, a B prolonged through the phrase extension, and that this connection focuses our attention on bar 20 as something more than the continuation of a two-bar measure. Or we might say that bar 20 becomes anacrusis to the phrase begun with bar 21 and is in this way detached from the beginning in bar 19. In any case, I think that there is some evidence of a further contraction of projective focus to the "level" of a single bar measure. And I believe that the process of contraction in bars 9–20 contributes very significantly

to the rhythm of the whole piece. If a contraction or a reduction to smaller measures can be felt, the recapitulation of the first phrase in bars 21–28 will have a breadth or spaciousness—a sense of expansion and relaxation—that was not felt in the beginning of the piece.

The reduction to smaller measures in bars 16–20 could also enhance the possibility of hearing in the course of the entire second section a process of contraction culminating in bar 20. Earlier, I said that to intensify a feeling of an eight-bar measure in bars 9–16 we might attempt to hear a second beginning with bar 13 as weak or continuative. However, I maintain that such an attempt may, in fact, detract from our perception of "large-scale meter." For many reasons bars 9–16 are considerably more fragmentary than bars 1–8, more easily breaking into two- and four-bar units. (Compare, for example, the connection of bars 3–4 to bar 5 with the subito piano in bar 13.) Thus, I would argue that the relative fragmentation and compression in bars 9–16 *as past* become relevant for bars 16–20, and that for a process of fragmentation and compression in bars 9–20, as present, the relative breadth of bars 1–8 becomes relevant.

The especially fragmentary character of bars 16–20 is also linked to a process of liquidation or "motivic" abbreviation. As is indicated in example 12.7, the repeated melodic fragments in bars 16–19 can be interpreted as abbreviations of a descent from E to B in bars 15–16. This line in bars 15 and 16 contrasts sharply with what we may regard as a failure of the melodic descent from E in bar 12 to close on B in bar 13 (the beginning of a new four-bar measure and a beginning again with respect to bar 9). By contrast, the descent from E to B in bars 15–16 takes place within a bar-measure projection in which B is now a continuation and a completion. The par-

EXAMPLE 12.7 Mozart, Symphony no. 35, K. 385, Trio, bs. 9–24

Acceleration and completion   Condensation

ticular urgency of the descent to B in bar 16 can be attributed to the relevancies of both the preceding small phrase (bars 9–12) and bars 13–14. Compared to bars 9–12, the eighth-note descent takes place a bar earlier—in the third rather than in the fourth bar of the phrase. And compared to bars 13–14, the figure beginning with an anacrusis to bar 15 can be heard as a complex accelerated and completed repetition. Thus, the abbreviations in bars 16–19 together with a progressive reduction in projective potential we observed in example 12.6 continue a process of compression and acceleration that spans the entire phrase. We should therefore expect this process of compression to have some effect for the final phrase, a literal repetition of bars 1–8.

In the abbreviated descents from E to B in bars 16–19 the pitch D is omitted, and, although there are immediate descents from E to D in bars 9–15, the characteristic rising-third figure B–D,

C♯–E emphasizes an ascent to E. Because of the prominence of E in this phrase and especially because of its isolation in the phrase's extension, I believe we are more prepared in bars 21–24 than in bars 1–4 to focus our attention on a descent from E to A. And here the grace-note figure in bar 22 (E to D) can take on novel significance, emphasizing a D quite conspicuously omitted in bars 16–20. Certainly, the length and "evenness" of the descending line in bars 21–23 contribute to the expansiveness of the new phrase vis-à-vis the compression and stoppage of the preceding phrase. Furthermore, to the degree we can feel a novel (though "local") sense of closure in the arrival on A in bar 23, the continuity of the four-bar measure will be enhanced.

In the preceding analysis an eight-bar measure in bars 9–16 is taken to be real and functional—it constitutes a phrase (equal in duration to the first phrase) that is extended. And the special relevancies of four-, two-, and one-bar measures in the expanded second phrase do not conflict with the eight-bar measure. Again, we could speak of conflict only if these measures were regarded as autonomous "strata." Shall we say that the eight-bar measure (or, in the second phrase, a "basic" eight-bar measure expanded to twelve bars) is the dominant metrical entity, the expression of large-scale meter, and the limit of meter? From a projective perspective, such an assertion will have little meaning. From the standpoint of an extensive, segmental hierarchy, measures are nested "spans of time"—the largest spans *contain* the smaller spans. Here large-scale meter is identified with the largest spans. But unless we can identify a single measure that is the entire piece, meter cannot extend to the highest level of form. However, from the standpoint of projective process there is no limit to the efficacy of meter. Rather than blocks of duration, we are presented with events, the largest of which is the whole piece. Here, boundaries are not so sharply drawn. A small measure is not subsumed in a larger measure; rather, it is creative for what the larger measure will become. And any measure, of any size, has the "power" (*potentia*) to affect the becoming of a later or a larger event. From this perspective, what the largest event— the piece—becomes is nothing apart from the totality of metrical processes that led to its being this piece.

Some Small Examples

Needless to say, there are as many ways in which meter contributes to "form" as there are pieces of measured music. Although our perusal of the *Haffner* Trio has allowed us to make certain methodological generalizations, it would be a mistake to conclude that periods or phrases are invariably measures or that two-, four-, and eight-bar measures (or three- and six-bar measures) necessarily arise from the repetition of one-, two-, and four-bar measures. Before turning to examples that feature larger projections, I would like to consider several examples in which we may question the mensural determinacy of relatively small phrases.

For an identification of measures larger than a bar, the opening of Vivaldi's "Spring" Concerto from *The Four Seasons* (example 12.8) is more problematic than the *Haffner* Trio. Shall we speak of a three-bar or a six-bar measure here? Certainly, we can hear the equality of bars 1–3 and bars 4–6. But cannot the seven-bar consequent (bars 7–13) be heard in some sense as equal to the six-bar antecedent (bars 1–6)? If there is a three-bar measure, is it triple unequal? Are the three-and-one-half-bar phrases in the consequent expansions of three-bar measures or contractions of four-bar measures? More generally, are the criteria for measurehood we developed for the Trio applicable here?

The gestural/projective world of the Vivaldi is radically different from that of the Mozart. The Vivaldi is much more energetic and compressed (as befits the depiction of spring), though hardly "small-scale." Of course, Mozart could also compose highly contracted projections (as we shall see in the next example), but the particular differences between the two pieces also reflects a difference in style. Although I will not attempt to delineate this stylistic difference, I would point out that a style is more than a set of conventional devices or techniques, forms or procedures—it is above all an environmentally (culturally and personally) specific manner of feeling duration.

In terms of mensural determinacy, we might (rather loosely) compare the three-bar beginning of the Concerto to the eight-bar measure that begins the Trio. That is, the degree of mensural determinacy (resulting in clear feelings of strong and weak) that can be felt in the two- and four-bar measures of the Mozart is limited to one-bar measures in the Vivaldi. Thus, I find little evidence of deferral with bar 3. This is not to deny that we can hear a three-measure phrase and that a feeling of "threeness" is involved in our perceptions of equality or adequacy.

That mensural determinacy is drawn so short here arises in part from repetition or "beginning again" in bars 1–2 and in part from an emphasis on or directedness toward continuation in each bar measure. The arrest on the second half of each bar is a goal that focuses our attention on ending; and, although the beginning of each bar is preceded by anacrusis (as is each second half-note beat), each beginning is a beginning again—a

EXAMPLE 12.8 Vivaldi, Il Cimento dell'Armonica e dell'Inventione, Concerto
no. 1 in E Major ("Spring"), bs. 1–10

dominant beginning rather than the continuation of a greater mensural determinacy.

That bars 1–3 are potentially reproducible as a mensurally determinate duration is proved by the fact that they are reproduced in bars 4–6 and that we can presumably feel a repetition of durational quantity. However, since the reproduction is virtually literal, the reproduction does not in itself attest to a high degree of durational determinacy. If the third small phrase (bars 7–10) is felt in some sense as equal in duration to the first two phrases—and I suggest that this phrase sounds more equal than it looks—this correspondence, in fact, argues against a high degree of mensural determinacy for the first phrase. If we grant a correspondence, we might ask whether the phrases of the consequent are expansions or contractions of those of the antecedent. In example 12.9 I have represented both possibilities.

From a hypermetrical standpoint (ex. 12.9b) the third phrase is presumably an expansion of the prototypical earlier phrases. From a projec-tive standpoint (example 12.9c) we might also speak of a contraction—four completed "bar" measures elided through a reinterpretation of metrical accent. (Incidentally, this reading points to a compressed version of the accelerative pattern long–long–short–short–long, shown in example 9.7 and example 9.8.) Although I deny the *metrical* extension shown in example 12.9b, I do not deny the relvancies shown there as correspondences between the third phrase and the first two phrases. Nor do I deny that these correspondences are largely responsible for our feeling that the phrases are similar in their durations. By comparison, the third phrase is expanded, both in the sense that it is made longer by the insertion of an "extra" half-note beat (the second beat of bar 8 or the first beat of bar 9) and in the sense that we may have some feeling of a larger duple equal measure (second half of bar 8—first half of bar 10). In light of the comparison, there is no contradiction between expansion and contraction. The contraction shown in example 12.9c serves the expansion by contributing to a

EXAMPLE 12.9 Vivaldi, Il Cimento dell'Armonica e dell'Inventione, Concerto no. 1 in E Major ("Spring"), bs. 1–3 and 7–10

sense of intensification, acceleration, and closure (i.e., an acceleration aimed at a continuation as ending).

The correspondences between the three- and three-and-one-half-bar measures are so compelling we may be only dimly aware of the difference in length. But I suggest that this assimilation to equality can occur only because these measures are not highly mensurally determinate and that a high degree of determinacy is reserved for one-bar measures. Thus, if there were a strong feeling of deferral in bars 4–6 (a feeling, crudely put, of strong/weak rather than "one-two-three") I doubt that we could accept bars 7–10 as a near-reproduction. I have continued to speak of these small phrases as measures, but I wish to distinguish them from one-bar measures as relatively indeterminate potentials for duration.

In the opening of Mozart's Piano Sonata, K. 311 (example 12.10), we can identify a period, the first phrase of which ends on scale degree 3 (F♯) in bar 4. Like the Vivaldi, the phrases are

three bars long, but here there is even less evidence of a three-bar measure and no evidence of a six-bar measure. The first bar is a measure, and the beginning of bar 2 projects the duration of a bar measure (P'). However, the second half-note beat of bar 2 also functions (or comes to function) as a new beginning—the beginning of a second "bar" measure or a whole-note duration (R). Deprived of its continuation, the beginning of the second notated bar can now become continuation of a first measure begun with the second half-note beat of bar 1 (Q). This reinterpretation is confirmed in a third "bar" (R'), which forms the cadence. In bar 4 the performer has the option of either simply completing the projected R' or retrieving the notated bar by accenting (or separating) the downbeat as a new beginning. (The grace note here is helpful for making such an articulation.) If a beginning again with bar 4 is suppressed, the period will be quite continuous, and the three-"bar" unit will emerge more clearly as a measure. However, I

EXAMPLE 12.10 Mozart, Piano Sonata in D Major, K. 311, first movement,
bs. 1–8

believe the second option is preferable in that it enhances a feeling of projective expansion introduced in the second large phrase (or sentence, bars 7–16) and thus contributes to a feeling of "large-scale meter." In either case, we can feel the durational correspondence of the first two small phrases. But by interrupting the first phrase with a new beginning on the downbeat of bar 4 we will (re-)focus attention on the smaller bar and "bar" measures. Since at the level of half-note measures there is no interruption or elision and no reinterpretation, were we to focus our attention on half-note measures we might suppress to some extent the feelings of interruption and reinterpretation—feelings that arise from thwarted attempts to grasp larger durations.

By contrast, the second large phrase begun with bar 7 (and here a feeling of interruption is unavoidable) presents a clear two-bar measure supported by the distinction strong/weak. These distinctions were not apparent in bars 1–6— even if we attempt to interpret the downbeat of bar 3 as the beginning of a bar measure, it will be extremely difficult to hear deferral. I suggest that a three-bar measure has very little relevance for the new phrase and that the relevance of the preceding passage is, more generally, that of a

tightly compressed projective field involving one-bar projections opening to expanded projections involving two-bar measures (and later, perhaps, four-bar measures).

In presenting cases in which the mensural determinacy of the phrase seems questionable I have, not coincidentally, chosen three-bar phrases. To retain a strong projective potential, a potential that does not demand a high degree of conformity in projected realization, a triple measure must offer a feeling of deferral or a feeling of strong and weak. This latter requirement is the same for duple measures, but in the case of duple measures mensural determinacy can be enhanced by an "earlier" projection. Thus, in example 12.11, although the duple projection (R–R') is longer than the triple, it may be more highly determinate. With the beginning of Q' a duration larger than the beat is promised, and there is no deferral of projective potential. In the triple there is no realized projection that mediates pulse and measure.

Large triple unequal measures are difficult to bring off—as mensural determinacy becomes attenuated it seems that we are not willing to defer projection and that we are inclined either to realize a projection with the third beat or to

EXAMPLE 12.11 Contrast of mensural
determinacy in unequal and equal measure

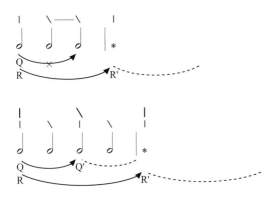

settle for smaller measures that present a high
degree of determinacy. However, measurehood
or projective potential is not determined exclusively by "length" (or clock-time duration), but
also by clear distinctions of metrical accent—
the distinctions of beginning and continuation.
If there is ambiguity in these distinctions, we
may focus our attention on smaller measures
even where there is the possibility of hearing a
larger duple equal measure.

The opening phrase of the Allegro from

Haydn's Symphony no. 88 (example 12.12) is
eight bars long and consists of two four-bar subphrases. If we can clearly feel a durational correspondence, we must say that there are two four-
bar measures (and perhaps even an eight-bar
measure). However, depending on our performance of the passage, such a feeling of durational repetition may, in fact, be quite vague, and
our attention may be drawn instead to the repetition of two-bar measures. The two-bar measures at the beginning of the passage seem to
hover between two interpretations—a beginning with bar 17 as indicated by the bar lines in
example 12.12 (interpretation 1), or a beginning
with the notated second beat of each bar and
indicated by dotted bars (the "bar" measures of
interpretation 2). Even with a dynamic accent
on the downbeat of bar 17, the distinction between beginning and continuation will remain
somewhat ambiguous. A clear conformity of
measure to notated bar occurs only with bars
23–24. The beginning of bar 22 will then have
become the beginning of a bar measure and,
possibly, the continuation of a two-bar measure.
But if there is such a reinterpretation, the metrical correspondence of the two four-bar phrases
will have been obscured, and we may attend to

EXAMPLE 12.12 Haydn, Symphony no. 88 in G Major, first
movement, bs. 17–24

four two-bar measures. As a result of the reinterpretation, the cadential fourth (two-bar) measure will be detached from the third. But even if there were no reinterpretation (if interpretation 1 were uncontested), the emphasis on the high A in bar 22 and the change of register will inhibit the formation of a four-bar measure (if the end of bar 22 is interpreted as anacrusis).

A pull toward two-bar measures also arises from the initial metrical ambiguity—any ambiguity at the "half-note level" will detract to some extent from the determinacy of a larger projective potential. Interpretation 2 especially invites a hearing of two-"bar" measures because of its emphasis on continuations as endings. Here the immediate melodic goals, G (bars 17–18) and A (bars 19–20), appear as continuative second "bars," and activity is suspended with these continuative quarter-note endings (a pattern, short-short-long, we shall later characterize as metrically closed). Here, too, there is no anacrusis connecting the two-"bar" measures. In interpretation 1, the anacrusis in bar 18 enhances the possibility of hearing a second two-bar measure as continuation. Comparing interpretations 1 and 2, we might say that the first is more fluid and the second is square or choppy. If there is some ambiguity—if something of both interpretations can be felt—these divergent qualities will be combined and will contribute to the particular energy of this phrase. Here we may properly speak of conflict, but this will be a metrical conflict and not a conflict of meter and rhythm. As a result of this conflict, the rhythmic gesture of the phrase involves a movement from projective ambiguity to clarity. And this gesture itself is repeated in the exposition in the formation of two larger events: the modulation to the dominant (bars 45–61) and in the following large phrase cadencing in the dominant (bars 61–77). Although metrical ambiguity and the emphasis on continuations as endings contribute to a reduction in projective range, they also contribute to the energy of the phrase as a whole. It should be clear, then, that the compression of this passage in no way detracts from the large-scale rhythm or meter of the phrase or from the relevance of this phrase for later or larger events.

As a final example I would like to consider the opening of Elliott Carter's Sonata for Violoncello and Piano shown in example 12.13. In comparison with the preceding examples, mensural determinacy here is drawn extremely short. The effect of this contraction of projective range is not "smallness," but rather an intensely energetic and dramatic continuity. The complexity and volatility of the projective field in this piece are by no means incompatible with the emergence of a "long line." Indeed, such complexity serves continuity in two ways: (1) by eliding individual gestures through overlapping and (2) by providing a variety of what might be called "projective behaviors"—contrasting metrical/rhythmic procedures that can characterize phrases, sections, or even instrumental lines.

If metrical notation is, in general, an unreliable guide to projective activity, it is especially so in music such as this, which aims for kaleidoscopic projective reinterpretations and effects of rubato and improvisatory freedom for which our notational system is quite unsuited. For this reason we should guard against allowing the notation to deafen us to the projective complexities that enliven this passage. If we choose to do so, we can (with some effort and given a score) hear the notated bar measures, supplying virtual beats in bar 2. In fact, if we are reading this passage rather than listening to a performance and counting rather than responding to rhythmic gesture, such an interpretation might well correspond to our hearing. However, in view of the pattern formed by the new staccato figure beginning in bar 3, it might be tempting to depart slightly from the notation to hear 4/4 measures beginning on the second half of bar 1. In this case, the first half of bar 1, since it is projectively incomplete, can fairly easily be heard as anacrusis. (Note, too, that this first half-bar sounds very much like dominant harmony resolving outward to B major.) It might also be claimed that at least two two-"bar" measures are formed in such a hearing—the second measure beginning with the new staccato figure in bars 3–4 (E–G–F♯, etc.) and confirmed by the beginning of a repetition in the second half of bar 5. However, while such an interpretation of the first few bars might (initially) serve the purposes of a performer, I believe that the perceptions of an unprejudiced but attentive listener will more re-

EXAMPLE 12.13 Elliott Carter, Sonata for Violoncello and Piano, first movement, bs. 1–7. Copyright © 1951, 1953 (renewed) by Associated Music Publishers, Inc. (BMI). International copyright secured. All rights reserved. Reprinted by permission.

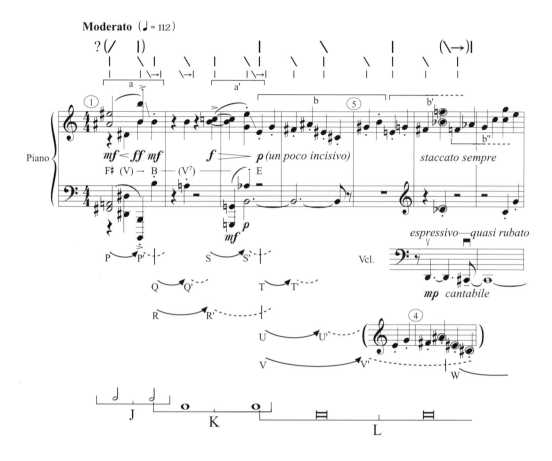

$$J = P – P'$$
$$K = R (Q–Q') – R' (S–S')$$
$$L = V (U (T–T') –U') –V'$$

semble the interpretation indicated in example 12.13. Later we will return to the general question of a possible disparity between the perceptions of performer and listener. But first I would like to comment on my construction of "the listener's" interpretation shown in example 12.13.

Initially, the last quarter in bar 1 will be heard as an afterbeat, a sort of rebound after the fortissimo climax on B. Likewise, the following attack in bar 2 (B, A♮) will presumably be heard initially as an offbeat. However, a correspondence quickly emerges that will alter the projective field. As I have indicated with the symbols "a" and "a'," a

repetition of the first bar measure in bars 2 and 3 will turn the fourth quarter-note attack of bar 1 into a projective beginning. (Note, too, that the introduction of A♮ in bar 2 turns the B-major "tonic" into a dominant for the following E-major/minor sonority in bar 3.) Because of the processive nature of projective reinterpretation, it is difficult to determine by introspection precisely *when* these changes occur (and if "when" means "at a point in time" the question will have little meaning). But once the new measure is formed, there will never have been a time *this* duration (realized in the projection Q–Q') did not begin urgently as an interruption of the projection P–P'. Indeed, the word "*re*interpretation" may be misleading to the extent that it suggests going back to a *past* construction and replacing it with a new construction (as if the past were still active, becoming, or *present*). It should be remembered that what I have called "reinterpretation" can take place only in the realization of present potential.

Similarly, in bar 3 the new beginning of what will become the projective duration T or U emerges to interrupt the projections S–S' and R–R'. However, because of the diminuendo in bar 3, the beginning of a new measure T (or U) may seem less interruptive than the beginning of Q (or R), in spite of the sustained B in the left hand. In any case, the new "staccato music" very quickly reorganizes projective potential through its contour and intervallic patterning, breaking as it does into "half-note thirds" (E–G, F♯–A♯, etc.). I have also indicated in parentheses the possibility of a reinterpretation of the first half-note beat in bar 1 as anacrustic. Here it seems that, in spite of the interruptive character of the overlapping, the extended prolongation of B in bars 1 and 2 allows this first half-note beat to function as anacrusis (in which case, the third and fourth quarter-note beats of bar 1 would actually coalesce as a single dominant beginning).

The remarkably intense character of the new "staccato music" beginning in bar 3 surely owes something to the energetically compressed gestures in bars 1–3 from which it emerges. Compared to the preceding two-note staccato figure (mezzo forte) in bars 1 and 2, the new figure will be heard to move twice as quickly; and as a successor to the mercurial projective reinterpretations in bars 1–3, the new figure will be met with heightened attentiveness on the part of a listener who closely follows this already volatile course of events. Nevertheless, as the music continues there can also be felt some measure of relaxation with the expansion of projective potential. Because of the repetition beginning in the second half of bar 5 indicated by the symbols "b" and "b'," a relatively large, four half-note-beat measure seems to be formed in bars 3–5 (projective potential V). One indication of this measure is the trace of earliness we can feel in bar 6 when a transposed replica of the initial fig-

ure (b": F♮–A♭–G–[C]) enters four quarter notes "too soon." (Note also the collapsing of the sequence A♯–E♯–C♯ from bar 4 in the simultaneity B♭–F♮–D♭ in bar 6 and the overlapping of figures b' and b" in bar 6 through the shared F♯/E♯.) This mildly interruptive overlapping and the immediate repetition of the melodic figure (E♭–G♭–F♯) a half step higher (F♮–A♭–G) help to refocus the listener's attention on the piano line following the entrance of the cello in bar 6.

Although I have ended the example with bar 7, I should say something about the continuation of this large phrase. (Indeed, the pervasive overlapping in this piece makes it very difficult to isolate discrete units for analysis.) The metrically and tonally unfocused cello line that begins in bar 6 remains (projectively and intervallically) separated from the sharply focused piano line for several bars. In fact, because of this disparity, the cello line is virtually ametrical until bars 12–15. Having risen in register to meet the piano in bar 11, the cello now interacts tonally and projectively with the piano to present its first "thematic" statement—a very carefully "written-out" rubato figure freely repeated throughout the movement.

The particular fluency or continuity of this piece is achieved in part by a blurring of phrase boundaries. For example, a focal cello "phrase" surfaces for our attention in bars 12–15; but we cannot say precisely when this gesture began to take shape. In example 12.13 we can point to an introduction composed of two overlapping gestures—J and K—leading to L, the new "staccato music"; and yet, since the beginning of this new phrase is foreshadowed in the preceding staccato figure (initiating K) and continues a larger process of overlapping, we may feel here more continuity than meets the eye. Indeed, throughout this movement foreshadowing is combined with a blurring of boundaries to produce quite remarkable rhythmic experiences. Characteristic is the experience of finding ourselves in a new "place" (i.e., a new phrase or section) only to realize that we have been there/ here for some time without knowing it. Such novel temporal and rhythmic experience draws upon ambiguities of sameness and difference in all musical domains. But without the very vivid metrical distinctions that help to particularize and articulate this fluency, the music would be robbed of its energy and vitality and collapse into a relatively incoherent and homogeneous experience in which tonal distinctions, too, would be flattened. To imagine that meter is less important here than in a piece composed of sixteen-bar periods in 4/4 time or that meter is of secondary importance compared to pitch relations would be to quite unrealistically ignore the force of Carter's rhythmic invention.

In chapter 9 I commented briefly on differences in our perceptions of meter that arise in playing and listening. In twentieth-century musics that aim for more complex projective distinctions than our notational system can accommodate, this disparity is considerably widened. Indeed, this is one of the more problematic aspects of "progressive" modern music and one to which we shall return in chapters 14 and 15. To play accurately (i.e., the right notes, in time, with appropriate dynamics), the performer may very well be forced to "count"; and without a great expenditure of time devoted to preparing a performance, counting can replace hearing. On the other hand, if the performance is accurate, the listener may be able to make a projective sense of the performance that is hidden from the player. For this reason, playing accurately with little comprehension is, in general, much better than

playing inaccurately and with little comprehension but with "feeling." Nevertheless, a performer who plays "by ear" (though this may also involve some form of counting) can communicate a much more vivid and engaging rhythmic/projective sense using all the articulative resources his or her technique provides. Clearly, this "sense" is not notated in the score and cannot have been fully grasped by the composer who could not possibly conceive of the limitless variety of experiences a composition makes possible. Each experience of "the" piece is an interpretation chock-full of the decisions that particularize that experience.

My "listener's interpretation" in example 12.13 (which may also be taken as a listening performer's interpretation) is very general. Even so, it is not so general as to be beyond dispute. Nor, of course, are such problems of interpretive latitude limited to twentieth-century repertories—all of the interpretations in this book are questionable. But I do not regard this as an analytic shortcoming. An adequate theory of meter cannot pretend that there are no choices to be made or that there is a single correct interpretation formed in the composer's "intention" and encoded in the score. This fact of musical life is challenging for the performer, the analyst, and the composer.

THIRTEEN

Overlapping, End as Aim, Projective Types

In the preceding section I considered several examples in which phrases do not form measures or, at least, very definite measures. And I attempted to show that failure to form large measures does not detract from the efficacy of meter in the creation of large-scale rhythm. I would now like to consider several passages from a single composition in which relatively large measures are formed. The following discussion is as much theoretical as analytic and involves the introduction of several new topics pertaining to projection.

In the Allegro from the first movement of Beethoven's First Symphony, two large phrases or periods compose the exposition. The first of these (bars 13–52) is a virtually unbroken gesture. The second period (bars 53–109), though more broken, is also a highly continuous gesture. Although there is a sharp break between the two periods, there is little (immediate) discontinuity between the second period and the repetition of the first. There is a very sharp tonal break with the beginning of the development section. This second large period begins as an interruption of the goal promised by the conclusion of the exposition. The interruption here might be regarded as a sort of deferral or a rupture that is subsequently healed with the beginning of the recapitulation. The recapitulation, in contrast to the exposition, is unbroken and emerges as a single large period. These various continuities and discontinuities arise in part from projective processes that I would like to discuss in some detail. My choice of detail is motivated by opportunities to clarify some of the notions introduced thus far and to consider a number of questions concerning projection that have not been addressed.

Our first topic will be "overlapping," conceived most generally as the joining of ending and beginning. Throughout this study we have been concerned with this crucial juncture in events; but having concentrated so much on beginning, we have given insufficient attention to the question of closure. Since tonal continuities and discontinuities play an essential role in overlappings, we shall have to consider more closely the interaction of tonal and projective potential and the notion of end as goal. I will conclude this theoretical discussion with a rudimentary theory of "projective types" or durational patterns that present more or less specific possibilities for overlapping. Rather than offer a catalog of types, I will explore the uses of one type that is prominently featured in the first movement of the Beethoven symphony—a "directed closing" type of the form long–long–short–short–long, which we first encountered in example 9.8.

Overlapping

In *Phrase Rhythm in Tonal Music*, William Rothstein offers the following definition of "overlap": "Simply stated, two phrases may be said to overlap when the last note (or chord) of the first phrase acts simultaneously as the first note (or chord) of the second phrase" (1989, p. 44). Restricting the process of overlap to the entities of phrase and subphrase, Rothstein distinguishes this process from that of "metrical reinterpretation":

> Reinterpretation is to metrical structure approximately what overlap is to phrase structure. Reinterpretation occurs when the last bar of one hypermeasure is treated simultaneously as the first bar of a new hypermeasure. (Occasionally two bars are reinterpreted in this way, though this is much less common.) When a bar is reinterpreted, one measure that "should" have occurred does not: the last bar of a hypermeasure, rather than being followed by a new first bar, *becomes* that first bar. (Rothstein 1989, p. 52)

These distinctions are carefully conceived and, in general, quite useful. For example, in the first movement of the Beethoven symphony we are about to consider there is a cadential overlap in the end of the introductory Adagio and the beginning of the Allegro, and until bar 53—the beginning of the second period—all phrase connections involve harmonic or tonal overlap. These deferrals of tonal closure are crucial for the rhythmic coherence of the exposition. And yet, the merits of Rothstein's terminology notwithstanding, I will propose that the notion of overlapping be broadened to refer to any situation in which we wish to point to the "simultaneity" of end and beginning. Ambiguities of ending and beginning can arise in events of any duration and in any sort of music—"tonal" and "non-tonal," metrical and ametrical. Moreover, from a projective point of view—or, more generally, from a temporal point of view—we will have little reason to isolate measure from phrase. Although we can make a real categorical distinction, phrase (itself a notoriously fluid category) and measure arise together and are inseparable in their interactions. Thus, Rothstein's tonal overlap will be a factor in the emergence of projec-

tive/projected potential, and, reciprocally, projective distinctions will play a formative role in our perceptions of tonal overlap. If we can view tonal "overlap" as a factor that can be involved in overlapping in general, we can view Rothstein's "metrical reinterpretation" also as a feature that can contribute to the particularity of an overlapping (as, for example, in the overlappings we observed earlier in the opening of the Carter Sonata). Of course, we should also have to alter Rothstein's definition, replacing "last and first bar of a hypermeasure" with (very loosely put) "continuation and beginning of a projection."

By overlapping I shall mean, most generally, a process in which an articulation serves as both continuation and beginning. Of course, any new musical event is a continuation of the piece that is present and in the process of becoming until it ends. But in the course of this becoming, any part or smaller event will become past and in itself no longer present and becoming. A succeeding event will then be present in itself and present also as a continuation of the piece as a whole. Thus, overlapping is an "operation" that characterizes all temporal process. Earlier I described the inseparability of end and beginning as a sort of overlapping. However, in the following discussion we will consider more specifically the overlapping of metrical phrase events and situations in which there is some ambiguity in feelings of continuation and beginning. Thus far, I have given more attention to beginning than to end. In approaching the question of overlapping, I shall have to redress this imbalance. But before taking up the question of end as aim or goal, I would like to consider several instances of overlapping in bars 13–52 of the Beethoven.

Among the many overlappings that might be identified in example 13.1, most striking are the articulations of the events that begin in bars 17 and 19 and bars 23 and 25. These pairs of overlappings draw upon a great variety of musical domains for their particularity: tone, contour, dynamics, metrical projection, register, and instrumentation. In example 13.1 I indicate in each case a reinterpretation in which a projected potential of four bars (P' and U') is interrupted by a new beginning. In the first case, the reinterpretation is quite abrupt. Although there is con-

EXAMPLE 13.1 Beethoven, Symphony no. 1 in C Major, first movement, bs. 13–27

tinuation in woodwinds' tonal resolution to D at the beginning of bar 19, the transposed repetition by the strings of the beginning of the Allegro (anacrusis included) almost immediately creates a new beginning and a beginning again. Here the repetition of bar 13 in bar 19 introduces marked changes in dynamics (subito piano), instrumentation, and register that intensify the feeling of discontinuity. Moreover, because of this "immediate" correspondence, the relevance of bars 13–16 for the new beginning in bar 19 gives to this beginning a real potential for realizing a duration of four bars. This potential, too, must contribute to our feeling of interruption.

If the new phrase event beginning with bar 19 is a *second* beginning, how shall we interpret bars 17–18? Were this two-bar event projectively detached from bars 13–16, it might come to function as an anacrusis to the longer (four-bar) measure that emerges in bars 19–22. Because of the projective overlapping in bar 17, this does not happen. The projection P–P' involves both the registral and instrumental discontinuities introduced in bar 17 and the continuity of the first violin line that ends on the octave C at the beginning of the new measure. Note, incidentally, the history of this latter gesture. Each of the projections P–P', Q–Q', R–R', S–S', and T–T' is enhanced by an anacrustic B (or G–B) that leads to a new beginning in C, repeating the immediate connection of the Adagio introduction to the Allegro (bars 12–13). Indeed, this gesture is repeated a whole step higher (C♯–D) to initiate the new small phrase in bar 19. But in noting the immediate tonal connections of end and beginning in bars 18 and 19 (C♯–D in flute, G–F in oboe) we should not ignore the interruptive character of the new beginning with bar 19 and the return of the first violins a whole step above the beginning of the preceding phrase in bar 13. With this second beginning, bars 17–18 are absorbed into a highly compressed and energetic small phrase (bars 13–18) whose final incompleteness is itself the promise of a larger event.

Although in many respects a repetition of bars 13–18, the following phrase in bars 19–24 is less sharply separated from its successor. In example 13.1, I have indicated a projection U–U'

interrupted by a new four-bar measure beginning with bar 25. Notice, however, that compared to bar 19 projective reinterpretation here is less abrupt. For many reasons, it now takes the emergence of a new projection (W–W') for a reinterpretation to be effected. All those aspects of difference that served to articulate a new beginning with bar 19 are present here, but each is now mollified: in bars 23–24 strings are now added to winds, the crescendo is no longer interrupted, and tonal boundaries are now relatively permeable in the sense that the pitches D and F in bars 23–24 can be absorbed into the following dominant harmony. (Note especially the bass descent, D–C♯–B, in bars 23–25.) This last factor is perhaps the most effective in softening a feeling of interruption here. In bars 23–25 there is an immediate connection A–A♭–G corresponding to the line C–C♯–D (or G–F) in bars 17–19, but there is nothing here that corresponds to the articulation created by moving up a step from C to D to begin a new phrase in bar 19. Less interruptive than the second small phrase and less sharply detached from its predecessor, the third phrase (bars 25–32, example 13.2a) continues this process of expansion opening into a grand arpeggiation of dominant harmony that in its eight bars effectively doubles the proportions of the opening gestures of the Allegro. In examples 13.1 and 13.2 I have indicated this homology in an identification of the patterns long–long–short–short–long (hereafter abbreviated LLSSL) in bars 13–16, 19–22, and 25–32.

If there is a broadening of gesture and an enlargement of projective potential in bars 25–32 (shown in example 13.2), there is also a quickening of pace and a dramatic intensification in the tutti climax leading to a new large phrase with bar 33. In the overlapping of these two large phrases we find a clear instance of tonal "overlap." The tonic in bar 33 that might resolve the immediately preceding dominant seventh chord and the prolonged and arpeggiated dominant seventh of bars 25–32 breaks off as a new beginning. In this complex mixture of continuity and discontinuity, projective distinctions play a crucial role.

The anacrustic half-note group of bars 31–32 promises a tonal close that is, in fact, realized

EXAMPLE 13.2 (**a**) Beethoven, Symphony no. 1 in C Major, first movement, bs. 25–35; (**b, c**) recomposition of bars 31–34.

EXAMPLE 13.3 Beethoven, Symphony no. 1 in C Major, first movement, bs. 8–13

with the beginning of bar 33. But because of the highly discontinuous changes in orchestration, texture, and melodic figure introduced with bar 33, the beginning of a new large phrase quickly emerges. This emergence, however, is not instantaneous, and in the gap opened by the process of reinterpretation, the new beginning takes on an especially urgent or interruptive character. To more clearly see the contribution of meter to this immediate effect, notice how crucial the anacrustic second beat of bar 32 is. In example 13.2b I have omitted this beat, allowing the phrase to close on the dominant at the beginning of the bar.

On the larger scale, we may note that if a tonal closure with the beginning of bar 33 were allowed to stand and thus to extend the first large phrase (instead of initiating a second phrase), a two-bar measure (Y') would suffice to exhaust projected potential, as in example 13.2c. Indeed, the possibility for a projection Y-Y' here shows how tenuous the relevance of a projective duration V becomes in the course of bars 29–32. In any case, the initiation of a new beginning with bar 33 promises a duration larger than four bars. And to the degree this new beginning emerges as a second beginning for the Allegro, it will promise a duration more or less commensurate with that of the first large phrase. Such a promise would seem to be enhanced by the relevance of the overlapping of Adagio and Allegro. As can be seen from a comparison of examples 13.2 and 13.3, bars 31–33 reproduce in many respects the cadential elaboration that led to the overlapping of the introduction and the begin-

ning of the Allegro (bars 8–13). By comparison, the cadence in bars 31–33 happens very quickly; it is not impeded, as was the end of the Adagio, delayed by the deceptive resolution in bar 10 and retarded by the prolonged dominant of bars 11–12. In each case, the promise of closure ends in a new beginning.

I would like to consider one other overlapping from this first period of the exposition since it involves a metrical reinterpretation quite different from those we encountered in bars 19 and 23. The conclusion of the period is shown in example 13.4a.

In the first four bars the acceleration and directedness of the line to G establishes the beginning of bar 45 as the end or goal of the progression begun in bar 41. Note here that the connection of A and F♯ to G in bars 44–45 is brought into special focus by contrast with the thwarted resolutions of scale degrees 6 and/or 4 in the previous overlappings shown in examples 13.4b–e. As a result of many factors—tonal as well as durational—a very definite four-bar projected potential is given to the new beginning at bar 45. Beneath bars 47 and 48 in example 13.4a I offer a simple realization of this potential substituting bars 51–52 for 47–48. To my ear, this alternative does not sound too short to satisfactorily complete the phrase. It does, however, seem too short to complete the period. In Beethoven's continuation, an eight-bar measure emerges in bars 45–52, exceeding the four-bar projected potential and thus, in a sense, detaching itself from the preceding small phrase with which it is overlapped. This gradual detachment

EXAMPLE 13.4 Beethoven, Symphony no. 1 in C Major, first movement, (**a**) bs. 41–56, (**b**) bs. 1–7, (**c**) bs. 10–12, (**d**) bs. 17–19 and 23–25, and (**e**) bs. 30–38

Continued

EXAMPLE 13.4 (*continued*)

is, as it were, the converse of projective interruption, but it is a metrical reinterpretation nonetheless.

As the new measure is formed in bars 45–52, the durational relevance of bars 41–44 comes to be felt in the expansiveness or breadth of the final phrase (and perhaps in a feeling of anacrustic directedness toward the new, larger measure).

Not only is there an expansion from four to eight bars, but also there is an acceleration in bars 45–52 that reproduces the accelerative pattern of bars 41–44 in proportionally expanded values. An important difference is that whereas the acceleration in bars 41–44 opens to a new measure and an overlapping with bar 45, the acceleration in bars 45–52 ends in projective closure. In bars 45–52 two instances of the pattern LLSSL can be identified. This large measure (or at least the best candidate for larger-than-four-bar measurehood thus far) is closed in the projective sense that the accelerative "shorts" lead to a continuative "long"—a cessation of activity in ending. Here, for the first time in the piece, the end of a measure is not directed toward a new beginning. And in the entire movement there is no distinction between end and beginning as sharp as this articulation of the two parts of the exposition.

Nevertheless, in my use of the term, there is an overlapping of the two periods of the exposition if only because the movement continues. More specifically, the large phrase begun with bar 53 is a prolongation of the goal of the phrase ended in bar 52—an opening to the dominant that continues the goal reached with bar 45. The second period takes this "end" as a beginning. The eight-bar sentence that begins with bar 53 (repeated in bars 61–68) replicates the LLSSL pattern of bars 45–52, and this correspondence may enable us to feel for the first time something resembling the projection of an eight-bar measure. However, it should be pointed out that this projective correspondence may, in fact, contribute to the separation of the two periods. In light of the distinctions of projective "scale" discussed in the preceding chapter, such a conclusion will not appear at all paradoxical. If bars 45–52 form a closed eight-bar measure and a more or less clearly defined projective potential realized with the beginning of a new phrase, the projective potential given to the beginning in bar 53 will be quite vaguely defined. Since the logic of this conclusion is so basic to a projective perspective and so counterintuitive from a "hypermetrical" or extensive-hierarchical perspective, I will briefly review the projective situation at the beginning of the exposition's second large period. Assuming that bars 45–52 form a measure, the new beginning with bar 53 will be predisposed to reproduce the large and therefore less sharply determinate eight-bar duration begun with bar 45, rather than the more immediate and vivid four-bar duration of bars 49–52 or the even more vivid two-bar duration of bars 51–52, which, in the context of the eight-bar measure, are continuations and so *cannot* function projectively for the new beginning with bar

53. Moreover, if an eight-bar projected potential is to be realized, it will take some time for sufficient correspondences to emerge that would support such a realization. Thus, in spite of the possibility that a large eight-bar reproduction may eventually be realized here, projective overlapping in this case is minimal. It may even be that the beginning of a new large phrase and a second period with bar 53 has the effect of detracting from the projective relevance that bars 45–52 have for bars 53–60.

I have offered brief analyses of these several passages primarily to show that overlappings on the durational order of phrase generally involve some projective (and, often, tonal) reinterpretation. As we saw in the preceding chapter, large projections require the emergence of conformity throughout the projected phase and especially in the early stages. This is another way of saying that a new projectively weighted beginning can be open to considerable reinterpretation. And, in general, the larger the projective potential, the longer it may take for a corresponding projected realization to escape the field of smaller projective potentials that would offer more security for our "prediction" of the future course of events. To break with the past event and to invest our attention in a new, dominant beginning with a relatively distant horizon we will need many reassurances, and when reassurance is lacking we must be ready to revise our expectations. The cases we have reviewed show considerable variation in the time it takes reinterpretation to be effected—as extremes, the event begun with bar 19 is almost immediately interruptive, whereas the event begun with bar 45 may take several bars to disengage itself from the projective potential of the preceding measure.

Another purpose in analyzing these passages is to point to the variety and particularity of overlappings and to show that tone and meter are inseparable in creating this particularity. If these two determinations—the tonal and the metrical—cannot be parted in their combined rhythmic effect, they can, nevertheless, be contrasted in their effectiveness, or "power." Mensural determinacy has relatively narrow durational limits. Tonal determinacy is limited only by the duration of the composition in which a tonal quality can be prolonged. (Here I would ask the reader to recall the difference between tonal and durational determinacy discussed under the heading "Projection and Prediction" in chapter 7.) Crudely put, if pitch classes are introduced with definite intervallic or scale-degree qualities, "they" (or any of their "representatives") can retain these qualities. And if these qualities are viewed as potentials, then it must be said that tonal potential can be effective for much greater durations than can be metrical-projective potential.

End as Aim

In speaking of the realization of tonal potential, I have frequently used the term "goal." And throughout this discussion I have used the term "end" ambiguously—sometimes to mean "become past" and sometimes to mean "terminus," "goal," or "aim." This ambiguity arises from differences of perspective—the differences of what an event is for itself; what it is for a successor; and what, together with a successor, it is for the emergence of a greater event. A new beginning necessarily ends the becoming of its predecessor. With the beginning of the development section the first *Hauptperiod* is now past and no longer becoming. Certainly, for the development section as an event, the exposition as past is relevant in countless ways; but for the development section as an event, relevant also are countless other events or experiences. Still, the exposition is part of a movement that is in the process of becoming, and this emerging whole is not past. And it is from this perspective that the becoming past of the exposition is not an end. Clearly, when there is a beginning of what will become the introduction there is also the beginning of what will become the movement, and the beginning of what will become the development section emerges from a movement already begun. The promise of becoming (for this movement) ends only when there is a movement. "End" in this sense means an annihilation of potential for becoming. We have already encountered the notion of "levels" of becoming in discussing the formation of a measure. Thus, the first beat of a measure ends or is past when there is the beginning of a second beat; but the measure is not past, and its beginning is still a potential for a

mensurally determinate duration. The second beat is continuative, and the overlapping of end and beginning here results in a greater mensurally determinate duration.

It is from the perspective of a new beginning or a new becoming that end will be understood to mean "become past." From the perspective of present becoming, end cannot be past, and it is from this perspective that end will mean "goal." The aim or goal of an event is to become an event or, rather, the particular event toward which its becoming is directed (but not predetermined). Thus aim implies the futurity of becoming—a future that is real because there are real, more or less definite potentials. We might say that the future of a becoming is to become past, but this would be to speak of two becomings. To say that an event "becomes" past is to say that it is now past for a present becoming. There is no past event apart from a present becoming that takes the past event as a datum, a given that in itself is completely determined and no longer realizing a potential for becoming—in short, an event with no future of its own. The aim of an event is not its annihilation as becoming, but the realization of its potential for becoming. In this sense, the end of an event is always future, much as the beginning of an event is always past. This end is the promise of completion or wholeness.

What I have called the more or less definite potential of beginning is the promise for a present becoming; and yet, a beginning is also a definite decision—an irreversible fait accompli. The emergence of the event is a fulfillment of this promise of beginning in the course of which novel, unpredetermined relevancies are brought into play. The end of the event is, from the beginning, the promise that initial and emerging potentials for becoming will be realized. This realization is the end or goal of the event—an aim toward completion or wholeness. When this event is ended it is past, and whatever completion or wholeness it has attained is fixed and unalterable. But its end was the attainment of completion or wholeness in the process of becoming—a *fait accomplissant* in which potential is being realized. If we were to posit a durationless instant, we could say that there is a moment when realization is accomplished—when there is no longer becoming but, rather, a purely "present" being in which the event has ended and yet is not past. But in this case the whole event would seem to be collapsed into a present being without duration—a single point of pure presence. If, on the other hand, we identify presence with becoming, completion will be an activity, not a state, and end will be a continuous making actual of an event in response to emerging potential(s) for becoming. If there emerges a new beginning that ends this becoming, the event will be past and its potential for becoming will be annihilated. And just as a present event will have been made a past event, a present end or aim for becoming will have been made a past or prior aim—the new beginning now makes the entire process of becoming, and whatever potential has been realized, past.

Too, whatever wholeness or completion that *was* being attained is now past. Thus, by wholeness or completion I mean something that pertains to the event itself as a goal of present becoming. A new beginning, as a new beginning, does not complete a past event (though, as continuation, a new beginning must perforce function for the completion of a present event engendered with a prior or "dominant" beginning). Whatever completion an event has attained belongs to that event either as present or as past for another event. Clearly, completion or wholeness is relative. By completion I mean the realization of potential. A complete realization of (all) potential would result in complete closure—an extinction of potential, becoming, and future. The fact of temporality denies such a closure—an absolute perfection that would bring an end to time. At the opposite extreme, a total absence of completion or the realization of potential would deny the possibility of an event and of becoming, and thus also abolish time; for however incomplete an event is, it is still the realization of a potential for duration and a potential for becoming an event. Obviously, the completeness of any event will lie somewhere between these extremes.

In the domain of measure, completion or wholeness is the realization of projection, and degrees of completeness are differentiated in various metrical "levels." For example, the realization of a projection involving two bar measures is a completion, but if there is a potential for a two-bar measure or a four-bar measure, projective potential is not exhausted in this realization, and projection will be incomplete. The realization of the two-bar projection will also be an opening for a two-bar projective potential (or a three-bar potential if there is deferral) and for a projection involving four bars in which the second bar—a completion of the smaller projection as the realization of a one-bar projected potential—will function as continuation. The completeness of measure depends upon mensural determinacy. If there is any possibility that mensural determinacy can be extended, what has been realized is incomplete and could yet offer itself as projective potential. Mensural determinacy is the possibility for achieving a more or less definite, reproducible duration or durational quantity—a potentiality that may be realized in an actual duration but never exhausted in a realization. The denial of a potential for mensural determinacy is the forfeiture of that potential. Mensural determinacy is forfeited in the realization of a duration that is no longer capable of providing a definite measure.

It is precisely because mensural determinacy admits of degrees and is not fixed that we cannot precisely determine the durational limits of measure. The reason I could not discount the possibility of an eight-bar measure in the *Haffner* Trio (or even a sixteen-bar measure in recomposition) in spite of the lack of any clear evidence of the distinction strong/weak is that there seemed to be the possibility for feeling durational equality—a feeling that could arise only from some degree of mensural determinacy. That such a feeling could arise and yet be sincerely doubted as metrical attests to the vagueness of the bounds of mensural determinacy and thus to *the inherent incompleteness of any projection.* And because of this incompleteness, projection always involves overlapping and the crossing of boundaries. We can identify situations in which mensural determinacy can be clearly felt (situations where there is a clear distinction between beginning and continuation, strong and weak) and situations in which mensural determinacy has clearly been forfeited (situations where there is no feeling of durational equality). But between these extremes there are often situations in which the decision to call a duration a measure is far from clear (in which case it might well be asked what is to be gained in deciding!). And even where mensural determinacy is clearly forfeited, there is the projective potential of "commensurate length." Thus, the beginning of the second large phrase of the first part of the Allegro (bar 33), as a second beginning (and perhaps, in some respects, a beginning again), promises a duration more or less commensurate with that of the first phrase. In fact, each of the two phrases is twenty bars long, but surely they are not felt as precisely equal. The beginning of a second phrase does not promise equality, but it does, I think, promise something larger than a duration on the order of the smaller phrases that compose the first phrase. And if we were to tamper with this composition and reduce the second phrase to four or eight bars (either closing with tonic or again opening to dominant), our small phrase might easily become assimilated to the first phrase as continuation. (And it could be argued that something like this happens in the recapitulation if the phrase of bars 178–205 is interpreted as an enlargement in correspondence to the phrase of bars 13–32, rather than as a contraction of the phrase of bars 13–52.) If there is such a promise of greater duration, then this, too, is a sort of projection. And to acknowledge this as a projection is to argue more strongly for the incompleteness of mensural projection and thus for its openness for the becoming of large-scale events.

I have attempted to clarify the notion of "end" in part to lay some groundwork for a discussion of questions of tonal goal and tonal completion. If we are to continue our investigation of overlapping and mensural projection, these questions must be addressed, if only cursorily. Since I cannot offer a theory of tonal projection, my comments on this topic will be sketchy at best. But as a beginning I would suggest that tonal function might be understood in terms of potential (more or less along the lines of Leonard Meyer's or Eugene Narmour's idea of "implication"). In this way we could conceive

of tonic, for example, as an indefinite potential. Tonic "harmony" (for want of a better word) has no definite potential for becoming—a "I-chord" can be succeeded by any harmony, provided that its successor does not end in a denial of that tonic as tonic. Thus the repose or completeness of tonic could be viewed as the lack of a definite promise for the future. Other harmonies or other tones or complexes of tones give rise to more definite potentials—the dominant, a potential for tonic continuation; the interval of a tritone, a potential for "resolution" in a third or sixth; the leading tone, a potential for ascent to scale degree 1; an "augmented sixth," a potential for progress to dominant harmony. The relativity of consonance and dissonance is in this sense the relativity of completeness or the relative extinction of potential. Thus, the perfection of a perfect authentic cadence is the end of a becoming. An imperfect or half-cadence is also the end of a becoming, but an end that engenders potential for a new event, not only for an immediate successor, but for a greater event—much as a realized mensural projection opens the possibility for a greater projection. Thus, the relativity of consonance as completion or wholeness is also the relativity of eventhood. I cannot hope to provide an adequate account of the tonal contribution to the formation of phrase events (or, for that matter, an adequate definition of phrase). But I will venture to describe several projective situations in an attempt to clarify some of my remarks concerning tonal overlapping.

In a typical parallel period, the first phrase closes with dominant. The phrase is, in fact, closed—it is completed and is made past with the beginning of the consequent. It is tempting to think of this last chord or sonority (V) as the goal of the phrase, and it is most convenient to speak of this chord as the goal. But this chord is itself an event with a beginning and end. It is not the phrase event and is not itself the goal of the phrase. That goal is the becoming of this phrase, which ends in an opening to dominant.[1] If the

---

1. Indeed, I believe it is a sense of the falsity of regarding "goal" as a thing, event, or state that inclines us to distrust the concept of goal. As a thing, event, or state, "goal" can seem to have a (determinate) being that could be detached from becoming and from the openness or indeterminacy of becoming. In the following discussion I shall sometimes (simply as a linguistic convenience) speak of events as goals, but I would ask the reader to under-

EXAMPLE 13.5 Beethoven, Symphony no. 1 in C Major, first movement, (**a**) bs. 33–45, (**b**) diagram for the first period of the Allegro

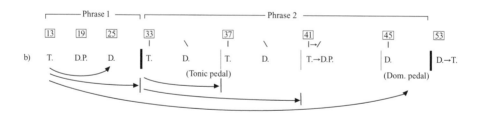

final chord of the phrase were itself the goal, then the immediately succeeding tonic of the consequent phrase would realize the tonal potential of the first phrase and result in closure—in effect, an enlargement or expansion of the first phrase. Clearly, this is not the case. The promise is that engendered by a first phrase for a second phrase, and when that more or less definite promise is fulfilled (when there emerges a second phrase that closes with tonic), there is now an event whose goal is to attain completion as a period—much as the goal of a second beat as continuation is to attain a mensurally determinate duration whose beginning is not the beginning of a first beat, now past. In itself—that is, not viewed as continuation—the beginning of the second

stand that this is a loose way of speaking and that by "goal" I mean a process that takes place throughout the entire duration of the larger event and not something that can be identified as a discrete part of that event.

phrase is a beginning again, and in the case of a parallel period an impression of beginning again is considerably enhanced by the conformity of the two beginnings. But whether parallel or not, the beginning of the second phrase as a new beginning is cut off from the first phrase, which, as a phrase, is now past.

If the second phrase were to repeat the first by closing again in dominant, we could still speak of a period—a larger phrase composed of smaller phrases—but the separation of the two phrases would be greater. The tonal goal of the period would be indistinguishable from the goals of the two phrases viewed as distinct events. To the extent the second opening repeats the first, we may speak of two tonal goals, not one—a period whose goal is repetition.

In the exposition of the Beethoven a repeated opening can be found in the first eight bars (33–40) of the second large phrase shown in example 13.5a. The second small phrase (bars 37–40) does not realize the potential of the first phrase for completion, and here the overlapping of the two phrases is made especially disjunct by the failure of F (bar 36) to resolve. Certainly, the resolution of B, the tonic pedal, the anacrusis figures, and countless other factors contribute to the continuity of the overlapping, but the completion of the two-phrase event is, nevertheless, a deferral of wholeness and the promise of a completion that is achieved in an overlapping with the following phrase. The tonic beginning in bar 41 is a new beginning but not a beginning again like bar 37. (It may, however, be a different sort of beginning again to the degree that it repeats features of the beginning of the Allegro.)

Through overlapping, this new beginning immediately realizes the promise for a resolution of dominant harmony. Yet, this new phrase, too, emerges as an opening to dominant and not as tonic completion. This gesture of opening repeats that of the first two small phrases (bars 33–36 and 37–40), but with the difference that the opening to dominant with bars 45–52 (example 13.4a) is now the goal of a large phrase begun with bar 33 (and of a still larger phrase begun with bar 13). In contrast to the beginning with bar 45, the dominant openings in bars 35–36 and 39–40 were projective continuations. In light of these metrical and tonal contrasts, we might say that for the larger phrase as a whole (bars 33–52) the attainment of dominant as an end of the passage becomes a goal that emerges from the failed completions of the earlier dominants—dissonances (for the phrase) that end in a relatively consonant dominant harmony at the end of the phrase.

In the diagram shown as example 13.5b I have represented failed completions in bars 33–52 as interruptions (bar 37 and bar 41) and have indicated an interruption also in the overlapping of the two large phrases (bar 33). To the extent that the beginning with bar 33 emerges as a beginning again, the opening of the first large phrase remains a promise for completion (not completed with the tonic beginning of the second large phrase in bar 33). That the second phrase as a whole repeats this gesture could be taken as an argument for the separation of the two phrases. However, these dominants (like all the dominants represented in the diagram) are hardly equivalent in their projective potential. The tonal goal of the first large phrase is an opening to a dissonant seventh chord; the goal of the second is an opening to a relatively stable dominant triad. On the other hand, it might be argued that the beginning with bar 33 comes to close or realize the potential of the preceding opening and that the two phrases are joined in progress to a single goal—the opening of the first part of the exposition. But it is not necessary to decide between these interpretations. This ambiguity is precisely the overlapping of the two phrases. In this large gesture the beginning again with bar 33 becomes continuation as the end of the period emerges.

The opening again with bar 33 creates two distinct phrases that can be joined in a single becoming. That the second opening is not a repetition of the first allows this opening to become the goal of the larger phrase. On the other hand, in the repetition of the exposition a tonal opening is quite literally repeated. This repetition functions, as do such repetitions in general, to bring to light the openness and incompleteness of the exposition's end and not to create a greater event through overlapping. However, the repetition of this large period also involves an immediate overlapping that very sharply focuses our attention in a moment of return to the

EXAMPLE 13.6 Beethoven, Symphony no. 1 in C Major, first movement, bs. 100–17 (in repetition)

highly compressed and energetic opening of the Allegro.

As is shown in example 13.6, the last phrase of the exposition in a sense comes to an end with the beginning in bar 106—a beginning that promises a two-bar continuative measure that will complete the phrase (and period and section) and complete or realize the projected potential of a two-bar continuation. This completion is interrupted by the emergence of a new projection and a reinterpretation of bar 106 as the beginning of a four-bar measure. At the same time, (with the appearance of F♮) there is a

reinterpretation of G as dominant rather than tonic. The promise of end has thus turned to a promise of beginning (\ →|). Tonally, there is completion in the return to tonic—a new beginning with bar 13 that is also a resolution or realization of the potential of the dominant harmony of bars 106–109. This reinterpretation in bars 106–109 recalls in many respects bar 12—the last measure of an introduction that prolonged an opening to dominant (example 13.3). There is a new beginning and a beginning again with bar 13, and with the measure begun at bar 17 this new event opens and will open again and again. But through overlapping, the new event begins as completion.

Metrically, too, there is completion—that of an eight-bar projection (P–P') in bars 106–16. The tonal overlapping is greatly enhanced by the projective overlapping shown in example 13.6. This projective acceleration in bars 106–16 repeats the accelerative pattern (LLSSL, bars 100–107) its beginning interrupts. The goal of acceleration here is the completion of projected potentials P' and Q' and thus the *closure* of an eight-bar projection (bars 106–16) and a four-bar measure (bars 13–16). And yet, in bar 16 the anacrustic (and possibly accelerative) first violin figure clearly functions as an opening that directs our attention toward a new beginning with bar 17. Mixed in this complex eight-bar duration are moments of opening and closing that together will shape the immediate overlapping with a new measure begun in bar 17.

To discuss the role played by projection in processes of overlapping, we must consider questions of metrical closure in more detail. Metrical closure is a concentration of potential in the continuation or completion of a measure. Openness is a concentration of potential in the promise of a new measure and, thus, in the promise of a projective overlapping. The reason I did not explicitly raise the question of end as goal in introducing the notion of projection is that *projective potential is not itself a goal*. Rather, projective potential (if realized) is a definite durational quantity taken by a successor in the form of a more or less definite projected potential. It is this latter potential that can function as a goal for the becoming of durational quantity, for it is only now that we can speak of a present event with a more or less definite potential for duration and therefore a more or less definite aim or goal for completeness. It is also only now that we can accurately predict a new beginning; and to the extent our attention is directed toward the possibility of a new beginning, the present projected potential is an opening and the promise of an overlapping of end and beginning.

Earlier, in chapter 6, I raised the question of prediction but did not discuss the factors that might direct our attention toward the possibility of a new beginning. Clearly, there are a great many such factors, not least among which are tonal potentials and the relevancies of past events—the very factors, indeed, that contribute to the determinations of projective beginning and continuation. Of the more purely quantitative durational factors, most effective are acceleration and anacrusis. For example, a measure that "ends" with anacrusis (or what promises to become anacrusis) is an opening, directed toward a new beginning. If there is a new beginning, the promise of anacrusis is realized, and this realization will play a role in the overlapping of two measures. The anacrusis will function both as continuation for the completion of the first measure and as a promise for continuation that detracts from the completeness of the first measure. (And as I pointed out earlier in this discussion, no measure is absolutely complete—projective potential is always, however vaguely, a potential for continuation.) Similarly, if in a measure there is a process of acceleration, this is the promise for an overlapping, and this promise is part of the particular incompleteness of the first measure.

Projective Types

To simplify our analysis of mensural closure, I offer a rudimentary typology based on the distinction open/closed. In example 13.7a I have allied this distinction with that of duple/triple (or equal/unequal) in the representation of four types. Although the examples shown here are concrete (i.e., performable), they are intended as symbolic representations of abstractions. Thus, the quarter notes in the duple opening type represent projected realization in which there develops a potential for anacrusis or an acceleration that promises a new beginning. Although the duple closing type might be represented by two equal durations as in the second figure of example 13.7b, I have chosen to symbolize this type in example 13.7a by dividing the projective duration to show a directedness toward the beginning of the projected phase, on the assumption that such directedness might focus our attention on the projected realization as an end and thus detract from its potential as anacrusis. The remaining patterns in example 13.7b show a few of the innumerable possibilities for this type. In

EXAMPLE 13.7 General projective types for unequal and equal measure

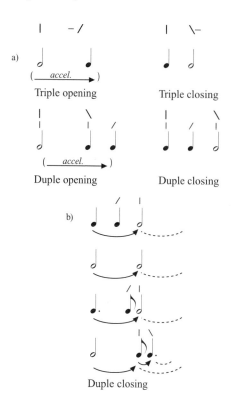

speed as repetition is highly variable. And as a continuation that breaks away from the dominant beginning to promise a new beginning, anacrusis is often distinguished by a move to shorter note values.

In view of the considerable overlapping in these distinctions, we might say more generally that the directedness indicated in the opening types arises from projective activity that emerges too late to be acted upon in the time we have left for the present event, but not so late that we cannot use this information to prepare for a new event. It is in the sense of being too late for action in the present event that anacrustic figures can be said to be "superfluous" or "not needed" for the realization of projected potential. And it is in the sense of being so late that we have no time to prepare for a new beginning that very brief anacruses do not seem to detract from projective closure. In example 13.4a, for instance, notice that the quarter-note anacrusis to bar 53 does not result in a projective opening for the preceding four- or eight-bar measure. This measure is more closed than any other measure of the movement, save the last measure (a measure, by the way, that exceeds the notation by two "bars"). In a real sense, this anacrustic quarter belongs to the next measure. To use a visual-spatial metaphor, it is as if the anacrusis to the new measure were superimposed upon the projective completion in bar 52. Again, this sort of overlapping will seem to place measure and phrase in conflict only if duration is viewed extensively or spatially as a "span of time" rather than heard temporally as process.

The abstractions represented by these two-times-two types can be drawn from innumerable actual measures, but in any particular instance a clear distinction between opening and closing will be mitigated by countless relevancies. Projective closure is always particular, always conditioned by emerging potentials, and, thus, to some extent always equivocal and open to "reinterpretation" (especially in the case of relatively large measures). Since the simple distinction opening/closing admits of degrees, it will in most cases be an oversimplification to classify a measure as simply open or closed. And in any case, it should be borne in mind that overlapping always involves both closing and opening.

We might gain more specificity were we to

example 13.7a I have distinguished two categories of opening: accelerative and anacrustic. However, in experience, these categories are often not clearly separated. In an acceleration there can be anacrusis. And although anacrusis is not itself an acceleration, it resembles anacrusis in that it "ends" in arrest or the immediate succession short–long. The distinction I wish to make between acceleration and anacrusis is this: acceleration involves repetition and anacrusis does not. Earlier, I described acceleration as an invariance under transformation—several beats heard as repetitions of "the beat," a beat that changes by becoming faster. Anacrusis can be repeated and there can be an acceleration of anacruses, but anacrusis itself is not a product or a process of repetition. Earlier I contrasted acceleration with "speeding up"—an increase of activity and, metrically, a division of the "same." However, this distinction, too, is far from clear-cut. An acceleration is also an increase of activity, and the degree to which we feel a change of

EXAMPLE 13.8 Latin motet, *O Natio/Hodie Perlustravit* (Wolfenbüttel), bs. 1–16, from Jeremy Yudkin, *Music in Medieval Europe* (1989). Used by permission.

identify types on the basis of durational "pattern." Thus, the type identified as duple-opening in example 13.7a would find instantiation only in measures reducible to the general form long–short–short (LSS) or, more accurately, to a projection in which the projected duration is divided and in which this division opens the possibility of anacrusis or acceleration. If we treat more complex patterns as types, we could posit a large number of types, all of which would be repeatable but few of which would be repeated. However, there are several "typical" patterns that can be found in abundance within pieces and repertories and across repertories. One especially prevalent pattern can be located at the beginning of the Allegro (and perhaps even in the first four bars of the introduction). This pattern, which I have labeled LLSSL, is repeated throughout the Allegro and together with the pattern LSS (in bar 3, for instance) plays a decisive projective role in practically all the phrase overlappings in this movement.

Instances of this type can be identified in countless pieces of music. Our earliest documentations of its use are in clausulae, discant sections, and motets from the Notre Dame school

where the patterned tenor seems to be instrumental in supporting the closure of the discant's phrase-measures (and their overlapping), as in example 13.8.

Earlier, I discussed the possibility of interpreting this pattern as an acceleration (example 9.7) and briefly considered its involvement in the sentence phrase type (example 9.8). I also suggested that the particular virtue of this pattern is that it can be used to create a strongly directed metrical closure—a directedness toward the final beat as continuation of two (simultaneous) measures. In line with my earlier discussion of acceleration, in example 13.9a I have analyzed the pattern in bars 13–16 as an overlapping of two closures of the form SSL (short–short–long).

Although the designations "SSL" and "LLSSL" are convenient, they are not very informative (and can be quite misleading if taken literally as a simple succession of note values). As a more descriptive designation we might substitute for the type SSL "directed closing" and for LLSSL, "compound (directed) closing."[2] The compounding of closure shown in example 13.9a is perhaps too specific an interpretation. In this type we need not feel "compound closure" as repetition

---

2. The type short–short–long is recognized by Theodor Wiehmayer (1917) as one of the two *Haupttypen* for four- and eight-bar phrases: 1+1+2 or 2+2+4. The other *Haupttypus* is 2+2 or 4+4.

EXAMPLE 13.9 "Nested" repetition of closure in compound closing type

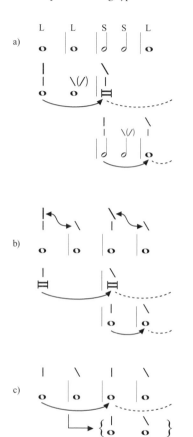

also be the last beat of the large measure as continuation of a continuation.

The distinction I have made between these two interpretations is not at all rigid. The pattern, at least in the form given in example 13.9a is composed both of four beats and of five beats. The distinction I have drawn is between acceleration and anacrusis. But acceleration and anacrusis are not mutually exclusive, and in many instances of the type I have labeled "LLSSL," both can be felt in a directedness toward closure or arrest in the continuation of a continuation that characterizes the type. If acceleration and anacrusis are often inseparable in contributing to a directedness toward closure, there is, nevertheless, reason to point to acceleration as a characteristic feature of the type in cases where fairly large measures are involved. In large measures, where mensural determinacy is attenuated, acceleration can play a decisive role in making the final beat the continuation of a continuation. In fact, the pattern LLSSL is usually found in relatively large projective units—measures (or phrases) of four, eight, or sixteen bars. The usefulness of the pattern for large durations lies in its contribution to mensural determinacy. In a small projection, the second (projected) duration can easily emerge as continuation of a dominant beginning. However, in a larger projection where mensural determinacy is attenuated (and thus where the distinction strong/weak is less clearly felt), the beginning of the projected duration can easily emerge as a new beginning and not as continuation. But if there is some process begun with the projective phase that finds completion with the projected phase, the possibility of feeling projective continuation will be enhanced. Thus, the pattern LLSSL can enhance the possibility of hearing a large measure if we can feel a process of condensation in the repetition of pattern and/or a process of acceleration. In fact, the ubiquity of the type suggests its utility in the formation of large compound projections—duple equal measures composed of duple equal measures. And in such compound projections, even without the pattern LLSSL, there is a compounding of closure, as I will now attempt to show.

In example 13.9b we will assume that the second two-bar measure is heard as continuation of a four-bar measure. In this case, the fourth bar

of pattern, but simply as a continuation of a continuation. If there is any feeling of pattern repetition (repetition of the pattern SSL), there will be a feeling of acceleration, but as I speculated earlier, without a special effort of attention (amply rewarded, in many instances) it is unlikely that we will very clearly feel this special repetition. However, even if we discount such a repetition we may still speak of acceleration if in this pattern we feel five beats rather than four (equal) beats. In this case, "the beat" accelerates, and the goal of this acceleration is the fifth beat (or what will become the fifth beat)—an end to acceleration and, projectively, a continuation of a continuation. If, on the other hand, we feel four equal beats (the four *bar-measure beats* in example 13.9a) there will be no acceleration. But if the articulated (half-note) continuation of the third beat functions as anacrusis, the goal of anacrusis will is necessarily continuation of a continuation. Since there is a uniform succession of whole notes, there is no distinctive "pattern" that could be heard repeated. Nevertheless, there is a repetition of closure if we can speak of the "continuation of a continuation." With the beginning of the third bar there is now a projective potential of a breve, and in the realization of this potential there is a repetition in whole notes of the relation of the two breves. As a continuation of a continuation the fourth beat is not a repetition of the second beat—the second beat is a continuation of a "strong" breve. There is, to be sure, a more obvious sense in which the fourth beat is a repetition of the second beat in the context of two-bar measures. Example 13.9c shows this repetition. However, the repetition in example 13.9c will emerge whether there is a four-bar measure or not. Since a four-bar measure, in distinction from a succession of two two-bar measures, can be formed only if the fourth bar emerges as continuation of a continuation, any factors that support this compounding of closure contribute to the creation of the large measure and enhance projective potential. In the domain of durational quantity, the pattern LLSSL can contribute to this double closure by creating a process of acceleration that supports continuation and by forming a pattern that can make the repetition more explicit. Thus, I would suggest that this schema is a "natural" solution to the problem of forming a large duple measure and, consequently, a large projective potential for a still greater projection.

Having designated the pattern type LLSSL a "closing" type and having acknowledged that closure is relative, we should now take the opportunity to explore something of the range of possibilities (along the axis open/closed) available to our type. After all, the reason we proposed the concept of pattern type was to gain more specificity and refinement in our categorization of closure. The following survey of instances from the exposition will disclose some of the closural possibilities of our type.

Although the pattern LLSSL is directed toward completion in its final continuative phase, closure here emerges relatively late—in the last quarter of the measure as continuation of a continuation. This delay in closure detracts to some extent from the conclusiveness of the measure, and for this reason the pattern is not, as a rule, used for the ending of a piece. Indeed, this delay offers the opportunity for an anacrustic opening at the end of the measure that will intensify its overlapping with a succeeding measure and enhance its projective potential. An overlapping of this sort is found in the beginning of the Allegro (example 13.1 and example 13.6). If we are to regard this as an instance of the LLSSL type, acceleration must come to an end with bar 16. And if we prefer to interpret the second beat of bar 15 as solely anacrustic (and not also accelerative), this anacrusis is directed toward continuation and completion. In any case, bar 16 is both continuative and anacrustic and in this overlapping of functions serves both to complete the four-bar measure and to direct our attention to the beginning of a new measure. Because of this directedness and determinacy of projective potential, the beginning with bar 17 is the beginning of a four-bar projected potential (interrupted by the new beginning in bar 19). The overlapping of these two small phrases also involves an interruption in that what promises to become a continuation quickly dissolves in bars 17–18—the change of instrumentation and register together with the focus on scale degree 3 in the oboe (note the dynamic markings in winds, example 13.1) leaves something of the promise of bars 13–16 unfulfilled. This interruption with bar 17 quickly followed by the much more intense projective interruption with bar 19 sustains for the phrase the energy and intense compression created by acceleration in the first four bars.

The fine balance of closing and opening that must be struck in situations such as this requires a relatively clear distinction of the directedness that leads to the final (continuative) measure from the directedness that leads to a new beginning. The fact of such a separation clearly points to a multiplicity or "polyphony" of projected potentials within the measure. In the case of bars 13–16 the separation of potentials is achieved largely through a distinction of instrumental components—the directed closure of the lower strings in bar 16 against the continuity of the first violin line. Although "instrumental" differentiation (including "line," texture, timbre, register, etc.) is a primary means of diversifying projective potential, other means can also be very effective. For instance, in the eight-bar LLSSL pattern of bars 25–32 (example 13.2a) the immediate resolution into tonic harmony with the beginning of bar 31 preceded by the anacrustic figure in the winds is almost entirely responsible for the traces of projective closure that can be heard in this passage. (Note again in this connection how radically altered would be the effect of this passage were the anacrusis in bars 31–32 to be omitted.)

An especially subtle balance of opening and closing can be heard in the opening of the Adagio (shown in example 13.4b). Although the first four bars do not form a measure, they can be regarded as an instance of the type LLSSL directed toward the attainment of dominant harmony in bar 4. Projectively, the first bar measure is closed, as is the second bar measure. Tonally, the second bar is less closed than the first and reveals an openness in the first bar. Although durational determinacy is highly attenuated here, we should be able to speak of the emergence of a two-bar projective potential if bars 3–4 can come to feel commensurate with bars 1–2 and if bar 4 can be felt as a durational continuation. At the extremely slow tempi that are often taken in performances of this piece, continuation might not be spontaneously felt were it not for a special relevance of the first two bars. Having heard in bars 1 and 2 the resolutions of dissonant "dominant seventh" chords as projective continuations, we are disposed to hear a repetition in bars 3 and 4. But we will hear congruence in this third chord pair only by "slowing" to a two-bar measure in which there is at the same time an acceleration toward resolution and projective closure. And although the continuative eighth notes in bar 4 would seem to be directed toward a new beginning in bar 5 rather than to complete the present measure, there are grounds for ambiguity here that could be taken advantage of in performance. Following the tutti arrival in bar 4, the piano violin line continued in bars 5–7 could seem to break off from a moment of ending. And yet, the violin line also continues the chromatic ascent from E in bar 1 up to an A, which remains unresolved, reappearing in bar 10 in the final opening gesture of the introduction (example 13.3). With the help, perhaps, of a

slight crescendo to the high A, the violin line in bar 4 can come to seem suspended between continuation and anacrusis, leading us into a huge elaboration of dominant harmony in bars 5–12 that, nevertheless, seems like a continuation or reverberation of the dominant we reached in bar 4.

It sometimes happens that the pattern LLSSL is itself repeated at the end of the measure or phrase, making the projective goal the continuation of a continuation of a continuation (as in example 9.8). In this case, the delay of closure pushes the final continuative phase closer to a new beginning and can also function for an opening to a new measure, particularly if an anacrusis to the new measure seems to grow out of the prior anacruses and continues a process of acceleration or speeding up. This internal repetition of the type is especially useful for the creation of relatively large projective events and is often found in instances of the "sentence" phrase type. In the Beethoven, this double compounding of closure occurs with any clarity only in eight-bar durations. Instances of such repetition are shown in examples 13.4a (bars 45–52) and 13.6 (bars 106–16). If we allow our type to greatly exceed the bounds of mensural determinacy, we might also recognize an instance in the first large phrase, or sentence of the Allegro (bars 13–32 shown in example 13.1 and example 13.2). In this case, the pattern LLSSL would be expressed in the following durations (measured in bars): 6(4+2) – 6(4+2)–2–2–4. Here, as we have seen above, the continuation 2–2–4 (bars 25–32) displays the pattern LLSSL.

For our final analysis of the type, I would like to consider a clear but hardly "typical" use of the pattern in the beginning of the second large phrase of the second period shown in example 13.10. Here I have included the overlapping end of the first phrase in bars 75–76 to show its similarity to the end of the first phrase of the first period in bars 29–32 (example 13.2). Although set up very much like the phrase begun in bar 33, the new phrase in bar 77 begins as a subito piano repetition in minor of the period's opening sentence (bar 53). This sudden softness, which turns to intimacy with the entrance of solo oboe, is matched by a relaxation of rhythmic drive and an unusual expansion of duration. Through a systematic use of the LLSSL pattern,

EXAMPLE 13.10 Beethoven, Symphony no. 1 in C Major, first movement, bs. 75–90

several small phrases are overlapped to create a relatively large and unbroken duration that gains intensity as it leads to a strongly overlapped close on G in bar 88.

The phrase begins, like bars 53–56, with the promise of a relatively closed four-bar measure. The entrance of the oboe could well be continuative, but it emerges as the beginning of a four-bar measure in which the pattern LLSSL appears in the bass, supported by the oboe's quarter notes. The promised continuation in bar 82 becomes a beginning, and the pattern is repeated—to be again interrupted and repeated in bars 85–88. The pattern is most clearly expressed in this third occurrence, and for the first time its continuative phase is a tonal closure, but

a closure overlapped with the beginning of a new phrase. This very continuous overlapping around bar 88 resembles in many respects the overlapping of the final phrase of the first period around bar 45 (example 13.4a). In both cases it will take some time for the projective reinterpretation to solidify and for the new measure to break away from the old.

Since our topical analysis of the exposition has led us to concentrate on relatively local events, I would like to conclude this discussion of overlapping and projective type in the Beethoven with a broad survey of the larger projections in the development section. Among the many aspects of this section I shall ignore are the relevancies of the exposition for projections in the development. These conditioning past events play an essential role in the formation of metrical gestures in the new section and should be considered in a closer analysis. Since our quick flight across this section will not permit us to take account of much detail, I have greatly simplified the score in my reduction to two staves in example 13.11. In the sequential passages of bars 110–121, 122–129, and 144–155 I have further abbreviated the patterned repetitions.

The development section begins with a non sequitur—an A major six-three chord. Nevertheless, the first small phrase (bars 110–113) answers the four-bar projective potential of bars 106–109 with a projected potential of four bars, and the eight-bar projection reveals an instance of the pattern LLSSL (or, more precisely, the type "compound directed closing"). This pattern, however, is without issue—the second and third small phrases (bars 114–117 and 118–121) repeat the pattern of the first phrase, the closed pattern SSL (or LSSL). The projective closure of these phrases is enhanced by the relatively static and homogeneous character of their concluding two-bar measures, in which syncopations arrest the accelerative drive of their initial two-bar measures. These three small phrases do not form a mediated unequal measure. It may be argued that an eight-bar measure is formed by bars 110–117, and that to hear a connection of A in the first phrase and G in the third phrase (perhaps with the promise of a C3 in the fourth phrase) will be to hear two beginnings. Evidence for such a perception will be a feeling that the beginning of the fourth small phrase in bar 122 as the beginning of a second large phrase is an interruption. But even if there is some evidence of an eight-bar projective potential in bars 110–117, the projective closure of the four-bar measures and the lack of tonal focus make this phrase chain the most fragmentary of any passage in the movement. Granted, each phrase is connected to the following one as an "applied dominant," but no tonal integration emerges. The A major and D major triads do not properly belong to C minor—C minor is not the goal of this three-phrase unit. And if there is some feeling of interruption with bar 122, such a feeling might arise as much from the change of mode and melodic contour as from a denial of projected realization.

The new large phrase (beginning with bar 122) does, of course, overlap with the preceding phrase—the descending fifth sequence is, in a fairly abstract sense, continued, and bars 118–121 provide a dominant for C minor. But with bar 122 there is for the first time a feeling of tonal stability (or *tonic*)—the preceding sequence of major triads is now broken and the new phrase is introduced with root-position chords. The goal of this large phrase is E♭ major, and the harmonies of the phrase—C minor, F minor, and B♭ major—form a cadential progression in this key, as does the larger counterpoint. In contrast to the previous four-bar measures, the four-bar measures of the second large phrase are projective openings strongly directed toward new beginnings. And these measures themselves cohere as an opening to a third phrase begun with bar 136 in an overlapping in which bar 136 enters as the completion of a large accelerative LLSSL pattern. In relation to phrase 1 (bars 110–121) there is a sort of quickening in bars 122–135—a change from half-note beats to quarter-note beats. This quickening is not, I think, acceleration, but rather a release into broader, more fluid gestures unimpeded by the closures and restraining syncopations of the previous 4(2+2)–bar measures. And this fluidity contributes to the expansiveness and continuity of the second phrase.

The projectively overlapped third phrase is even more coherent, both tonally and projectively, than the second phrase. It consists of a single harmony—the dominant of E♭—which emerged as the goal of the second phrase—and it forms a very clear instance of the pattern LLSSL in an expression that recalls several instances of this pattern in the exposition (especially bars 45–52, the end of the first part of the exposition). The promise of this dominant is realized in the beginning of the second period of the development (bar 144). The new beginning with bar 144 recalls the beginning of the development, except that rather than being a tonal interruption, it is a tonal goal, similar in this respect perhaps to the resolution effected by the repeat of the exposition that was denied the second time around with the beginning of the development. Although the small phrase in bars 144–147 returns us to something resembling the closed pattern SSL and the syncopations of

EXAMPLE 13.11 Beethoven, Symphony no. 1 in C Major, first movement, bs. 106–179

Continued

EXAMPLE 13.11 (*continued*)

bars 110–113, the phrase has also assimilated features of the second and third phrases of the first period: the ascending repetitions of the figure B♭–D–E♭ through three octaves recall the repeated arpeggios of the second phrase, and the opening quarter-note anacrustic figure in bar 147 (and bars 151 and 155) clearly corresponds to the figure in bar 125; and from the third phrase there is a continuation of the nervous eighth notes (a quickening in the third phrase that results not in increased fluidity, but in contraction and intensification).

The new large phrase in bars 144–159, like the first phrase (bars 110–121), presents three four-bar measures in sequence (now ascending by step every four bars rather than every eight), but adds to these a fourth measure (bars 156–159) more sharply divided into two two-bar measures and four one-bar measures—an acceleration that leads to the dominant of A minor in bar 160. I would suggest that in this overlapping the condensation in bars 156–159 and the relatively abrupt focusing of tonal potential (say, compared to bars 132–135) open the possibility for bars 158–159 to function projectively for the beginning with bar 160, and that bars 160–161 could realize a two-bar measure as projective continuation.

For this reason, the four-bar measures that open this second and final phrase of the second period (phrase 5 of the section) are projectively somewhat ambiguous. The second two-bar measure (bars 162–163), to my ear, seems to break from the four-bar measure as a new beginning and not a continuation. Bars 160–161 open metrically to bars 162–163. In turn, bars 162–163 open to bars 164–165. I feel here a peculiar sort of overlapping, as if bars 162–163 were "superimposed" on a four-bar measure that they, in fact, complete. Although I find it difficult to adequately describe this sensation, I think it arises, in part, from tonal interruption. The entire phrase (like the final phrase of the first period) is

a "standing on the dominant." In bars 162 and 166 there is an apparent tonic resolution. But since the goal of bars 162–163 and 166–167 is the dominant, there is, in fact, no resolution for the four-bar measures, and the tonics are interruptive. Nevertheless, to respect the ambiguity and complexity of this passage I have provided two interpretations in example 13.11—one that recognizes four-bar measures (interpretation 1) and another that reduces these by half (interpretation 2). The choice between these hearings will significantly affect the connection of the development and recapitulation.

If (as in interpretation 1) we recognize four-bar measures, the end of the development will resemble the end of the exposition, where with bar 106 a projective continuation is reinterpreted as dominant beginning (see also example 13.6). In this interpretation the large acceleration in bars 164–171 will lead to a dominant beginning with bar 172. As a result, the projected potential of the beginning with bar 172 will be for a duration of four bars. (Note here that the sforzando in bar 172 and the change to woodwinds could help to signal such a beginning.) Since bars 174–177 emerge as a measure, the beginning with bar 174 will be reinterpreted as a dominant beginning (rather than the beginning of a continuation), and the overlapping of development and recapitulation will involve the overlapping of projective function. Here bar 174 will be reinterpreted at the same time that the F of bar 174 is reinterpreted—from scale degree 6 in A minor to scale degree 4 in C.[3] Moreover, such a projective reinterpretation could lead us to a heightened attentiveness born of uncertainty and so prepare us for the explosive return in bar 178. If, on the other hand (as in interpretation 2), bar 166 is not continuation, there will be an acceleration to bar 172, and bars 172–173 will fully exhaust projected potential. In this case, the four-bar measure in bars 174–177 will be relatively detached from the end of the devel-

---

3. Notice that it is only with the pitch G♮ in bar 177 that A minor dissolves and F becomes scale degree 4; were this a G♯, bars 174–177 would arpeggiate a VII7 in A minor and thus repeat the tonal contour of the woodwinds in bars 163–164 and 167–168.

opment as a very relaxed transitional figure leading a surprisingly loud return in the recapitulation. Obviously, performance will decide which of these two general interpretations is to be heard. Although I find interpretation 1 preferable to the comparatively tame interpretation 2, I admit that its realization will take some special effort. If this passage is simply "played through," the chord change with bar 174 is likely to obscure the possibility for a dominant beginning with bar 172 and thus deny us a deeply engaging moment of projective reinterpretation in the overlapping of development and recapitulation.

FOURTEEN

Problems of Meter in Early-Seventeenth-Century and Twentieth-Century Music

Modern studies of meter have generally been restricted to eighteenth- and nineteenth-century practices and have developed theories of meter based upon notions of regularity observed from these practices. I have argued, however, that even in "Classical style" the appearance of metrical regularity or homogeneity is largely the result of abstraction. Since from a projective standpoint, meter is characterized by novelty rather than by repetition of the same, styles that feature a high degree of metrical ambiguity and severely limited mensural determinacy must be regarded as no less metrical than styles in which we can observe the "rule" of a single mensural type.

Because of limitations of space, it is impossible here to give adequate attention to any style or, more generally, to discuss the relevancy of meter to questions of musical style. Since this study can, in any case, touch upon only a few of the analytic and aesthetic problems posed by measured music, I would prefer to leave the eighteenth century (and leave the nineteenth century untouched) and devote the remainder of this book to a discussion of meter in some practices that have received considerably less attention in studies of rhythm and meter. From the early seventeenth century I have chosen compositions by Monteverdi and Schütz, and from the twentieth century compositions by Webern and Babbitt. Certainly, this is a very narrow selection. From the twentieth century, I especially regret omitting a discussion of music by Stravinsky and Bartók. However, a glance toward Webern and Babbitt will allow us to consider some issues of meter that appear more problematic and will better serve as a transition to musics in which projection is largely suppressed.

Monteverdi, "Ohimè, se tanto amate" (First Phrase)

Monteverdi's "Ohimè, se tanto amate" from the fourth book of madrigals presents a metrical subtlety rarely encountered in eighteenth- and nineteenth-century music. Here the projective field is very mobile, and mensural determinacy is restricted to relatively small measures. For this reason it will be necessary to consider projective engagements in considerable detail. The opening four bars (shown in example 14.1) raise several analytic questions.

If there are two two-bar measures here, we may ask when the first of these becomes a measure. It may be only with the emergence of a second two-bar measure at the end of bar 3 that the first two-bar unit can come to function as a measure. In the first bar there is a completed projection—the quarter note serves as anacrusis to a half-note continuation, thus forming a relatively closed unit. However, for bar 2 no beginning is sounded—a "silent beginning" emerges only with the second half-note duration, and only now is there a projection and a second bar measure. Again the emphasis is on continuation (or closure) in the upper voices, but the half note in the bass functions or, rather, comes to function also as anacrusis for the next bar measure, repeating the descending third (D–B♭) of the preceding anacrusis figures. Only the word boundary— *mè / Ohi*—detracts from the anacrustic function of the bass half note.

Because of the emphasis on continuation in bars 1 and 2, the projective potential of the first two bars is not very definite and, thus, with the beginning of bar 3 it is not clear whether a projected duration of one or two bars is promised. However, with the entrance of the upper voices in bar 3 the projection is clarified—the repetition of bar 1 and the change of harmony mark this bar as a second beginning and not the continuation of a three-bar measure. With bar 4 the projection is realized and we are presented with two two-bar measures. This means that bars 3–4 can offer a two-bar projective potential for a new beginning with bar 5.

The eighth-note rest in bar 5 is confirmed as a silent beginning in the resolution of the following anacrustic group—the first three eighth notes of bar 5 pointing to the focal stressed syllable of "a̲mate." The conformity of this figure to the "Ohimè" figure in bar 3—both anacrusis to half-note continuation—may enhance a two-bar projected potential beginning with bar 5. (Note that in bars 6–7 these two figures are sung simultaneously—"ohimè" in the upper voices and "se tanto amate" in tenor.) On the other hand, there is no correspondence in bar 5 to the clear beginnings in bars 1 and 3. There is, indeed, a silent beginning with bar 5 and the beginning of a duration larger than the durations begun with silence in bars 2 and 4, but there is also a special openness and continuity here—an overlapping in which the half-note anacrusis at the end of bar 4 (corresponding to the anacrusis at the end of bar 2) remains unresolved and, in a sense, "prolonged" through the suspension of the pitches F, A, and C across the bar.

The sort of projective activity I have attempted to describe in these bars does not much

resemble eighteenth-century metrical practice but can, I think, be observed in many sixteenth- and seventeenth-century compositions. Characteristically, measures are small—projective units of four "bars" are often reserved for cadential passages and are rarely repeated as measures (i.e., as projective/projected potential). Characteristic also is a prevailing ambiguity of projective boundaries. Certainly, much late Baroque and Classical music presents great metrical ambiguity, but there "reinterpretation" generally takes place in a field of larger projections. There is, I think, a connection here between small projective scale and ambiguity or openness of projective potential. The suspension of definite potentials and the delay of projective realization can serve projective gestures of relatively large scale by delaying closure. If definite projective decisions can be put off until late in the phrase, such a delay of resolution can contribute to a sense of directedness for the completion of the phrase. And to keep the larger projective field in suspension it will be necessary to limit clear mensural determinacy to very small measures.

An analysis of the first large phrase of "Ohimè, se tanto amate" (bars 1–19) will serve to illustrate this procedure. If in bar 5 there is now any evidence of a projected potential of two bars, the realization of this measure is interrupted in bar 6, where a new measure, overlapping the old, is begun with the second half-note beat on "dir." (For convenience I will label this beginning bar "6" for the upper voices and bar "[6]" for the lower voices.) As a result, the beginning of bar 5 has become the beginning of a triple unequal measure (bar [5]) and thus an expansion compared to the preceding duple bar measures. If the first half-note beat of bar 6, "-tir," becomes anacrustic deferral (|→ — /) with the emergence of a new beginning with "dir," we may come to feel the entire phrase "se tanto amate di sentir" as an anacrustic group and perhaps even as a continuation and development of the anacrustic promise initiated at the end of bar 4. But the finer distinctions of continuation and anacrusis aside, an immediate effect of the metrical reinterpretation in bar 6 is the fact that "dir" has replaced "-tir" as a downbeat. This reinterpretation lends some urgency to "dir" and to the syntactical unit "dir ohimè."

EXAMPLE 14.1 Monteverdi, "Ohimè, se tanto amate" from Madrigals, Book IV (1603), bs. 1–21

Continued

239

EXAMPLE 14.1 *(continued)*

The line of Guarini's verse is itself broken by the introduction of a new clause with "deh." Here the adjacent stressed and rhymed syllables "-mè"/"deh" (and the punctuation) should further encourage the reader to pause in the middle of the second line.

> Ohimè! se tanto amate
> di sen*tir dir* Ohi*mè, deh*, perché fate
> chi dice Ohimè morire?
>
> (Alas! if you so love
> to hear one say Alas, then why do you cause
> the one who says Alas to die?)

As we shall see, Monteverdi takes full advantage of this internal rhyme. He also takes advantage of the rhyme formed by the preceding adjacent syllables "-tir" and "dir" to create a musical spondee (one that would not, of course, be performed in speech). Accenting both "-tir" and "dir" has the effect of uniting the words "dir ohimè" and breaking this phrase from the line.

Notice that the first "ohimè" is an interjection; the second is a reflection on *saying* "alas" and the third "ohimè" turns to a reflection on what this saying "alas" signifies ("morire"). The spondee "-mè"/"deh" breaks the line to introduce a second clause answering "if" with an implicit "then." Monteverdi introduces the new text phrase very gradually. It begins first in the canto in bars 8–9, where "deh" is obscured by the active alto and the tenor's repetition of "ohimè." A second "deh" appears more clearly in bar 10 in quinto and basso but is still somewhat obscured by the focal "ohimès" and the coincidence of vowels at the beginning of bar 10; that is, the interjection "deh" is to some extent masked by the rhyming syllables "-mè" and "-te." It is only with bars 12–13 that the new phrase emerges in full clarity; and as a transposed repetition of bars 10–11, bars 12–13 make bars 10–11 the first of what will be three statements to create an overlapping within the large phrase— an overlapping of bars [6]/ 6 (or [5])–11 as a "dir ohimè" phrase and bars 10–15 as a "deh, perché fate" phrase.

Projective activity follows a similar course. Bars 6 /[6]–11 present considerable projective ambiguity, whereas bars 10–15 realize definite two-bar measures. Because the complex arrange-

ment of metrical patterns in bars 5–11 is difficult to see from the score, I have simplified the notation in example 14.2 to show a double canon. As can be seen from the reduction, this small phrase is composed of (1) a threefold (overlapping) repetition of the "se tanto amate di sentir" figure beginning with canto and quinto in bar 5 and forming three successive unequal measures in "bars" [5], [6], and [7]; (2) a threefold repetition ("out of phase") of the "dir ohimè, ohimè, deh, perché fate" figure, each of which forms equal measures; and (3) a line in the basso composed of both figures, the second of which ("dir ohimè, ohimè, deh, perché fate") appears initially in augmentation to support the unequal measures of bars [5]–[7] and then to support equal measure in bars 10–11.

Obviously, we cannot feel all these conflicting projective potentials simultaneously with equal clarity. But obviously, too, these various potentials do not cancel one another out to leave the passage unmeasured or projectively undifferentiated. Rather, this small, seemlessly overlapped phrase presents us with considerably more differentiation than we can keep track of. Very broadly, the effect of this passage is quite clear, though (as is always the case) difficult to describe. Prolonging the anacrustic drive that (with bar 5) led us out of the relatively closed introductory measures, this knotted intensification of the large phrase gradually dissolves in the homophonic two-bar measures that in bars 10–15 emerge as the climax of the phrase. To give a more specific account of this process we might attempt to trace some of the projective engagements that contribute to the broader effect.

The upper voices beginning in bar 6 could, as a repetition of the opening measures (bars 1–2 and 3–4), form a two-bar measure, bars 6 - 7 . However, the lower voices, as a repetition of bar [5], could be heard to form an unequal measure, bar [6]. In any case, the repetition of "se tanto amate di sentir" in the tenor (bar [6]) contributes to an overlapping by now making bar [5] the beginning of a second small phrase. The choice between the two measures, bars 6 – 7 and bars [6]–[7], is not at all clear. If we hear bars 6 – 7 , the new beginning with bar [7] will be interruptive, "too soon." If we hear bar [6], the second "ohimè" in the upper voices will receive

EXAMPLE 14.2 Monteverdi, "Ohimè, se tanto amate" from Madrigals, Book IV (1603), bs. 5–13 ("double canon")

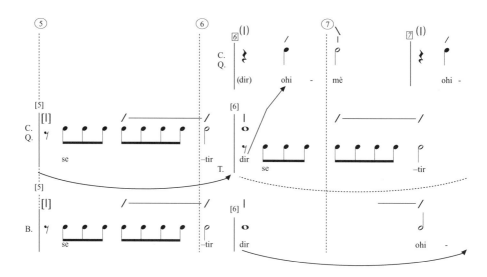

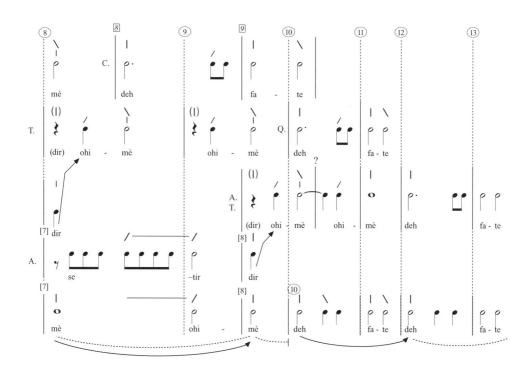

EXAMPLE 14.3 Monteverdi, "Ohimè, se tanto amate" from Madrigals, Book IV (1603), contrapuntal repetitions of "bars" [5]–[6] in bs. 10–11, 12–13, and 14–15

a metrical stress different from the first, "-mè" now falling on a beginning rather than on a continuation. Rather than choosing, we might simply say that there is here an intensification of the overlapping, reinterpretation, and ambiguity first introduced in bars 5 and 6. Ambiguity increases in bars 9 and 10 and is resolved with bar 11, itself a definite bar measure. "Before" bar 11 the projective situation is not at all clear. Once there is a bar measure 11 there is now a relatively clear two-bar measure, bars 10–11, confirmed with bars 12–13. Bar 10 is now an interruption of an emergent bar [8] and/or bar 9 introducing the new "deh, perché fate" phrase (the third small phrase). Although the phrase begun with bar 10 is in many respects detached from the preceding phrase, it should be noted that the new sequential pattern in bars 10–15 repeats the contrapuntal connection of bars [5] and [6] that served to initiate the unequal "se tanto amate" measures and to signal the emergence of the second small phrase. (See example 14.3.)

In bar 11, the syllable "-mè" of "ohimè" is now definitely stressed as the beginning of a bar measure and is followed by a stressed "deh" in bar 12. The new, thrice-repeated phrase unit is enclosed in the rhyme "deh . . . (fa)-te," which will rhyme with the final syllable of the large phrase "(mo-ri-)-re." There is a causal connection that motivates the rhyme "deh/fate/morire." And the causal link is made through the saying

of "alas." In the final, cadential phrase the vowel repetitions in "di̱ce," "o̱hi̱mè," and "mo̱ri̱re" are intricately overlapped to permit the word "morire" to blossom at the end of the phrase. Projectively, there is expansion and perhaps simplification or relaxation in the close of the phrase. Bars 16–19 form a large and newly expansive four-bar measure. Here the beginning with bar 18 is clearly continuative. In bars 10–15 there is no question of a six-bar measure, nor do the beginnings again with bars 12 and 14 function as continuations of four-bar measures. Note, too, that the concluding four-bar measure of the phrase is without issue. The second large phrase beginning in bar 20 ("S'io moro") is separated from the first by projective hiatus.

Schütz, "Adjuro vos, filiae Jerusalem"

Since our analysis of "Ohimè, se tanto amate" was restricted to a single section divorced from the context of the piece as a whole, I would like to consider projective contributions to "large-scale" rhythm in another composition from this style-world. Schütz's concertato motet "Adjoro vos, filiae Jerusalem" from the *Symphoniae sacrae*, Book I (1629), presents us with the pleasure of extremely subtle rhythmic detail and great projective contrast used in the service of a compelling larger gesture. Here, as in the Monteverdi, the repetition of small melodic figures is used for the creation of complex projective fields that serve the continuity of phrases and sections. The following analysis will be very detailed, especially for the first phrase (bars 1–11). It is, after all, a central thesis of this study that the small cannot be detached from the large. But beyond the attempt to illuminate the rhythmic particularities of this piece, a close analysis will help to further acquaint the reader with the sorts of distinctions a theory of projection would make available.

The form of this work cannot be easily captured in our customary schemata. Projective (and other) distinctions create several types of music; but the central distinction is between two types, the second of which begins with the phrase begun in bar 36 and endures to the end of the piece (bar 92). This second type is a setting of the words "(quia) amore langueo," with an emphasis on the word "langueo" ("I am faint," akin to *laxus*). However, there is also a textural (rather than a textual) division that would put the bipartite division of the piece in the neighborhood of bar 52. We will later have an opportunity to consider this overlapping more closely. The form of the piece can be most clearly seen in the form of the text (which Schütz himself probably composed):

Adjuro vos, filiae Jerusalem,
si inveneritis dilectum meum, ut nuncietis ei,
quia amore langueo.

(I charge you, daughters of Jerusalem,
if you find my beloved, tell him,
that I languish for love.)

For now we will identify the first section with the setting of the first line, "Adjuro vos, filiae Jerusalem" (bars 1–27), extended perhaps to include the following transitional passage—a recitativelike setting of the second line (bars 28–35).

The first section begins with an instrumental introduction, shown in example 14.4. (Since the two treble instruments are unspecified, I will refer to the upper and the lower line simply as "instrument 1" and "instrument 2.") This large, highly continuous phrase is composed of four intricately overlapped small phrases. Each phrase

begins with anacrusis, and while the first three phrases articulate a half-note continuation in their final bar measures, the last phrase closes on tonic in an unbroken whole note. Although it would be an overstatement to say that the first small phrase "comes out of nowhere," there is some indeterminacy in this beginning that serves the larger gesture. In example 14.4 I have shown anacrusis to a dominant beginning with the tied half note in bar 1. But notice here that the projective field is in suspense (undetermined) until a new beginning emerges in bar 3. This new beginning and this tonal opening to the dominant are goals of the small phrase brought into sharp focus by the anacrustic and accelerative deferral in bar 2.

Since a projection Q–Q' has been created, the beginning of a new small phrase in bar 4 will be interruptive. Note that a first half-note beat of bar 4 could have realized the projected potential Q' and the tone D in the bass could have resolved the dominant harmony of bar 3. Thus, it is only when there is in bar 4 some evidence of the emergence of a new measure and a new phrase that a metrical and tonal interruption can be felt. It must be said, however, that metrical interruption is not likely to be very intensely felt here, because unequal measures at this tempo and in this projective environment are not highly determinate. Compared to the preceding unequal measure, the duple equal measure in bar 3 may be felt as contracted and intensified, followed in bar 4 with a new measure that enters with a special quickness or urgency. Or, to put the matter more generally, if a triple unequal measure is somewhat unstable, we may seize the opportunity to gain greater determinacy in a smaller, equal measure without altogether giving up our ability to make a prediction based on the duration of the unequal measure now past. (A similar situation was encountered in example 11.2 in bars 111–112 of the Wolpe.)

I have dwelt on the character of this interruption in some detail because the schema we have identified in this first small phrase—a two-measure, "five-beat" pattern divided 3+2 or unequal/equal—is a characteristic projective feature of bars 1–35 of "Adjuro vos." Since it is frequently encountered, this general arrangement can be regarded as a projective type that we

EXAMPLE 14.4 Schutz, "Adjuro vos, filiae Jerusalem," from Symphoniae sacrae, Book I (1629), bs. 1–11

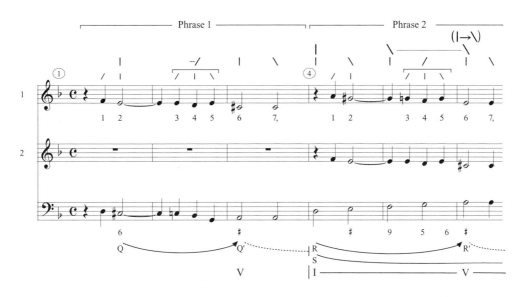

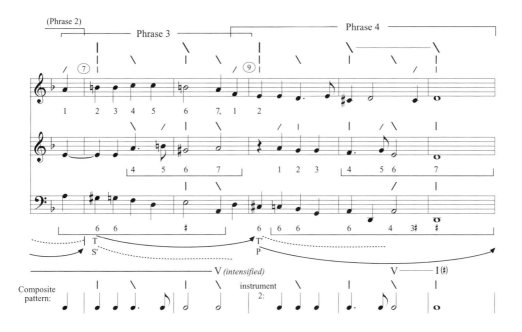

might, for convenience, refer to as "unequal contractive," or simply "3+2." Another instance of this type can be identified in bars 4–8, involving the second and third small phrases, if phrase 2 can be interpreted as a three-bar measure and phrase 3 can be interpreted as a two-bar measure. Should we imagine a correspondence

between these two 3+2 beat complexes such that phrases 2 and 3 might appear as an expanded repetition of phrase 1? As conceptually appealing as this sort of correspondence might be, I find no evidence for it.

We can, however, very easily hear a repetition of the first phrase in the second. The descending tetrachordal bass (D–A) in the first phrase is answered by an ascent from D to A in the second phrase, and the upper voice of the first phrase is repeated (in instrument 2), now with the addition of a new upper line (instrument 1) that itself repeats the previous bass at the interval of a fifth. A peculiar difference here is that the tied half note in bar 4 comes to be interpreted as *continuation* and so takes on the energy of a syncopation—a deferral of closure or suspension of activity that here contributes to the mobility of the phrase. By contrast, in phrase 1 the beginning of the tied half note was (or came to be) the *beginning* of an unequal measure. But it should be remembered that this first beginning was very open and that much of the excitement and mobility of the first phrase derives from the delay of projective focus until the new beginning with bar 3 and from the acceleration to this beginning. On this comparison, the tied half note of phrase 2, in fact, closely resembles *in its effect* the tied half in phrase 1: in the second phrase the syncopation in the upper voices creates a suspension of activity that is fully "resolved" only in the acceleration to bar 6. Indeed, it is because the beginning of the tied half in bar 4 is interpreted as continuation that the second phrase can match the first phrase in intensity. (Note in this connection that performing a half-note D in the bass at the beginning of bar 1 to match the beginning with the half-note D in bar 4 will deaden the entire passage.)

If this projective reinterpretation of phrase 1 in phrase 2 serves to sustain the energy of the larger emerging phrase, there is another difference between phrases 1 and 2 that would seem to lead to a reduction of intensity. In phrase 1, the projected potential Q' is cut short by the beginning of phrase 2. However, in phrase 2, bar 6 can be interpreted as deferral, in which case phrase 2 will form a large measure and there will be little sense of urgency in the beginning of the third phrase. (In example 14.4 a deferral in S is shown as the denial of projection R–R'.) Although the projective potential S shown in the example may overstate the mensural determinacy of a three-bar measure formed by the second phrase, this duration must have some relevance for our feeling of compression or contraction in the shorter third phrase. To claim deferral

here is to acknowledge some degree of expansion and relaxation in comparison to phrase 1. Expansion can also be heard in the tonal domain. Thus, in contrast to the disjunctive tonic beginning that sharply separates phrase 2 from phrase 1, there is no tonal break between phrases 2 and 3—phrase 3 continues the dominant to cadence on an octave A in bar 8.

These two factors—one projective and the other tonal—that led to the special urgency in the beginning of the second phrase now contribute to the continuity of phrases 2 and 3. There are, however, other factors that more than compensate for this loss of energy. In comparison to the beginning of phrase 2, phrase 3 enters the duration of a half note too soon—before the third bar measure of the second phrase is completed. This interruption is much more intense and exciting than the interruption with the beginning of phrase 2, and for this reason it creates another sort of continuity, the continuity of a growing intensity or urgency in the overlapping of phrases. It should be understood that although these two interruptions arise for different reasons, the second is also a type of projective interruption (drawing on the relevances of the first two phrases) and for both the category for feeling is the same—that the new event begins too soon, earlier than anticipated. (And, as I have pointed out before, increased familiarity need not detract from this feeling.)

A second factor that contributes to the vitality of the phrase involves melodic correspondences. In this respect, the third phrase is a highly compressed repetition of the prior phrases. The bass of the new phrase repeats, in a tightly compressed form, the upper line of the second phrase and the bass of the first phrase (a fifth higher), and a new upper line reflects the bass in inversion to form the climax of the large phrase. In its abbreviations of the melodic figures of phrases 1 and 2, phrase 3 has omitted the suspended "tied half notes." Now there is no arrest—no suspension and accumulation of energies released in the accelerative, anacrustic groups that led to closure in phrases 1 and 2. Instead, the line rushes to a projective closure in the continuation of a two-bar measure—in fact, the line keeps moving on into the continuation of this continuation (the second half of bar 8) to end in a cadential arrest on A. Corresponding to the bass line of the first phrase, which took a duration of seven quarters to descend a fourth from D to A in a tonal opening, the bass in the third phrase descends a fourth from A to E after five quarters and then closes on A as the continuation of a bar measure. This cadence on A at the climax of the phrase sharply focuses our attention on relatively brief durations and on a very active scale degree 5. The cadence also leads to overlapping with the final small phrase.

If the cadential fourth phrase returns us to a three-bar measure, it is an expansion that nevertheless sustains the energy of the large phrase to its end. I would now like to address the question of how this is accomplished. To my ear, the beginning of the fourth small phrase is no less urgent than the entrance of the third phrase. As was suggested earlier, by identifying phrases 2 and 3 as an instance of an "unequal contractive" or "3+2" type there should be some urgency in the beginning of a new measure with bar 9. But it is the immediate undercutting of the cadence on A in phrase 3 that makes the beginning of the fourth phrase especially interruptive. The cadential resolution itself is very late, in the sense that the octave A in bar 8 arrives as the continuation of the continuation of a two-bar measure. The new phrase begins with an anacrusis to bar 9, even before this final half-note continuation of bar 8 has had a chance to play itself out. In its earliness the fourth phrase resembles the third phrase, which also began (in a different sense) too soon and before the preceding measure was completed. Although the fourth phrase also very clearly resembles the first phrase, it is this initial resemblance to the third that sustains the energy of the (small and large) phrase. In fact, it may be only quite late in the phrase that the feeling of a three-bar, unequal measure matures in our ear.

Contributing to the intensity of the fourth phrase is the close imitation between the upper voices. In pitch, the dux (instrument 1) repeats the upper line of phrase 1 and the comes (instrument 2) repeats the upper line of phrase 2 over a bass repeated from phrase 1. Note also that instrument 2 of phrase 4 picks up the pitch A from the abandoned upper line of phrase 3 (cut short by the anacrustic beginning of phrase 4) and very rapidly negotiates the descent from A to D.

In duration, each of these upper voices in phrase 4 repeats the composite pattern of phrase 3 made distinctive by the dotted quarter figure in bar 7. (Instrument 2 is an exact repetition.)

Because phrase 4 begins in many respects as a clear repetition of phrase 3, it also begins with the potential for forming a two-bar measure (T' in example 14.4). In bar 10 this potential is denied by the prolongation of dominant harmony; that is, instead of closing on D in bar 10 and thus preserving the correspondence with the cadence on A in bar 8, the bass in bar 10 returns to A in the second half of the bar. With bar 10 the small phrase begins to lengthen to a three-bar measure, slowing to a close on D as a deferred continuation. From the perspective of the large phrase, it may be said that the tonal/metrical rupture that broke the first small phrase from the second and that has been preserved in the growing intensity of dominant harmony is now healed as A (together with E and C♯) resolves to D in the psychologically unitary duration of this final three-bar measure. In the large phrase there is one other situation in which a comparable resolution takes place: bar 8. And it is largely through the correspondence of these two cadences that the fourth small measure can come to equal, if not to exceed, the intensity of the earlier phrases.

At the end of phrase 3 the resolution of E (and B and G♯) to A is truncated. Here A in the bass is an afterbeat or continuation of the (projectively) dominant beginning with E. By contrast, in phrase 4 these relations have been inverted in the sense that D in bar 11 can be felt as a dominant beginning in relation to the immediate resolutions of the tones of dominant harmony—in other words, from the perspective of bar measures the final cadence (A to D) is "weak-strong," as opposed to the "strong-weak" cadence of phrase 3 (E to A). This change of projective relations entails a comparative lengthening and deceleration in phrase 4—an expansion to three bars compared to the two-bar measure of phrase 3. But, fortunately, the bass and instrument 2 here help to sustain the energy of the phrase right up to bar 11 by drawing upon more specific features of this very correspondence between phrases 3 and 4.

If the cadence on D at the end of phrase 4

can be said to arrive "a half note late" in comparison to the cadence on A in phrase 3, we can say also that instrument 2, which carries the upper voice closure, enters a half note late in imitation of instrument 1. It is this delayed entrance in bar 9 coupled with a reinterpretation of the bass that will concentrate our attention in the moment of cadence. In example 14.4 I have used brackets to indicate a strong resemblance between the combined lines of phrase 3 and the conjunction of instrument 2 and the bass beginning with the second quarter-note beat of bar 9. If the line beginning with A in bar 9 (instrument 2, A– G – G – F) could be heard to begin as an inverted repetition of the line on A that opened phrase 3 (instrument 1, A–B♮–B♮–C) this correspondence will be considerably enhanced as instrument 2 in bar 10 repeats the very distinctive sequence of durations that concluded phrase 3 in instrument 2—dotted quarter–eighth–half. (Remember here that instruments 1 and 2 will not be so distinguishable in audition as they are on paper.) Because of this resemblance, our attention can be shifted to a corresponding bass line also beginning with the second quarter of bar 9. Again, like the bass of phrase 3, the sequence of durations will be repeated—five quarters followed by a half. But equally important for our inclination to be lured into this shift toward the end of the bass line in phrase 4 (and away from the clear repetition early in the line) are correspondences of contour. Having once been enticed to follow instrument 2 in phrase 4 as a repetition of instrument 1 in phrase 3, we can easily come to feel some similarity of contour in the cadential basses in their final two beats: down–up–*down* in phrases 3 (F–D–*E*–A) and 4 (A–D–*A*–D).

All of these correspondences working together produce in the final cadence an echo of the cadence of phrase 3. As a result, the intensity attained in the climactic third small phrase is not dissipated in the fourth and there is no trace of enervation at the close of the large phrase. Note also that, as a result of this "half-note shift" in phrase 4, projective functions have been reversed in the corresponding figures we have been observing. Obviously, this contrast between a cadence to A in phrase 3 that recedes from a dominant bar measure beginning (| \) and a final cadence that resolves a continuative A in a dominant beginning D (/ |) will enhance the closure of the large phrase. Indeed, this particular contrast cannot be isolated from its history or from a larger context in which the final bar measure of each phrase but the last has been increasingly destabilized in its moment of ending.

As a technical detail, this procedure in phrases 3 and 4 of reversing projective function is reminiscent of the change from beginning to continuation we observed in connection with the tied half notes in phrases 1 and 2. The effectiveness of this procedure depends on the repetition of relatively small segments or sequences that can retain sufficient identity under transformation for them to serve as measures of a transformation into novel character—that is, to serve as measures of particularity and novelty. In this style, close repetition (including all sorts of "imitation") creates opportunities for extremely subtle and mobile projective engagements. Among the many characters of a sequence that can be repeated under transformation, I wish to mention "number" here as an especially useful one. In example 14.4 I have numbered the beats of the phrases as I did earlier in the E♭ Courante. The repetition of "7" contributes to many of the metrical distinctions and correspondences we have observed and greatly enhances feelings of acceleration and deceleration (especially in the climactic third small phrase).

To give some indication of the variety of projective activity in this piece and the large-scale rhythmic effects this activity supports, I will present a somewhat less detailed analysis of the remainder of this section and two passages from the second section (or part) of the piece. This reduction of detail, while not perhaps sufficient to greatly spare the reader's patience, will nevertheless result in some oversimplification—of both the rich ambiguity of projective decisions and the manifold relevances of past events. Throughout the first section there are many repetitions of projective situations we have encountered in the instrumental introduction. Since I will point out only a few of these, I wish to alert the reader to the abundance of repetition (and transformation) in this section and throughout the piece.

EXAMPLE 14.5 Schutz, "Adjuro vos, filiae Jerusalem," from *Symphoniae sacrae*, Book I (1629), bs. 11–27

Continued

The second large phrase (bars 12–27) is tonally and projectively more broken than the first. In example 14.5 I have ventured to identify three small phrases, each composed of two smaller constituents. (In a closer reading that would better reflect the overlappings that join these constituents as a single event, we should also have to consider a beginning again with bar 21 and, thus, a division into two parts, each composed of three constituents.) The first small phrase begins as a repetition of various characters of the previous large phrase (bars 1–11). In fact, it most closely resembles the second small phrase (bars 4–6) in the half-note ascent in the bass and the anacrusis to a syncopated (tied half-note) continuation in the upper voice. I mention these resemblances to point out the special relevance of a three-bar projective potential for the beginning with bar 12. The projected potential for a three-bar measure (locally, P') is, I believe, sufficiently realized to create a projective overlapping with the beginning of a new two-bar measure (Q) in bars 14–15. The result is an extension or elongation of the small subphrase (bars 12–14) brought about by the reinterpretation of a de-

ferred continuation as a new beginning with bar 14 ($—\backslash \Rightarrow |$). To interpret this complex simply as a four-bar unit would be to ignore its particular quality of suspense and the new feeling of elasticity now given to the piece.

The two-bar measure (R) begun with bar 16 as a realization of Q' might have been a tonal and projective continuation. Instead, it emerges as a new beginning and a (relatively mild) tonal interruption—in part, because of the return in instrument 2 to the beginning of the phrase (D–C–B♭–A) and in part because of developments in bars 17 and 18. On the other hand, it would be an unfortunate oversimplification here to entirely ignore the immediate closure on D in the bass at the beginning of bar 16, for although a potential Q' is realized, there is also clear evidence here of a contraction to the bar measure with the vocal entrances in bars 16 and 17. This contraction is shown in the example as a projection S–S' interrupted by the new line of text ("filiae Jerusalem") in bar 18. (It should be pointed out here that a projection S–S' can take place only at the expense of a projective potential R. This

EXAMPLE 14.5 (*continued*)

issue was discussed in chapter 9 in connection with example 9.5.)

Because of the projective break in bar 18 and the immediate tonal redirection to B♭ in bar 20, I have identified here the beginning of a second small phrase extended through bar 23. This phrase begins with a mediated or triple unequal measure leading to what at first appears to be a duple equal bar measure in bar 20 and, thus, another instance of our "unequal contractive" or "3+2" type. Notice that the beginning of the new small phrase in bar 18 is not perhaps so interruptive as the interruption of the bar-measure projection S–S' would suggest with its two dominant beginnings separated by a half-note duration ("vos" in tenors 1 and 2 and "filiae" in tenor 2). I attribute this mollification to a newly emerging conformity brought about through a reinterpretation of the end of the preceding phrase. Example 14.5 shows in parentheses the realization of an *unequal measure* (T) in the intensely contracted repetition of "Adjuro vos," beginning with the anacrusis to bar 17. As a result of this overlapping of the two small phrases, there is no break in the address, "Adjuro vos, filiae Jerusalem." Rather, there is a very urgent naming of the addressees—a naming that will

be made even more urgent at the end of the large phrase. In this connection notice also the accelerated repetition of the melodic descent from D to A in tenor 1 (bars 17–18) and tenor 2 (bar 18).

After the cadential arrest in bar 20, the now familiar syncopated suspension in tenor 1 on "-ju-" in bars 21–22 would seem to repeat the projective characters of bar 12. In this environment it will be difficult initially to suppress the feeling of a dominant beginning with bar 21. However, as the small phrase closes we can now come to hear a subtly overlapped unequal measure (W) beginning with the second half note in bar 21, and, thence, a concluding "3+2." Two factors may be named in the creation of this remarkable projective reinterpretation: (1) the tonal change (and resolution) in the middle of bar 21 from B♭ (scale degree 6) to A (scale degree 5); and (2) the relevance of the previous "Adjuro vos" figures from the end of phrase 1 (bars 16–17), which present very similar projective functions. In this reinterpretation in bars 20–22, it would seem plausible to imagine that the projected potential U' is realized after all (as I have indicated with the symbol ---+---), but in view of the complexity of our perceptions here and

EXAMPLE 14.6 Schutz, "Adjuro vos, filiae Jerusalem," from Symphoniae sacrae, Book I (1629), bs. 28–35

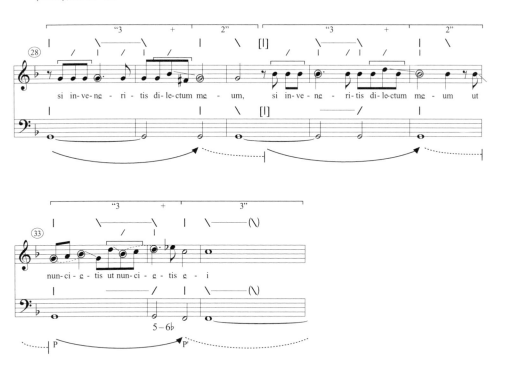

the difficulty of sorting out distinctions of "before" and "after" in the simultaneity of these projective events such a decision may remain questionable.

The final phrase (bars 24–27), which repeats the text of bars 18–20 ("filiae Jerusalem"), elaborates the two measures of bars 18–20, opening the large phrase to G much as the small phrase (or, perhaps, the first "half phrase," A) opened to B♭ in bar 20. After the complications of the previous projections and, especially, the contractions of bars 16–20, this phrase seems very expansive and fluid. Among the factors that contribute to continuity here, note the complex overlapping of measures created by ambiguities in grouping. If we attend only to the vocal parts, we will hear in bars 24–26 two unequal measures (Y and Z), the second of which leads to a duple measure in bar 27. If we follow the instrumental parts in their continuation of an ascending line running parallel to the bass (A–B♭–C–D), we can hear duple equal bar measures, at least in bars 24 and 25. Notice that we are encouraged to follow the instrumental line

in bar 25 because the instruments continue the pattern, while tenor 2 in bar 25 breaks the pattern and drops away from the rising contour. But notice, too, that if we attend to instrument 1 in bar 25 we will be attuned to the immediate repetition in bar 26 by tenor 1 (D–A–A–B♭–A), and in this case we may well be inclined to reinterpret the second half-note beat of bar 25 as beginning and come to feel an unequal measure. If we do, we are rewarded with a very close correspondence (in many respects) between the end of this phrase and the "3+2" setting of the same text in bars 18–20.

The address is now completed, and its completion is a tonal opening for the matter of the address which is delivered in the following phrase (bars 28–35, example 14.6). This message to the daughters of Jerusalem is, in fact, a request to deliver another—a message to the physically absent beloved. For solo tenor, this passage presents a change of style for the piece. Projectively, the third large phrase is simpler and more continuous than the second. And yet, by this same comparison it continues the movement toward fluidity and expansion initiated with bars 24–27. This continuation and numerous other correspondences between bars 24–27 and the new phrase begun with bar 28 create a very effective overlapping of the two large phrases. Note also that the overlapping here resembles the overlapping in the first two phrases—for example, in the retention of harmony across phrase boundaries (D in bars 11–12 and G in bars 27–28) together with the change from major third to minor third (F♯ to F and B to B♭).

Although the three small phrase constituents indicated in example 14.6 are very clearly articulated, the large phrase is highly continuous. I suggest two reasons for this continuity: the immediate overlappings created by the "irregular" bass and a larger tonal expansion coupled with acceleration in the final small phrase. Because of the incontrovertible repetition of the first small phrase (bars 28–30) in bars 30–32, the suppression of a new beginning in the bass in bar 30 should not prevent the beginning of a new measure on the second half. (Moreover, I believe that an attentive keyboard player, realizing this bass, will strongly feel the urge to supply a right-hand attack on the second half of bar 30.) The effect of this suppression is similar to the suspense of a syncopation, and it may be that this suspense is not fully resolved until bar 33, where the bass supports the metrical beginning of a new small phrase (bars 33–35). Or perhaps the special intensity of the new beginning with bar 33 is more directly the result of the interruption of projected potential by the bass in bars 32–33 compared to bars 29–30, where no new beginning is sounded in the bass. However we choose to weigh causes, the complex interaction of bass and voice keeps this large phrase mobile until its end. With the final small phrase there is for the first time in this piece a clearly completed projection (P–P') involving two large unequal measures.[1]

Leading to the close of the large phrase and welding the three small phrases into a continuous gesture, the rising melodic sequence in bars 28–34 greatly accelerates in the final small phrase. In example 14.6 I have circled several focal moments in the arpeggiation from G up to D. The third small phrase repeats in great compression the closing figures of the two previous phrases (the two descending thirds B♭–G and D–B♭ indicated by short diagonal lines in the example). There is also compression or acceleration within the third phrase as a result of the sequential repetition of the initial four-note figure, B♭–G–A–B♭ ("ut nuncie-"), a third higher (D–B♭–C–D). To match the first figure projectively the second would have had to enter a quarter note later. As it stands, the second "ut nuncie-" enters too soon, as a sort of interruption. Also because of this "quarter-note shift" (and taking advantage of the interruption) the second "ut nun-ci-e-" returns us to the more mobile anacrustic groups of the preceding phrases: "si inve-ne-" and "di-lec-tum me-." Notice that in this comparison our second "ut nuncietis" in bars 33–34 repeats the first part of phrases 1 and 2 ("si inveneritis"): a group of three anacrustic eighth notes leading to a dotted quarter followed by an eighth-note anacrusis to the beginning of another half-note beat. (And I believe the second part of phrases 1 and 2, "dilectum meum," can also be heard to begin too soon, though the feeling of interruption here is less intense than in bar 33.) Such a correspondence will contribute to a special sense of compression in the ending of the large phrase.

In example 14.6 I have underlined the vowels "e" that coincide with the circled tones of the arpeggiation. One effect of the "quarter-note shift" in the third small phrase is an intensified focus on the vowel "e," enhanced by the very quickly completed stepwise ascent from G to D arrested on B♭ ("e") in bar 33. This development lends a special sense of urgency to the repetition of "e" that begins the final (unequal) measure. Thus, tone, meter, melodic contour, and even vowel harmony lead to the crucial word "ei" and the climax of the phrase. I draw attention to this complex interaction of domains because in bars

---

1. Although the bass pattern in bars 33–35 is not repeated in the piece, it is a closural form ("LSSL" or "unequal compound closed") frequently encountered in un-

equal measure. Another instance of this type was pointed our earlier in the first two bars of the E♭ Courante shown in example 10.9.

28–35 mismatches between syllabic accent (whether by stress or length) and what accentual/extensive theories call "strong" and "weak" *parts* of meter might again raise questions of metrical/rhythmic conflict. But again I remind the reader that for a projective theory there can be no isolation, and therefore no conflict of "metrical accent" and "phenomenal accent," meter and grouping, or rhythm and meter. Whatever projective potentials are created and whatever relevancies are brought into play in a newly emerging event must bear the specificity of all the qualitative/quantitative distinctions that are available for feeling.

We now come to the end of the text—*the* message, "amore langueo," introduced by a new and very distinctive figure on the connective, "quia" (see example 14.7). The new large phrase ending in bar 50 is composed of two closely overlapped small phrases. Each of these consists of a long, drawn out cadence on "langueo" emerging seamlessly from the little "amore" figures that play in close imitation with the bass. Because of the way in which the two smaller phrases are overlapped, we seem to be caught in a single extraordinarily spacious cadence. The first small phrase leads us to a cadence that is beautifully erased in bars 43–44 as the tenor's sustained D is immediately absorbed into a more closed G minor harmony, which then slips into D minor as the bass continues moving "down" in bar 44 to lead us back into "amore" imitation and thence to a transposed repetition of bars 39–43, ending with a cadence on A.

With this new large phrase we enter a new projective world. From here to the end of the piece every bar is unambiguously a measure, and there are long stretches in which two-bar measures can be quite clearly felt. The remarkably evocative character of this setting of "amore langueo" draws deeply on projective contrast with the music of bars 1–35. In this first part of the piece our attention is focused on intricate and mercurial projective groupings of half-note durations and the lively play of equal and unequal measures. Far from fragmenting the larger phrases, this complex projective activity in bars 1–35 works as a centripetal force overlapping relatively small constituents as phases of intensely focused larger events. By comparison, the new

"langueo" music is very relaxed and less sharply focused. The relative homogeneity, ambiguity, and slowness introduced in bars 36–50 have a centrifugal effect that will be magnified in the final section of the piece (bars 55–92), in which the various "nows" of small phrase, large phrase, and phrase group seem to coalesce in a present of remarkably uncertain extent. Indeed, the great gesture of this piece (and a gesture that wonderfully reflects the text's contrast of exterior and interior, public and private) is this particular movement from a relatively focused, highly differentiated projective field to a diffuse and homogeneous field—a diffuse present—in which projective aim is largely suspended.

In example 14.7 I have indicated projective decisions that most significantly affect the course of the phrase. Since there is little ambiguity in the formation of bar measures, possibilities are now opened for the formation of larger, two-bar measures. These two-bar (four-"beat") measures are larger than any of the measures we have encountered heretofore in the piece, but they are also less determinate. "Final" distinctions between beginning and continuation (i.e., the largest durations for which such distinctions can be made) are much less definite now than they were when measures were smaller. Nevertheless, I believe there is ample evidence of a two-bar measure beginning with bar 36. There is clearly a new beginning with bar 36 and nothing to prevent us from hearing bar 37 as continuation. The "quia" figure in the voice is directed toward closure or toward a second bar measure as continuation, and a new measure is initiated in bar 38 as the bass (and harmony) moves from F up to G and the voice begins the new "amore" figure. In example 14.7, I have represented this state of affairs by the projection Q–Q'. I have also shown a reinterpretation in bar 39 as a new projective potential R arises from the emergence of the beginning of a half-note descent in the bass. Owing to the weakness of a two-bar projective potential in this environment, the sense of reinterpretation here is subtle, but I believe that an attentive hearing will reveal evidence of the projective detachment here of a second and markedly slower event beginning with bar 39 and crystallizing around the word "langueo." The tied half-note continuation initiated in bar 39 is,

EXAMPLE 14.7 Schutz, "Adjuro vos, filiae Jerusalem," from *Symphoniae sacrae*, Book I
(1629), bs. 36–57

by now, a familiar feature of this piece. What is quite novel here is the fact that this suspended continuation is, in a sense, not resolved for *four* bar measures—that is, until the octave cadence is achieved in bar 43.

If there is a two-bar projected potential realized in bars 43–44, there will be, presumably, a two-bar projected potential initiated with the beginning of the second small phrase in bar 45. The bass seems to realize this possibility by beginning a half-note descent that clearly corresponds to the measure begun with bar 39. However, as the second small phrase unfolds, evidence of a correspondence between bars 46–50 and bars 39–43 emerges. Bars 46–50, in fact, very nearly replicate bars 39–43 a fourth lower. In example 14.7 I have shown the possibility for two-bar measures beginning with bar 45 as interpretation 1 and a beginning with bar 46 as an alternative interpretation 2. I submit that there is genuine ambiguity here created by the lack of correspondence between immediate projective potential, which would favor interpretation 1, and the relevance of the first small phrase, which would favor interpretation 2. If there is such ambiguity, it will work to detract from the mensural determinacy of two-bar measures in the second small phrase. Indeed, an indication of such ambiguity and its consequent reduction of mensural determinacy will be a perception that the beginning with bar 50 promises nothing beyond the completion of the bar measure. One effect of projective ambiguity in this phrase is to heighten its contrast to the phrases of the first section—here, rather than an intensification toward the end of the large phrase, there is relaxation and a diffusion of projective potential. Such contrast is crucial for the effectiveness of the text setting.

Because projected potential is exhausted with the whole-note duration of bar 50 and there is no new beginning, the notated rest in bar 51 is an unmeasured silence of waiting, a hiatus in which the projective field is for the first time broken. And because bars 52–53 form a strongly closed two-bar measure (of the type SSL) there is also hiatus with bar 54. The "quia" figure that introduced the fourth large phrase in bars 36–37 now returns in bars 52–56 to introduce a much larger five-phrase group that will close the piece. In fact, the rest of the piece can be understood as a single extended meditation on the subject introduced in bars 36–50. Although I have identified two large sections, bars 1–35 and bars 36–92, this is obviously a great oversimplification. Large-scale overlapping in this composition is very complex. Notice, for example, that bar 52 returns the full ensemble, which has not been heard since the completion of the address in bar 27. There is a sense, then, in which bars 28–50 cohere as a section that spans the delivery (by solo tenor) of the message: "si inveneritis dilectum meum, ut nuncietis ei, quia amore langueo." As was mentioned earlier, the kernel of this message or the message within the message—"amore langueo"—now becomes the subject of a meditation that for a duration of thirty-six bars

(56–92) continuously repeats the figures of the fourth phrase (bars 36–50).

I will not attempt to discuss the conclusion of the piece in detail. In some ways this music is more complex than any other we have observed in the piece. Projective decisions are made extremely subtle because of an attenuation of mensural determinacy and an expansion in the durations of phrases, and because massive repetition now presents an almost overwhelming universe of relevancies. The novel character of the fourth phrase (bars 36–50) is greatly amplified in its expanded repetition within this closing section. It is as if the entire closing section were a single complex cadence, as if we were "timelessly" suspended in a moment of ending that nevertheless keeps going on. The effect might be compared to that of a turning barber's pole in which the stripes continually move upward in the same space, except that here the "illusion" is one of stasis rather than of movement. To give some idea of the novel expansiveness of this music, I have reproduced the fourth phrase of the closing section in example 14.8.

Since I have not provided score for bars 56–72, a brief account of this passage will help provide some context for the phrase shown in example 14.8. Remember that the projective field is broken in bar 51 and in bar 54 (example 14.7). The statement of "quia" in bars 52–53 is thus relatively isolated and stands as an arrest in the piece's progress. In bar 55 a second "quia" returns us to activity and introduces a largely unbroken, projectively overlapped succession of phrases. From bar 55 through bar 72 there is an uninterrupted succession of relatively clear two-bar measures. The new phrase begun with bar 73 continues this succession of two-bar measures until bar 80, where there is a reinterpretation and thus a projective overlapping (shown in example 14.8). But this reinterpretation hardly results in the articulation of a "small phrase," and, in any case, imitation between tenor 1 and tenor 2 further overlaps these cadential figures.

Although I have drawn attention to two-bar measures as the largest bearers of more or less definite projective potential, it must be said that these projections are by no means as sharply defined as the smaller projections in the first part of the piece. As in bars 1–34, a high degree of

EXAMPLE 14.8   Schutz, "Adjuro vos, filiae Jerusalem," from *Symphoniae sacrae*, Book I (1629), bs. 72–84

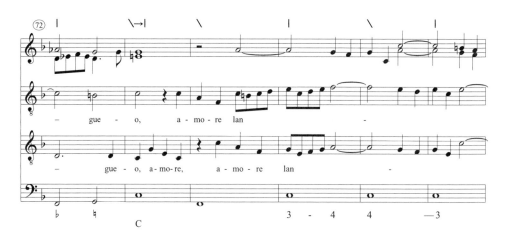

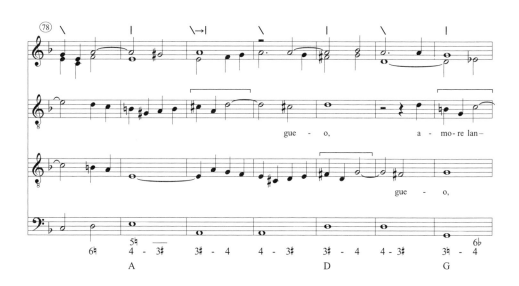

mensural determinacy is reserved for bar measures. (Note, too, that the bar-length imitation in bars 74–78 between the instruments and voices also weakens the articulation of two-bar measures.) However, in contrast to the first part of the piece, the "langueo" music is projectively relatively homogeneous. Gone now are the complex reinterpretations and interruptions that in the earlier music functioned to articulate phrase constituents and to overlap these constituents in a vividly felt whole. As a result of projective homogeneity in bars 73–84 we find ourselves in a large, relatively unsegmented but fully metrical

phrase whose beginning we can no longer "remember" and whose end seems always to be slipping from our grasp.

If we get lost projectively, we also get lost tonally. The preceding three phrases in bars 57–73 cadenced on D, G, and C. Apparently conforming to this pattern, the new phrase promises to cadence on F (at the climax of the phrase and perhaps of the entire piece), but in bar 77 tonal function is redirected through several especially ravishing dissonances to bring us, quite magically, to A in bar 80. This cadence is then averted to lead to D at the beginning of bar

82. The first tenor's D in bars 80−82 is very promising as a close and can draw on the relevance of the long descending line begun with the suspended F in bar 75 (F−E−D); but again the cadence is averted and the phrase ends on G. And yet, even though the tonal direction of the phrase is being redirected in a most unpredictable fashion, the phrase has been cadencing—has been ending—since bar 75. Indeed, the piece has been ending for a much longer time (perhaps from as long ago as bars 36−50), and it will continue ending. Notice, by the way, that in the overlapping of the final phrase in bar 84 the "amore" figure that always initiates the new phrase is now itself assimilated to a *closing figure* through its explicit repetition of the cadential pattern exposed in bar 82 and bar 80. If we can feel in some sense "lost" in a moment of ending, it is very tempting to call this feeling of a suspension of duration an experience of "timelessness." And, as I shall argue later, a sort of "getting lost" leads to the effect of timelessness or the concentration in an eternal now, which is often said to characterize our experience of much music of the postwar avant-garde.

Webern, Quartet, op. 22

In "Ohimè, se tanto amate" and "Adjuro vos, filiae Jerusalem" we observed a projective world of relatively small measures and considerable mobility and ambiguity. In some music of the twentieth century we find much smaller measures and much greater ambiguity. To illustrate the new style, I would like to consider the first movement of Webern's Quartet, op. 22. Especially striking here is the absence of a clear pulse. Indeed, the projective field is so volatile there might be some question whether this music is genuinely metrical, particularly if we equate meter with regularity. In Renaissance and early Baroque music there is often great freedom granted to the grouping of *battute* (half notes in the preceding examples) and thus variation in felt *takt*, but within the phrase, divisions of these beats present constant distinctions of strong and weak. In the Webern there is no projective constancy. There is a "smallest value"—the sixteenth note—but the metrical grouping of sixteenth notes is highly

variable and often ambiguous, with the result that in many cases it is difficult to say whether a sixteenth note is beginning or continuation. Moreover, hiatus or unmeasured durations can occur within the phrase to articulate its constituent events. Because this music raises new questions concerning projective and tonal potential, my discussion of the first phrase will be very detailed and will engage some general issues of performance and analysis.

The first phrase from the Quartet (bars 1−5) is shown in example 14.9. (See also example 14.10 for a more detailed analysis of this passage.) Here I have identified four or possibly five small constituents. The final constituent, broken by hiatus from the preceding events, functions as a cadential (opening and closing) figure that serves the overlapping of phrases. In the absence of clear tonal potentials and because of the brevity of the figures, it does not seem appropriate to call these small, fragmentary gestures "phrases." "Phrase" connotes some degree of completeness or closure that is denied these "shards" or "splinters" (to use Georgiades' expression). Nevertheless, these fragments are clearly articulated, and their very incompleteness and brokenness serve the continuity of the phrase by leaving possibilities for connection open. To some extent this procedure resembles the uses made of the reduction to small measures for the formation of phrases in the older music.

In bars 1−4 a process of condensation and acceleration provides some direction for the becoming of the phrase—the figures grow increasingly shorter and succeed one another ever more quickly and fluently. (And it is as the final stage in this process of abbreviation that the two-note clarinet figure in bar 4 might be regarded as a fourth constituent and an end of sorts.) The final constituent in bar 5 will then appear relatively detached. As a slower, more relaxed answer to constituents 3 and 4, it comes to function as a conclusion to the first phrase; and yet, as a reversal of the process of acceleration, it also functions to introduce a new phrase. Not fully a continuation of the first four bars and not fully the beginning of the next phrase, this very distinctive figure is an agent for the overlapping of the two phrases. Against this interpretation, it might be argued that the phrase is composed of

two parts on the basis of instrumentation—an alternation of the wind/string ensemble and piano in bars 1–3 repeated in bars 4–5. Doubtless, the reappearance of the piano in bar 5 contributes to the extension or reopening of the phrase. However, to hear the passage simply as an alternation of instruments, we will have to be deaf to the rhythm that joins bars 1–4 as a unit and ignore Webern's efforts to incorporate the timbrally anomalous piano into the ensemble. Certainly, we can hear the alternation, but the two piano constituents are functionally quite different.

EXAMPLE 14.10 Anton von Webern, Quartet, op. 22 first movement, bs. 1–7.

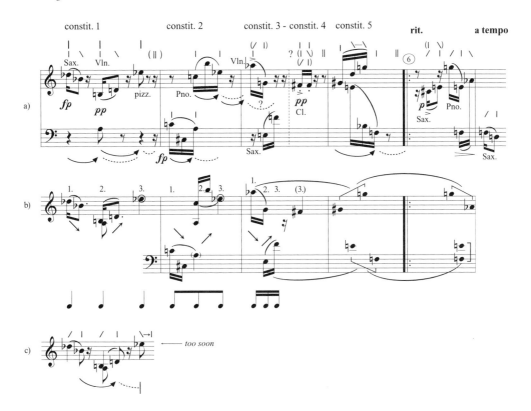

I would now like to consider the tonal and projective progress of the first phrase and its overlapping with the second phrase in more detail. In examples 14.10a and 14.10b I have redrawn bar lines to correspond to the beginnings of our phrase constituents. Although this barring obviously will not serve the needs of the performers, it does no violence to the projective sense of the passage and will simplify our reading.

The first two notes of the phrase are metrically somewhat ambiguous. Although Webern has countered this tendency with his metrical notation and dynamic markings, the first note can easily emerge as anacrusis. However, in the context of the first constituent as a whole, this Db is a beginning, and a "quarter-note" beat emerges. To be sure, two three-note figures in saxophone and violin are here overlapped, but the presence of two events is more apparent to the eye than to the ear, and I suggest that in

hearing three beats we hear three (overlapped) events. Above the duration of the quarter note (here about one second, according to Webern's metronome marking), projective potential is relatively indeterminate. It is not at all clear if this is a measure of 2/4 or 3/4. The projected duration of the quarter note, on the other hand, is highly determinate. As a result, the second constituent enters a sixteenth too late, creating a projective break. This brief hiatus in itself gives some closure to the first constituent—nothing follows that will be a continuation of this constituent. And yet, the hiatus also intensifies the openness of the first constituent for the formation of a larger event. This first constituent is an opening for the piece, and its final event—the single high Eb—is not itself an especially compelling close (unless our attention is focused exclusively on the imitation). If there is openness or the possibility for continuation, and if the third beginning with the pizzicato E♭ has acquired a projected and a projective potential for a quarter-note duration, the delay of the second constituent will be charged with expectation.

Before we turn to the overlapping of the first two constituents, I would like to consider a different metrical interpretation of the first constituent (example 14.10c) and discuss some of the problems this music raises for the performer (and, hence, for this writer and for the reader). If the saxophonist and the violinist lengthen their second notes (the eighth notes B♭ and D) and if the saxophonist plays the A in bar 2 very softly or does not make a clear distinction between forte and piano in bar 1 (as, for example, in the performance by Tashi, RCA ARL1-4730), the sixteenth notes D♭ and B can be felt as anacruses. In this case, the final note, E♭, could be heard as an offbeat or as a beginning projectively detached from the first two events. There will still be a hiatus between the first two constituents (a silence of waiting), but there will be considerably less metrical coherence for the first constituent, and this constituent will have less projective relevance for the second.

How should the passage be performed? I prefer the interpretation shown in example 14.10a, but it must be admitted that even such basic projective distinctions are far from self-evident here. Aside, perhaps, from the uses Webern makes of beaming (often against the bar and against the signature), the metrical notation provides very little information about meter. For example, the signatures in the first phrase—3/8, 5/8, 4/8, 3/8—do not indicate metrical types but, rather, serve to identify four phrase constituents by means of bar lines and to divide the phrase into "readable" units without doing too much violence to its rhythm. Certainly, Webern makes the best use he can of the notational system (and of dynamic and articulation markings), but the system is incapable of both reflecting the metrical complexity of this music and providing the performers with a grid for timing their actions. For this reason, Webern's notation presents considerable problems for the performers. A performance adequate to the metrical subtlety of this music will require playing by ear rather than merely counting and improvisation rather than premeditation. And yet, the problems of coordi-

nating the ensemble will make counting a necessity unless a great amount of rehearsal time can be lavished on the piece (and perhaps, as well, on other pieces by Webern in order to gain an ear for the "style" of this music). Without such preparation for improvisation, opportunities for sharply felt ambiguity can be lost to an anaesthetic reduction of particularity and a tedious homogeneity of tone and meter. To the extent particularity is not felt, tones will become "uniform gray" by being absorbed into an undifferentiated "total chromatic," and metrical distinctions will become submerged in a relatively undifferentiated stream of "attack points." To the extent ambiguities are felt as definite potentials to be affirmed or denied in actualization, we can enjoy a highly rhythmic experience marked by considerable directedness (and redirection) in the formation of phrases.

Let us now return to our closed/open first constituent and its relevance for a successor. Constituent 2 begins with the energy of a delayed connection, renewing projective activity and reducing the duration of the beat by half. If we have heard a quarter-note beat in constituent 1, we can now hear acceleration in a new eighth-note beat. A feeling of acceleration here is strongly supported by the contour and pitch repetitions shown in example 14.10b. Notice that each of the two constituents is composed of three beats: a descending dyad, followed by an (overlapped) ascending dyad, ending with the single pitch E♭. The impression of increased speed and fluency in constituent 2 is further enhanced by contrast with the suspended continuations that lead to closure in the first two beats of constituent 1. In each of these first two beats, the energy of an initial sixteenth note is arrested in a long continuation. In constituent 2 there is an unimpeded flow of sixteenths and a flow that leads to a new constituent.

Now there is no delay—constituent 3 begins as a fourth eighth-note beat. However, projective continuity here should not allow us to ignore the suddenness of this new beginning. In view of the relative closure of constituent 2 vis-à-vis constituent 1 and the projective separation of these first two constituents, the entrance of violin and saxophone seems almost too soon. This new figure is highly compressed, and although I have shown a continuation of the eighth-note beat, the overlapping of violin and saxophone makes this projection less clear than those in constituent 2. The entrance of saxophone in its low register and the coinciding of the two voices on the second sixteenth-note beat of the figure (E – G) will tend to reinterpret the first sixteenth of the violin as anacrusis, as I have shown in parentheses. Notice here that the coinciding of two voices on a second beat is a familiar gesture from the first two constituents — in constituent 1 this happens on the second quarter-note beat (again in saxophone and violin), and in constituent 2 on the second eighth-note beat. I would suggest that this ambiguity in constituent 3 serves to reduce the beat to the sixteenth note for a closing fourth constituent.

The clarinet figure in bar 4 is extraordinarily ambiguous from a projective standpoint. I speculated in chapter 9 that the first of two very brief sounds played in isolation will tend toward anacrusis; that is, all things being equal, we will tend to hear closure (/ |) in such situations rather than indefinitely extended opening (| \) — indefinite because mensural determinacy far exceeds such brief durations. In the case of constituent 4, the first note is dynamically accented to counteract this tendency. And since constituent 3 is projectively too ambiguous to decide the issue, the distinction between beginning and continuation (or, more specifically, anacrusis) for the clarinet is virtually annihilated — in effect, two immediately successive sixteenth-note beginnings, or an undifferentiated sixteenth-note beat! Our attention is now focused on very small units, and projective ambiguity now concerns the metrical grouping of sixteenths rather than eighths (constituent 2) or quarters (constituent 1). If the clarinet figure continues a process of abbreviation and metrical reduction, it also ends this process — there follows a relatively long unmeasured silence, and the final constituent is, by comparison, expanded. This constituent also expands registrally, opening from the registral contraction of constituent 3. The pitch-class repetitions shown in example 14.10b contribute to this feeling of expansion and opening.

The immediate sense of closure effected by the clarinet in bar 4 could be attributed also to two other factors that I feel obliged to consider here: F♯ completes the chromatic and is the midpoint or "axis" of a registral symmetry formed by all the pitches of the phrase. These are undeniable facts, as is, I think, the feeling of relative closure in bar 4. However, I maintain that these special features of the pitch F♯, though doubtless significant for Webern, have little, if any, bearing on closure. I know this assertion will find resistance in many quarters, and certainly I cannot prove that these intervallic relationships that can be ascribed to F♯ are not the principal cause of closure. But neither, I think, can proof be offered to support such a claim. Will a feeling of closure be greatly diminished if we substitute F♯3 or E4 for F♯4? Certainly, the choice of F♯4 has consequences for the particularity of this closure. We may indeed sense a convergence of the violin and saxophone lines in this pitch, a half step below G and a half step above F, and perhaps even sense something resembling a "tonicization" of F♯. (Incidentally, I would ask the reader to play or sing a B♮ after this F♯ to test the "focal" quality of the tone.) These connections certainly contribute to the continuity of a single gesture in Webern's bar 4. But whether this F♯ is also heard to be the "center" of the entire phrase or the midpoint of the other constituents cannot be so easily determined. (This is, of course, not to say that this particular "symmetry" does not contribute to the intervallic particularity of pitches.)

A better case might be made for chromatic closure. The intervallic homogeneity of the "total chromatic" argues for tonal closure with F♯, as does Webern's statement in his essay "The Path to Composition with Twelve Tones" (in Webern 1963) that, prior to working with the twelve-tone method, he was aware of the closure associated with the completion of the chromatic. Speaking of the composition of the Bagatelles for String Quartet, op. 9, Webern writes: "Here I had the feeling: When the twelve tones have elapsed, the piece is ended" (1963, p. 51). On the thesis of chromatic homogeneity, the F♯ in bar 4 will neutralize tonal particularity and thus reduce tonal potential to zero; that is to say, the presence of all pitch classes is equivalent to the presence of a single pitch and thus results in a dissolution of tonal potential — a genuine *a*tonality. However, I would argue that it is too late for F♯ to accomplish this—that more or less definite tonal potentials have already functioned for the becoming of the phrase and cannot now be brought to naught. Moreover, I argue that the brokenness of the projective field is a compositional necessity that serves to diversify the chromatic and thus to assure the tonal particularity of pitches—that is, precisely to avert homogeneity. I do not deny the sincerity of Webern's statement or the truth of his musical intuition, but would suggest that a choice of pitches that complete the chromatic might arise from an aversion to repetition and from the novelty and freshness of pitches that have not recently been sounded. In the continuation of the passage quoted above, Webern writes: "In my sketchbook I wrote out the chromatic scale and crossed off the individual tones.—Why?—Because I convinced myself: this tone was already there." Indeed, Webern's habit of "crossing out" itself may cast some doubt on the aesthetic force of such closure.

After the close on F♯ in bar 4, constituent 5 might well function to begin a new phrase. However, it is prevented from so functioning by the saxophone in bars 6 and 7, which, by repeating the minor thirds of bars 1–2, clearly marks a new phrase as a beginning again. If this Janus-faced piano figure in bar 5 is thereby brought into the sphere of the first phrase to articulate an ending, its gesture of opening also promises continuation, in a manner analogous, perhaps, to a half-cadence.[2] As is shown in example 14.10b, the overlapping of the new phrase in bars 5 and 6 involves a repetition of pitches in the two piano figures (and not merely pitch classes, as in the connection of constituents 3+4 and 5). The "ritardando . . . a tempo" also serves the overlapping, as does the piano figure in bar 6, which clearly resembles constituent 3.

An important factor in this overlapping, but one that for all its obviousness might easily be overlooked, is the gradual emergence of a new

instrumental and rhythmic texture. (See example 14.11.)[3] In this repeated second phrase beginning with bar 6, there are virtually no silences (no hiatus) except for that preceding the "cadential" piano figure in bar 15, and constituents are continuously overlapped. Continuous also is the long line played by the saxophone—a focal *Hauptstimme* accompanied by the other instruments. There are now three "instruments": saxophone, piano, and violin/clarinet. And although instrumental alternations are much more rapid than in the first phrase and the character of the music is more agitated, larger constituents emerge. In fact, the three events I have identified in example 14.11a might now more appropriately be called small phrases.

To find our way through the complexities of the second large phrase, it will be helpful first to make some general observations. The articulation of three overlapping small phrases is accomplished by the combination of two factors: the immediate projective reinterpretations that occur in the saxophone at the end of bar 8 (\ → |) and at the beginning of bar 12 (\ → |), and the gradual emergence of "motivic" repetitions in (small) phrases 2 and 3. These distinctions can be more easily seen in example 14.11b, where I have attached motivic labels (lowercase letters) to the two- and three-note figures of the saxophone line and aligned phrase 3 beneath phrase 2 to show the correspondences. These two- and three-note figures (drawn from bars 1–5) are combined with small figures in the remainder of the ensemble to form the phrase constituents shown in example 14.11a. In each case, the saxophone initiates the constituent that is completed by the "accompaniment"—usually a three-note figure closely resembling constituent 4 from the first large phrase.

Although much could be gained from a closer analysis, it will suffice here to comment on several of the projective decisions that enliven the rhythm of this phrase. In example

---

2. For a different reading of this passage and for a list of other published analyses of Webern's op. 22/I, see Mead 1993.

3. As in example 14.10, in example 14.11 bar lines have been redrawn in order to show more clearly the articula-

tion of small phrases and their constituents. The violin, clarinet, and piano parts are here reduced to two staves beneath the saxophone *Hauptstimme*. To conserve space, I have not in this case included a reproduction of the score. I have, however, indicated the position of Webern's bar numbers to facilitate a comparison with the score.

EXAMPLE 14.11 Anton von Webern, Quartet, op. 22, first movement, (**a**) bs. 6–15. Copyright © 1932 by Universal Edition. © Copyright renewed. All rights reserved. Used by permission of European American Music Distributors Corporation, sole U.S. and Canadian agent for Universal Edition; (**b**) motivic analysis of phrases 1–3.

Continued

EXAMPLE 14.11 (*continued*)

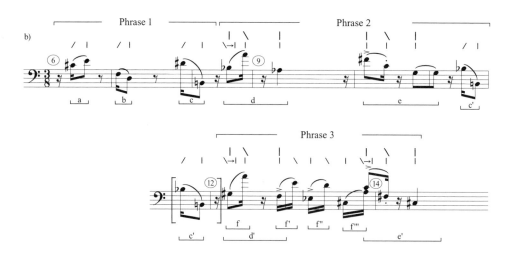

14.11a I have provided a fairly detailed labeling of projective distinctions. The phrase begins with an especially poignant ambiguity in the saxophone's opening dyad (a). Because of the ritardando and the fresh relevance of the saxophone dyad from bar 1 (there forte piano) we will be inclined to hear the C♯ as beginning rather than anacrusis. However, as the phrase develops, the first notes of the following saxophone dyads in bars 7 (b) and 8 (c) will come to be heard as anacruses, and as a result we may well be inclined to reinterpret the figure in bar 6(a) in the present of the small phrase. The effect of such a reinterpretation, though subtle, is far from negligible—as tempo is regained in bar 7 the projections of the small phrase will coalesce as we are led into the opening of a new large phrase. (Here again, I would ask the reader to listen very attentively to an accurate performance of the piece.) Somewhat oversimplifying this process, I have indicated from the beginning of the phrase a repeated "pure unequal" measure of 2+3/16 (in bars 6–7) made especially mobile by a maximization of anacrustic potential. (Note, too, that, for reasons discussed at the end of chapter 9, the unequal "2+3" measures will inhibit the formation of strong projective potentials.) On this interpretation, the third and final constituent/measure is interrupted by a new constituent and new measure beginning with figure d in bar 8.

Since there is little evidence of closure in the first small phrase, the new constituent (d) might be incorporated into the first phrase as an interruptive fourth constituent. It will take some time for this constituent to become the beginning of a second phrase. Only when a second phrase actually emerges as a new becoming will the constituent initiated with figure d be a new beginning. This occurs with the formation of a constituent e in bar 10, which "answers" d projectively as a three-note figure introducing a new eighth-note beat. Notice also the urgency with which figures d and e in the saxophone are joined by the small unequal measure (3/16) formed by clarinet and violin at the end of bar 9. Following figure e in the saxophone, the "accompaniment" continues an eighth-note (and possibly, a quarter-note) beat to mesh with figure c' in the saxophone. This projective continuity promises the absorption of figure c' into the second small phrase. This promise is fulfilled when a new small phrase begins with a second projective reinterpretation in the saxophone in bar 12. Notice here that the second phrase ends in a sort of rhyme (c-c') with the end of the first phrase (each closing on low B in saxophone).

Because of the rhyming of the end constituents c and c' the new phrase begun in bar 12 can become detached from the second phrase as soon as the saxophone's G♯ is reinterpreted as a projective beginning. However, the correspondence of this phrase to its predecessor shown in example 14.11b does not become entirely clear until the end of the phrase. Just as evidence of a third phrase (a beginning again with d') emerges, there also emerges a peculiar overlapping within the new phrase that temporarily obscures the relevance of phrase 2 (and figure d). Although the continuation of the saxophone's line in bar 13 supports the reinterpretation of the G♯ in bar 12 as a projective beginning, this continuation also reinterprets the trichordal segmentation (G♯–A♮–F) of figure d' in bar 12. Now it appears that the line is composed of an accelerated succession of dyads (figure f). This reinterpretation effects an overlapping within the third phrase. The clarinet now takes over the dyad sequence (C♯–A) from the saxophone, and the saxophone reemerges with a striking projective interruption (\ ⇢ |) in bar 13 supported by the piano in bar 14. The interruptive three-note figure in the saxophone (e') now reestablishes the correspondence with the second phrase shown in example 14.11b: d, e / d', e'. This is a correspondence promised by the initial trichordal segmentation of bar 12 (i.e., d' rather than f).

Now, for the first time in the large phrase, there is a projective hiatus—a slight break at the end of phrase 3—followed in bar 15 by a version of the "cadential" figure we observed in bar 5. Although this final constituent does not continue the process that is completed with the saxophone's figure e', it nevertheless belongs to the large phrase as an echo (transposed) of the saxophone's closing figure and as a repetition of the piano's "three-note" closing figure that overlaps the saxophone in bar 14. (It is largely because of this latter repetition that the figure in bar 15 receives the projective interpretation I have indicated in example 14.11a.) Notice also that, unlike the final constituent of the first large phrase in bar 5, the figure in bar 15 has no *pitches* in common with the first piano figure in bar 6 (only pitch classes).

In the preceding analysis I did not consider row forms, and I did not discuss tonal relations in any detail. Rectifying the latter omission would shed much more light on the rhythm of the piece and would considerably enhance our understanding of projections (as would a careful consideration of pitch contours). An analysis of row forms and their relations might reveal some-

thing of Webern's intentions and his compositional procedure and would, in any case, lead to an appreciation of the constraints under which he worked. Certainly, an analysis of serial relations may be useful in our efforts to discover tonal potentials and tonal functions, and in gaining an appreciation of correspondences and repetitions in the work we can hardly ignore the repetitions of rows and row segments. However, I do not believe that an analysis of row structure per se is likely to shed much light on the question of rhythm. Conceived as a systematic totality, row structure presents us with a largely determinate order for the organization of pitches and pitch classes. This is not to say that an analysis of rows must ignore other domains (though in practice these other domains are generally treated as secondary). It is to say, however, that indeterminacy and the vagaries of becoming can easily be replaced by a static being in which elements and relations are fixed in the whole they constitute. There is emergence—the piece unfolds "in time"—but this is the emergence of a preformed whole enfolded in the prior act of composition (or perhaps even in "precomposition"). What cannot so easily be captured with the concept of structure is performance, or the actual process through which a musical whole is formed in experience.

It is a general feature of analysis that musical process tends to be represented by (and thence reduced to) terms of a static arrangement and that tonal or pitch relations come to be treated as the primary cause of musical intelligibility and order. That this latter tendency has been especially prevalent in the analysis of so-called "atonal" or "posttonal" music and "twelve-tone" music may have some connection to the loss of tonal determinacies that had informed the theory and practice of earlier styles. It is perhaps understandable that a weakening of tonal potential should have created very strong anxieties concerning pitch and interval on the part of some theorists and composers, and, in some cases, overcompensation for a practical (and conceptual) loss of determinacy. But whatever the causes of this fascination with pitch, I would argue that meter is no less important for the intelligibility and coherence of Webern's twelve-tone music. I have attempted to demonstrate this importance in the preceding analysis of bars 1–15 of the Quartet, but to catch a glimpse of the importance of rhythmic distinctions for Webern's compositional labor, I would like to examine a few of his sketches for an unfinished movement that was to be part of opus 22. In order to provide a more general context for this analysis I would first like to consider, very briefly, Webern's conception of the determinacy provided by the row.

In his collection of lectures published as *Wege zur neuen Musik*, Webern identifies "two paths to 12-tone composition," two types of law. These two types are *Materialgesetze* and *Darstellungsgesetze*—laws of material and laws of presentation.[4] *Reihengesetze* are the particular material laws that govern the structure of rows and the structural possibilities for combining row forms. However, when he uses the singular form, *Reihengesetz*, Webern often means an ideal lawfulness. The row guarantees the unity of the composition, but "row" here does not refer to any particular row or even to the total arrangement of row forms. It is, rather, an immanent organizing principle, real as manifested in particular rows and ideal as transcending any particular form. Unity does not arise from a systematic order of pitch elements and relations, but from a continuously expanding gesture of repetition and development. Although the row may form part of the material of this gesture, the notion of material is not limited to pitches and intervals abstracted from other domains. In a letter to Hildegard Jone describing the form of his Variations, op. 30, Webern traces a process begun with six notes, or rather the particular gestalt formed by these notes:

> Imagine this: 6 notes are given, in a *shape* determined by the sequence and the rhythm, and what follows (in the whole length of this piece lasting about 20 minutes) is nothing other than this shape

over and over again!!! Naturally in continual "metamorphosis" (in musical terms this process is called "variation")—but it is nevertheless the same every time.

Goethe says of the "*Urphänomen*":

> ideal as the limit to what can be apprehended,
> real as apprehended (*),
> symbolic because it comprehends all instances,
> identical with all instances (**)
>
> (ideal als das letzte Erkennbare,
> real als erkannt,
> symbolisch, weil es alle Fälle begreift,
> identisch mit allen Fälle)

(*) In my piece that is what it is, *namely the shape mentioned above*! (The comparison serves only to clarify the *process*).
(**) Namely in my piece! That is what it does!

> First this *shape* becomes the "theme" and then there follow 6 variations of this theme. But the "theme" itself consists, as I said, of nothing but variations (metamorphoses of this first shape). Then as a *unit* it becomes the point of departure for fresh variations. . . . Such and such a number of metamorphoses of the first shape constitute the "theme." This, as a new unit, passes again through such and such a number of metamorphoses; these again, fused into a new unit, constitute the form of the whole. Thus, roughly, the shape of the whole piece. (Webern 1959, p. 47)

Although Webern insists that "composing with twelve-tones" is a spontaneous and necessary historical development, he recognizes that the total chromatic presents a truly new material and that the new laws for the material are not connected to the old laws (beyond certain acoustical givens). What bridges this gap are the laws of presentation. These are very general laws governing the form of music and ensuring its *comprehensibility* ("the highest law of all"). If the laws of the material are laws of "what," the laws

---

4. The productive, dialectical relationship of material and presentation is a central thesis of Webern's lectures, forming the basis for a construction of music history that would make twelve-tone composition a natural or spontaneous development of Western musical tradition. A concise statement of this dialectic also appears in Webern's May 3rd, 1941, letter to Willi Reich, which is appended to *The Path to the New Music* (Webern 1963, pp. 61–62). For an insightful discussion of Webern's understanding of the row and a more detailed analysis of the two "paths" than we shall undertake here, see Zuber 1984.

EXAMPLE 14.12 Rows "III" and "II" extracted from Webern's sketches for an uncompleted variation movement for the Quartet, op. 22

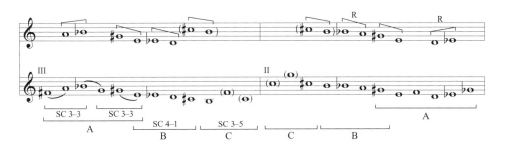

of presentation are laws of "how"—they concern the ways in which the constituent parts of a composition are articulated and held together. Webern identifies many types of presentation—for example, motivic connection, developing variation, imitation, the differentiation of melody and accompaniment, "pure polyphony." Although these diverse types do not appear in all musical epochs, Webern maintains that the laws of presentation are, in essence, universal—in their most basic forms (repetition, contrast, development, phrase articulation), these procedures are to be found in all music. Stylistic diversity arises as the fundamental laws of presentation are adapted to changing materials. For Webern the variable laws of an ever-changing material and the universal but flexible laws of presentation (universal precisely because of the *limits* of human understanding) create through their dialectical relationship the continuity of musical tradition. Therefore, we must take Webern at his word when he writes, echoing Schoenberg, "one composes as before, but on the basis of the row; on the basis of this fixed series one will have to invent" (Webern 1963, p. 53):

> Until now, tonality has been one of the most important means of establishing unity. It is the only one of the old achievements that has disappeared; everything else is still there.

> We want to say "in quite a new way" what has been said before. But now I can invent more freely; everything has a deeper unity. Only now is it possible to compose in free fantasy, adhering to nothing except the row. To put it quite paradoxically, only through these unprecedented fetters has

complete freedom become possible. (Webern 1963, pp. 42, 55–56)

If this "deeper unity" is to be "given" by the row, it must be taken in an act of selecting from the myriad possibilities contained in a fixed series of pitch classes those that will serve rhythm. We can observe some traces of this act in sketches for the beginning of a movement that Webern intended to include in the Quartet, op. 22. On August 20, 1930, six days after completing what was to become the first movement, Webern began work on a new movement, which was to occupy him for the next three weeks. Eight pages of sketches (plates 25–32 in Moldenhauer 1968) document Webern's composition of a phrase that was apparently conceived as the "theme" for a set of variations to be placed as the first movement of op. 22.

I count nineteen versions of the phrase altogether, though there are often variants attached to these versions. From these sketches I have selected six for close analysis—by my count, version nos. 1, 2, 7, 11, 16, and 19. To facilitate comparison with the notebook, correspondences with Webern (1968) are as follows: plate 25, nos. 1, 2, and 7; plate 27, no. 11; plate 32, no. 16; plate 31, no. 19. (See also Smalley 1975 for faithful transcriptions of all the sketches we shall consider here.) In examples 14.13 and 14.14 are transcriptions of what appear to be the first two versions of the "theme." In each case I have added a rudimentary projective and constituent analysis.

Example 14.12 is a representation of the two row forms employed here, labeled "III" and "II" by Webern in the sketches. The second row

EXAMPLE 14.13 Version no. 1 [on Plate 25], from Anton von Webern, Sketches (1926−1945). Copyright © 1968 by Carl Fischer, Inc., New York. All rights reserved. Reprinted by permission.

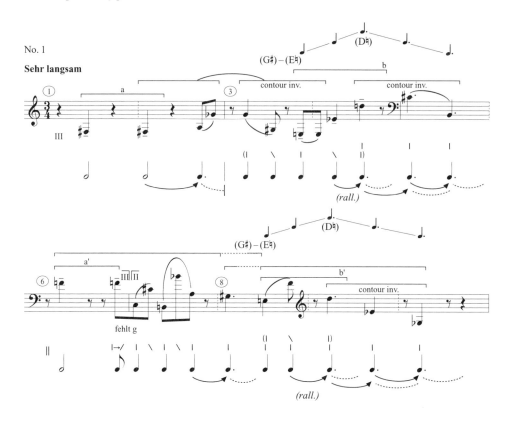

form is a retrograde inversion of the first which returns to F♯ (G♭). In his composition of the saxophone line, Webern chose to fix the registers of the twelve pitch classes and to omit several pitches from the line, reserving them for piano. In no. 1, G is missing, and in the revision of no. 2 reproduced here, F, C, and G are excluded. I would like to suggest one possible motivation for these omissions.

The row presents three relatively distinct intervallic groups: roughly stated, the first few pitches expose "thirds," pitches 6−9 form a chromatic segment, and the last three (an instance of set class 3−5) present the intervals of "fourth" and tritone. This last group is especially distinctive and, as we observed above, functions in the first movement as a "cadential" figure — that is, a figure that marks the end of the row and the ends of phrases. This intervallic heterogeneity can make "the row" recognizable as a unit

with a relatively distinct beginning, middle, and end. In the first movement such distinctiveness characterizes the first and third large phrases and serves to contrast phrases 1 and 3 with phrases 2 and 4 where phrase articulations cut across these boundaries. In the sketches we are now considering (examples 14.13 and ex. 14.14), Webern's omission of pitches eliminates the distinctive 3−5 trichord to produce a more continuous and homogeneous line. There is a tritone in no. 1 (B−F), but the F in bar 6 is detached from the preceding B as a beginning again. In no. 2, F is eliminated. Reserving the pitches F, C, and G for the piano will also have other consequences for the articulation of the phrase. Doubtless, Webern was aware of these possibilities and had already decided on the two row forms he would use for the "accompaniment."

In examples 14.13 and 14.14 I have indicated several correspondences among constituents.

EXAMPLE 14.14 Version no. 2 [on Plate 25], from Anton von
Webern, Sketches (1926–1945). Copyright © 1968 by Carl Fischer,
Inc., New York. All rights reserved. Reprinted by permission.

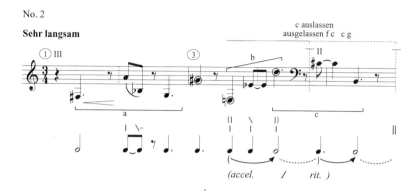

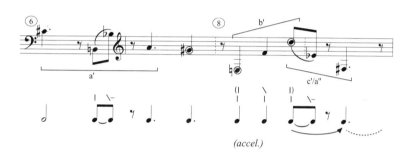

However, at this stage possibilities for segmentation are quite open, and without the "accompaniment" and a clearer determination of projective potentials it is difficult to develop a satisfactory analysis of small constituents and their
rhythmic functions. Although I cannot speculate
on how Webern may have felt projective potentials (or, indeed, at this early stage of sketching,
how clearly he had yet come to feel such potentials), I have indicated continuities and discontinuities in the succession of beats and in some
cases have ventured an interpretation of metrical
accent. (The distinction between solid and dotted bar lines is Webern's.) But even if an analysis
of small constituents is problematic, we can, nevertheless, draw some conclusions regarding the
general shape of the phrase in these two versions. Incidentally, I should point out that the
possibility of hearing the retrograde relation of
the two row forms is excluded here, in part be-

cause of the "givens" of the row layout. Example
14.12 shows above the two row forms the ordered repetition of three dyads, a repetition
made more palpable by the fixing of registers.

In no. 1 (example 14.13) there is a very clear
two-part division—a compressed and relatively
energetic beginning again in bar 6 signaled by
the immediate pitch repetition (figures a and a'),
and an end rhyme created by the two components labeled "b" and "b'." The projective and
constituent analysis shown in the example should
be more or less self-explanatory, and I will not
pursue a more detailed analysis of this phrase. I
would only note here the close interaction of
duration, pitch, register, and contour in the articulation of this two-part rhythmic gesture.

Phrase articulation in version no. 2 (example
14.14) is less clear. If the pitches C♯ and B in bars
4–5 are connected to the preceding constituent
as in version no. 1, the large phrase will offer nu-

No. 7

Sehr langsam

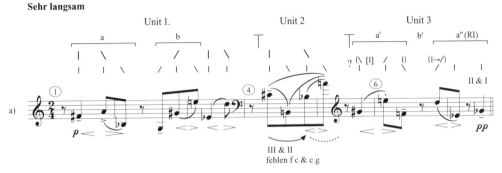

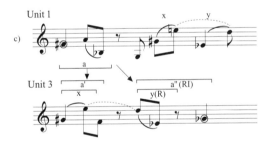

merous possibilities for the overlapping of constituents. In this case, a second phrase will begin with bar 6 in an overlapping with the end of the first phrase. This second phrase begins with a contour inversion of bars 1–2 (a and a') and repeats the durational pattern of the first phrase, overlapping this repetition with a final constituent, c', that accelerates constituent c in a rhythmic figure that recalls the last three beats of figures a and a'. On the other hand, Webern may have intended to break the phrase with the initial C♯–B in bars 4–5, in which case this small constituent could serve either to separate the two small phrases begun with a and a' or to begin a second phrase (bars 4–9). In succeeding

versions Webern will choose to break the phrase and will try out both of these possibilities.

In versions 3–6, Webern experiments with various rhythmic adjustments and meter signatures (4/4, 5/16, 2/2, and 2/4). This initial stage of sketching ends with version no. 7 (example 14.15), a determination of a saxophone *Hauptstimme* that remains unaltered in the following five versions.

The phrase is now divided into three parts but retains some feeling of two phrases in the correspondence of parts 1 and 3. For the second constituent ("unit 2" in example 14.15) Webern has indicated in this sketch three different articulations: two two-note slurs, a three-note slur isolating the first note, and a four-note slur. Were a three-note slur chosen, the ascending eighth-note figure (B−B♭−A) in bars 4−5 could be heard to repeat the beginning of the constituent I have labeled "b." As is shown in example 14.15b, this correspondence could serve an overlapping of the three units. However, Webern finally chooses two-note slurs. The result of this decision, I think, is to separate unit 2 from units 1 and 3, and in the next three versions this separation is underscored by the piano. In light of this articulation we might call units 1 and 3 small phrases.

The "two parts" of no. 7 (units 1 and 3) do not, however, exhibit the sort of clear correspondence we observed in the small phrases of version nos. 1 and 2, largely because of projective asymmetry. Although Webern has notated the figures in bars 1−4 as syncopations and metrical "displacements," a continuous series of quarter-note measures and perhaps even half-note measures will tend to arise here. Indeed, Webern's beamings and articulation markings generally support such a projective continuity. In any case, this degree of regularity contrasts sharply with the projective diversity of version nos. 1 and 2, in which metrical differentiation was used to support a fairly clear antecedent-consequent relation in the two small phrases. If in no. 7 the placement of bar lines does not reveal an underlying evenness in the projective course of units 1 and 2, neither does it very clearly show the considerable ambiguity of unit 3. Although I have ventured a projective interpretation of this unit, the choices are not so clear-cut. The result of this ambiguity for the rhythm of the phrase is, I believe, to create a highly compressed "consequent" to unit 1 whose resemblance to that unit is palpable but not at all obvious. Even if the figure labeled "a'" in unit 3 were clearly a projective repetition of figure a in unit 1, the coupling of a' and a" would unsettle a sense of obvious repetition. Constituent a' repeats the contour and duration pattern of a, and a" is a retrograde inversion of a (now taking advantage of the relation of the row forms). Since unit 3 shares four pitches with constituent b of unit 1, it can also repeat aspects of this second constituent of unit 1. In example 14.15c I have indicated a sort of compression of unit 1 in unit

3. All of these correspondences contribute to the closure of the large phrase in the return to F♯ (G♭).

In the next set of sketches, Webern composed a piano accompaniment made up of sixteenth-note "offbeats" to the saxophone *Hauptstimme* of version no. 7. After several revisions of the piano part, Webern arrived at a finished version (*gilt*) in no. 11 and began sketching the first variation. Example 14.16 shows only the "theme." In general, the piano supports our constituent analysis of version no. 7, as well as the abbreviation and compression we noted in the second small phrase—unit 3. However, as we shall soon see, the piano part of version no. 11 also opens a new possibility for the form of the large phrase.

In terms of row layout, the piano plays row II against the saxophone's row III in the first half of the phrase and then row III against the saxophone's row II in the second half. (Row indications in example 14.16 are Webern's.) In unit 2 the piano takes the pitches missing from the *Hauptstimme* (C-G and F-C) to synthesize a new form of set class 3−5 (G−C−F♯, a form of row segment "C" in example 14.12) and a new trichordal sonority, set class 3−8 (G−C−F), not heard within the row. At the end of the phrase set class 3−5 appears again (now as the last three notes of row III), and Webern manufactures a corresponding form of 3−8 by introducing a new row form starting on F (a transposed retrograde of row III labeled "28" by Webern continued in the first variation). This repetition of trichord pairs 3−5 and 3−8 unsettles the symmetry of two complementary small phrases (units 1 and 3) articulated by a "middle" segment (unit 2). Although the piano figure in bars 4 and 7 could well function to mark the ending of two small phrases—units 1+2 and unit 3—there is also a tendency for the two piano figures to begin and end a second small phrase as a sort of frame for the *Hauptstimme* in bars 5−7. This latter possibility will become more explicit in versions 16−19.

There is also considerable metrical ambiguity in this passage. Although the saxophone line will tend to dominate in the distinction between eighth-note beat and sixteenth-note offbeat, these distinctions are not always entirely clear, particularly in bars 3 and 5, where the saxo-

EXAMPLE 14.16 Version no. 11 [on Plate 27], from Anton von Webern, Sketches (1926–1945). Copyright © 1968 by Carl Fischer, Inc., New York. All rights reserved. Reprinted by permission.

No. 11

Langsam

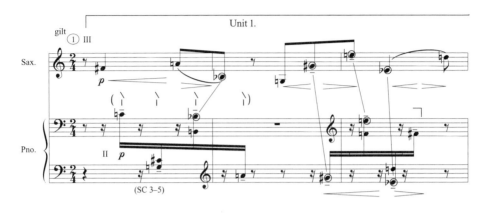

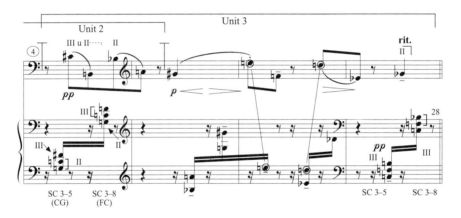

phone sustains a comparatively long quarter-note duration. The difference of timbre and the "regularity" of the piano will contribute to this ambiguity, as will pitch relations. Notice, for example, the effect of pitch repetition between the two instruments made possible by the invariance of dyads in rows III and II shown above the row forms in example 14.12 (A–B♭, G♯–E, and E♭–D). In example 14.16 I have circled the immediate repetitions to show the alternations of saxophone and piano in taking the first of these pitches.

This tension between hearing highly charged offbeat "suspensions" in the piano and hearing

eighth-note "piano beats" sporadically surface is very effective in sustaining continuous rhythmic energy throughout the phrase. However, as a result of this ambiguity, mensural determinacy is greatly reduced, as is the variety of projective engagements. Coupled with the general flatness of register, this degree of projective homogeneity has a rather mechanical effect, which may perhaps have contributed to Webern's later dissatisfaction with the rhythmic texture he had so carefully developed in version no. 11. In any case, following a revision of no. 11 that lightens the piano part with grace notes, Webern abandoned this conception of the phrase in no. 13

EXAMPLE 14.17 Version no. 16 [on Plate 32], from Anton von
Webern, Sketches (1926–1945). Copyright © 1968 by Carl
Fischer, Inc., New York. All rights reserved. Reprinted by
permission.

N. 16

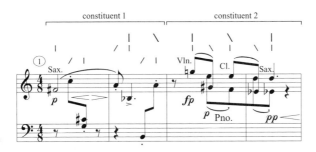

(August 27) and began altering the *Hauptstimme*,
distributing the line among all the instruments
and experimenting with novel phrase articulations. As Roger Smalley (1975) suggests, Webern's aim was now to break down the rigid
melody and accompaniment texture and create a
more integrated ensemble. In no. 14 (August 29)
Webern returned to saxophone and piano but
radically altered the saxophone line and introduced considerable metrical ambiguity in the
Hauptstimme itself. The next complete version to
appear in the notebook is dated September 9
and is very close to the final version (again
marked *gilt*) composed the following day. These
two versions are shown in examples 14.17 and
14.18 in a reduction to two staves.

Apart from the change of meter signature,
the most conspicuous alterations of version no.
16 involve the notes of bars 3 and 4, which are
lowered in register in no. 19 (the first note, G,

by two octaves), and the group of overlapping
2-note figures in bars 7 and 8, which in no. 19
(bar 6) is compressed in duration. This registral
change in version no. 19 is, by the way, Webern's
first departure from the rule of fixed register.
Note also two other changes: the B♭ in bar 2 of
no. 16 is transferred from saxophone to piano in
no. 19, and in no. 19 the violin plays its first two
notes (G – A♭) *pizzicato* rather than arco. As we
shall see, these changes create a far tighter and
livelier phrase in version no. 19. In order to facilitate our analysis of this final version, I have labeled two types of constituent based on the distinction between long and short: "A" labels a
composite of a long two-note figure and a short
two-note figure, and "B" labels a composite of
overlapping short two-note figures.

The large phrase is now divided more or less
clearly into two small phrases marked by a brief
hiatus in bar 4. In the second small phrase the

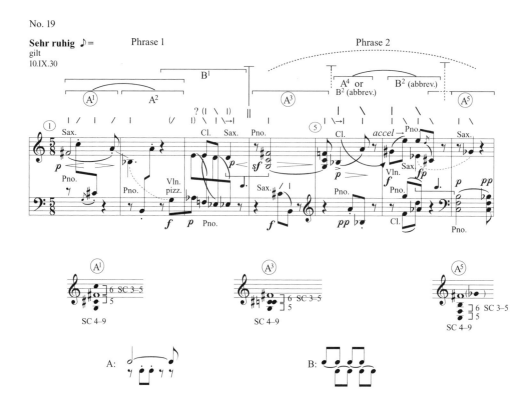

"frame" created by the figures A³ and A⁵ serves to isolate a "middle" constituent in bars 5–6. Notice that this constituent, flanked by A³ and A⁵, could itself be heard as a compressed and abbreviated repetition of the first small phrase. The clarinet/piano figure in bar 5 (A⁴) resembles the saxophone/piano figure in bar 1 (A¹), and yet it also becomes assimilated to the figure labeled "B²" in bar 6. Adding to the complexity of overlapping here, the correspondence of A¹ and A³ (reversing piano and saxophone as "middle") urges a correspondence of A² and A⁴.

Version no. 19 is projectively more complicated than version no. 16, presenting novel ambiguities that serve the larger rhythmic gesture of the phrase. To trace this gesture, let us now follow some of the projective distinctions that emerge with the articulation of the phrase. The last note of bar 1 (the pitch A) becomes anacrusis with the beginning of bar 2. Since in bar 1

there is no articulation of a fourth (eighth-note) beat and no clear beginning for which this "fifth" beat might be a projective continuation, I would draw attention to a feeling of projective "suspension" here. Webern's notation of 5/8 is quite appropriate and continues to inform version no. 19 in its departures from no. 16. As a result of the changes made in version no. 19 (i.e., giving the B♭ to the piano in bar 2 and lowering the violin by two octaves) the pizzicato G in the violin can now form the interval of a minor third with the piano's B♭, thereby echoing the minor third F♯ – A in saxophone and forming a repetition of figure A¹ in the figure A². As I have shown in example 14.18, these changes in no. 19 create an overlapping of two constituents that in no. 16 were clearly separated. As a result of this overlapping (and changes of register, etc.), projective distinctions in constituent B¹ of version no. 19 are much less clear than those of constituent 2 of no. 16. (Incidentally, the dynamic marking of forte given to the pizzicato G at the end of bar 2 in no. 19 will not suffice in this context to create an unambiguous projective beginning.) In the absence of a clear metrical grouping of eighths in constituent B^1, there will be an unmeasured duration or hiatus separating this component from the following small phrase begun with A^3.

If at the end of constituent A^3 the second chord of the piano in bar 5 is not clearly anacrustic, the following B♭ in clarinet will be reinterpreted as a projective beginning, and such reinterpretation will further serve to join the figures in bars 5 and 6 as a single constituent (B^2). In terms of projection, this is by far the least ambiguous constituent and the only constituent thus far to present a relatively clear quarter-note beat. As a result, the registral and dynamic climax in bar 6 will be accompanied by sudden rhythmic fluency in a highly compressed and accelerated gesture closely overlapped with figure A^5. Notice, by comparison, the relatively tame equilibrium of version no. 16, where bars 7−8 repeat bars 3−4 in register, dynamics, and projective activity.

In following Webern's labor of giving shape to the given pitch-class "material" in these few sketches, we should have no illusions of having followed Webern's thought process—much less of having divined his "compositional intent." And yet, in a much broader and, I think, truer sense, we have followed his intent, which was to work with this phrase until it satisfied him with its particular "comprehensibility" or beauty— when it seemed finished enough to warrant a *gilt*. Why Webern abandoned this movement we shall likely never know. Nor shall we likely know how many versions preceded a finished form of the two phrases of the first movement (bars 1−15) with which we began our analysis. It should be clear, however, that no less care was taken in the shaping of projective process and that, in general, a keen sensitivity to projective distinctions was inseparable from Webern's "feeling of form."

From the listener's or the player's point of view, it must be said that projective determinacy in the Quartet is often highly attenuated, and to feel the distinctions and the contrasts I have suggested (or distinctions I have not suggested) will require a concentrated act of attention. If there is

any lapse in attentiveness, this music may appear nonmetrical. But I believe that to the extent we do not perceive metrical distinctions, we will be deaf to a rhythm and a beauty Webern painstakingly sought to achieve. This is not to deny that there can be nonmetrical music or to suggest that such music is inferior to a music whose rhythm is informed by meter. And in the conclusion of this study I will briefly consider some of the aesthetic consequences of an abandonment of projective activity in the creation of a nonmetrical yet fully rhythmic musical experience. This turn in compositional practice, though not without precedents, took place in the two decades following Webern's death and, at least in its early stage, appears to have been inspired by Webern's example. But before turning to this development, I would like to consider a highly metrical composition by Milton Babbitt, which presents analytic problems we did not encounter in the Webern.

Babbitt, Du

In op. 22, and in most of Webern's twelve-tone music, a constant "smallest value" broken by hiatus (and sometimes lost in a larger beat) serves as a basis for metrical groupings, much like the "beats" of the Renaissance tactus, only much smaller and more evanescent. As inadequate as traditional notation proved in representing to the performer the complex projective groupings of these units of duration, it nevertheless provided a representational system in which notated pulses could often be felt as beats. However, in much twentieth-century music notated pulses and their subdivisions often do not correspond to beats. In such cases conventional notation can be used to indicate with great precision variations in pulse (rubato, acceleration, and deceleration) that cannot be so precisely indicated with more conventional uses of the notation. The opening of "Wankelmut," the second song from Babbitt's cycle *Du* (1951), illustrates such a practice (see example 14.19).

The song begins in bar 15 with a gesture that is metrically much more comprehensible than it looks. My renotation of this bar, though not so precise, produces a result that I think is quite similar to that produced by Babbitt's notation— anacrusis to a "dotted" figure and an accelerated

EXAMPLE 14.19 Milton Babbitt, Du, "Wankelmut," bs. 15–22. Copyright © 1957 by Boelke-Bomart, Inc. Reprinted by permission.

II. Wankelmut

quarter-note pulse. The beginning with F, of course, "becomes" anacrusis only when there *is* a beat begun with C♯, made past with the final D. Similarly, the arrangement of so-called "stresses" in the verbal phrase "Mein Suchen sucht!" emerges only when there is a phrase.

I have chosen an example with text to facilitate our analysis. But although the text enhances the determinacy of this projection, it does not produce it—our feeling of projection would be much the same if this figure were sung on "la." Again, the flexibility of mensural determinacy frees projective activity from the narrow confines of "precise" equality. But, again, this flexibility should not be equated with imprecision. The very precisely felt processes of acceleration and deceleration and feelings of early and late that can arise from relatively minute differences in duration attest to a very fine discrimination of durational quantity and to the efficacy of such discrimination in the perception of projective potentials.

David Lewin (1981) cites an experiment performed by Jeanne Bamberger that seems to illustrate the assimilation of inequality to a determination of projective potential (note especially the perception of anacrusis in the incomplete "4/4 bar" with which the series begins):

A sound synthesizer had been programmed to generate a series of identical pulses, separated by successive durations of 2, 3, 4, and 5 time units, at a brisk tempo. The listener expected to respond to the stimulus as an ametrical phenomenon, simply following the acoustic pattern symbolized by (5.1).

(5.1)

Instead, he was surprised to discover, in his own perception, a very strong metric response to the stimulus, which he "heard" as in (5.2).

Bamberger herself experienced the sense of (5.2) strongly, and I think it is reasonable to suppose that many listeners will be able to respond easily to the objective stimulus of (5.1), at a brisk tempo, in the mode of (5.2). (Lewin 1981, pp. 101–102)

The acceleration in bar 15 involves a "quarter-note" beat. In fact, the eighth-note D "(Su)-chen" is a bit slow. I have indicated an initial quarter-note projection in the piano interrupting the voice, but this interpretation becomes more tenuous as the passage develops, and I suggest that there is little, if any, projective continuity in the overlapping of voice and piano. The connection of voice and piano is largely one of contrast—free/strict, slow/fast, metrical/ametrical. Although the piano constituent begins with a clear eighth-note pulse and affords constant sixteenth-note divisions, there is little projective order, and the passage sounds relatively chaotic. On the other hand, because of its constant division, the piano presents us with a fixed tempo; and because there is so little metrical grouping, this tempo is very quick. It might be said that both the acceleration in the vocal gesture and the sudden jerk into a fixed and very fast tempo serve the text, lending a feeling of great urgency to the verbal exclamation.

The second vocal constituent, projectively disconnected from the preceding piano figure, presents a new pulse now supported by the piano. If these three beats correspond to the "quarter note" of bar 15, the vocal tempo will be faster, but whether or not we make this connection, the voice is still "slower" than the piano, which again interrupts the realization of projected potential. The third vocal constituent, "wandeln Ich!," again disconnected from the piano, also accelerates. Whether this is to be heard as a "slow" triple or a "fast" duple is a choice for the singer to make. The latter interpretation will better serve the rhyme with "Und halte Dich!" in bars 20–21.

A new small phrase is begun at the end of bar 18 ("Ich taste Ich") with a "return" to bar 15. Here the piano is no longer projectively detached—the voice enters as continuation of a piano beginning (in bar 18). In bar 20 the soprano interrupts herself to sing "und fasse Du" very quickly (and with no rubato) in the tempo of the piano. This is the climax of the large phrase (and here the correspondences with the opening in bar 15 may hold the connection of "Suchen" and "Du").

In this music, great demands are placed on listeners and, especially, on the performers. If there is a lapse in attention to projective detail, rhythm will be lost. In "Wankelmut" (fickleness), appropriately enough, tempo fluctuates rapidly and the projective field is highly fragmented. In the first song, "Wiedersehen" (example 14.20), there is considerably more projective and tonal continuity.

In the first constituent (bars 1–2) voice and piano are metrically coordinated, and there emerges a clear quarter-note pulse that matches the 4/4 time signature. There is even some evidence of a half-note projection: in addition to the crescendo, there is also directedness toward a second half-note beat in the resolution of the initial suspended anacrusis in piano, right hand. And if we can sense the repetition of thirds in piano (E–G) and voice (E♭–C), the voice could then be heard in relation to the piano as an overlapping and accelerated resolution of anacruses— slow for E–G and fast for E♭–C. Acceleration continues in the second half-note beat with the triplets and the oscillating figure formed of these triplets (shown in brackets above piano). Following this intensification, the phrase ends quietly in "bebt" as "Schrei-" turns to "Schreiten."

The beginning of bar 2 with "bebt" promises a projected duration of at least a quarter note. However, the piano subtly shifts pulse by a sixteenth note, minimizing the relevance of this projected potential. As a result of this shift, there is a projective interruption with the entrance (too soon) of the voice at the end of bar 2 ("In Schauen"). This interruption functions to separate the two vocal constituents ("Dein Schreiten bebt / In Schauen") and will allow the second vocal constituent to become the beginning of a larger constituent ("In Schauen stirbt der Blick"). To the degree bars 3–8 cohere as a continuous gesture, "In Schauen" might refer not only to "Blick" in bar 4 but also to the play of wind (bars 4–6) and to "you turning away" (bar 7). But phrase articulations are by no means clear-cut here (or in Stramm's verse). Six vocal

constituents form the large phrase (bars 1–8) and are joined in four syntactic units (bars 1–2, 2–4, 4–6, and 7), but various overlappings serve to draw out syntactic and acoustic connections that cross these boundaries. In example 14.20b I have indicated a connection of the last four vocal constituents of the phrase. The chromatic descent (G–F♯–F–E) in bars 4–7 links "Blick," "Wind," "Bänd-," "Du," and "wend-." A registral wedge narrows to "Du" and then opens in "wendest fort!" The acoustic connections are subtle but effective: "der Blick" and "der Wind" are parallel and rhyme in vowel; and although "*Wind* spielt" and "*Bänd*er" do not make a very close rhyme, the sound of both "Wind" and "Bänd-" is repeated in "wend-." Notice, too, that the closing wedge in the voice reverses and greatly expands (in duration) the opening wedge of the piano (left hand) in bar 4.

The vocal constituents in bars 2–6 are articulated by various projective breaks with the piano. But with the last constituent ("Du wendest fort!") piano and voice are more clearly coordinated metrically; and after a moment of hesitation in a sustained continuative suspension on "Du" in the soprano of bar 7, a clear pulse comes into focus in "wendest fort!" and is continued in the piano through the following bar. In example 14.20c I show imitative reiterations of the voice's closing constituent in the piano in bars 7 and 8 leading to an overlapping with the next phrase (D–C–F♯ in piano). If this complex repetition of contour, interval, and duration can be heard, it will contribute to a (precisely notated) rallentando, introducing the slower tempo rubato of the voice's final phrase, "Den Raum umwirbt die Zeit!" Because of the very clear closure in bar 8 of a process begun perhaps as early as bar 2 ("In Schauen"), the new vocal line ("Den Raum umwirbt die Zeit!") seems to break off from a large phrase in bars 1–8 to begin a second phrase continued (à la Schumann) by the piano and closed in bar 14.

A discussion of the interruptions, overlappings, and changes of "speed" that might arise from the interpretation of projective functions I propose in example 14.20 (and also an account of the contribution of tone to rhythm) would involve us in a more detailed analysis than we need to undertake here. Suffice it to say that we are presented with a

EXAMPLE 14.20 Milton Babbitt, Du, "Wiedersehen," bs. 1–11. Copyright © 1957 by Boelke-Bomart, Inc. Reprinted by permission.

I. Wiedersehen

Continued

EXAMPLE 14.20 (*continued*)

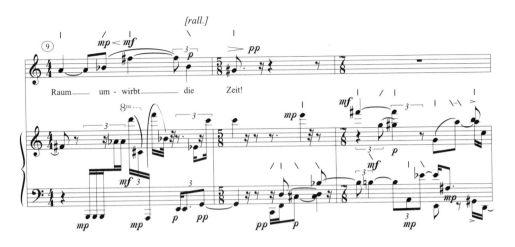

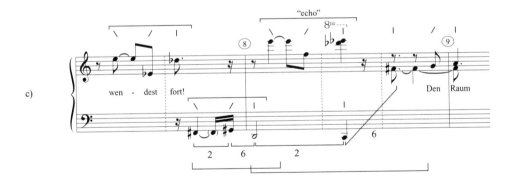

projective field of great complexity and a highly continuous overlapping of very small constituent gestures. The gestures themselves appear quite discontinuous, broken as they are by very rapid projective fissures and reinterpretations. However, phrases here and throughout the cycle are large— not by clock time, but in our experience of an extraordinarily contracted and dense present. If such phrases can be felt, it will require a high degree of attentiveness to comprehend a becoming

so projectively fragmented. And without a relatively high degree of attentiveness we will, I think, be denied an appreciation of the rhythmic particularity of this music. In fact, this level of attentiveness might itself be said to contribute to the particularity of our aesthetic experience.

Because of the compression of the projective field, even a relatively small lapse of attention can require an active refocusing of attention, and if we are unwilling to make this effort (perhaps repeatedly), we may lose interest and find the music incomprehensible — that is, uninteresting. This refocusing can be quite demanding in light of the brokenness of constituents. And if we lose track, we are not given many opportunities to recover our bearings and reenter the course of such volatile phrases. Nevertheless, small constituents and the phrases they compose are, in general, clearly articulated (though often overlapped) and offer numerous opportunities for comprehension. Such opportunities for comprehension (provided that we find them sufficiently "attractive") serve as lures for our attention. Where a discrimination of projective potentials does not lead to a grasp of larger durations or where we are not enticed to make the effort we may well withdraw our attention from an active engagement with the dance of meter.

FIFTEEN

Toward a Music of Durational Indeterminacy

The intense reduction (or compression) of projective potential we observed in Webern's op. 22 and carried even further by the brokenness of the projective field in Babbitt's *Du* invites comparison with efforts in the years following the Second World War to eliminate meter's hold on the attention and its involvement in the formation of those more or less determinate sonic durations we call "phrases." Here our choice of pieces is especially difficult because of the wide variety of experiments (instrumental and electronic) undertaken in recent decades aimed at suppressing the durational determinacies of measure and phrase. I have selected Boulez's *le marteau sans maître* in part because its nine movements offer a great variety of approaches to musical continuity: sections in which there is neither pulse nor phrase articulation, pulsed music with little or no phrase articulation, loosely integrated phrase-like units articulated only by ruptures in continuity, phrases that draw upon projective distinctions for their coherence, and phrases that do not.

Thus far we have considered projection from the standpoint of its contribution to the formation of phrases. However, meter is not required for the formation of phrase, nor does the emergence of pulse or the clear distinction of projective functions create phrase articulations. Indeed, in *le marteau sans maître* it is in the most clearly

pulsed sections that phrases are often most difficult to grasp. In examples 15.1, 15.2, 15.3, and 15.4 I have quoted excerpts from several sections: the openings of no. 1 ("avant 'd'artisanat furieux'") and no. 2 ("commentaire I de 'bourreaux de solitude'"), a passage from no. 4 ("commentaire II de 'bourreaux de solitude'"), and the beginning of no. 9 ("'bel édifice et les pressentiments' *double*"). These examples will lead us to the end of the present study—a consideration of rhythm in music that has renounced meter's efficacy in the formation of phrase. An examination of these excerpts will also allow us to consider some more general questions of rhythm and some of the novel experiences offered by "the New Music." In order to address these questions it will be helpful first to discuss the distinction of "constituent" and "phrase" in more detail. This discussion will provide us with an opportunity to consider more explicitly questions of determinacy in relation to differences of durational "span."

Throughout this study I have used the term "phrase" very loosely. My reason for doing so was to avoid reifying phrase as a definite durational type that can be identified in all instances. It is clear that music (or even a single piece of music) presents us with events that vary in size and in their degrees of closure and overlapping. If we define phrase too narrowly, we will then have to define other types and enter into questions of classification that will eventually become a matter of hairsplitting. Such questions will, I think, have less to do with perception than with problems set up by our categories.

Although I have given wide berth to the term "phrase," I have followed conventional usage in not calling very brief events "phrases." In the twentieth-century pieces we have considered, I have called such events "constituents" as an abbreviation of the term "primary constituents" I have employed elsewhere (Hasty 1984). By "primary" I mean the "first grouping" of beats (or, in some cases, a single beat) in an event that does not exhaust the limits of what psychologists have identified variously as "immediate," "primary," or "auditory" memory. These differences of nomenclature reflect a wide variety of interpretations of this "span" and its duration. Since acts of attention are so various, it is impossible to say precisely what these limits are. But we might, nevertheless, offer as a very rough estimate an upper limit of three to five seconds. Most of the events we are likely to regard as phrases are at least this long, if not considerably longer. By virtue of their brevity constituents lack the fixity or stability of articulated phrases. Much as metrical beats will tend to expand measured duration to form a larger measure, such small segments of music (whether metrical or not) will tend to coalesce as a single event—a phrase.

Earlier I said that phrases are characterized by some feeling of completeness or wholeness and that such completeness arises in the present becoming of the event and not simply in its having become past. In this process of becoming, variously articulated "segments" are adjusting to a novel event that is not a mere addition of parts. Although our language and habits of thought make the task difficult, we should try to avoid thinking of the "segments" or "parts" of the emerging whole (substantives seem unavoidable here) as discrete, fully determined objects. It is true that as an individual event each segment becomes *in itself* past and fully determined, but the whole, too, is an event and is not fully determined until it ends. Indeed, it may be taken as a definition of "larger event" that component segments are not for themselves.

To argue in this way against the fixity of the

components of an event in passage is to argue for real novelty in becoming. This has been the central argument for the theory of metrical projection I have developed in the preceding chapters, finding its most obvious expression in the notion of mensural determinacy and the substitution of "beginning" and "continuation" for the notion of "strong and weak *beats*" or "accented and unaccented *parts*." If this perspective can shed any light on the question of measured duration, it must also be applicable to questions that concern the becoming of events whose durations are not so "precisely" measured (and, as we have seen, it is very difficult to draw a sharp line between these two categories). Just as the openness of mensural determinacy allows for the formation of a larger event in the continued expansion of measured duration, there appear to be durational limits for the perceptual construction of events in general and a similar openness in the determinacy of the relatively brief events I have called "constituents."

From a rather different perspective, psychological interpretations of the concept of "immediate memory" (or "echoic memory" in Neisser 1967) also point to a degree of incompleteness or a special sort of mobility or openness in events of relatively brief duration. Psychologists often speak of a temporary storage of contents in a relatively uninterpreted or "unsegmented" form. For example, Ulric Neisser, taking the perception of spoken language as a model, writes:

> In ordinary speech the context necessary to obtain a segment may come *after* it, so segmentation itself can often be profitably delayed. Or, if it has not been delayed, it may still be corrected by information arriving subsequently. Some persistence of the echo would greatly facilitate this retrospective analysis of what has been heard. . . . Of course, we must admit that context can still be useful even if it comes after the echo has faded and only labeled segments remain. In such cases it helps by suggesting how to reinterpret them. It will be far more helpful, however, if the unsegmented information is still accessible and can be restructured. (Neisser 1967, pp. 201–202)

Or as G.A. Miller writes:

> If complete storage is necessary even after lower-level decisions have been tentatively reached, why

bother to make the lower-level decisions first? Why not store the message until enough of it is on hand to support a higher-level decision, then make a decision for all levels simultaneously? (Miller 1962, p. 81)

Here "labeling," "decision," and "segmentation" correspond, more or less, to my "determinacy." I should also note that the size of this "transient storage mechanism" or "buffer" corresponds roughly to the limits of a highly determinate projected potential (one where we can appeal to the test of "silent continuation") or the limit of a relatively brief two-bar measure advocated by many theorists. Moreover, the possibility of a reinterpretation of projective function as well as the formation of a *functional* "silent beginning" for anacrusis also seem to lie within this limit.

Constituents are incomplete on account of their length. On the hypothesis of immediate memory, the determinacy or closure that would end the becoming promised by a very brief event is either deferred to a greater becoming involving its successors or, if there is no immediate successor, realized in a duration in which the event will become fixed and no longer subject to reinterpretation. In the case of a group of constituents such as might form a small phrase, I suggest that later constituents will generally be less "open" than earlier ones because the special relevancies offered by earlier constituents in the course of a single becoming will narrow the possibilities for "segmentation" or determinacy. That is, as more context develops, definite potentials narrow interpretive possibilities. (This, in any case, was the assumption I made in chapter 12 when discussing the possibility of large measures.) Here we cannot separate the determinacy of constituents from the emerging determinacy of the greater event they are in the process of forming (or, for that matter, from the relevancies of past events). And this greater event on account of its duration is relatively fixed. It is true that the overlapping of phrases often involves some openness in the interpretation of the final constituent(s). But this openness is inseparable from the openness of the phrase as a whole. Such constituents do not break away from the phrase as autonomous events.

Given opportunities for grouping small con-

stituents, we will apprehend larger units—small phrases or "subphrases." We could perhaps define as a "primary phrase" a first grouping of constituents. But such categories are difficult to apply in all cases. As we have seen in the opening of the Carter Sonata, Webern's op. 22, and "Wiedersehen" (and in Haydn, Mozart, et al.), groupings of constituents can be quite ambiguous and mercurial. And in such cases overlappings can make a rigid analysis of constituents problematic. In short, becoming cannot be broken down into a neat hierarchy of parts. But we need not invoke a "segmental" hierarchy to note the efficacy of articulation and grouping for the comprehensibility of events that exceed the limits of immediate memory.

Immediate memory has sometimes been viewed as a sort of movable container through which a continuous stream of stimuli pass, rather like the window of a train. However, most research suggests an *atomic* interpretation—articulated units or "chunks" of stimuli. And where "chunking" is inhibited, our ability to comprehend or recollect larger events seems to be impaired. In music, such articulation can arise, in part, from the formation of mensural units on the durational order of bar measure (or "bar" measure if this "medium-sized" measure does not correspond to a notated bar). Where such mensural units are not formed, constituents can be articulated by a great variety of other means. However, where there is no articulation of constituents immediate memory may, in fact, more resemble a movable container—a window of uncertain dimensions through which largely unsegmented stimuli pass. Or if immediate memory is intrinsically atomic, it may be that an absence of articulation and grouping will inhibit our acts of "segmentation" or detract from determinacy and particularity. The beginning of *le marteau* may serve as an illustration.

In bars 1–10 of example 15.1 there are virtually no metrical beats. Since, from the page, it looks as if we might be able to distinguish projective functions, I would refer the reader to a recorded performance. Here and elsewhere in this piece, grace notes are especially effective in neutralizing the projective field. I have said that it is virtually impossible to suppress projective distinctions in the realm of "middle-sized" or

EXAMPLE 15.1 Pierre Boulez, *le marteau sans maître*, no. 1, "avant 'l'artisanat furieux',"
bs. 1–13. Copyright © 1932 by Universal Edition (London) Ltd., London. © Copyright
renewed. All rights reserved. Used by permission of European American Music Distributors
Corporation, sole U.S. and Canadian agent for Universal Edition (London) Ltd., London.

mensurally determinate durations—durations that do not exceed the limits of immediate memory. But the speed of this passage coupled with the complexity and noncongruence of these very quick figures obscures any feeling of projective determinacy. If definite projective functions do not emerge in this passage, we may take this as an example of what Boulez has called "amorphous" or "smooth time," as opposed to "pulsed" or "striated time" (Boulez 1971). If there are constituents here, they are exceedingly small and, in their overlappings, relatively indistinct. There is an articulation by silence at the end of bar 10. The event ends here—or rather stops, cut off in the midst of a flurry of activity. In bar 11 activity is resumed in a passage that in many respects could sound like a continuation of the preceding music. In fact, we might hear the silence simply as a break in continuity, an interruption in the progress of a relatively homogeneous activity. It must be said that in this case there is also contrast, which detracts from a feeling of interruption—clearer examples of an "interrupted continuity" can be found later in this movement and in bars 54–102 of the second movement (where there is, incidentally, more evidence of pulse).

If we do hear the silence as interruption, there will be little sense of closure or completeness in the first event. Shall we call this event a phrase? If we do not, we shall have to find another name for it and then say precisely what constitutes a true or proper phrase. This would prove a difficult and, I think, unrewarding task. Nevertheless, in its homogeneity and lack of closure this event does not seem to possess characteristics we normally attribute to phrase. To make a distinction, I will call this an "unsegmented" (or relatively unsegmented) phrase. "Segmentation" here will refer not only to the articulation of constituents, but also, more in line with Neisser's usage, to the emergence of definite "meanings" or potentials in the joining of constituents (such as we will later observe in no. 9, "bel édifice"). This dual perspective is, I think, inescapable—as James has pointed out (for instance, in his examples of bamboo and thunder, quoted in chapter 2), segmentation is at once a cutting *and* a joining. In bars 1–10 I would argue that in the absence of clear segmentation

the phrase is relatively amorphous and homogeneous, and that this homogeneity detracts from the determinacy or "particularity" of its becoming. However, by thus stating the matter in purely negative terms I do not wish to detract from the novelty and particularity of the experience Boulez has offered us or from his compositional ingenuity. Without a relatively high degree of homogeneity we could not feel the silences as interruptions and phrases as beginning in medias res. Nor could we feel the kaleidoscopic effect of fleeting gestures that continually escape our grasp.

Other "phrases" or sections of this movement (bars 24–41, 42–52, 53–80, and 81–95, all articulated by brief silences) present somewhat more clearly defined constituents, but some are much larger, and their constituents (where such can be identified) are continuously overlapped without forming definite groups. Here I would suggest that this protracted suspension of articulation results in a highly diffuse present, broken by resumptions of activity rather than by new beginnings. This activity can, as I have said, be heard as relatively homogeneous. But to say this is to focus on a broad and, as it were, "generalized" continuity, or rather to point to the possibility of losing our ability to focus our attention on detail. If we attend to a very narrow present, we will hear gestures of considerable heterogeneity and particularity. To do so, however, will require great concentration, and by continually blurring the boundaries of such possible "presents" Boulez has not made this an easy task. Nor was this an easy task in Babbitt's "Wiedersehen," but there the lure of a large and highly "segmented" phrase could more readily focus and hold our attention (and, of course, the song is quite short).

The next piece (example 15.2) is something of a relief. There is now a rarely broken sixteenth-note pulse, and therefore the first section (bars 1–53) can be taken as an example of Boulez's "striated time." However, this pulse serves to create another continuous activity in which segmentation can be suspended. We can now much more easily attend to detail, and if we follow projective activity this detail will be very small indeed. The projective field here is relatively well defined, but projective gestures are

EXAMPLE 15.2 Pierre Boulez, *le marteau sans maître*, no. 2, "commentaire I de 'bourreaux de solitude'," bs. 1–12. Copyright © 1932 by Universal Edition (London) Ltd., London. © Copyright renewed. All rights reserved. Used by permission of European American Music Distributors Corporation, sole U.S. and Canadian agent for Universal Edition (London) Ltd., London.

287

minute (and often quite ambiguous). Indeed, the projective field is so complex and compressed that if our attention is not sharply focused, we may perceive a largely undifferentiated and homogeneous continuity. As Boulez remarks, "a static distribution in striated time will tend to give the impression of smooth time" (Boulez 1971, p. 94).

The alto flute plays small phrases that are composed of a relatively comprehensible ensemble of constituents. However, the "percussion" ensemble of xylorimba, tambourine, and pizzicato viola presents what could be heard as a relatively "static distribution" of pulse groupings; and, in general, beginnings and endings of flute phrases do not disrupt the continuity of the other instruments. If we regard the other instruments as "ground" and the flute as "figure," we may hear a piece in which there are flute phrases intermittently played over a background of continuous and homogeneous activity provided by the percussion ensemble. Not to overstate this separation, I should mention that within this section there are two articulations that involve all the instruments—in bar 11 the ending of a flute phrase and in bar 34 the beginning of a flute phrase. Incidentally, both articulations involve a descending minor third, which for this piece characteristically functions as a "cadential" or closing gesture (as in bar 7 of "bel édifice," see example 15.4a).

On the other hand, we need not hear a distinction of "figure" and "ground." If we attend to the music of the percussion ensemble in its heterogeneity and particularity (and not as a "static distribution"), we might hear an alternation of segmented and relatively unsegmented phrases. Or if we attend to a continuity of metrical groupings that is not broken by flute entrances, we may be less inclined to hear the passages without flute as separate phrases. In this case, rather than speaking of phrases, we might speak of a continuous becoming diversified but not broken by alternating ensembles. Among the flute phrases or segments there are many subtle repetitions (of contour, interval, and projective function), and we may have the impression of several "beginnings again" initiated with the flute. But if we can perceive a continuous becoming, these "beginnings again" may seem more

like being again in "the same place" than initiations of new becomings. Likewise, although the percussion phrases or segments are highly diversified in their detail, as units they are quite homogeneous, and it is difficult to avoid a feeling of being in "the same place" when we hear their returns. Thus, I suggest that while we can avoid "amorphous time" in attending to detail we may hear something resembling a "static distribution" in larger events.

In example 15.2 I have offered a projective analysis. To arrive at this interpretation I had to listen many times to recorded performances of these few bars (Boulez's and Craft's). Although this effort reflects the complexity and smallness of the projective field, it should not suggest that the effects of such distinctions as I have indicated cannot be felt in a highly focused first hearing. Nevertheless, the difficulties I encountered do, I think, point to a peculiarity of "scale" here. In order to determine projective function, I was forced to stop the recording at intervals of two or three seconds, durations that do not exhaust the limits of immediate memory. Thus, I speculate that the metrical "units" here are continuously overlapped and available for reinterpretation by immediate successors without attaining the fixity of past events. In this case, we might say that the distinction between past and present in the immediate successions of "beats" is not very sharply drawn.

The projective interpretation I have offered here is based on Craft's faster and more metronomic performance. Boulez's recorded performances are somewhat freer and tend more toward tempo rubato in the flute. However, in terms of projective function there are relatively few differences among these performances. The most significant differences occur in bars 6 and 8, and I will discuss the rhythmic effects of these alternatives in my comments on bars 1–11, a unit that might be regarded as a first phrase. Although my projective interpretation is in many respects an oversimplification, it can be used to point to several characteristics of this music.

The effects of projective distinctions in the flute line in bars 1–3 seem to hover between feelings of rubato (to the degree the flute is heard in isolation from the other instruments) and feelings of interruption, delay, suspension, et cetera, in reference to a strict pulse supplied by the other instruments. For the other, nonsustaining instruments there is no feeling of tempo rubato. In bars 4–6, complex, heterogeneous (and often ambiguous) metrical groupings do not give rise to an articulation of constituents. The groupings are too small and fluid to be themselves regarded as constituents; rather, they constitute fleeting and "irregular" beats. And to the extent we can feel the play of these beats we will be less inclined to hear this music as a homogeneous background over which the flute is laid or, in passages where the percussion ensemble plays alone, as an amorphous period of waiting for a new beginning with flute. In fact, the new beginning by the flute in bar 6 is prepared by or overlapped with the immediately preceding music. In Craft's recording the three eighth-note beats of the flute (recalling bar 1 sans anacrusis) follow three eighth-note beats of the tambourine, interrupting the tambourine's pulse by entering a sixteenth too soon. However, the flute does continue the xylorimba's pulse, which now, continued by flute, can emerge reinterpreted as a pulse and not as a succession of "offbeats." In Boulez's 1968 recording there is no reinterpretation—the three eighth-note beats of the xylorimba (shown in parentheses) are "accented" from the start.

I would draw attention to two other features of the new "phrase" or segment. In Craft's performance, at the end of bar 8 there is a projective break and a hiatus articulating a second flute constituent—a pause in a quarter-note duration, which here could be felt as unmeasured in the absence of sixteenth notes. In Boulez's recordings there is no projective break with bar 9—bars 8 and 9 in flute form a single constituent in tempo rubato. Finally, at the end of bar 11 there is a close in all parts articulated by silence. This is the first such break, and the xylorimba's repetition of the alto flute's (sounding) C♯ at the end of bar 11 contributes to a sense of closure here. (Note, too, that the flute's descending minor third rhymes with the close of the preceding movement.) As a result of this articulation we might hear a second phrase begun with the percussion ensemble in bar 12. And if we do hear this as the beginning of a second large and relatively unsegmented phrase, we will

be less inclined to hear the flute entrance in bar 16 as a new beginning over a homogeneous percussion "ground."

If in bars 1–43 of this second movement the alternating ensembles do not clearly emerge as phrases, they are also too long to be regarded as constituents. I would argue that here, as in the first movement, a focused attentiveness to detail will result in a relatively diffuse present in the becoming of larger events. Feelings of definiteness or particularity would then arise in a relatively narrow present whose boundaries are not sharply drawn. And since these fleeting "presents" so closely resemble one another, the larger becoming may seem relatively static—again to use a spatial metaphor, it might be said that the "place" we find ourselves in at any moment is more or less "the same place" we have been in all along.

In the fourth movement ("commentaire II," example 15.3), Boulez employs a very different procedure, but to similar ends. In the first part of the movement (bars 1–47), we are presented with clearly articulated segments on the durational order of constituents. Articulation is accomplished either by silence or by a sustained final sound, usually in vibraphone. In Boulez's recorded performances there is virtually no trace of pulse or projective function, and long pauses articulate constituents. In Craft's recording, metrical groupings often arise and pauses are much shorter. Here constituents are still clearly articulated, but we are given less time to savor their particularity.

If we wish to call these units primary constituents, we must acknowledge that these "first" groupings are to a large extent "final" groupings that do not coalesce in clearly defined phrases. Separated by fermatas, these "units" often achieve a considerable degree of autonomy and closure, and as each ends we can retain the completed gesture in a more or less vivid "echoic" present. In this "arrest" constituents can become relatively fixed as completed events.

In view of this determinacy and closure, might we then call these units small phrases? To do so would be to ignore a degree of incompleteness that arises primarily on account of their brevity but also because of connections that emerge in their overlapping. Here pitch repeti-

EXAMPLE 15.3 Pierre Boulez, *le marteau sans maître*, no. 4, "commentaire II de 'bourreaux de solitude'," bs. 4–11. Copyright © 1932 by Universal Edition (London) Ltd., London. © Copyright renewed. All rights reserved. Used by permission of European American Music Distributors Corporation, sole U.S. and Canadian agent for Universal Edition (London) Ltd., London.

tions, intervallic connections, and similarities of "content" serve to bind these units together in a single, continuous, and continually broken becoming. Not to overstate the homogeneity of this section, I should point out that there is great variety in the connection of constituents and their degree of closure. There is also considerable variety in the character of constituents. Sometimes constituents of highly contrastive character and length are juxtaposed. Sometimes there is a succession of several relatively homogeneous constituents. But these differences and similarities do not result in an articulation of constituent groupings as discrete events with definite beginnings and ends. Between section and constituent there are no determinate events. And since constituent events do not exceed the limits of immediate memory, I would suggest that we are offered here an experience of a present becoming with no clear beginning and end—a becoming in which there is a continual renewal of vividly present "moments."

Finally, in the beginning of no. 9, the second version of "bel édifice et les pressentiments," we find an example of a relatively closed, clearly "segmented" phrase in bars 1–8. It must be said, however, that even among vocal phrases in *le marteau* this degree of closure is not typical.

In example 15.4a I have identified several constituents, but because of overlappings this analysis is a considerable oversimplification (as any line drawing must be). In bars 3–6 various possibilities for overlapping result in a highly continuous gesture. Although the vocal climax in bar 4 is connected to the preceding sequence of ascending figures in the voice and thus continues a beginning in bar 3 (and in bar 1), "morte" also seems to break off from this event as a beginning continued in the following descent ("vagues"), reflecting the spondaic break in the poetic line—"mer"/"morte." Notice, too, that projective distinctions contribute to the continuity of the line from bar 1 and to a feeling of interruption with "mor-(te)," which enters too soon. There is a relatively clear articulation separating bars 2 and 3, but tonal and projective overlapping here makes the beginning of the second constituent group (bars 3–6) much more elusive than it may look from the page (see example 15.4b). The possibility of hearing a repe-

tition of the whole step C–D ("mar-cher") in the ascending whole step of xylorimba and vibraphone, G♯–B♭—that is, of connecting B♭ and G♯ across the intervening silence—and of reinterpreting beginning as anacrusis (provided that the silence is not too long) could lead to the sense of a new beginning with "dans mes jambes" and a beginning again with the sustained E♭ in viola. Consulting example 15.4b, notice that there is an intervallic correspondence that enhances this possibility: in the imitation shown here, the pitch C in the voice acquires the tonal quality of tritone from the preceding F♯, and a similar quality is given to the xylorimba's G♯ by the D in voice. The effect is not only that of an overlapping, but also that of energetic suspense in the delayed connection across an unmeasured silence. Indeed, in performance the silence should be long enough to maximize suspense, but not so long that a connection might be lost and with it the opportunity for projective reinterpretation.

In bars 1–8 of "bel edifice" many such overlappings act together to form a relatively long, segmented phrase. I will not attempt to catalog the manifold relevancies that come into play in the course of this phrase's becoming. Suffice it to say that throughout this phrase, later constituents derive their determinacy and particularity from potentials engendered by preceding constituents. Most broadly, this process can be heard in the rise and fall of the vocal line coordinated with acceleration and deceleration, crescendo and decrescendo, and, finally, a return in bar 7 to the initial gesture of the phrase in bar 1 (sans maraca). The maraca figure in bar 8, released from its former captivity in the first constituent, belongs to this phrase as an articulation of its end and overlaps with the beginning of the following phrase.

Although the determinacy of projective potentials is highly attenuated in the large phrase, more or less definite projective functions (beginning, continuation/anacrusis) can often be felt. Now at this "middle-sized" *tempo* of events it is virtually impossible to completely suppress the discrimination of projective function (again, given some minimum degree of attentiveness). But these functions are often not coordinated among the several "instruments." For example, in bar 1, while the first tone of the voice becomes ana-

EXAMPLE 15.4 Pierre Boulez, *le marteau sans maître*, no. 9, "'bel edifice et les pressentiments,' double" bs. 1–8. Copyright © 1932 by Universal Edition (London) Ltd., London. © Copyright renewed. All rights reserved. Used by permission of European American Music Distributors Corporation, sole U.S. and Canadian agent for Universal Edition (London) Ltd., London.

Continued

EXAMPLE 15.4 (*continued*)

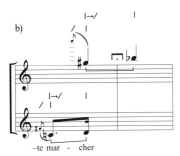

b)

–te mar - cher

crusis, the first beat of the xylorimba can become anacrusis only to the second beat (B♭) and is thus detached from the voice's beginning. (A similar detachment can be heard in the vocal entrance in bar 3.) Also, in bar 1, the maraca is projectively detached from guitar and viola. The timbral diversity of Boulez's ensemble obviously favors such a superimposition of relatively autonomous projective gestures, and this technique of projective noncongruence is used throughout *le marteau* to suppress a clear feeling of "downbeat" and clear projective potentials. In the phrase we have been examining, the only cases of clear coordination of instruments and voice occur in bars 4 and 5—the beginnings, "mor-(te)" and "va-(gues)"—but there is no evidence here of a projection.

It would be an overstatement to say that no projected potential emerges in this passage—that there are no traces of rubato or no traces of potential denied in feelings of "too early" and "too late." However, in the absence of clear realizations of projected potential there is, I think, comparatively little relevancy for mensurally determinate durations. What vestiges there are of meter reside primarily in the distinctions of projective function, and these distinctions are essential ingredients in the formation of the phrase, contributing as they do to the particularity of constituents and to their overlappings.

In his essay on "musical technique," Boulez remarks on the difficulty of attaining "amorphous" or "smooth time" in performance (1971, pp. 93–94). Given our irrepressible inclination to pick up projective potential, meter can be suppressed only if durations exceed the limits of mensural determinacy or if in a succession of

very small durations we are deprived of opportunities for grouping. And as I have attempted to show in connection with example 15.2, if our attention is highly focused, we can feel traces of meter in very complex arrangements where we are given few cues for grouping. As psychological experiments have shown, people find it very difficult to produce ametrical or "arrhythmic" sequences. Commenting on the problem of asking performers to produce the effect of "smooth time" from a "chronometric" notation (i.e., approximate values related to the measurement of seconds), Boulez writes:

> The performer, instead of producing smooth time, will automatically return to striated time, where the unit of reference is the second—he will fall back on the metronomical unit equal to 60; this confirms how false and illusory directly chronometric notation is in most cases, since the result will directly contradict the intention. True smooth time is that over which the performer has no control. (Boulez 1971, p. 94)

The difficulty of escaping meter is reflected in the extraordinary complexity of "metrical" notation in *le marteau*, which places daunting obstacles in the way of the performers' projective sensibilities. Of the many solutions to the problem of creating an ametrical music, I would like to present, as our final example, an excerpt from Lutosławski's *Jeux Venitiens* (example 15.5).

The "chronometric" notation of this passage does not succumb to Boulez's criticism. Even if the conductor and/or the instrumentalists gauge their progress in terms of seconds, this "measure" will not be communicated to the listener. And it seems clear that Lutosławski does not intend for the performers to rely on a feeling of pulse. As he writes in the performance instructions, "The bar lines, rhythmic values, and metre are intended merely for orientation: the music should be played with the greatest possible freedom. The number of notes at places like the third bar of section B in the first viola depends on the strength of the player's bowing (*spiccato* or preferably *ricochet*)."

Here feelings of meter are averted by an articulation of durations that often exceed the limits of mensural determinacy. There are, to be sure, smaller intervals. For example, in bars 3–5, reading successive attacks beginning with viola I (followed by contrabass II, etc.), we can find the following sequence of durations, measured (approximately) in seconds: 1, 2, 1.5, 1.5, 2. However, the variety of "attacks" here results in the articulation of much longer durations. And al-though the violin in bar 4 resembles the viola I in bar 3 and cello I in bar 5 (in contrast to the less obvious articulations in the other voices), the reemergence of the violin in bar 5 results in a first "violin event" of approximately 3.5 seconds duration and a span of 6 seconds between

EXAMPLE 15.5 Witold Lutosławski, *Jeux Venitiens*, first movement, section B. Copyright © 1962 by Moek Verlag. © Copyright renewed. All rights reserved. Used by permission of European American Music Distributors Corporation, sole U.S. and Canadian agent Moeck Verlag.

the viola I and cello I beginnings. We can certainly sense an increase of activity in bar 5, and perhaps a "speeding up" in the rate of articulations, but the brief emergence of projective activity in the violin is without issue. Finally, I would note that the unmeasured spiccato or ricochet attacks coming to rest in a sustained sound seem designed to make the beginnings of these new pitch events ambiguous.

In this passage, Lutosławski has clearly taken great pains to avoid groupings or processes that would fulfill expectations based on any emerging pattern. This section is highly unpredictable, as are the other sections of this movement. There is nothing here we could identify as a constituent. Certainly, the little ricochet events are constituentlike, but their boundaries and affiliations are loosely defined. After their initial articulations, these pitches are then absorbed into a slowly changing but relatively static sonority. Here again we are presented with a continuous and relatively homogeneous and diffuse becoming. In this greatly extended present, our attention is drawn to the sporadic twitterings of bouncing bows and between these to the changes in a sustained sonority effected by the assimilation of new pitches. These "events" do indeed articulate and diversify the larger becoming, but they do not create boundaries that would distinguish individual becomings.

EXAMPLE 15.5 (*continued*)

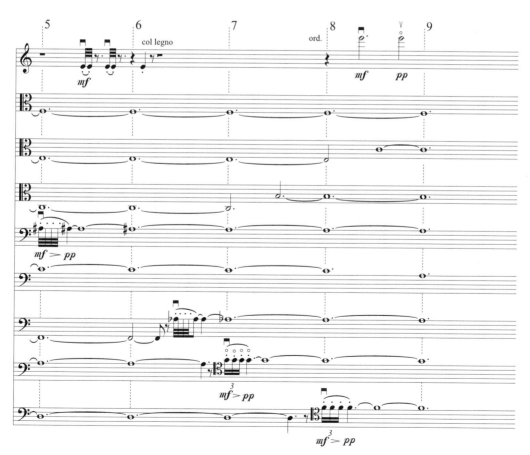

SIXTEEN

The Spatialization of Time
and the Eternal
"Now Moment"

In commenting on these examples of non-metrical or barely metrical music I have allowed myself the liberty of speculating on questions of rhythm. Here I have attempted to characterize rhythmic experiences using the notions of becoming and determinacy that have guided our investigations of meter. Although I believe that such notions could provide a basis for the investigation of much broader questions of rhythm, I do not claim to have done more than to hint at the direction such investigations might take. To address more general questions of rhythm or even to formulate these questions far exceeds the scope of this study. If meter is inseparable from rhythm it is, nevertheless, only one ingredient in rhythm, and a dispensable ingredient at that.

In connection with the Boulez and Lutosławski examples I have spoken of a relatively "diffuse" becoming and a relatively narrow present for the feeling of determinacy and particularity. Although a suppression of meter may favor such experiences, it is the suppression of the "segmented" phrase that seems to be the decisive factor in concentrating our attention on what Stockhausen has called "the consecrated moment." Thus, I would argue that although meter is highly attenuated in the first phrase of "bel édifice," we are here given the opportunity to experience an event in which constituents are as-similated to a larger becoming and in the process of adjusting to a new composition contribute to the determinacy and closure of this larger becoming. On the other hand, I have argued that in the pulsed and much more clearly metrical music of "commentaire I" there is little determinacy and closure in larger becomings. Fleeting articulations of very small metrical groupings and intermittent flute entrances diversify the becoming of the section but do not give rise to clearly segmented phrases. And although we may identify a phrase in bars 1–11, this event relies primarily on silence for its articulation and on immediate or "local" detail for its closure. Here smaller events are assimilated to a relatively homogeneous becoming and in the context of the whole contribute more to homogeneity than to determinacy and closure. We might also point to examples of so-called "process" music (for instance, Steve Reich's *Violin Phase*) where repetitions of pulse and "bar" measure are employed to create a relatively continuous and homogeneous becoming free from the consolidations of phrase.

The novel experiences offered by the New and post-New Music have been the subject of considerable speculation concerning the temporality of postwar compositions and our experience of "time" in general. These speculations have centered on two characteristics that distinguish the new music from the old: the spatialization of time and the experience of the moment as an autonomous, timeless, or eternal present. And although our present study of meter is at an end, I would like to briefly consider the attribution of spatiality and timelessness to musical events. We encountered these notions in earlier discussions of *structure* and of meter conceived as cyclic return. There I argued that the spatialization of time and the autonomy of a present freed from becoming are products of conceptualization. However, in postwar avant-garde aesthetics these categories are adamantly applied to perceptual acts.

It is in Webern's music and his use of palindrome and pitch symmetries that early apologists for the New Music find the first signs of a spatialization that will be fully realized in the work of the Darmstadt school. In an essay that describes the "paralysis of the flow of time" in works of Boulez and Goeyvaerts, and in Messiaen's "nonretrogradable rhythms," György Ligeti writes:

> Webern's music brought about the projection of the time flow into an imaginary space by means of the interchangeability of temporal directions provoked by the constant reciprocity of motivic shapes and their retrogrades. . . . This projection was further strengthened by the "grouping around a central axis, which implies a conception of the time-continuum as 'space' [Eimert]", and by the fusion of the successive and the simultaneous in a unifying structure . . . Webern's structures seem, if not to move forward in one direction, at least to circle continuously in their illusory space. (Ligeti 1965, p. 16)

Here retrograde as the "interchangeablity of temporal directions," the "spatial" symmetry of pitches, and the "unifying structure" of the row (indifferent to succession and simultaneity) all contribute to the suspension of time, albeit an "illusory" or "imaginary" suspension.

George Rochberg locates spatialization in the brokenness of becoming. Rochberg writes of Webern's music, and then of music inspired by Webern's example:

> The beat and meter is now a frame, not a process—a frame on which to construct symme-

tries of pitch and rhythm . . . uniform, discrete, individual units of time which have no more relation to each other than the seconds which a clock ticks off.

> By subordinating duration to space, music no longer exists in its former state of anticipation of the future. It projects itself as a series of present moments, holding up to aural perception each spatial image as the self-sufficient object of perception as it occurs, not as it will realize itself in some future event. (Rochberg 1984, pp. 111–112, 132)

For Stockhausen, the autonomy of the moment, although it annihilates time, does not result in an image of space, but rather in an experience of eternity:

> In recent years musical forms have been composed to which one cannot from the present predict with certainty the direction of development; forms in which either every present counts or nothing counts at all; forms in which each now is not regarded untiringly as a mere result of the immediately preceding one or as the prelude to the one that is approaching, that one expects—but rather as something personal, autonomous, centered, independent, absolute; forms in which an instant need not be a segment on a time-line nor a moment a particle of measured duration. Forms in which the concentration on the now—on each now—makes, as it were, vertical slices which cut across horizontal time experience into the timelessness I call eternity: an eternity that does not begin at the end of time, but that is attainable in every moment. I speak of musical forms in which nothing less is being attempted than to explode, yes, to overcome the concept of time or, more precisely, the concept of duration. (Stockhausen 1963, pp. 198–199)

Boulez, on the other hand, has little interest in eternity and, in describing the "instantaneous" listening required in the new style, points to the prospect of an "irreversible" time (here, presumably, memory is the agent of time's "reversibility"):

> Western music has ingeniously developed recognized "markers" within recognized forms, so that it is possible to speak of an "angle of hearing" as we speak of an angle of vision, thanks to a more or less conscious and immediate "memorizing" of what has gone before. But with the object of keep-

ing the listener's attention alerted, these "markers" have become increasingly unsymmetrical, and indeed increasingly "unremarkable", from which we may conclude that the evolution of form characterized by such points of reference will eventually end in irreversible time, where formal criteria are established by networks of differentiated possibilities. Listening is tending to become increasingly instantaneous, so that points of reference are losing their usefulness. A composition is no longer a consciously directed construction moving from a "beginning" to an "end" and passing from one to another. Frontiers have been deliberately "anesthetized", listening time is no longer directional but time-bubbles, as it were. (Boulez 1986, p. 178)

Although there is little consensus on the precise nature of the new moment isolated from memory and anticipation, there is general agreement that its defining characteristic is novelty. Like Georgiades' Classical "here and now," the new autonomous moment is absolutely new. It owes nothing to the past or the future, for if it were conditioned by the past or creating conditions for a future it would no longer be autonomous. It may be that this pursuit of autonomy and novelty is in some way a reflection of the avant-garde's ambition for an absolutely new art completely dissociated from tradition (and perhaps protected from a future of becoming old—certainly, the designation of postwar music as "*the* New Music," like the earlier "music of the future," bespeaks a desire for perpetual novelty and originality). But from either perspective— history or "immediate," unmediated experience —we must ask if "now" can be cut off from becoming in an unconditioned "present" moment.

Certainly, there are religious and meditative practices aimed at "stopping time" (see Eliade 1965). Meister Eckhart's eternal *Nu* and the Buddhist *sono-mama* state, for example, point to the possibility of a transcendence of becoming and an experience, paradoxically, of eternity "in" time (*sub specie aeternitatis*). Describing such a "transcendental" experience, D. T. Suzuki writes:

> "Was" and "will be" must be in "is." What is finite must be carrying in it, with it, everything belonging to infinity. We who are becoming in time, therefore, must be able to see that which eternally "is." This is seeing the world as God sees it, as Spinoza says, "*sub specie aeternitatis.*"

> Those who live in the light of eternity always are and are never subjected to the becoming of "was" and "will be." Eternity is the absolute present and the absolute present is living a *sono-mama* life, where life asserts itself in all its fullness. (Suzuki 1957, pp. 107, 126)

The becoming of which Suzuki speaks is not the becoming of which I have spoken; it refers, rather, to the separation of "was" and "will be" from what "is"—a separation that is the product of intellect. And although Suzuki speaks of an "absolute" present, it is not unconditioned, but rather infinitely conditioned by the whole of time. Suzuki translates *sono-mama* as "suchness," what we might also call an extreme "particularity" or "novelty" (and what Joyce with Aquinas called *quidditas*). This "suchness" is absolute precisely because it is conditioned by the whole. It is most definitely not autonomous—where there is isolation and an intellectual analysis of before and after there is no *sono-mama*.

If such an experience is attainable through the medium of music, it would make little sense to identify an eternal now with an isolated moment or a succession of moments or to link such an experience to a particular style or compositional technique. Indeed, homogeneity (or "static distribution") and a blurring of the boundaries of events would seem to lead to an undifferentiated becoming devoid of particularity. I do not suggest that in the music of Boulez, Stockhausen, Ligeti, et alia, there is any dearth of particularity. But I would argue that whatever vividness and novelty we hear in this music is the result of a highly diversified becoming and not the result of an isolation of autonomous moments. Without an effort to connect, we are likely to lapse into inattentiveness and regard this music as relatively homogeneous and arrhythmic. However, if our interest is drawn to the heterogeneity of detail and we do "follow" this music, we are rewarded with experiences of rhythm quite unlike those of any earlier musics.

In view of the general lack of enthusiasm with which the New Music has been greeted, it must be said that "following" does not come easy. Examples of the new style often present us with an extraordinarily narrow focus for our acts of attention. And I think it could be said that the particularity or novelty we can hear in these fleeting and concentrated "moments" often arises from a concentration of becoming in a vivid now of relatively brief duration. When Stockhausen writes that "either every present counts or nothing counts at all," I take this to mean that if we cannot grasp the uniqueness and originality of the moment, musical process will collapse in a diffuse and homogeneous becoming from which nothing of interest can emerge. And although the same could perhaps be said of any music, the large-scale homogeneity of much postwar music makes such collapse a more immanent danger.

I have said that the desideratum of the moment is novelty (though apologists have not used this term). But it might be said that novelty is required for all rhythmic experience. As I have used the term throughout this study, "novelty," far from being the product of an isolation of the present from past and future (memory and expectation), is a mark of the greatest integration of "moments" of becoming. Where "now" involves the relevancies of remote "pasts" and the definite potentials of distant "futures," becoming is most particular and most spontaneous. As Milič Čapek writes, concerning the relevancy of the "immediate" past:

> [The] qualitative difference between two successive moments both *separates* and *links* them; for the mnemic link which joins the present to its immediate ancestor is precisely the act by which the novelty of the present is constituted; for it is an immediate recollection of the antecedent moment which makes the present different from it and it is the emergence of this qualitative difference which is *the very essence* of novelty. The whole paradoxical nature of duration consists of this relation *which separates as well as unites* in an act which is both a retention of the past and the emergence of the present. (Čapek 1971, p. 220)

Čapek's comments are specifically directed toward an analysis of Bergson's concept of "durational tension" or the "rhythm of duration." And although this concept engages questions that lie far beyond the bounds of our study, it can, I think, shed some light on the issues we have been considering throughout this study.

In his earlier works, Bergson makes a sharp distinction between the spatial and the temporal or durational and regards the "spatialization" of time as a misunderstanding of temporality and a falsification that arises from a mathematical and predominantly visual approach to temporal experience. In later works (*Matter and Memory* and *Creative Evolution*), Bergson does not relax his critique of spatialization, but he does attempt to correlate different degrees of spatiality with different degrees of "durational tension." To account for the extensive character of our perceptions in terms of duration, Bergson speaks of "extended" or "diluted" duration. "Extended" here does not mean "long"; it refers instead to a duration that approaches *extensivity* or spatiality—a "diluted" form of duration. In fact, extensivity for Bergson arises from the reduction of duration's temporal span in "moments" of extreme brevity. Such a reduction or narrowing of the present can happen only when successive moments become external or exterior to one another—that is, when there is a reduction in the relevance of the past. Where moments do not participate in a "larger" becoming, succession will more resemble juxtaposition. And since the juxtaposed, "exteriorized" terms are cut off from one another as relatively autonomous "nows," contrast is reduced and the series itself becomes homogeneous. "Past," "present," and "future" distinguish the terms of the series, but we can now more justifiably regard past simply as "earlier than" and future as "later than"—terms applied to a homogeneous and, thus, a *determined* order. In the following passage, Čapek relates homogeneity and a concomitant determinism to the question of novelty:

> The reduced tension of duration brings up another effect: *the reduction of novelty itself.* For, since the novelty of the present is due to the quality which differentiates it from its antecedent context and is thus inseparable from the mnemic link which joins it to the past, an attenuation of this link means a reduction of the qualitative difference between two subsequent moments; the novelty of the present is less pronounced and the successive phases will tend to be *more similar* to each other. Thus together with the reduction of the temporal span and the tendency toward exteriorization, there are two other concomitant features characterizing 'extended' or 'diluted' duration; the tendencies toward *homogeneity* and toward *determinism*. A present moment, being, by virtue of its lesser

degree of novelty, less differentiated from its ancestor, will yield itself more easily to the deductive effort which will derive it from its antecedent. For any consistent rigorous determinism, such as that of Democritus, Spinoza and Laplace, implies a *complete* negation of novelty. Its successful application is possible only when the irreducible difference between successive phases—call it an element of contingency, of novelty, of indetermination—can be neglected for practical purposes. (Čapek 1971, pp. 220–221)

The "deductive effort" of which Čapek speaks refers to the method of modern scientific inquiry and to the strict derivation of "present" from "past" as effect from cause. This purely conceptual derivation implies an equivalence of cause and effect. Since there is mutual determination, we can reverse the process and derive cause from effect to deny the "arrow of time":

A complete equivalence of cause and effect, i.e., the mutual deductibility of one from another regardless of 'the direction of time', was the ideal of classical deterministic explanation. The principle of *causa aequat effectum* graphically shows how closely the homogeneity of successive phases and strict determinism are correlated. (Čapek 1971, p. 221)

This conceptual "timelessness," of course, has no bearing on perceptual experience. In terms of experience, the homogeneity of "diluted" duration results in a degree of passivity and a relaxation of attention. The future is not, in fact, determined, but the "externality" of successive moments and their homogeneity dulls expectation. It is only in conceptualization that we can imagine a strict causal determinacy and place past and future in a timeless "present."

Although I have used speculations on the autonomy of the musical moment and the "spatialization of time" to introduce Bergson's analysis of extension, I do not mean to suggest that our experience of new music should be characterized by passivity and inattentiveness. I do suggest, however, that a narrowing of the present may be responsible for judgments that such music is uninteresting, arrhythmic, or "uneventful." In such a judgment there would not be a feeling of too much novelty, but of too little. From a Bergsonian perspective, the notions of autonomy and spatiality do not characterize

rhythmic experience but, rather, point toward an intellectual analyisis that would make experience its object. Rhythmic experience is to be found elsewhere. At the opposite extreme from extended duration is an experience of "pure" (i.e., non-"extensive") duration in which the past is most fully involved in present becoming. Bergson describes such an experience as follows:

Let us then concentrate attention on that which we have that is at the same time most removed from externality and the least penetrated with intellectuality. Let us seek, in the depths of our experience, the point where we feel most intimately within our own life. It is into pure duration that we then plunge back, a duration in which the past, always moving on, is swelling increasingly with a present that is absolutely new. But, at the same time, we feel the spring of our will strained to its utmost limit. We must, by a strong recoil of our personality on itself, gather up our past which is slipping away, in order to thrust it, compact and undivided, into a present which it will create by entering. Rare indeed are the moments when we are self-possessed to this extent: it is then that our actions are truly free. And even in these moments we do not completely possess ourselves. Our feeling of duration, I should say the actual coinciding of ourself with itself, admits of degrees. But the more the feeling is deep and the coincidence complete, the more the life in which it places us absorbs intellectuality by transcending it. For the natural function of the intellect is to bind like to like, and it is only facts that can be repeated that are entirely adaptable to intellectual conceptions. Now our intellect does undoubtably grasp the real moments of real duration after they are past; we do so by reconstituting the new state of consciousness out of a series of views taken of it from the outside, each of which resembles as much as possible something already known; in this sense we may say that the state of consciousness contains intellectuality implicitly. Yet the state of consciousness overflows the intellect; it is indeed incommensurable with the intellect, being itself indivisible and new. (Bergson, *Creative Evolution*, pp. 199–200)

This experience (which for Bergson is not absolute, given the limitations of human memory) closely resembles Suzuki's characterization of *sono-mama*. And it could be said that music offers extraordinary opportunities for such experience by creating events of great duration, "condensing" past into vivid presents that far exceed the bounds of "immediate memory."

The intellectuality of which Bergson speaks cannot be excluded from musical experience or from consciousness in general. However, where intellectuality and the aim of abstraction and conceptualization dominate we can imagine a transcendence of time by the fixations of intellectual analysis. Our ability to recollect, to re-present past events as present, leads to the conviction that past events can be isolated from becoming and preserved as "earlier" presents. Indeed, for the purpose of analysis we can and do make copies or models of events laid out as a "series of views" taken from outside time as process. The copies we make *resemble* the events in that they are constituted by whatever properties of the events we choose to regard as salient or essential. And our choice of properties is guided by the sorts of comparisons we wish to make. As Bergson says, the function of the intellect is to bind like to like—a process of abstraction in which common characteristics constitute the external relations that hold together "juxtaposed" terms in a conceptual order. This process itself is not atemporal. It is part of "life" and experience. The analytic choices we make are no less than any other experience guided by relevancies of past and future.

However, to preserve the "objectivity" of our analysis we must discount the contigencies of the analytic act and equate the analysis and the object of analysis. And since analysis requires that we preserve elements and relations from the indeterminacies of becoming, we have formed a concept of time modeled on the notion of space as a container of juxtaposed terms that are fully "present" for our inspection. In the following passage, Čapek argues with Bergson that "extended" duration when pressed to its *logical* extreme leads to a spatialized or extensive conception of time and to the notion of the durationless instant:

> The extreme theoretical limit of the process of distension of duration . . . would be, properly speaking, a *complete suspension of time*, or rather, its complete transformation into a homogeneous and static space. For by virtue of the increasingly restricted temporal span the successive phases of duration would become more and more *external*

to each other until their complete mutual exclusion would become equivalent to the complete externality of the juxtaposed terms. The present moment would shrink to a mathematical instant which, being without duration, would lose its concrete character of novelty and thus would be qualitatively equivalent to the past. The past itself, lacking any qualitative differentiation with respect to the present, would lose its constitutive character of pastness; it would be a purely verbal 'past', which instead of *preceding* the present, would *coexist* with it, since the essence of succession consists in the qualitative differentiation between the anterior and subsequent moments. This qualitative differentiation depends, as we have seen, on the fact of *elementary memory*, that is, on the elementary survival of the past in the present. But there is no such survival within a durationless instant; *mens momentanea* lacks *recordatio* [from Leibniz, "Omne enim corpus est mens momentanea sive carens recordatione"]. By the same token, the present deprived of novelty, and thus being qualitatively identical with the past, *would not follow it*, since its consecutive character would be purely verbal. Thus in such an obviously impossible limit case, the succession of heterogeneous phases would pass over into the juxtaposition of an infinite number of mathematical, qualitatively identical instants whose more appropriate name would be 'points'. This would be the timeless geometrical world of Spinoza and Laplace in which the future is not only necessary, but literally *pre-exists*, or rather, *co-exists*, alongside the so-called 'present' and the so-called 'past'. It would be an entity in all respects similar to classical space, that is, to the mathematical continuum of points without any qualitative differentiation and thus without succession. (Čapek 1971, pp. 223–224)

If the notions of an autonomous present moment, a spatialization of time, and an "overcoming" of time do not seem adequate for a description of rhythmic experience, they do, nevertheless, provide us with a conceptual order for the analysis of events from which becoming can be eliminated—an analysis in which what was, is, and will be are equally "present" for thought. For the progress of the physical sciences this order has proved highly productive—at least until the twentieth century, when discoveries in physics unsettled traditional notions of determinacy, "simple location," and the infinite divisibility of time. For the study of music a denial of the spontaneity and creativity of becoming has supported the construction of various theories of musical structure in which questions of temporality are averted by imagining an absolute present that contains elements coexisting in an ultimately fixed network of relationships. And for compositional practice, belief in a quasi-technological control over process has led to the notion that structure can be implanted in the work through acts of "precomposition," which might guarantee the aesthetic value of the product. Where such concepts have proved less successful is in addressing the question of musical rhythm.

As I indicated at the beginning of this study, by naming the rhythmic we point to something that cannot be captured in schematic or numerical representations. Mattheson called this elusive factor in musical experience *Bewegung*—a matter of "feeling" that "cannot be captured by the pen." And yet, by naming the rhythmic we necessarily enter into the realm of concepts and intellectual distinctions. Bergson, too, undertook what must be call an *intellectual* analysis of the limitations of intellectuality. And Suzuki has written many closely argued essays that criticize the hegemony of "mere" intellect. However, such undertakings are not as circular and hopeless as they may appear. For Bergson, for Suzuki, and for William James, the habits of intellectual analysis, though grounded in features of perceptual experience, do not exhaust possibilities for thought or reflection. That certain habits of thought, transmitted through culture, have hardened in beliefs concerning time and "objective" reality does not preclude the possibility of breaking these habits and attaining new perspectives or attitudes. It may be appropriate here to repeat James's criticism of a return of the same—a crit-

icism that speaks also of the conservatism of language:

> The realities, concrete and abstract, physical and ideal, whose permanent existence we believe in, seem to be constantly coming up again before our thought, and lead us, in our carelessness, to suppose that our 'ideas' of them are the same ideas. . . .
>
> What makes it convenient to use the mythological formulas is the whole organization of speech . . . What wonder, then, that the thought is most easily conceived under the law of the thing whose name it bears! (James 1890/1981, pp. 225, 230)[1]

An alternative perspective does not, of course, transcend intellect and the limitations of analysis, but it may permit us to overcome some of the limitations to thought posed by that particular form of intellectual analysis presented by our scientific-technological culture. In this essay, I have attempted to present an alternative to customary views of musical meter as habit, as return of the same, and as a homogeneous medium and determined order used but transcended by rhythm proper. In this regard, I have followed Riemann in attempting to bring meter closer to the spontaneity and "mobility" of rhythm. Whether or not this attempt is judged at all successful, I would hope at least to have raised questions of time and process that might place traditional problems of musical form and musical analysis in a new light. In fact, it is in this same light that the shortcomings of my analysis of meter will be seen. The concepts and typologies I have been developing are aimed at an analysis of the "sensible flux" of musical experience. And although they strain against linguistic habit, they, too, succumb in the end. The creative, synthetic process of rhythmic

---

1. For a spirited defense of Bergson's critique of intellectualist thought, see also James's long footnote to the fifth lecture of *A Pluralistic Universe*, from which the following quotation is drawn: "In using concepts of his own to discredit the theoretic claims of concepts generally, Bergson does not contradict, but on the contrary emphatically illustrates his own view of their practical role, for they serve in his hands only to 'orient' us, to show us to what quarter we must *practically turn* if we wish to gain that completer insight into reality which he denies that they

can give. He directs our hopes away from them and towards the despised sensible flux. *What he reaches by their means is thus only a new practical attitude.* He but restores, against the vetoes of intellectualist philosophy, our naturally cordial relations with sensible experience and common sense. This service is surely only practical; but is a service for which we may be almost immeasurably grateful. To trust our senses again with a good philosophical conscience!" (James 1977, p. 339).

experience tempts the intellect that would comprehend it but will ever evade intellect's grasp.

Indeed, it was in a similar spirit of Mephistophelean skepticism that we began the first part of this study. But having given the devil the first word, we are under no obligation to let him speak the last. If we can keep in mind the limitations of analysis, our attempts to understand and describe rhythmic experience need not end in a denial of process and a naming of parts (or any gesture of surrender wherein we say at last, "Verweile doch! Du bist so schön!"). The static charms of the formula or schema (or of the timeless "now moment") will lose their fascination if it can be understood that our theorizing about music is itself a part of music and no less temporal than this most unruly and recalcitrantly temporal product of the human imagination. Indeed, in its resistance to schematization, music may hold important clues for our understanding of process and open questions of temporality that have not found a favorable environment for exploration in our present intellectualist climate. Were such a "musical turn" possible, thought about music might profoundly contribute to a more general theorizing that would take time seriously. But to suggest this possibility is to extravagantly open our more specialized study at its proper end.

References

Benjamin, William. 1984. "A Theory of Musical Meter." *Music Perception*, I, pp. 355–413.

Benveniste, Emile. 1971. *Problems in General Linguistics*. Trans. Mary Elizabeth Meek. Coral Gables, Florida: University of Miami Press.

Berg, Alban. 1965. "Why Is Schoenberg's Music So Difficult?" In Willi Reich, *Alban Berg*. Trans. Cornelius Cardew. London: Thames and Hanson, pp. 189–204.

Bergson, Henri. 1911. *Creative Evolution*. Trans. Arthur Miller. New York: Henry Holt.

Boulez, Pierre. 1971. *Boulez on Music Today*. Trans. Susan Bradshaw and Richard Rodney Bennet. Cambridge: Harvard University Press.

———. 1986. *Orientations*. Trans. Martin Cooper. Cambridge: Harvard University Press.

Bücher, Karl. 1924. *Arbeit und Rhythmus*. Leipzig: Emmanuel Reinicke.

Burtt, Edwin Arthur. 1959. *The Metaphysical Foundations of Modern Science*. London: Routledge and Kegan Paul. (Garden City: Doubleday, 1954.)

Čapek, Milič. 1961. *The Philosophical Impact of Contemporary Physics*. Princeton: Van Nostrand.

———. 1971. *Bergson and Modern Physics*. Boston Studies, 7. Dordrecht: D. Riedel.

Cassirer, Ernst. 1951. *The Philosophy of the Enlightenment*. Trans. Fritz C. A. Koellin and James P. Pettegrove. Princeton: Princeton University Press.

Cone, Edward T. 1968. *Musical Form and Musical Performance*. New York: Norton.

Cooper, Grosvenor and Meyer, Leonard B. 1960. *The Rhythmic Structure of Music*. Chicago: University of Chicago Press.

Eliade, Mircea. 1965. *The Myth of the Eternal Return: or, Cosmos and History*. Trans. Willard R. Trask. Princeton: Princeton University Press.

Fraisse, Paul. 1956. *Les structures rhythmiques*. Louvain: University of Louvain.

———. 1963. *The Psychology of Time*. New York: Harper and Row.

———. 1982. "Rhythm and Tempo." In Diana Deutsch, ed., *The Psychology of Music*. New York: Academic Press, pp. 149–180.

Georgiades, Thrasybulos. 1951. "Aus der Musiksprache des Mozart-Theaters." *Mozart-Jahrbuch*, 1950 (Salzburg), pp. 76–104.

———. 1953. "Zur Musiksprache der Wiener Klassiker." *Mozart Jahrbuch* 1951 (Salzburg), pp. 50–59.

———. 1974. *Musik und Sprache*. Heidelberg: Springer.

———. 1982. *Music and Language*. Trans. Marie Louise Göllner. Cambridge: Cambridge University Press.

Halm, August. 1926. *Einführung in die Musik*. Berlin: Deutsche Buch-Gemeinschaft.

Handel, Stephen. 1989. *Listening—Introduction to the Perception of Auditory Events*. Cambridge: MIT Press.

Hasty, Christopher F. 1984. "Phrase Formation in Post-Tonal Music." *Journal of Music Theory*, vol. 28/2, pp. 167–190.

Hauptmann, Moritz. 1873. *Die Natur der Harmonik und der Metrik*. Leipzig: Breitkopf und Härtel.

Henneberg, Gudrun. 1974. *Theorien zur Rhythmik und Metrik*. Mainzer Studien zur Musikwissenschaft, 6. Tutzing: Hans Schneider.

Houle, George. 1987. *Meter in Music, 1600–1800*. Bloomington: Indiana University Press.

Imbrie, Andrew W. 1973. "'Extra' Measures and Metrical Ambiguity in Beethoven." In Alan Tyson, ed., *Beethoven Studies*. Vol. I. New York: W. W. Norton, pp. 45–66.

James, William. 1977. *A Pluralistic Universe*. Cambridge: Harvard University Press.

———.1890/1981. *The Principles of Psychology*. Vol. 1. Cambridge: Harvard University Press.

Koch, Heinrich Christoph. 1787/1969. *Versuch einer Anleitung zur Composition*. Vol. 2. Leipzig, 1787; facsimile, Hildesheim: Georg Holms.

———. 1983. *Introductory Essay on Composition*. Trans. Nancy Kovaleff Baker. New Haven: Yale University Press.

Kramer, Jonathan.1988. *The Time of Music*. New York: Schirmer.

Kuba, Fritz. 1948. "Studie in zwei Teilen über das Verhältnis von Takt und Rhythmus in philosophischer, ästhetischer und fachwissenschaftlicher Hinsicht." Ph.D. dissertation, University of Vienna.

Lerdahl, Fred and Jackendoff, Ray. 1983. *A Generative Theory of Tonal Music*. Cambridge: MIT Press.

Lewin, David. 1981. "Some Investigations into Foreground Ryhthmic and Metric Patterning." In Richmond Brown, ed., *Music Theory: Special Topics*. New York: Academic Press, pp. 101–37.

Lieb, Irwin C. 1991. *Past, Present, and Future*. Urbana and Chicago: University of Illinois Press.

Ligeti, György. 1965. "Metamorphoses of Musical Form." *Die Reihe 7, Form-Space*. Trans. Cornelius Cardew. Bryn Mawr: Theodore Presser.

Lorenz, Alfred. 1924/1966. *Das Geheimnis der Form bei Richard Wagner*. Vol. I. Tutzing: Hans Schneider.

Lussy, Mathis. 1966. "Die Correlation zwischen Takt und Rhythmus." *Vierteljahrsschrift für Musikwissenschaft*. Volume I. 1885; rpt., Hildesheim: Georg Olms, pp. 141–157.

Mattheson, Johann. 1735/1980. *Kleine General-Baß-Schule*. Hamburg, 1735; facsimile, Hamburg: Laaber-Verlag.

———. 1739/1981. *Der vollkommene Capellmeister*. Hamburg: Christian Herold. Trans. Ernest C. Harriss. Rpt., Ann Arbor: UMI Research Press.

Mead, Andrew. 1993. "Webern, Tradition, and 'Composing with Twelve Tones.'" *Music Theory Spectrum*, vol.15/2, pp. 173–204.

Miller, G. A. 1962. "Decision Units in the Perception of Speech." *I.R.E. Trans. Information Theory*, IT-8, pp. 81–83.

Narmour, Eugene. 1990. *The Analysis of Cognition of Basic Melodic Structures*. Chicago: University of Chicago Press.

Neisser, Ulric. 1967. *Cognitive Psychology*. New York: Appleton-Century-Crofts.

———. 1976. *Cognition and Reality*. San Francisco: W. H. Freedman.

Neumann, Friedrich. 1959. *Die Zeitgestalt: Eine Lehre vom musikalicshen Rhythmus* (in two volumes). Vienna: Paul Kaltschmid.

Newton, Sir Issac. 1729/1968. *The Mathematical Principles of Natural Philosophy*. Trans. Andrew Motte. London: Printed for Benjamin Motte; rpt., London: Dawsons of Pall Mall.

Piaget, Jean. 1971. *Structuralism*. Trans. and ed. Chaninah Maschler, New York: Harper and Row.

Printz, Wolfgang Caspar. 1696. *Phrynis mitilenaeus, oder Satyrischer Componist*. Dresden and Leipzig: Riedel.

Ratz, Erwin. 1973. *Einführung in der musikalischen Formenlehre*, 3rd ed. Vienna: Universal Edition.

Riemann, Hugo. 1900. *Die Elemente der Musikalichen Ästhetik*. Stuttgart: W. Spemann.

———. 1903. *Musikalische Rhythmik und Metrik*. Leipzig: Breitkopf und Härtel.

Rochberg, George. 1984. *The Aesthetics of Survival*. Ann Arbor: University of Michigan Press.

Ross, Robert Christopher. 1972. "*Rhuthmos*: A History of its Connotations." Ph.D. dissertation, University of California at Berkeley.

Rothstein, William. 1981. "Rhythm and the Theory of Structural Levels." Ph.D. dissertation, Yale University.

———. 1989. *Phrase Rhythm in Tonal Music*. New York: Schirmer.

Schachter, Carl. 1980. "Rhythm and Linear Analysis: Durational Reduction." *Music Forum*. Vol. V. New York: Columbia University Press, pp. 197–232.

———. 1987. "Rhythm and Linear Analysis: Aspects of Meter." *Music Forum*. Vol. VI, part I. New York: Columbia University Press, pp. 1–59.

Schenker, Heinrich. 1935. *Der Freie Satz*. Vienna: Universal Edition.

———. 1979. *Free Composition*. Trans. Ernst Oster. New York: Longman.

Seidel, Wilhelm. 1975. *Über Rhythmustheorien der Neuzeit*. Neue Heidelberger Studien zur Musikwissenschaft, 7. Bern: Franke.

Smalley, Roger. 1975. "Webern's Sketches (II)." *Tempo*, no. 113, pp. 29–40.

Stockhausen, Karlheinz. 1963. *Texte zur elektronische und instrumentalische Musik*, vol. 1, *Aufsätze 1952–1962 zur Theorie des Komponierens*. Cologne: M. Du Mont Schauberg.

Sulzer, Johann-Georg. 1792. *Allgemeine Theorie der schönen Künste*. Vol. 2. Leipzig: In der Weidmannschen Buchhandlung.

Suzuki, D. T. 1957. *Mysticism, Christian and Buddhist.* New York: Harper and Row.

Toch, Ernst. 1977. *The Shaping Forces in Music.* New York: Dover.

Webern, Anton. 1959. *Briefe an Hildegard Jone und Josef Humplik.* Vienna: Universal Edition.

———. 1963. *The Path to the New Music.* Trans. Leo Black. Bryn Mawr: Theodore Presser.

———. 1968. *Sketches (1926–1945).* New York: Carl Fischer.

Whitehead, Alfred North. 1978. *Process and Reality.* New York: Free Press.

Whitrow, G. J. 1961. *The Natural Philosophy of Time.* London and Edinburgh: Nelson.

Wiehmeyer, Theodor. 1917. *Musikalische Rhythmik und Metrik.* Magdeburg: Heinrichhofen's Verlag.

———. 1926. "Über die Grundfragen der musikalischen Rhythmus und Mertik." *Bericht über den I. Musikalischen Kongress der Deutschen Musikgesellschaft in Leipzig.* Leipzig: Breitkopf und Härtel, pp. 445–459.

Yeston, Maury. 1976. *The Stratification of Musical Rhythm.* New Haven: Yale University Press.

Yudkin, Jeremy. 1989. *Music in Medieval Europe.* Englewood Cliffs, N.J.: Prentice Hall.

Zuber, Barbara. 1984. "Reihe, Gesetz, Urpflanz, Nomos." *Musik-Konzepte Sonderband, Anton Webern II.* Munich: edition text+kritik, pp. 304–336.

Index

acceleration, 87–88, 111–113, 164, 225–228

accent: dynamic, 107,127; metric, 15–20, 52–55, 101–102, 104, 175; rhythmic, 15–20, 50–55

aesthetic experience, 4, 6

ambiguity, 173–174, 205–206, 261

analysis, 67–68, 154–155

anticipation, 69, 80, 92

Aristoxenos, 35–36, 37

Augustine, Saint, 68

Babbitt, Milton: *Du*, "Wankelmut," 275–278; *Du*, "Wiedersehen," 278–280, 286

Bach, J. S.: Suite for Unaccompanied Cello in C Major, 154, 155–162, 165–167; Suite for Unaccompanied Cello in E♭ Major, 154, 155, 161–167, 248, 252 n.1

Bamberger, Jeanne, 277

Beethoven, Ludwig van: Piano Sonata op. 2/1 in F Minor, 79, 83, 113–115; Symphony no.1 in C Major, 130, 210–236

Benjamin, William, 18, 19, 106

Benveniste, Emil, 10–11

Berg, Alban, 68 n.2

Bergson, Henri, 4, 46, 68, 300–301, 302 n.1

Boulez, Pierre, 193, 197–198; *le marteau sans maître*: "avant 'l'artisanat furieux,'" 284–286; "bel edifice et les pressenti-ments," 288, 291–293 , 296; "commentaire I de 'bourreaux de solitude,'" 286–289, 296; "commentaire II de 'bourreaux de solitude,'" 289–291

Brahms, Johannes: Third Symphony, 125 n.3

Bücher, Karl, 42

Burtt, Edwin Arthur, 10 n.2

Čapek, Milič, 7 n.1, 299–301

Carter, Elliott: Sonata for Violoncello and Piano, 206–209

Cassirer, Ernst, 26

Chopin, Fryderykc: Prelude in E♭ Major, 54–55

clock, internal, 169

Cone, Edward T., 34, 48–51, 55, 58, 175, 176, 183, 197

Cooper and Meyer, 20, 48, 50–57, 175

Craft, Robert, 288–289

cyclic return, 56

deferral, 133–135, 139, 142–145, 147, 204–205

Dehnung. *See* expansion

denial, 91, 133–135, 150–151, 188

dominant beginning, 104, 115

Eliade, Mircea, 298

end, 74–75, 219–223

environmental determinacy, 94–95, 141, 147, 151, 168

Epstein, David, 16

eternity. *See* timelessness

expansion, metrical, 176–181, 197–199, 202

extension, 119, 299

extensivity, 299–301

Fraisse, Paul, 92, 108 n.2

Galileo, 10 n.2
Georgiades, Thrasybulos, 43–47, 257, 298
Gibson, J. J., 94 n.1
goal, 219, 221–222, 225
Goethe, Johann Wolfgang von, 48, 266
Guarini, Giovanni Battista, 241

Halm, August, 41–42
Handel, Stephen, 124–125, 173
Hasty, Christopher, F., 283
Hauptmann, Moritz, 34–35, 36, 38, 100–102,
    135, 197
Hauser, Franz, 35
Haydn, Franz Joseph, 43 n.2, 44; Symphony no.
    88 in G Major, 205–206; Symphony
    no.101 in D Major, 128–129
hiatus, 88, 129, 170, 191
hierarchy: extensive, 18–19, 49–50, 56,
    115–118, 175; projective, 151
hypermeasure, 49, 51, 175, 179–183, 196–197

Imbrie, Andrew W., 17–18, 19
indifference point, 108 n.2
inertia, 168
instant, 7, 16–19, 38, 56–57, 70–71, 73, 301
internal clock, 170
interruption, 138
intrinsic quantity (*quantitas intrinsica*), 27–28,
    105

James, William, 31–32, 286, 302
Jone, Hildegard, 266
Joyce, James, 46, 298

Kant, Immanuel, 45
Koch, Christoph Heinrich, 21, 26–32, 50, 69,
    83, 105, 106, 116
Kramer, Jonathan, 16–17
Kuba, Fritz, 42

laws of material and laws of presentation,
    266–267
Lerdahl and Jackendoff, 20, 56–59, 63 n.3, 129,
    176

Lewin, David, 277
Lieb, Irwin C., 7 n.1
Ligeti, György, 297
Lorenz, Alfred, 34, 48, 175
Lussy, Mathis, 16 n.4
Lutosławski, Witold, *Jeux Venitiens*, 293–295,
    296

Matteson, Johann, 21, 22–26, 28, 30–31, 32,
    69, 116, 302
Mead, Andrew, 262 n.2
Meister Eckhart, 298
memory, 12, 81, 94 n.1, 283–284, 299, 301
mensural determinacy, 80–83, 95
Messiaen, Olivier, 297
Meyer, Leonard B., 197. *See also* Cooper and
    Meyer
Miller, G. A., 283–284
Moldenhauer, Hans, 267
Monteverdi, Claudio, "Ohimè, se tanto amate,"
    237–243
motion, 12, 20–25, 37, 49, 57–59, 62–63, 175
Mozart, 43, 44; Piano Concerto in C Major,
    K.467, 179–181; Piano Sonata in D
    Major, K.311, 203–204; Symphony no. 35
    in D Major (*Haffner*), K.385, 177–178,
    184–191, 194–196, 198–200, 201, 220;
    Symphony no. 40 in G Minor, K.550,
    53–54; Symphony no. 41 in C Major
    (*Jupiter*), K.551, 53

Narmour, Eugene, 111
Neisser, Ulric, 94, n.1, 283, 286
Neumann, Friedrich, 38–41, 48, 96–100
Newton, Sir Isaac, 9–10
now, 43–46, 72, 76–78, 151
number, 9–10, 16–19, 30, 38–39, 60

pedagogy, 5, 130, 152
performance, 48, 130, 152, 209, 260, 293
phrase constituent, 283
Piaget, Jean, 67 n.1
Plato, 10–11, 26, 35
Pollock, Jackson, 68
Printz, Wolfgang Caspar, 105, 135

Ratz, Erwin, 198
Reich, Steve, 296
Reich, Willi, 266, n.4
reinterpretation, 119, 218
relevance, 77, 81, 84, 93–95, 110, 150–151, 169–173
reproduction, 80–82, 92, 94, 150–152, 184
rhuthmos, 10–11, 20
Riemann, Hugo, 35–38, 39, 44, 50, 98, 100, 129, 191, 302
Rochberg, George, 297
Ross, Christopher, 11 n.3
Rothstein, William, 176, 177, 179–181, 211
Rousseau, Jean, 23–24, 31
row structure, 265

Schachter, Carl, 17, 176–179, 180, 182, 198
Schenker, Heinrich, 61–61, 63 n.3, 176–177, 179, 195
Schönberg, Arnold, 68 n.2, 113, 267
Schütz, Heinrich: "Adjoro vos, filiae Jerusalem," 243–257
segmentation, 283–284
Seidel, Wilhelm, 24–25, 26–27, 35
sentence, 113, 230
silence, 75–76, 78–79, 90, 169–170, 184
simultaneity, 75
Smalley, Roger, 267, 273
sono-mama, 298
space, 7, 38 n.1
Stockhausen, Karlheinz, 46, 68, 296, 297, 299
Stramm, August, 278
structure, 4, 64, 67
subjective grouping, 27–28, 131–132, 141, 147

Sulzer, Johann-Georg, 26–27, 30, 32, 106
suspense, projective, 127, 136–137, 157
Suzuki, D. T., 298, 300
syncopation, 119, 152. *See also* suspense, projective

tactus, 23
time: absolute, 7 n.1, 9–10, 59, 98; relational, 7 n.1; smooth and striated, 286, 293
timelessness, 9, 24–25, 46, 61 n.2, 257, 297–298, 300
timepoint. *See* instant
time sense, 169
time signatures, 5, 26, 129
Toch, Ernst, 42–43

virtual articulation, 89, 110, 120, 130, 152–154
visual experience, 12
Vivaldi, Antonio: "Spring" Concerto from *The Four Seasons*, 201–204

Webern, Anton, 261–262, 266–267; Quartet, op. 22, 257–265; sketches for op. 22, 267–275
Whitehead, Alfred North, 65, 69
Whitrow, G. J., 7 n.1, 10 n.2
Wiehmeyer, Theodor, 102, 227 n.2
Wolpe, Stefan: Piece in Two Parts for Violin Alone, 169–174, 244

Yeston, Maury, 69, 106
Yudkin, Jeremy, 227

Zeno, 60
Zuber, Barbara, 266 n.4